Feather River Country Adventure Trails

Feather River Country, Adventure Trails

100 Fun Hikes within the Region of the Upper Middle Fork, Lakes Basin, and the North Yuba River

by Tom DeMund

Know DeFeet Publishing Co.
Graeagle, California

Published by
Know DeFeet Publishing Company
P.O. Box 296
Graeagle, CA 96103

Front cover: Sierra Buttes beyond Deer Lake
Title page: Seven lakes in the center of the Lakes Basin that are visited by several trails: *from left to right, top row,* Mud Lake (a tiny one surrounded by green), Long Lake; *middle row,* Silver Lake, Cub Lake; *bottom row,* Round Lake, Little Bear Lake, Big Bear Lake

Cover and Interior Design by Pete Masterson, Aeonix Publishing Group, www.aeonix.com
All photographs and maps are by the author except the photographs on pages 4, 66, 69, 110, 113, 150, 152, 160, 170 and 185, which are by Woodward Payne.

Notice to Readers

Although utmost care has been taken to make this book as accurate as possible, Mother Nature and Old Man Time have a way of changing things. Floods, landslides, erosion, or bush growth may make a trail impassable or different from the description in this book. New "No Trespassing" signs may appear, so please heed them. All hiking has some inherent danger. Any of these hikes should be undertaken with the understanding that the hiker is assuming all associated risks and holds the author and publisher harmless from any liability arising from the use of this book. The difficulty ratings herein are meant to serve as a general guide. Each hiker must be responsible for determining his or her own level of fitness and ability to do any of the hikes in this book.

Publisher's Cataloging-in-Publication Data

DeMund, Tom
    Feather River Country Adventure Trails / 100 Fun Hikes within the Region of the Upper Middle Fork, Lakes Basin and the North Yuba River : Tom DeMund
        p.   cm.
    Includes index.
    LCCN 00-111991
    ISBN 0-9679740-0-3
    1. Hiking—Sierra Nevada Mountains (Calif.)—Guide-books. 2. History—Sierra Nevada Mountains (Calif.). 3. Sierra Nevada Mountains—Description and travel—Guide-books. I. DeMund, Tom. II. Title.
    GV

Printed and bound in Singapore by Star Standard Industries, Ltd.

Contents

Part One: About the Area and the Book

Part Two: The Hikes

Hike Distance
(in Miles)

Hike Distance
(in Miles)

Hike Distance
(in Miles)

Fern Falls (Hike GL-28)

Preface

The Sierra just can't be beat! Over the years, I've hiked most of it, from where the mountains start in Southern California to where they end in the north. In my view, no other place in the Sierra begins to compare with the Feather River country for easy access, moderate altitude, beauty, lack of crowds, and a huge variety of trails. It's not just the pine-scented, super-healthful air that caresses you; it's not merely the sounds of the multitude of bird species or the wind in the conifers; it's not the green kaleidoscope of the area's many tree varieties and seemingly infinite variety of wildflowers; nor is it only the rustic places to stay and the quaint eateries of the area. It's a unique combination of all these things, and much, much more, that makes up the mountain paradise we call the Feather River country.

Short, easy hikes; all-day-to-the-mountaintop hikes; or numerous in-between hikes—the Feather River country provides wonderful outdoor experiences for almost everyone. Many visitors to the mountains are lowlanders, so the moderate elevations of the area (4,000 to 6,500 feet altitude for most of the hikes in this book) mean easier breathing, less risk of altitude sickness, less chance of "high Sierra weather" (but no guarantees), and fewer physical dangers than most other parts of the Sierra range.

Because the Feather River country is so rich in history, for many of the trails I have included some history of the route or its surroundings.

The bull's-eye of the region is the quaint town of Graeagle, located in the center of Mohawk Valley, 49 miles north of Truckee, California, via State Highway 89. All but two of the hikes in this book are within a 15-mile radius (as the crow flies) from Graeagle, and all but two trailheads are less than a 45-minute drive from town.

I hope you will enjoy many of the "old faithful" trails as well as some of the more obscure, hiker-free routes.

Always remember to take it easy, plan ahead, and stop often to enjoy the grandeur around you.

Lava fromations on Sugar Loaf Mountain (Hike RP-1)

Acknowledgments

Although, in preparation for this book, I solo hiked over one-third of the trails described in these pages, I always preferred company. Fortunately, my wonderful wife, Mary, tromped many of these trails with me, patiently waiting while I photographed, made trail notes, or checked locations with my GPS. Her company, enthusiasm, lunch-making abilities, and wildflower cataloging (as well as many other things) are appreciated by me to the max.

My good friend David Vena was my companion on many of these trails, particularly all of the cross-country jaunts. His wife, Sally, joined Mary and me on others, excluding, however, those of the cross-country variety. My Graeagle neighbor Dr. Herb Longnecker has also been a good hiking buddy, with his wife, Wanda, occasionally accompanying us. The list of other hike companions includes Rick and Jennie Atkins, Dann DeMund, Brad and Kay Bradway, David and Sue Hirsch, Dick and Gael Paddack, Doug and Donna Hill, John Hokenstad, Don and Carole Jehling, and Peter Anderson. My longtime best friend (since fourth grade) Woody Payne, along with Beverly Anderson, joined me and Mary on any number of these hikes. Several of their better-than-mine photographs are included in the book.

Once I elected to go the self-publishing route, I had to assemble a team that could do the book production jobs I couldn't do myself. Jeannie Yee was of enormous help, typing the manuscript and keeping me organized. Zipporah Collins and Mark Woodworth did a fine editing job and provided many useful suggestions. Pete Masterson of Aeonix Publishing Group did my layout work and cover design and guided me through much of the production process. Excellent proofreading was done by Diane Gibbs, and the index was created by Andy Jerron. Fei Chen with Star Standard Industries was a terrific coordinator for all the printing activities. I owe a huge "thank you" to each of them.

My last word of thanks (which I give each day) goes to our Creator, who has provided the majestic, open-air temple through which these hikes wander. I also daily acknowledge God's help in giving me my great love for the mountains, together with the physical ability to tromp through them over whatever terrain presents itself. And all the Feather River country hikers shouted, "Amen!"

Dixie Mtn

LAKE DAVIS

Taylorsville Road

Beckwourth

Crocker Mountain

CM

Horton Ridge

GV-1

CM-2

Beckwourth Road

GV-2

Genesee Road

Cow Creek

CM-1

Big Grizzly Creek

• Reconnaissance Peak

• Smith Peak

Grizzly Road

P-3

• Table Rock

RP-1

P

B-5

Lake Davis Road

P-4

• Sugar Loaf Peak

RP

70

BECKWOURTH

70

DELLEKER

Middle Fork

P-2

To Reno

Union Pacific Railroad

PORTOLA

Calpine Rd

Feather River

70

A15

P-1

A24

Union Pacific Railroad

B-2

B-3

Rd

A23

Mclears

Portola

• Beckwourth Peak

• Radio Tower

• Carman Saddle

Beckwourth

5

39

Sulphur

Carman Valley

Creek

CP

89

Lookout

CP-1

SIERRA

C-1

• Haskell Peak

CALPINE

C-4

CP-2

89

A23

EK

HV-4

• Deadman Peak

49

To Truckee

49 89

N

Legend

Paved Roads & Highways	————
Gravel or Dirt Roads	··············
Railroads	————
State Highway Numbers	49
County Road Numbers	A14
Trail Designations	SC-1
Topo Map Name Abreviations	HV
Town Name	CLIO
Creeks and Rivers	
Peaks	•

U.S. Geological Survey Topographical Map Designations

B - Blairsden
BN - Blue Nose Mtn.
C - Clio
CM - Crocker Mtn.
CP - Calpine
GL - Gold Lake
GV - Grizzly Valley
HV - Haypress Valley
J - Johnsville
MF - Mt. Fillmore
MI - Mt. Ingalls
P - Portola
RP - Reconnaissance Peak
SC - Sierra City
SG - Spring Garden

Map Symbols

▬▬▬▬	Paved Road	Church/site/remains
▬ ▬ ▬	Graded Gravel Road	Cemetery
═══════	Dirt Road	Cabin or Building
= = = = = = =	Jeep Road	Cabin Site/remains
▬ ▬ ▬ ▬ ▬	Main Trail	Meadow
▬ ▪ ▬ ▪ ▬ ▪	Alternate Main Trail	Marsh
▬ - ▬ - ▬ -	Main Trail Along Jeep Road	Golf Course
▬▬▬▬	Main Trail Along Dirt Road	Campground
▬ ▪▪ ▬ ▪▪ ▬	Cross Country Route	Backpack or Unimproved Campground
• • • • • •	Trail Other Than Main Trail	Point of Interest
〰〰	Creek or River	Locked Gate
▬ ▪▪ ▬ ▪▪	Intermittent Creek	Open Gate
〰≠〰	Waterfall	Mine
•〰	Spring	Bridge (with Dirt Road)
(49)	State Highway	Lake
⟨A14⟩	County Highway	North
△24	Forest Road	Forested Area
23N11	USFS Road	Gravel Pit
GL-3	Main Trail Number	
TH	Trailhead	
ALT TH	Alternate Trailhead	

Paved Road
Graded Gravel Road
Dirt Road
Jeep Road
Main Trail
Alternate Main Trail
Main Trail Along Jeep Road
Main Trail Along Dirt Road
Cross Country Route
Trail Other Than Main Trail
Creek or River
Intermittent Creek
Waterfall
Spring
State Highway
County Highway
Forest Road
USFS Road
Main Trail Number
Trailhead
Alternate Trailhead

Church/site/remains
Cemetery
Cabin or Building
Cabin Site/remains
Meadow
Marsh
Golf Course
Campground
Backpack or Unimproved Campground
Point of Interest
Locked Gate
Open Gate
Mine
Bridge (with Dirt Road)
Lake
North
Forested Area
Gravel Pit

Part One
About the Area and the Book

Chapter 1

Two Introductions to the Sierra, from a Century Ago

If the following two introductions were given to a present-day editor, each essay would be ripped to shreds as being too flowery and over-dramatic, with impossibly long sentences. Nonetheless, both of the authors do a better job of describing the Sierra than any other introductions I have ever read. So, here they are as written many years ago by a couple of fellas who knew their mountains.

The first narrative consists of excerpts from John Muir's landmark book *The Mountains of California,* written in 1894:

> The coniferous forests of the Sierra are the grandest and most beautiful in the world, and grow in a delightful climate on the most interesting and accessible of mountain ranges, yet strange to say they are not well known.... But few indeed, strong and free with eyes undimmed with care, have gone far enough and lived long enough with trees to gain anything like a loving conception of their grandeur and significance as manifested in the harmonies of their distribution and varying aspects throughout the seasons, as they stand arrayed in their winter garb rejoicing in storms, putting forth their fresh leaves in the spring while steaming with resiny fragrance, receiving the thunder-showers of summer, or reposing heavily-laden with ripe cones in the rich sungold of autumn. For knowledge of this kind one must dwell in the trees and grow with them, without any reference to time in the almanac sense.
>
> The giant pines and firs and sequoias hold their arms open to the sunlight, rising above one another on the mountain benches, marshaled in glorious array, giving forth the utmost expression of grandeur and beauty with inexhaustible variety and harmony.
>
> The inviting openness of the Sierra woods is one of the most distinguishing characteristics. The trees of all species stand more or less apart in groves, or in small irregular groups, enabling one to find a way nearly everywhere, among sunny colonnades and through openings that have a smooth park-like surface, strewn with brown needles and burs. Now you cross a wild garden, now a meadow, now a ferny, willowy stream; and ever and anon you emerge from all the groves and flowers upon some granite pavement or on a high, bare ridge commanding superb views above the waving sea of evergreens far and near.
>
> The different species are ever found occupying the same relative positions to one another, as controlled by soil, climate, and the comparative vigor of each species in taking and holding the ground; and so appreciable are these relations, one need never be at a loss of determining, within a few hundred feet, the

elevation above sea-level by the trees alone; for, notwithstanding, some of the species range upward for several thousand feet, and all pass one another more or less, yet even those possessing the greatest vertical range are available in this connection, in as much as they take on new forms corresponding with the variations in altitude.

Among the many unlooked-for treasures that are bound up in the depths of the Sierra solitudes, none more surely charm and surprise all kinds of travelers than the glacier lakes. The forests and the glaciers and the snowy fountains of the streams advertise their wealth in a more or less telling manner even in the distance, but nothing is seen of the lakes until we have climbed above them.

All the upper branches of the rivers are fairly laden with lakes, like orchard trees with fruit. They lie embosomed in the deep woods, down in the groovy bottoms of cañons, high

on bald tablelands, and around the feet of the icy peaks, mirroring back their wild beauty over and over again.

The weather of spring and summer in the middle region of the Sierra is usually well flecked with rains and light dustings of snow, most of which are far too obviously joyful and life-giving to be regarded as storms; in the picturesque beauty and clearness of outlines of their clouds they offer striking contrasts to those boundless, all-embracing cloud-mantles of the storms of winter. The smallest and most perfectly individualized specimens present a richly modeled cumulus cloud rising above the dark woods, about 11:00 A.M., swelling with a visible motion straight up into the calm, sunny sky to a height of 12,000 to 14,000 feet above the sea, its white pearly bosses relieved by gray and purple shadows in the hollows, and showing outlines as keenly defined as those of the glacier-polished domes. In less than an hour it attains full development and stands poised in the blazing sunshine like

A calm section of the Feather River upstream from its upper gorge (Hike B-3)

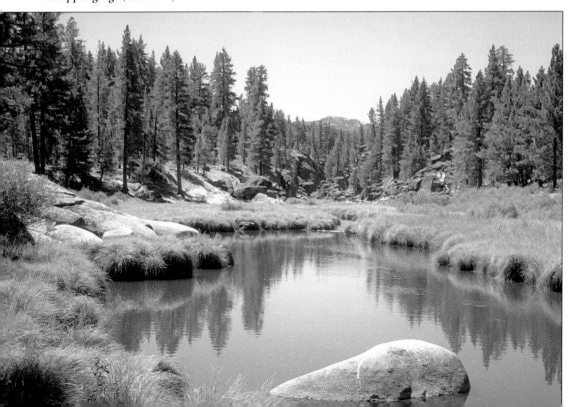

some colossal mountain, as beautiful in form and finish as if it were become a permanent addition to the landscape.

The second quotation is from *History of Plumas County, California,* written in 1882 by Fariss and Smith (oddly, their first names are not given):

Plumas is a county of mountains, whose lofty chains hold in their firm embrace many green and fertile valleys, as lovely as any that fall beneath the eye of Apollo in his daily round. Lofty peaks and sloping hills, rich with their robes of green, greet the eye; while winding through and around them are hundreds of clear mountain brooks, singing and babbling in their joy, as they hasten onward to unite their waters with the great streams that carry them onward to the valley and thence to the bosom of the mighty ocean. Three great divisions of the Feather river—the middle fork, the north and east branches of the north fork—have their sources in the county, and from their multitude of tributaries receive the water that falls as rain or snow on the lofty hills or imprisoned valleys, having their ramifications in every nook and corner of the vast expanse of mountains. High up among the peaks are lakes of clear, pellucid water, lovely mountain tarns, sweetly reposing in their secure abode far above the busy scenes of life below. Children of the glaciers, they carry the thoughts back to those distant ages when those immense fields of ice ground and furrowed their way over the mighty hills, plowing in their onward march the deep cañons and ravines that form our water-courses, filling the valleys with that alluvial deposit which creates a fertile soil for agriculture and ranching.

This region remained unknown and unexplored until the *ignis fatuus* of gold drew into the mountain recesses an eager band of adventurers, and opened to the world these grand mountains and lovely valleys.

The early history of Plumas properly begins with the naming of the river from which its name was derived, and whose arms and tendrils reach out into the county in all directions. Its patron stream, the Feather river, has been for years the fountain of its wealth and the source of its prosperity. In 1820 a Spanish exploring expedition passed up the valley, headed by Captain Louis A. Argüello. By this party the name Rio de las Plumas or Feather river, was bestowed upon the stream, because of the great number of feathers of wild fowl floating on its bosom. At the same time the Yuba river was christened Rio de los Uva. As the Spanish pronunciation of the word "Ooba," it is easy to see how it was Americanized into "Yuba" by the heedless miner.

Yes, these two writings serve as a fine preparation for your enjoyment of hiking in the Feather River country.

Chapter 2

What and Where Is the Feather River Country?

If you want to be technical about it, the Feather River country extends from the source of the river's numerous tributaries all the way downstream to Lake Oroville where the North, Middle, and South Forks flow into the lake formed by Oroville Dam. However, vacationers and hikers who prefer the cooler-in-the summer elevations above 4,000 feet usually refer to the Feather River country as that region of the northern Sierra in the vicinity of the upper portion of the river's Middle Fork. Folks living nearer the town of Oroville, though, and even those who reside near the river as it flows from Oroville Dam south to join the Sacramento River just north of Sacramento, may take exception to my description.

The "bull's-eye" for the region covered by this book is the town of Graeagle in Plumas County. The bumper sticker sold in local stores asking "Where the Hell Is Graeagle?" may be a fair question from people who aren't familiar with this part of the Sierra. Finding the answer is well worth it.

How to Get There

To reach Graeagle from places west of the Sierra, drive east on Interstate 80 to Truckee, and then turn north on State Highway 89. From Truckee, Graeagle is 49 miles away by scenic, two-lane, Highway 89, which receives prompt snowplow attention during winter storms. An alternate route, and a good choice when Donner Pass on I-80 is choked with snow, is via State Highway 70 from Marysville and Oroville easterly through Quincy to Graeagle. Driving from Sacramento in dry weather, the Highway 70 choice takes about one-half hour longer than the I-80 route, but in snowy conditions, Highway 70 is a better choice. The maximum altitude on Highway 70 is only 4,425 feet at Lee Summit, while Donner Summit on I-80 is 7,239 feet.

Traveling from Reno to Graeagle, the preferred one-hour route is north on US Highway 395, 30 miles to Hallelujah Junction, and then west on Highway 70 another 30 miles to Graeagle, passing through Portola.

The nearest airport with commercial flights is Reno International, in Nevada. Nervino Airport, 15 miles east of Graeagle on Highway 70, is the nearest airport for private planes. Passenger trains traveling the once-famous "Feather River Route" were discontinued many years ago. One Greyhound bus a day each way travels Highway 70 and stops at the junction of Highways 89 and 70 in Blairsden.

Shopping and Things to Do

Graeagle and its nearby neighbor, Blairsden, have no shopping centers, thankfully, to detract from their quaintness. Still, almost everything a vacationer may want is available in Graeagle and Blairsden, including a gas station, auto repair, grocery store, hardware store, US Forest Service Regional Ranger Station, medical clinic, several nice restaurants (most of which close in the winter), a couple of churches, a new post office, and a variety of other retail establishments. The kids will be glad to know that these towns also boast a pizza parlor, video store, miniature golf, Frostee, public millpond for swimming, and stables for horse rentals. Six golf courses are within a five-to-ten-minute drive of Graeagle, and several charming shops and art galleries in town are fun to visit. Naturally, real estate offices abound, and, wouldn't you know it, the community even has a lawyer's office and a bank ATM. Accommodations in the region are extensive, ranging from rustic lodges, motels, and bed-and-breakfasts to RV parks and campgrounds. Luckily there are no massive Hilton Hotels, Holiday Inns, Marriott Suites, or the like, to overpower the area with a convention atmosphere.

For more extensive shopping facilities, the town of Portola is only a 12-minute drive from Graeagle. Portola features a well-equipped regional hospital, supermarket, drugstore, and library as well as many other retail stores. The male members of your family, and perhaps even its female members, will enjoy the free railroad museum in Portola where the displayed engines and railroad cars can be climbed on and walked through. On select weekends, for a small fee, kids, or even rail-smitten adults, can drive an actual train (slowly) on a short loop track.

It's nice to know that, at the time of this writing, not one fast-food restaurant has located in the area, nor even any chain stores (with the exception of a NAPA auto parts store in Portola). The county seat, Quincy, a 25-mile drive west of Graeagle, is a different story, though. Chain stores abound there, and the town even has a

traffic light—the only one in Plumas County!

The Yuba River Area

Because several of the hikes in this book are accessed by taking Gold Lake Highway to State Highway 49 (a 30-minute drive from Graeagle) to the North Fork of the Yuba River basin, some people question whether this North Yuba region is really part of the Feather River country. Technically, I suppose they're right that it's not. However, these "Yuba area" hikes fit well with the rest of the hikes in this book, because the Yuba trailheads all fall within the "45-minute drive from Graeagle" criterion I use. Hence, I've lumped the Yuba area trails in with all the rest. (Try 'em—you'll like 'em.)

Northern California

Chapter 3

How to Use This Book

This book has three purposes:
- ❖ To help you select a suitable hike.
- ❖ To tell you how to get to the trailhead and how to follow the route of the trail.
- ❖ To describe some of the fun special features of each hike or to point out any parts where extra caution is needed.

I emphasize the word *fun*, because that's what hiking the Feather River country is all about. I hope your enjoyment of hiking here will be similar to mine.

Within the past two years, I have hiked each of the trails included in this book, so the write-ups should be fairly accurate. I used a handheld GPS instrument to plot trails that didn't show up on the topo map or whose route had been changed since the map was published. All of the USGS topographical maps (throughout this book referred to only as "topo maps") are, alas, out of date, with the very newest ones dated 1981 and the oldest ones dating from the early 1950s. I wonder why the US Government can map the moon and the planets but cannot see its way clear to publish updated versions of these maps used by many hikers—especially in an era when aerial and satellite photography, coupled with computer production techniques, can make updating easy and accurate. To know which topo map you need for each hike, please refer to the regional map just before Part One. However, although I have strived for accuracy, you may find, in walking a trail, that it differs from my description. Certainly, each person observes things differently, and Mother Nature has a habit of making physical changes.

Abbreviations Used

ATV	all-terrain vehicle
GPS	global positioning system
NCO	Nevada, California, and Oregon Railroad
OHV	off-highway vehicle (jeep)
PCT	Pacific Crest Trail
RV	recreational vehicle
SUV	sport utility vehicle
SVR	Sierra Valley Railway
topo	topographical map (from the USGS)
UPRR	Union Pacific Railroad
USFS	United States Forest Service
USGS	United States Geological Survey
WPRR	Western Pacific Railroad

Selecting Which Trails Might Be of Interest

Location of Trails —Each of us has certain criteria for selecting a trail. No matter what your trail wish-list includes, you should be able to find several good trails in this book that will fit the bill (unless, of course, you're a Mount Everest type). To find a trail near where you're staying, check the regional map just before Part One to discover which topo map or maps the trail appears on. Then, because the hiking chapters are categorized by the topo map on which all or most of the trail occurs, review the applicable chapter or chapters to determine which hikes sound best. A review of the "Directions to the Trailhead" part of the write-up of each hike will enable you to discover the degree of difficulty you'll experience in driving to the trailhead. Also check the List of Some of the Best Trails by Feature at the end of this chapter.

Distances —The distance description is for the entire hike, including both directions for out-and-back trails and for the round-trip for loops. In some instances, an alternate trailhead, alternate trail route, or trail shortcut is suggested, and, in such cases, the alternative distance is also listed. The hike chapters omit any description of how long it will take to cover the entire distance, because hiking speed varies from one person to the next. The physical condition of each person and the difficulty of each trail obviously play a large part in elapsed time. As a rule of thumb, I usually figure a hiking rate of 2 miles per hour for level hikes and 1½ miles per hour for hikes with minor elevation gain or a rougher trail. These walking rates include time for short rest breaks, view admiring, photo taking, and flower examining, but do not include time for a lunch break.

Elevation Gain—The listing of "Total Elevation Gain" lets you know the total number of feet you'll be walking uphill. Many hikes have several up-and-down sections, so the elevation gain description is the sum of all "up" portions.

Sunset on Little Deer Lake (Hike GL-9)

Difficulty—The "Difficulty" section gives you an idea of the toughness of the trail. Naturally, my classifications of "easy," "easy/moderate," "moderate," "moderate/strenuous," and "strenuous" are subjective. A flat short trail will land in the "easy" category. A flat 2- or 3-mile trail or steeper short trail will earn an "easy/moderate" rating. "Strenuous," on the other hand, means plenty of elevation gain, a rough trail, a long haul, or some combination of these factors. "Moderate," naturally, falls somewhere in between and probably means an elevation gain of less than 1,000 feet and a distance of less than 6 miles.

Trailhead—My "Directions to the Trailhead" descriptions all commence at the town of Graeagle, simply because Graeagle is the bull's-eye of the Feather River country covered by this book as well as the focal point of the summer homes and lodgings of the region. If you're traveling to the trailhead from somewhere else, consult a road map or one of the maps published by the USFS, available at any ranger station. The Plumas National Forest map covers the entire area included in this book, but the Tahoe National Forest map doesn't show any of the area north of Highway 70.

This section also lets you know when an access road becomes one for which a four-wheel-drive vehicle is a good idea. In such instances, the description will usually give an alternative parking location that will avoid the jeep road, although these alternatives usually require a longer hike. (I always chuckle about the days before four-wheel-drive vehicles came into vogue, when a plain-old two-wheel-drive passenger car or pickup truck would slowly and cautiously traverse roads that today would receive a four-wheel-drive-only rating.)

Comments—In the "Comments" part of each subchapter I briefly cover some of the high points of the hike (or low points, if any), to give you a taste for the hike without having to read the whole hike description. Often, this section will describe some

particular history that applies to the trail or the area it traverses.

Hike Description— "The Hike" portion gives a complete description of the suggested route, together with a notation of trail intersections, interim distances, and points of interest. The Graeagle Store, the Blairsden Mercantile, and the County Library in Portola each have a coin-operated copy machine for your use if you wish to photocopy the applicable pages of a hike to avoid having to carry the whole book.

Camping—If you plan to use the trail for backpacking with an overnight campout, the "Camping" portion of each hike write-up will describe locations, with water, that are campable. Naturally, many hikes lack backpacking potential, and camping is prohibited along all the streams or at any of the lakes within the Lakes Basin Recreation Area (with the exception of Smith, Grass, Jamison, and Wades Lakes). For the trails whose trailheads are near a car-camping campground, this section also provides such information.

Winter Use— In winter, a few of the trails have potential for snowshoeing or cross-country skiing; these possibilities are described in the "Winter Use" paragraph. None of the Feather River region cross-country ski trails are groomed, and you will often find yourself having the fun of breaking fresh trail. Following a snow-covered trail through the woods is no easy matter, though, and only a few routes have the little blue arrow signs posted high on the tree trunks to help a skier or "shoer" find the path. With winter travel, however, you can always turn around and follow your tracks back, unless the route disappears during a Feather River country blizzard, which can cover your tracks in an amazingly short time. Although skiing or "shoeing" in a snowstorm is exhilarating, I always turn back before my tracks back to the car have been obliterated by fresh snow. I also take along an emergency blanket, extra clothes, and emergency provisions, just in case.

What This Book Doesn't Cover

I would have liked to include several other subjects in this book. However, my knowledge of these subjects isn't vast, and I acknowledge that they're covered beautifully in other books:

Geologic History and Mineralogy—A comprehensive book titled *History of the Feather River Country, California,* by Cordell Durrell, the late professor of geology at the University of California–Davis, tells you everything you could possibly want to know (and more!) about the area's geology. Most of the trails in my book traverse geologic features described in detail in Professor Durrell's book. I bought my copy at the Plumas County Museum in Quincy.

Fishing—Andrew Harris's recently published *Plumas National Forest Trout Fishing Guide* clearly describes many of the good lake and stream fishing places. However, quite a few of the hikes located within Tahoe National Forest—an area not covered by Harris's book—are fishable. The fishable lakes within Tahoe National Forest are given in my book and include Deer Lake (GL-1), the Salmon Lakes (GL-2 and GL-20), the Spencer Lakes (GL-12), Packer Lake (SC-1), the Tamarack Lakes (SC-1 and SC-4), Saxonia Lake (SC-5), Volcano Lake (HV-2), and Deadman Lake (HV-4). Also fishable are the North Yuba River (HV-6, HV-8, and HV-10) and its tributaries, Williams Creek (HV-3), Milton Creek (HV-7), Butcher Ranch Creek (SC-3 and GL-11), Pauley Creek (GL-11), Howard Creek (C-2), and Chapman Creek (C-4)—but whether there are fish in them, I can't tell you. Toss in a line and find out.

Wildflowers—Although I describe various wildflowers on various hikes, you will encounter many more varieties. For more complete coverage of wildflowers and trees you should own a copy of Toni Fauver's book, *Wildflower Walking in Lakes Basin of the Northern Sierra.* My wife carries a copy along on all Feather River country hikes. The disadvantage of Ms. Fauver's book is that it is not in color, but the black-and-white illustrations done by Marion Steinbach are excellent. Ms. Fauver's book is sold at most of the same local places that sell *Feather River Country Adventure Trails.*

Meadow in Mohawk Valley

List of Some of the Best Trails by Feature

Best Bag-a-Peak Trails
GL-14, GL-15, GL-16, C-1, J-6, J-9, SC-1, SC-2, CM-2, P-1, CP-1, RP-1

Best Trails with Great Views Not from Peaks
GL-1, GL-7, GL-9, C-3, J-4, J-16, SC-4, HV-2, HV-10

Best Wildflower Trails
GL-3, GL-5, GL-22, GL-26, C-5, J-3, J-9, SC-3, HV-3, HV-10, MF-2, GV-1

Best Trails to Waterfall Views
GL-4, GL-17, GL-27, GL-28, J-17, HV-6, HV-8

Best Trails Along Streams
GL-5, GL-22, C-2, C-5, C-9, J-15, B-3, BN-1, SG-1

Best Trails to Lakes
GL-1, GL-2, GL-8, GL-9, GL-10, GL-18, GL-20, GL-21, GL-29, GL-30, J-3, J-10, J-14, SC-5, HV-4

Best Trails Along Meadows
GL-26, C-6, B-2, SC-3, BN-1, GV-1, GV-3, GV-4, CM-1, P-2, P-4, CP-2

Best Historic and Ghost Town Trails
GL-19, C-7, J-5, J-7, J-12, J-13, B-2, B-6, BN-3, GV-3

Best Trails Along Old Railroad Rights-Of-Way
B-1, B-2, C-1, P-3

Best Trails to Old Mines
GL-10, GL-17, GL-24, C-5, C-7, J-7, HV-1, HV-3, HV-9, HV-11, MI-1

Best Short Easy Hikes
GL-4, GL-18, GL-20, GL-28, C-3, C-9, J-3, J-10, B-4, HV-5, HV-8

Best Hikes With Some Cross-Country
GL-12, J-6, CP-2, RP-1

Best Trails for Spring Hikes
C-9, J-3, J-4, -8, J-11, B-2, B-3, B-4, HV-6, HV-8, HV-10, SG-1, P-2, P-4

Best Trails for Fall Color
GL-13, GL-14, C-8, C-9, B-4, HV-10, GV-1, GV-5, SG-1, P-4

Chapter 4

Nice Things to Know and What to Take Along

Safety

I know I may sound like your overly concerned mother (why isn't it the father who sometimes gets the bum rap for being overly concerned?), but *hiking safety is of paramount importance*. Although I venture to guess that the most dangerous part of any excursion on any of the trails described in this book is the drive to and from the trailhead, I want to review some do's and don'ts for Feather River country hikers.

Plan Ahead—Prior to beginning any hike with which you are unfamiliar (or even partially familiar), you should read about the hike and review its route on the map. Hikes usually take longer than you expect, so don't plan more than you can reasonably expect to accomplish within the time you have allocated for the hike.

Recognize Your Capability—Excessive fatigue on the trail may result in an unsafe situation. Avoid trails that sound more difficult than you or anyone in your party can accomplish relatively easily. Not only is trail distance a factor, but total elevation gain, the smoothness of the trail, and weather conditions dictate how tough the hike will be. Each hike description elaborates on all but the weather.

Research the Weather—Because most hiking in the Feather River country is done during the summer, planned hikes probably will not need to be canceled or shortened because of bad weather. However, every now and then, a freak spring snowstorm may occur in April, May, or even early June, and winter storms may start in late October or early November. Very cold or extremely hot weather can dramatically affect the length and complexity of your hike, as can a summer thunderstorm. Read the local papers, watch the weather channel (in the Graeagle area it's Channel 35 on cable), or call the USFS Mohawk/Blairsden Ranger Station, 9:00 A.M. to 5:00 P.M. (530/836-2575), to get up-to-date weather information. For summer hiking, I have rarely experienced lousy weather, except for infrequent thunderstorms. Such storms are most often an afternoon occurrence and come and go within an hour. Chapter 5 includes a paragraph on how to reduce your chances of being struck by lightning.

Be Prepared

For a quick, one-hour walk, you probably will be fine not taking along anything extra. However, the longer and more aggressive the hike, the more you need to take extra stuff with you, such as the following:

Extra Clothing—I usually hike in short pants and a polo or T-shirt, but, on all but short trips, I take along a light rain jacket. (I'm fond of the completely waterproof, windproof, and breathable kind, the most popular of which is made of Gore-Tex material.) If I expect to be out late in the afternoon toward nightfall, or if I'm hiking in spring or fall, I might carry along a fleece pullover and perhaps some Gore-Tex long pants too.

Toilet Paper and a Trowel—Poop should be buried, if possible, six inches underground and covered thoroughly to prevent animals from digging it up (it sounds weird, but they do). Merely turning over a rock, pooping, and putting the rock back in place is *not* sufficient. So, carry a small plastic trowel (backpack stores sell them), dig a hole, and try to aim accurately. Modern conservation theory says used toilet paper is best carried out in a Ziploc plastic bag rather than buried (same goes for facial tissue, sanitary napkins, dirty diapers, and so forth). Please poop and pee at least 100 feet from lakes, streams, and trails, and a long way away from campsites.

Early morning calm on Lower Salmon Lake (Hike GL-20)

Water—Although many of the trails in this book visit lakes, ponds, and streams, water should not be drunk directly from these sources because of the probability that they contain the *Giardia* protozoan and other contaminants. Even sparkling-clear, rapidly running water far from grazing livestock may contain *Giardia*. All of the mammals in the Feather River country are subject to being contaminated, and their feces, which transmit the protozoan, can get into even the remotest water sources. Because giardiasis is debilitating and difficult to treat, it is best to avoid taking a drink of that inviting-looking, cool water. The solution is to carry along your own water or plan on purifying the water from the wilds. For day trips, I merely carry my own supply and don't bother with using a hand-pump filter (many good light-weight brands are available in camping and backpack stores) or disinfectant tablets. The tablets take 20 to 30 minutes to treat the water, besides making it taste lousy.

I have read that some doctors recommend

drinking ½ quart of water for each hour of hiking on a hot day. On day hikes with good pre-hike hydration (I drink a glass of water before leaving the house), I will admit that I don't follow their recommendation and usually carry only one quart per day for an average-weight adult. On super-hot days I may carry one and one-half times, or even two times, that amount, using plastic water bottles. Electrolyte supplement drinks or "energy drinks" such as Gatorade are excellent supplements to pure water because they replace electrolytes in the body that are lost by heavy exercise. Soft drinks, the experts say, are not the best thing for a trail beverage and will not substitute for water; someday I may heed their advice and not have my usual diet soda for lunch. Cocktail hours, in any case, are best held after a return from a hike, not while on it.

Meals: Breakfast, Lunch, and Dinner—As delightful as it sounds, other than on overnight backpacks, I have never tried breakfast or dinner on the trail. However, having a picnic lunch at a lake, along a stream, or at some vista point is one of the reasons I love hiking. Avoid overeating and foods that are tough to digest. Some hiking books list a bunch of foods considered no-noes for the trail, but, I will admit, for day hikes, I pay no attention to these no-noes, so as not to diminish the pleasure of the hike.

Snacks—The old tried-and-true trail mix or "gorp" (a mixture of nuts, raisins, M&Ms, and the like) seems to be losing popularity. For a snack, I prefer dried fruits or raisins. Naturally, everybody has their own preferences. The new "high energy" bars such as Power Bar, Balance Bar, or Stoker Bar are gaining popularity. On hikes, I carry a couple for emergency purposes, but none of the hikes described in this book is so energy-sapping that consumption of such high-calorie bars seems necessary—suit yourself on this issue.

Pills, Ointments, and Medical Devices—Be sure to bring along any prescription drugs that you normally take during the hours of your planned hike. The Sierra sun is tough on the skin, so I suggest liberally applying sunscreen lotion with a SPF of 15 or higher. Such practice is highly recommended by the experts, and I faithfully follow their advice. Put it on 30 minutes before leaving to allow it to "settle in," and don't forget the tops of your ears and any baldish spots (unless you wear a brimmed hat). I have read that replacing last year's sunscreen with a fresh supply is a good idea; I guess someday I should do that.

If you need a drug for some unexpected occurrence (such as Benadryl for an adverse reaction to a bee sting, or an inhaler to treat an asthmatic attack in a flowery meadow), always take some along. And, yes, in the Feather River country you *will* find voracious mosquitoes around throughout the summer, especially in damper areas near streams, boggy meadows, or lakes. Unless you are one of the lucky people who are not bothered by mosquitoes, I suggest applying insect repellent *before* leaving for your hike. Read the label, because many brands should not be applied to skin that will be covered by clothing. I have read a lot about which brands are best, but I dare not delve into that big subject here other than to say that a high DEET content seems to do the best job. Mosquitoes are attracted to perfumes or nice-smelling lotions, so, for hiking, you might wish to smell *au naturel.*

My wife religiously carries along two other items in mosquito country, and, I have to confess, I now do too. The first item is anti-itch stuff. She likes a product called After-Bite (a bunch of other brands are readily available), which looks like a fountain pen except that under the cap is an applicator. All it takes is a dab on the bite, and, for some people (but not everyone), the itch goes away. The second item has caused me to be the recipient of much teasing from my backpack buddies, but, darn it, it does a good job of de-itching a mosquito bite. Here too, there are several brands on the market, although I stick with one called The Extractor. If you have never seen one, it is a "reverse hypodermic" type device that, when the plunger is pushed in, causes a suction in the suction cup stuck on the "business end" of the device. Place the cup over the bite, push in the plunger to cause a suction, wait a couple of minutes, and *voilà!* the sting disappears for good as the suction sucks out the venom. I know it sounds weird, and you do look goofy sitting there with this thing stuck by suction to your skin. Also, when removed, it leaves a round little "hickey" on your skin that looks funny and does not go away for an hour or more.

Altitude sickness, which might bring on a severe headache and nausea, is rare in the modest altitudes found in the Feather River country. Nonetheless, you may want to take along some ibuprofen pills (I take Advil, but there are several good brands), which are also useful to treat other types of pains or strains. (With all pills and ointments, be sure to check the expiration date on the container, and, if you transfer the pills into a smaller bottle for hiking, mark the new container with the name of the pill, expiration date, and recommended dosage.)

First Aid Kit—I always carry along a hiker's first aid kit, which is smaller than my backpacker's first aid kit. The smaller kit includes antibiotic ointment, Band-Aids in various sizes, a small compression bandage roll, a roll of tape, tweezers, blister stuff (see the next item), and any pills described in the above paragraph. I freshen up my kit every year at the start of the hiking season to make sure that everything is dated properly and is in good condition.

Blister Stuff—Perhaps you are one of the lucky people, like me, who do not get blisters, but, if you are not, be prepared. Many people take preventive measures before leaving on the hike rather than waiting until an evil blister occurs while on the trail. New blister spots, though, seem to pop up where they never have before, no matter what preventive measures have been taken, thus causing the blisteree to stop on the trail to doctor a "hot spot" or tend a newly forming blister (get 'em early!). My wife now swears by a recently introduced product called New Skin, which is sprayed or painted on (there are several other brands). It dries to a slick, flexible skin covering that lasts for the entire hike. One disadvantage is the time needed for it to dry, so plan ahead. Some of my backpacking buddies had it fail for them because they put on their socks and boots before waiting the several minutes for complete drying. It seems to work well on existing blisters too. The old time-tested moleskin (the mole-lovers lobby in Washington, DC, probably has been successful in changing the name to "blister adhesive") is still used by many hikers, as are other products like Second Skin. Use whatever works best for you.

Maps, Compass, and GPS—Throughout this book, I refer to two types of maps. The *topo maps* published by the USGS are the most useful. These can be purchased at most backpacking stores, at the Plumas County Museum in Quincy, or directly from the US Geological Survey. (See Appendix E for other locations where you can buy maps.)

Two *USFS maps* cover the Feather River country: Plumas National Forest for the northern part, and Tahoe National Forest for the southern part. Another dandy map recently published by the USFS is titled "Lakes Basin, Sierra Buttes, and Plumas-Eureka State Park." I highly recommend purchasing this map, which covers many of the hikes in this book. All USFS maps can be purchased at USFS ranger stations as well as in many backpacking stores.

I carry a small *compass* but almost never use it. If you don't know how to use a compass with a map, it isn't of much use anyhow.

Learning how to use a *GPS instrument* with a map is far better than a compass. However, the devices are pricey, and, for most of the trails in this book, a GPS may be a toy to bring along merely to impress your hiking companions.

Flashlight—For emergency use only, I suggest carrying along a small, one- or two-cell AA or AAA flashlight. An inexpensive model is fine. Be sure to put in a fresh battery at the start of each hike season, because a two-year-old battery may not provide much light anymore.

Other Stuff

For hikes to the top of mountain peaks, I take a small pair of *binoculars* along—otherwise I don't bother with them.

My *camera* is always with me on hikes, plus an extra roll of film. I often use a point-and-shoot pocket-size camera instead of my heavier and bulkier Nikon with its fancy lenses. Everyone has their own preferences as to what camera they like.

Extra socks are great for a quick change at lunch, or for when you slip off that mossy rock into the stream. My wife carries an extra pair because her feet sweat a lot. (She is going to have a fit when she finds out that I have mentioned her sweaty feet in this book.)

A *pocket knife* is always a good friend to have along. I carry a pared-down version of the Swiss army knife, because all I need is one sharp blade, a can opener, and an awl, and I don't want to carry the extra bulk of the giant one that has all kinds of nonessential "bells and whistles."

My *emergency rations* consist of a few energy bars described earlier in the paragraph on snacks.

I have not carried a *snakebite kit* for many years. Modern theory says do *not* cut into the wound or suck on it with your mouth or use a tourniquet. If the bitten person can get to a hospital or doctor within three to four hours (via a slow walk out and a quick drive to the hospital or doctor's office), that's the best bet. The Extractor suction device described in the "Pills, Ointments, and Medical Devices" paragraph of this chapter may be an effective tool if the hospital is too far away. Both Portola and Quincy have hospitals, and Graeagle has a weekday-staffed medical clinic (see Appendix E for telephone numbers and addresses).

I always carry some strike-anywhere *matches* in a waterproof case for emergency use, despite the fact that I have never lit a campfire in the Feather River country (even on overnight backpack trips). If you have to spend an unplanned night on the trail, you might want a campfire for warmth and security, but, otherwise, there is no reason to ruin the landscape with a blackened fire pit and risk a forest fire (to say nothing of any civil or criminal penalties that might arise).

As to a *cellular phone* for calling out in an emergency, I have tried mine on numerous Feather River country hikes, and the darn thing always says "No connection" because it is out of cell range. Perhaps your cellular company has better coverage of the area than mine (call in advance to inquire).

Chapter 5

Good and Bad Things Found on the Trail

Humans—Perhaps the scariest things you will find on the trail are other humans, especially hunters, drunks (in particular, drunk hunters), and out-of-control mountain bikers. I have come across a few hunters on autumn hikes in the Feather River country, but, fortunately, I have never been a target. In fact, the few I have encountered have been friendly, sober, and cautious. The hunting season varies, so, for autumn hikes, you may want to check with the California Department of Fish and Game for applicable dates. The Blairsden Mercantile folks might have this information, or the staff at the USFS Mohawk/Blairsden ranger station might know. There is no hunting within the Plumas-Eureka State Park, so fall hikes within that area are a safe bet.

I have heard horror stories about hikers on the Appalachian Trail in the East being robbed at gunpoint or molested. Never have I heard of a similar occurrence in the Feather River country. I have always felt super-safe from unwanted human intrusion while hiking any of the trails in this book.

Also, rarely have I encountered mountain bikers (except the parts of Hikes SC-3 and GL-11 along the Butcher Ranch Creek Trail, fondly called the Downieville Descent by bikers), and, without exception, the ones I've met have been polite and in control. Plenty of tales are told about hikers having been

run down by bikers, but here too I have never heard of any such happening in the Feather River country.

Snakes—The only poisonous snakes I have read about that might inhabit the Feather River country are rattlesnakes. Yet in 30 years of hiking the region, I have seen only one rattler, and that was up a ravine off a trail that isn't even included in this book. Of course, that is no guarantee that rattlers are not out there, but my experience tells me that they are rare. I will admit that I have talked to other hikers who claim that they have seen any number of them, so caution is advised anyhow. Rattlers are scared of humans and will try to avoid conflict. They will coil and give their easily recognized rattle if cornered or surprised. Remember, a rattlesnake cannot strike a distance farther than its length, so, if you encounter one on the trail and you need to pass, politely ask him (or her?) to uncoil so that you can calculate how big a detour you need to make. On hot days, rattlers like shade. I have been on numerous Arizona and Southern California hikes that included the company of rattlesnakes, but, as I have said, the good old Feather River country has, for me, been delightfully free of such unwanted company.

Bears—Until one fine day last June when a beautiful, cinnamon-colored bruin made an appearance in a far-off meadow, I could say that I had never encountered a bear on any of the trails described in this book. Oh yes, they are out there—black bears, of course, not grizzlies (the only grizzly you will see in California these days is on the state flag). On several of the Feather River country trails I have come across bear scat, some fairly fresh, some old. True, that answers the question, "Do bears do it in the woods?" but, while it increases my awareness, I figure that the pooper is long gone. I have never heard or read about any bear attacks in the region covered by this book other than those encounters described by miners over a hundred years ago. While backpacking in other parts of the Sierra I have had plenty of bear encounters, so I know that black bears (yes, it is strange that even a brown-colored bear is of the black bear species) are usually not threatening. If you do encounter one, particularly if it is a female with her cubs, make noise so that it is not unduly surprised by your presence, do not make sudden moves, and do not continue hiking toward the bear. Chances are the bear will hightail it, once it discovers your presence, as did the one I saw in the meadow. Do not panic, and do not run. If you're backpacking, hang (or place in a bear-proof container now available at camping stores) food and other stuff like toothpaste, lip ointment, and, last but not least, that bag of M&Ms you have been saving. If you do not know the technique for bear-bagging on a back-pack trip, you should learn how to do it by reading almost any book on backpacking. Alas, in the Feather River country there are no food-storage bear boxes or bear poles such as are encountered in the "bearier" parts of the Sierra; their absence tells you something.

Mountain Lions— Although I would love to see

one, I never have, other than in the zoo. The closest I came was fresh tracks in the snow one spring, high up above the Lakes Basin on the PCT. Sightings by others have been made, but these animals are very leery of humans and will do their utmost not to be involved in an encounter. However, if you ever see one at close range, do not run or try to stare it down. Make yourself look as large as possible by raising your coat or shirt above your head. Pick up small kids and put them on your shoulders. Stay calm (sure, sure!), and do not panic. Here, too, I have never heard of a Feather River country mountain lion accident. Although we once saw a bobcat behind our house in Graeagle, I have never encountered one while hiking.

Squirrels and Rodents—Huh? Squirrels and rodents dangerous? Well, maybe. Now, don't get turned off, but I must mention that over the past few years, in a few very rare instances, bubonic plague has been found in a dead animal in the Feather River country. As a precaution, signs were posted and a few campgrounds closed, but I do not recall any cases of human infection. When you are merely hiking down a trail, no sick animal is going to run up and bite you, nor will it attack your lunch spot except, perhaps, to beg for a handout from a

Beckwourth Peak rising behind Ross Ranch Meadow (Hike P-2)

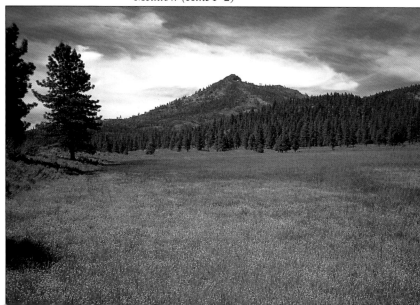

distance. I do not spend even 10 seconds a year worrying about a close encounter with such a critter. However, I mention it only to suggest that you not offer, in your hand, a morsel of your luncheon sandwich or snack to that cute, begging chipmunk.

Coyotes—Yes, we see them all the time. The past few summers, we have observed a lively coyote den near our house on the outskirts of Graeagle. Their family chorus on full-moon nights is a delightful, yet slightly chilling, sound. On the trail—no problem. Those coyotes I have encountered have made a fast getaway. I have never heard of a problematic Feather River country encounter between a human and a coyote.

Cattle—Yup, you will encounter them on a few of the hikes in this book. Where applicable, the description of the hike will tell which part of the trail might be shared with a member of the bovine species. Cows are big and mooey but not ferocious. A good yell and arm-waving usually makes them scram. The only negative about cows is the need to keep an eye out to avoid stepping on a meadow muffin.

Bugs and Such—I have been told that the region has a few scorpions and black widow spiders, but they are rare and I have yet to encounter either on any of the trails in this book. However, it does have plenty of bees and some wasps, so a bit of caution is advised if you encounter a hive. I have never run into one along a trail, but I know that they are out there somewhere.

The only flying pest of consequence is Ms. Mosquito (the only ones that bite you are the females—the males don't). Where there is water, particularly if it is not moving rapidly, mosquitoes will be found, but, for the most part, the trails described in this book will be mosquito-free.

I have never gotten a tick, but I do need to mention the buffalo gnat. This tiny no-see-'em insect is prevalent in grassy areas during late April, May, and maybe into early June. Their favorite parts of the body to attack are the ankles and around the back of the neck and back of the ears. Each unfelt bite develops a tiny red spot and then begins to itch. Several days pass before the itching stops, and I have yet to encounter a lotion or salve that relieves the infernal itching. On most trails, buffalo gnats will not be a problem unless you tread through a meadow or across a grassy field. Protecting the ankles with high-top boots or gaiters is one solution. They will not fly up neck-high if you are merely walking along, but if you are picnicking on a grassy field in May, I suggest a neck wrap and mosquito repellent around the neck. Somehow, they do not seem to like arms, faces, or fingers, and I have no knowledge of whether they care for fannies because, I assure you, I avoid pooping in meadows or grassy places (all year long).

I have never encountered anything but friendly dragonflies while taking a dip in any of the lakes of the area.

Plants to Avoid—None. To my knowledge the Feather River country has no poison ivy, poison oak, stinging nettle, or any other unfriendly plant.

Other Scary Stuff—The Feather River country does have summer thunderstorms with lots of lightning. The do's and don'ts for avoiding being struck by lightning are fairly well known. Do try for a forested area rather than open ground. Don't be on a mountain peak or in the water. Avoid standing or sitting under a lone tree, boulder, cliff edge, or overlapping rock ledge. If you are caught in an unforested area, crouching in a ditch or depression in the terrain helps to keep you from becoming a lightning rod 'til the storm passes.

Toxic Waste Sites—Who knows what kind of toxic stuff the old miners spread around? Still, I doubt if you will face much danger in this regard. For the one exception, Walker Mine and its ghost town, described in Hike MI-1, is the subject of one of the nation's all-time-longest and most complex cases of toxic waste litigation.

Chapter 6

History of the Feather River Country

Not much is known about the very early history of the first inhabitants of the region. Petroglyphs cut into rocks near Hawley Lake (Hike GL-26) have not been specifically dated and are of the Central Sierra style. Research by Dr. Robert F. Heizer and Dr. Albert B. Elsasser shows that such rock carvings in the region were likely created by a prehistoric group of Great Basin Native Americans who inhabited the area. The Maidu tribe replaced the prehistoric tribes somewhere between AD 1200 and 1800. Early interviews with Maidus in the nineteenth century could only elicit comments like "The petroglyphs have always been there." Dr. Heizer and Martin A. Baumhoff explored Plumas County in the 1950s and attributed the sites to the Martis peoples, who had settled in at least 21 camps or village locations within the county, each with as many as 50 inhabitants. More-recent tribes apparently did not create petroglyphs, possibly because such markings were thought to be "dangerous" and "taboo" or no longer needed to ensure hunting success.

The Maidu, about which a great deal is known, lived in many places throughout Plumas County. One of our neighbors in Graeagle has a fine collection of Maidu arrowheads he has found on his property.

The entry of whites into what is now California occurred long before explorers set foot in the Feather River country. Early Spanish and Mexican priests and explorers did not venture into this part of the Sierra. The trappers of Hudson Bay Company and American Fur Company who crossed the mountains in 1825, and frequently thereafter, did so farther south or by way of the Pit River much farther north.

The lower Feather River was first discovered by a Spanish exploring expedition in 1820, captained by one Louis A. Argüello. They named the river Rio de las Plumas (River of the Feathers) because of the large number of floating feathers. Eventually it became known simply as the Feather River. The same Spanish explorers also christened the Yuba River rather prosaically as Rio de los Uva. Uva was pronounced *Ooba* in Spanish, which soon was Anglicized into Yuba by the early miners. However, the Spanish never traveled up either of these rivers into the region covered by this book.

It has been speculated that Peter Lassen, for whom the mountain, county, and national park are named, was the first white man to set foot in what is now Plumas County. Records show that he visited the area in 1848 but may well have made earlier excursions into the region from his ranch north of Marysville. Emigrant parties followed either the Oregon Trail or Lassen's route over the Truckee River, which later became known as the Donner route, after the infamous leader of the doomed

Donner party of 1846–1847. Most immigrants in 1848 and the decade that followed were headed for the gold fields in the Sierra foothills above the Sacramento Valley. None ventured into the Plumas region until 1850, when a prospector named Stoddard and another man wandered through the area on a hunting expedition.

The Stoddard story is still shrouded in mystery, and several versions are related. However, it bears retelling from the account in Fariss and Smith's 1882 *History of Plumas County, California*. Stoddard and his pal became lost and wandered around for several days looking for their camp. In their wanderings they came upon a lake on whose shore they found some large chunks of gold. They pocketed the gold but were in such a panic to find civilization that they failed to note the location of the lake or its environs. The next day they were attacked by Indians, and supposedly Stoddard's companion was killed. Stoddard escaped but continued to wander, hardly stopping for rest, in hopes of find-ing help. At last, on the North Yuba River, he encountered some miners who gave him food and shelter. Before anyone could attempt to retrace Stoddard's steps, however, winter closed in, and any excursions to find the lake of gold were impossible.

During the winter, Stoddard and the miners who found him circulated throughout the Yuba and Feather River region, telling the story of Stoddard's find. Stoddard himself returned to the North Yuba and in the spring of 1850 attempted to form a party to hunt for his then-famous lake. Many thought him crazy, but his large gold chunks were powerful persuaders. Believers reasoned that the gold had washed down from the mountainside above the lake from a spot that would result in a record find of gold nuggets, simply lying there waiting to be picked up. From that point on, the story gains credibility as hordes of miners came to believe the story was true.

Lake Davis from the Crocker Mountain Trail (Hike CM-2)

Stoddard formed a party of 25 to go in search of the lake, although many more wished to go. (Fariss and Smith interviewed George Brittan, who, in 1882 when their Plumas history was published, was the only known survivor of the original party to start their search.) This party of 25 was followed by 500 to 1,000 men who had closely watched the preparations of the select few. They trekked up the ridge between the North Yuba and the Middle Fork of the Feather River (somewhere near the route of Hikes SC-3 and GL-11). As Fariss and Smith relate, "Wherever they went the crowd of miners clung to them like a shadow. Having reached the neighborhood where he supposed the lake to be, Stoddard appeared to know as little about its actual locality as any of his followers. He wandered about from place to place with his party, closely watched and followed by the crowd of hangers-on, who supposed that the apparently aimless movements were made for the purpose of throwing them off the scent and to tire them out."

They traveled over much of the area covered in this book, and finally it became clear that Stoddard could not find his lake of gold. Fariss and Smith relate, "The party was badly demoralized. Many of their animals had perished, some in deep snow, and others being dashed to pieces upon the rocks of some dark and precipitous cañon. For a number of days they had been discontented, and now they rebelled openly. A meeting was called to discuss the situation, and it was decided to hang the author of their woes at once. A few dissenters convinced the others to give Stoddard one more day to find the lake." That night, Stoddard snuck quietly out of camp and escaped back to the mines on the Yuba.

The news of Stoddard's party spread like wildfire throughout the mining camps of the Sierra (unaccompanied by the salient detail that the lake of gold had not been found). Gold fever set in, and men stampeded toward the Feather River country, some

in large parties, but most others in groups of two or three, hardly taking time to stock up on provisions. The epidemic extended way down to the southern Sierra. The prices of horses, mules, and oxen skyrocketed. Because neither wagon roads nor even trails existed, wagons were useless, and all supplies had to be brought in on the backs of pack animals.

The excitement lasted about a month, but it was sufficient to infuse the area with hundreds of gold-seeking men who naturally turned to prospecting for gold rather than returning to the hardscrabble mining areas they had left. In this manner, gold finds were made in numerous places throughout the region (although most of the early action took place on the Middle Fork west of the area covered by this book), and the next 80 years of historic mining in the Feather River country commenced.

Oh yes: whatever became of good ol' Stoddard? For several years he hung out around the mines on the Yuba River trying to form another search party. Most folks thought him crazy, and he never was able to get another group together. None of the Stoddard stories relates his fate.

When California became a state in 1850, the area that is now Plumas County was part of Butte County. In 1851, Quartz Township was formed as part of Butte County, its name coming from a gold mine discovered the previous year and later known as the Plumas-Eureka Mine. Appendix B describes the history of this famous producer of gold. In March 1854, the state legislature determined that a separate county, Plumas, should be carved out of Butte County to deal with Plumas's swelling population and the inaccessibility of its territory from the seat of government in Butte County.

By 1851, a few farmers had settled in Mohawk Valley, finding a good outlet for their produce (see Hike B-6). That same year Jim Beckwourth opened his famous emigrant trail, which lured travelers through the area on their way to the Sacramento

River Valley. (See Appendix D for the Beckwourth Trail history.)

For many years, mining was the principal industry of the Feather River country. A number of sawmills were built, although their output was destined for tunnel support beams in the mines and for constructing mine buildings and workers' cabins. By the 1910s, a few mines were still operating, but completion of the Western Pacific Railroad in 1908 opened the area to other possible industries. Cut lumber was in growing demand in Sacramento and San Francisco, so mills began shipping lumber out of Plumas County. Logging trains enabled cut trees to be brought from farther distances and in greater quantities than could be achieved previously by carts. So, as mining faded, lumbering took over as the region's main source of income.

The completion of State Highway 70 in 1937 (described in Hike B-6) provided better access to the area for tourists. Today, tourism and lumbering are the dominant sources of income for Plumas County.

Looking south across Charles Valley from the Charles Valley Trail (Hike P-4)

Part Two

The Hikes

Chapter 7

Gold Lake Topo

GL-1 Deer Lake Trail with Alternative Loop Back on the PCT

Distance: 5 miles out and back (with the Alternative Loop, 8 miles)
Highest Point: 7,068 feet (with the Alternative Loop, 7,435 feet)
Total Elevation Gain: 980 feet (with the Alternative Loop, 1,260 feet)
Difficulty: Moderate (with the Alternative Loop, moderate/strenuous)
Hiking Season: June or July through October

Directions to the Trailhead: From Graeagle, go south on Highway 89 for 1.4 miles. Turn right onto Gold Lake Highway, and, after 12.8 miles, turn right onto a paved road with a sign to Packer and Sardine Lakes. Just after this turn is a Y with the left branch going to the Sardine Lakes and the right toward Packer Lake; take the right fork. On your left, 2.7 miles from Gold Lake Highway, on a good paved road is the well-used USFS Packsaddle Campground. Turn in, and park in the hikers' parking area to your right across from campsite 1.

Comments: The pleasant hike to Deer Lake is on a well-traveled trail with a good bit of uphill. If you have the time and the energy, I highly recommend extending this hike from the Deer Lake Trail junction up to the PCT, then hiking south on the PCT to Forest Road 93, and completing the loop down 93 to your car. This part of the PCT offers outstanding views of Sierra Buttes and the basin containing Packer Lake. A short side trip from the PCT to Wallis Mine is also worthwhile.

The Hike: From the campground, walk back to the paved road, and go about 50 yards back the way you came. Cross the road, and commence north up the trail signed "Deer Lake Trail." Even though the topo map is one of the most recent USGS maps in the region, dated 1981, it calls this trail part of the "Pacific Crest National Scenic Trail." However, the PCT route has changed here from that shown on the topo, as it has in much of the area covered by this book. The trail winds uphill and soon crosses Packer Creek, the outflow from Packer Lake. The crossing on nonwobbly stones is easy. A bit farther, some dim trails intersect, but you can pick out the Deer Lake Trail because it is so well worn. Behind you is your first glimpse of Sierra Buttes, with their sharp profile cresting at 8,591 feet. Don't fret that you can't get a good buttes photo through the trees; you'll have much better opportunities a bit later.

Another ¼ mile brings you to a second creek crossing, also easily accomplished on good flat rocks. The trail continues uphill, levels a bit, and comes to a trail on the right with a sign "Grass Lake" (one of several lakes with the same name in this part of the Sierra). The lake is only about 300 yards away, so you may wish to detour and give it a look (although, on a scale of 1 to 10, I wouldn't give this one more than a 3). Along the south shore are some mediocre camping places, and, with the lake's marshy edges, I'll bet an early summer campout would include being visited by a million mosquitoes.

Don't be too disappointed though—Deer Lake will make up for Grass Lake's lack of charm. A few hundred yards after returning to the main trail you encounter Sawmill Creek, the outflow from Deer Lake. Here, you find no friendly rocks on which to hop across. You can either wade (the bottom isn't rocky, nor is the water too swift, but gets about two feet deep) or backtrack 30 yards, and cut back to the creek downstream. The place to cut back is getting pretty well trod, so you may easily discover the proper route. Your reward is a large log that handily spans the creek. Unless your balance is poor, you can carefully cross on the log and wind up with dry feet and a sense of accomplishment. It is easy to parallel the creek back to the wade-across crossing and pick up the main trail.

Soon, a four-way intersection appears. A sign on the side of the trail indicates right to "Upper Salmon Lake 1½," straight ahead to "PCT ½" and sharp left to "Deer Lake ¼." Naturally, you head off to the left. Climbing up a glaciated rock face, you pop over the top and behold exquisite Deer Lake below you. My inclination was to immediately whip out my camera but there are lots of better photo spots on the trail that follows the lakeshore. Because it has better views, I always choose the trail to the right, which follows the lake's

north shore, offering magnificent panoramas of Sierra Buttes in the distance across the lake. You'll seldom find a more scenic lunch spot. You might even try one of the sandy beaches if they haven't already been taken by other hikers. Yes, one of the few drawbacks is that during "the season" you have to share this lake with others who have found its fairly easy access and great beauty.

After enjoying Deer Lake, if you're not doing the Alternative Loop, return to Packsaddle Campground the way you came. However, I highly recommend the loop if you're not too tired and have a couple of hours before you need to be back at your car. To do the whole loop, continue around the northern edge of the lake on the shore trail. Just before it dead-ends at a large rock face, you find a well-used campground with a dim trail leading steeply uphill. The lower part of this trail seems to follow several routes, so, pick one, and continue uphill. Eventually you reach a crest above the lake, and just as your view of the lake disappears you

Deer Lake with Sierra Buttes in the distance

intersect with a trail that leads back to the four-way intersection to the right. To the left it continues up for ¼ mile to a T intersection with the PCT.

Just before reaching the T is a fine view through the trees to the north of Upper Salmon Lake. At the T, you find a PCT signpost giving no directions or distances. Turn left, and soon you will be awed by the view of Deer Lake below and, far beyond it, the spires of Sierra Buttes. A photographer will be mighty happy with the photo opportunities available on this next stretch of trail. The route goes south along the ridge above Deer Lake, and then suddenly intersects with a jeep road. "A jeep road way out here?" you mutter to yourself. Yes, and a description I read about the area says that a jeep trail even leads down to the western shore of Deer Lake, although I couldn't see where it would be and the topo map doesn't show it. Heaven forbid that

the beautiful serenity of Deer Lake be shattered by the roar of four-wheel-drive vehicles!

This intersection is confusing because the jeep road heads north (with signs saying it's for four-wheel-drive vehicles) and also south, more or less paralleling the PCT. Over the next several hundred yards, this jeep trail crosses, recrosses, and runs immediately adjacent to the PCT. Just stay on what looks like trail, not road, and you'll be OK. Finally, the jeep road cuts westerly downhill, and you're left with just the good old PCT.

The trail continues along the ridge west of Deer Lake, and, although the buttes are no longer the backdrop, the views are still "way above average." The purist in you will revolt at the sight of clear-cut logging as you head westerly below the crest. Old stumps of massive trees show that the loggers cut some "fine ones." Although this logging appears to have occurred quite a few years ago, the forest is just beginning to reestablish itself (the loggers obviously never replanted) and new trees are only a foot or so high. A bit farther along the trail, you notice that the loggers left a few large trees rather than completely clear-cutting. A lot of good this did! The few large firs were left without the shelter of their former neighbors, exposed to the high winds that occasionally roar up the ridge from the west. The result is dozens of giant red firs that have been snapped in two by gales. The winds would have had little effect if the full protective forest had still been in existence. Hardly a complete tree remains, and the area is littered with snapped-off tops—not little stuff, but full-grown trunks. At last, after passing this devastation, the trail commences a few gradual downhill switchbacks. You pass other PCT posts that are supposed to show mile markers, I believe. However, the deteriorating wood of some and the ruining knives of foes-of-the-forest on others have made them unreadable.

To add to your view-filled day, take a brief detour as a jeep road crosses the PCT. My map indicated that I needed to turn left for a short walk downhill to see what might remain of the Wallis Mine. Indeed, after crossing a fallen steel cable and following a couple of switchbacks, I came to some tailings and, off to the left, the mine entrance. Above the padlocked entrance door a sign read, "Golden Key Mine." I guess a subsequent owner decided that Mr. Wallis no longer needed to be recognized. Gold, I assume, was the goal, but the sole entrance and the diminutive tailings pile suggest that Mr. Wallis's find was not particularly productive.

Back on the PCT heading south, you find the last bit of wonderful view, to your left in the basin below: Packer Lake. During the summer, you might see specks on the lake—people lounging on air mattresses or rubber rafts. Please don't ponder, in your tired, hot, sweaty condition, how nice it would be to be floating on cool Packer Lake instead of tromping down the PCT. After you've gone ¼ mile from the Wallis Mine side trail, the PCT reaches Packer Saddle and a four-way road intersection (although it appears to be three-way, because the dirt road to the right is below the lip of the saddle).

If you were to continue on the PCT, you would cross the paved intersection. Alas, this is the end of the wonderful trail for your trip and the beginning of a steep mile-long descent on paved Forest Road 93. Turn left, and walk the narrow paved road downhill. Try at this point to focus on the wonderful trails you've been on for the past few hours and not to be peeved that this lovely day's hike finishes on a paved road. Keep truckin', and, without having to dodge much traffic on this lightly used portion of 93, you'll approach the dirt road turnoff to Packer Lake. Just before that turnoff on your left, a rocky jeep road angles off slightly to the right. Take this "cut-off" for the final few hundred yards to your car, to avoid spending any more time on the paved road.

Camping: At the trailhead, the USFS Packsaddle Campground offers good car camping. (It fills on summer weekends.) For backpackers, Grass Lake has some OK, but not spectacular, campsites, and Deer Lake has lots of good sites. Most of the sites are around the north side, but several dandies are on the east and south shores. Along the stretch of the PCT that you hike if you do the Alternative Loop, there are no good water sources, so camping on the ridge to the west above Deer Lake is generally done by folks driving in on the jeep roads with a good supply of water and perhaps other beverages. There is no camping at Packer Lake, although Packer Lake Lodge offers nice rustic accommodations for noncampers.

Winter Use: None.

GL-2 Upper Salmon Lake Trail to Summit Lake

Distance: 7¾ miles out and back with loops

Highest Point: 7,420 feet

Total Elevation Gain: 1,170 feet

Difficulty: Moderate/strenuous

Hiking Season: June or July through October

Directions to the Trailhead: From Graeagle take Highway 89 south for 1.4 miles, and turn right on Gold Lake Highway. Drive 11.3 miles, and turn right at the sign to Salmon Lakes. The paved road dead-ends in 1 mile at a parking lot adjacent to Upper Salmon Lake. If the lot is full, parking along the road is OK. RVs and trailers are not allowed to park in the lot.

Comments: This hike leads you by a series of lakes, each with a different charm and character. Upper Salmon, the largest of the four, is, in the summer, usually dotted with boats, rafts, inner tubes, and what-not. Its charming lodge, at the far end of the lake, is accessible only by boat or trail. Horse Lake is scenic but not one of the all-time best. Deer Lake *is* one of the best. Finally, Summit Lake, reached after a pretty walk on the PCT, rates in the bottom half of the beauty chart. You can't have every lake in the region a "wow" experience; I consider any lake away from the main road worth visiting.

The Hike: Don't be fooled into starting your hike on the lakeside trail from the western end of the parking lot. This fisherman's trail nearly touches the water in several places, but it eventually comes to a dead end with no access to the upper trail where you need to be. Instead, from the parking lot, walk back along the road about 80 yards. On your left is the correct trail, marked "Upper Salmon Lake Trail." It parallels the north side of the lake but is,

on the average, about 120 feet above lake level. You won't be terribly excited about all the rocks in the trail and the lack of shade, but these conditions last for only about ½ mile. Nice views of Upper Salmon Lake below you help to make this portion of the hike more enjoyable. You can see the main lodge and the widely spread cabins of Salmon Lake Resort at the western end of the lake. The trail in midsummer offers a rich variety of wildflowers; I'm always amazed at the colorful display, despite the fact that this south-facing ridge receives little water after the snowmelt ends.

Looping around the northwest corner of the lake, the trail finally drops down to lake level and passes the first of several lakeside cabins that are part of the resort. Stay on the trail at the side of the lake, and a short distance farther the lodge appears. Along this route, on the lake side, is a fine example of American dogwood, a shrub, not a tree, with small white flowers and beautiful red foliage in autumn.

The rustic lodge has recently been remodeled. Some updating was probably due, because it was originally built in the 1920s on old tailings from the long-gone Peck Mine, located on the mountainside high above the lake. The lodge originally catered to both miners and tourists, but tourists are, naturally, its only occupants now. Several of the cute cabins are remotely located on the mountainside above the lodge. Getting your luggage from car to cabin involves lugging it from car to dock, loading it in the lodge's shuttle boat for the ride across the lake, unloading it to a cart pulled by a mini-size tractor that slowly chugs up the rocky trail, and, at last, unloading it at the proper cabin. Fortunately, lodge employees help with all these logistics. Each unit has a different design and a spectacular view of the lake, making them unique among rentable Sierra cabins. They are absolutely not wheelchair accessible. All meals are served at the lodge.

The trail passes between the lodge's front steps and the lakeshore, and then immediately makes a right turn heading uphill, paralleling a creek. Where a trail branches right to the hillside cabins, a sign saying "Deer Lake Trail" and "Horse Lake ⅛" points the way to the left. The short stretch of trail you take to Horse Lake climbs at a moderate grade. Horse Lake's backdrop is the 600-foot-high ridge along which you'll later be walking on the PCT. The lake is completely surrounded by willows, some of which are the less "willowy" ligulate or Mackenzie's willow, whose male flower is fluffy, like a pussy willow. It would be difficult to fish Horse Lake, because the willows are so dense and completely encircle the water, allowing no shore access. You're treated to a wildflower display of great variety along the trail, especially in the vicinity of Horse Lake. Light pink sandwort, white six-petaled fawn lily, and blue wandering daisy were some of the more rarely seen varieties I found, joined by the more common lupine, paintbrush, sulfur buckwheat, spiraea, and cinquefoil.

Although the topo map (dated 1981, "new" compared to many of the region's way-out-of-date topos) shows a trail around the southern edge of Horse Lake leading up to the ruins of the Peck Mine, I couldn't find where it cut off from the main trail. It would be fun someday to work on reconstructing this now-obliterated trail to the historic mine.

The trail from Horse Lake to Deer Lake goes uphill at a fairly steep angle, with only a few small switchbacks to make the gradient less severe. To compensate, it is smooth, shady, and loaded with wildflowers. I saw a "haven't seen before" stonecrop, a low-growing plant with succulent-type leaves and a puffy pink cluster of flowers along a vertical red stem. (My flower book says the young leaves and plants are edible.) You continue ½ mile above Horse Lake to a four-way trail intersection. The sign shows Deer Lake ¼ mile in one direction, the PCT ½ mile in another, and Upper Salmon Lake 1½ miles back the way you came. It fails to point left to Packer Lake along the Deer Lake Trail (Hike GL-1). (I know, the sign at the lodge called the trail you just took the "Deer Lake Trail" too. Well, I guess they both go to Deer Lake, so why not—although the one from Packer Lake is the one commonly known as "the" Deer Lake Trail.) At this point, take the trail on the right to the PCT. Later you'll return to this point after completing the loop above Deer Lake.

The trail up to the PCT is easy to follow but not as highly used as others in the area. It climbs steadily, and, in ¼ mile, a faint trail (which you will take later) branches off to the left. Another ¼ mile brings you to a T intersection with the PCT with a typical PCT "post" bearing no directions on it. Behind you is a nice view of Deer Lake and Sierra Buttes rising majestically in the distance. Turn right on the PCT, and commence enjoying its smooth, fairly level, and very beautiful route. Soon, views of Lower Salmon, then Upper Salmon, and Horse Lake appear in the drainage basin below, to the east. A bit farther, and Gold Lake pops into view in a more northerly direction, identifiable by its larger size.

This part of the PCT differs from that shown on the 1981 topo map, and it passes on the easterly, not the westerly, side of Peak 7502. Indeed, this "new route" is welcome because it provides these lake views, which the topo map route didn't have. The trail begins a downhill stretch with a few gentle switchbacks. Before you reach what looks like the bottom of the canyon, the trail crosses a jeep road. I heard the on-off roar of a jeep engine being gunned, the sound made by someone trying to get

Horse Lake on the trail above Upper Salmon Lake

a vehicle unstuck. Sure enough, here it was the last week in July, and a jeep with big tires was stuck in a huge snowbank still covering the road. I'm sure that the driver eventually got through, but I decided to hike, not gawk.

At the jeep road intersection bunches of signs point in all sorts of directions. Although you'll hate not to continue along the accommodating PCT (see Hike GL-23 for the PCT north of this point), turn left on the jeep road, and in a few steps you'll find little Summit Lake nestled among the trees. One of the things that makes a lake pretty is a mountain backdrop, and poor little Summit suffers by not having any interesting mountains around it. Although at this point you could retrace your steps along the PCT, I suggest a mini-loop route, continuing on the road. As it passes Summit Lake it forks. Take the left fork with the sign "Deer Lake 2," and follow the lightly used jeep road along the ridge, now with views off to the west. In the distance you can see the ridges of Second Divide and Third Divide. On the topo map, this jeep road is shown as the PCT, but the current route of the PCT is the one you were on earlier.

In about 1 mile, the jeep road attains the crest of the ridge overlooking Deer Lake and intersects with another jeep road. You need to be alert at this point because your connection with the PCT back in a northerly direction is not immediately obvious. The intersecting jeep road cuts back sharply to the left, and the PCT just a few yards farther east also cuts back sharply to the left but slightly nearer the rim overlooking Deer Lake. Don't head south to your right. Travel north on the PCT for about ¼ mile, until you reach the T intersection you were at previously. Then head down the same trail on which you hiked up to the PCT.

About halfway back to the four-way intersection, a dim trail heads right. Take it for a mini-loop down to Deer Lake. The lake cannot be spied at this turnoff, but it soon comes into view. The trail down gets steep in parts as it nears the lake. In this lower section you'll also find a variety of routes; all wind up at the same place on the lakeshore, so pick the one that looks best to you. Upon reaching the lake, the trail crosses a large campsite, then goes left around the western and northern edges of the lake, and in some places is almost in the water. The view across the lake toward Sierra Buttes is terrific.

As you round the lake to its north shore, the trail cuts uphill, while a narrower trail hugs the shoreline. As you being to climb out of the lake basin, a tree on your left has an old double blaze. Blazing (cutting rectangular chunks out of the bark to mark trail routes) has long since been discontin-

ued as an ecologically unsound defacing of trees. Along the ¼ mile trail back to the four-way intersection you pass several ponds, which dry up by late summer. Along this stretch I saw some red mountain heather, a wildflower I hadn't encountered previously, although the flower book says it's not uncommon. It is distinctively different from other Sierra wildflowers, with fine petite pink flower clusters surmounting a 3-inch stem with short pine-needle-like "leaves."

The trail down from Deer Lake arrives at the four-way intersection, completing your mini-loop. The route back by Horse Lake to Upper Salmon Lake is perhaps even more enjoyable than on the way up because you're coasting downhill rather than chugging uphill. On the final stretch back to your car, above Upper Salmon Lake, you may well decide to join the people lounging in the sun on a raft in the lake or on one of the lake's two islands after your big day's hike.

Camping: Summer weekends bring backpackers to Deer Lake, and many of the good camp spots on the lakeshore will be taken by midday on Saturday. Horse Lake and Upper Salmon Lake do not offer camping possibilities. At the point where the PCT meets the jeep road, I've encountered jeep folks camping, but, because this spot has no water, it's probably not a site for backpackers. Summit Lake also offers (mosquito-laden) camping for either backpackers or the four-wheel-drive crowd, but most backpackers prefer camping where vehicles aren't.

Winter Use: None.

GL-3 Gray Eagle Creek Trail

Distance: 4¼ miles out and back

Highest Point: 5,800 feet

Total Elevation Gain: 463 feet

Difficulty: Easy/moderate

Hiking Season: June through October

Directions to the Trailhead: From Graeagle take Highway 89 south for 1.4 miles to Gold Lake Highway, turn right, and drive 3.3 miles to a wide spot in the road on your right with a sign saying "Gray Eagle Creek Trail." There is plenty of room for parking.

Comments: This is one of my favorite hikes with friends who don't want a long, bumpy, dusty road to the trailhead and a very difficult long hike but do want pretty scenery. If you don't want to hike but want to visit a pretty mountain stream, you might try the first ¼ mile only: although it is a bit steep and rocky, just go slowly until you get to the footbridge over Gray Eagle Creek. Spend a few minutes at the footbridge admiring the creek as it tumbles along before you turn back. For nice picnic spots, this is tough to beat. Some fine streamside boulders plus a tiny sand beach a few yards downstream from the footbridge on the eastern side of the creek are swell places for a noon meal (hey, even breakfast or dinner here wouldn't be bad).

The Hike: The trail leads west from the south end of the parking area. The first ¼ mile down to the footbridge is not flat or smooth, but the trail is well traveled and can be negotiated by almost anyone who can climb stairs. If you take pictures on your hikes, you certainly will want to click off a few of Gray Eagle Creek from the footbridge.

You may wonder why "Gray Eagle," the name of the creek, is two words and "Graeagle," the name of the town, is one word. The town

was originally named "Davies Mill" after the owner of the sawmill (he also owned the entire town). In 1921, Davies sold out, and the new owners wanted a new name. There are conflicting stories about how the new name was coined, but the name-the-town contest described at the beginning of the Hike B-6 is the most enjoyable.

You reluctantly leave the footbridge and its nice view of the creek, continuing on the zigzag trail uphill for a short distance to a trail intersection. Here a sign points right to "Graeagle 2¼" and left to "Gray Eagle Lodge 2" and "Smith Lake 3½." Before reaching this intersection, you may spy what looks like a trail leading to the right, but there's a pile of brush across it to tip you off that it's not your route. Turn left toward the lodge, and proceed uphill a bit farther on the rocky trail; soon it becomes smoother and less steep. Overhead, a thick black telephone line appears. It is attached to the trees along the way, which is fine because telephone poles would definitely impair the feeling of wilderness. But the problem with using trees as attaching points is that they occasionally topple over. Indeed, one early spring when I took this hike, one line-holding tree had finished the winter in a horizontal position, putting several hundred feet of phone wire on the ground. Somehow, the line had stretched and not snapped. I was glad the line was telephone, not electrical, because the latter would have created a very dangerous situation.

The trail parallels the creek for the entire remainder of the hike to the turnaround point, but, because the creek is somewhat below trail level and plenty of foliage is growing in the area between the creek and the trail, no sight of the water is available. On the other hand, the sound of the creek never disappears, so you'll have some of the joy of walking near a creek. Another aspect of walking near the creek is the company of the aggressive Gray Eagle Creek mosquitoes. I suggest putting on mosquito repellent before you start this trip.

About 1½ miles from the footbridge, your surroundings get greener, with ferns and water-loving plants. Underfoot, you begin to encounter water on the trail and need to detour to keep your footwear dry. (The latest environmental magazine articles say don't detour because the "new trail" just causes more damage to foliage. Instead, tromp through on the wet trail, getting your boots muddy.) In spring, this area can become quite waterlogged, and, on one spring hike, my companions and I had to turn back here, because there was too much wet footing to cope with. One benefit of all this dampness is that it creates a different environment for wildflowers. In midsummer we identified several varieties not seen earlier along the route. We particularly enjoyed the lady's thumb, a two-foot-tall stem capped with a two-inch-long tightly packed cluster of white round flowers. About ¼ mile after leaving the damp

Footbridge over Gray Eagle Creek

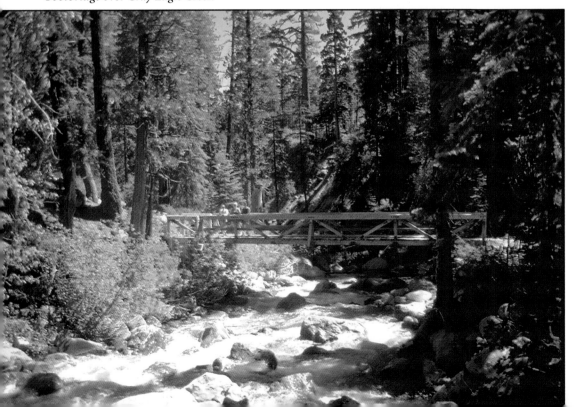

area, the trail intersects a dirt road, the entrance road to Gray Eagle Lodge. The lodge itself is several hundred yards farther, and the parking area and trailhead for the Smith Lake and Smith Creek Trail (Hikes GL-5, 16, and 22) is just to your right.

If you wish, detour 250 yards on the road to see the lodge, which is wonderfully constructed of massive logs. Be sure to go inside to see the rock fireplace and large exposed ceiling beams. (The small rustic bar might be a good "watering hole" before you head back.) Then turn around and retrace your steps back to the trailhead.

Consider planning this hike in midsummer for late afternoon, and walk to the lodge for dinner (reservations are a must, 530-836-2511). Gray Eagle Lodge is one of my favorite places to take guests for

an excellent dinner. The owners take special pride in their good, although not extensive, wine list. After an early dinner, you will enjoy the evening walk back along the trail to your car (with plenty of mosquito company, however) before darkness sets in. As an alternative, you could take the dirt road for ½ mile back to the Gold Lake Highway and walk the pavement, which makes a right curve and then heads almost in a beeline for your car.

Camping: None. (Car camping is found at the USFS Lakes Basin Campground 3 miles beyond the trailhead off Gold Lake Highway.)

Winter Use: None. Gold Lake Highway is not plowed as far as the trailhead. However, the unplowed highway is a favorite route of snowmobilers.

GL-4 Frazier Falls Trail

Distance: 1 mile out and back

Highest Point: 6,180 feet

Total Elevation Gain: 25 feet

Difficulty: Easy

Hiking Season: May through November

Directions to the Trailhead: From Graeagle, take Highway 89 south for 1.4 miles to Gold Lake Highway. Turn right, and drive 1.6 miles to a road on the left with a sign saying "Frazier Falls 4." Take this paved but narrow road for 4.2 miles to a parking lot with a sign "Frazier Falls Observation Site" and another "Frazier Creek ¼, Frazier Falls ½."

Comments: Well, the falls in Yosemite are mighty spectacular, but, for little old Plumas County, Frazier Falls isn't bad, particularly in the spring and early summer when Frazier Creek is in full flow. The falls are still falling in late summer and autumn, but they are nowhere near as spectacular as earlier. The trail has some ups and downs, but toddlers and

Frazier Falls

The trail winds around and over rocks that were polished by the glacier that filled this canyon around 10,000 years ago. In ¼ mile, the route crosses a nice footbridge over Frazier Creek. For a view from the top of the falls, turn left off the main trail here. This path isn't a maintained trail, but enough people have taken it so that it's like a trail. Stay to the left of the polished rock face, and follow the creek downstream. In about 200 yards, wow, there you are at the place where Frazier Creek disappears over the edge of the canyon in a mighty roar. This is one place you shouldn't bring the kids—it's way too dangerous. One slip and the rushing creek will sweep the tyke over the edge in a blink. The rocks at the edge of the brink are uneven and slippery, so even adults should exercise extreme caution. I was appalled to see how close to the edge some people were going—in sandals, yet. Overenthusiastic and rambunctious teenagers might also best be shepherded along the main trail and not introduced to this side trip. The return from the top of the falls to the main trail is along this same route.

From the bridge, you go only another ¼ mile to a left turn in the trail that ends at the viewing spot. Fortunately, 3-foot-high fencing encloses the viewpoint, so that kids and drunks can't slip over into the abyss. Now that you're there, you too will "ooh" and "ah" at the beauty of the falls. The site is directly across the canyon from the falls and far enough away so that your conventional camera in vertical position can perfectly capture its full length. Because the viewpoint looks almost directly west toward the cascade, photography in the late after-

great-grandmothers are seen traversing it with ease. Dogs on a leash are welcome on this trail. Hey, your pooch might enjoy the view, but I bet he or she will be more interested in grasshoppers. The sign at the start of the trail points out that the route is for foot traffic only.

The Hike: At the trailhead, on a fine summer weekend, you'll find gobs of cars. This is one of the few hikes in this book on which you'll meet a bunch of hikers. Families with little kids are particularly plentiful and welcome. The trailhead area has picnic tables and some typical USFS no-flush restrooms.

noon, looking into the sun, is not the best. For good photos of the falls, do this hike in the morning or early afternoon.

The stream's vertical drop of 176 feet is one of the highest in California. As the water crashes at the bottom, it creates a cloud of spray, which casts a glow of rainbow colors, when the sun is on it. A bold friendly Steller's jay usually greets people at the viewpoint, begging for a handout, of course. However, for this bird, like all wildlife, the rule is "No feeding, please."

As you watch, the effect of the cascade is almost hypnotizing. You'll need to pull yourself away from the scene for the short hike back to the car.

Camping: None.

Winter Use: The road from Gold Lake Highway to the falls is one of my favorite snowshoe routes. Since a new snowmobile parking lot has been opened farther south on Gold Lake Highway, that road will probably be plowed past the Frazier Falls Road turnoff. The plows usually create a wide-enough space so that snowshoers can park at this intersection.

GL-5 Smith Creek Trail to Plumas Pines

Distance: 5 miles one way with a car shuttle back; Alternative Hike, 4½ miles out and back; side trip to Smith Lake adds ½ mile

Highest Point: 6,079 feet

Total Elevation Gain: 289 feet; Alternative Hike, 1,344 feet

Difficulty: Moderate; Alternative Hike, moderate/strenuous

Hiking Season: June through October

Directions to the Trailhead: See Hike GL-16.

Comments: To do this hike one way, using a car shuttle, first drive two cars .5 mile past Mohawk, which is 1 mile from Graeagle on the Graeagle-Johnsville Road (County Road A-14). Just before reaching the right turn onto Poplar Valley Road, which goes into the Plumas Pines Estates, turn left onto a well-graded gravel road with the number 2413 nailed to a tree. Park within 200 yards of A-14, and leave car number one there. Drive in car number two to the Hike GL-16 trailhead. You'll finish the hike at car number one. Drive it home or to your lodgings. Then, just before dinner, drive car number one up to Gray Eagle Lodge, located ¼ mile from the trailhead. Eat dinner at the lodge's rustic dining hall made of huge logs (make a reservation several days in advance, 530-836-2511). The food is usually excellent and the wine list not bad (con-sidering this is the boondocks) and fairly priced. After dinner, drop off a driver at car number two, and drive both cars back down the hill. Naturally, dinner at the lodge is not a necessity for making the day enjoyable, but it certainly adds a nice touch.

To do the Alternative Hike out and back, drive directly to the GL-16 trailhead. A nice, but longer, loop trip goes along part of this route in Hike GL-22.

The Hike: The trail to Smith Lake leaves from the western end of the parking area. Two other trails leave from this same general area (the turnaround for Hike GL-3 and the end of Hike GL-16), so make sure you start on the proper one. The well-used trail is a bit rocky and shadeless, but it is only about ⅓ mile up to where the trail crosses Smith Creek (for the first time), at which point the uphill, rocky part is all behind you. After an easy stream crossing, you reach a trail junction where good signage points left to "Smith Lake ¼, Mount Elwell 3¼" and right to "Mohawk 3¾."

I recommend doing the ¼-mile side trip to Smith Lake. It has a beautiful setting snuggled between steep hills on each side. If you take the side

trip, you'll come to another well-signed trail junction that directs you to Smith Lake or up to Mount Elwell (Hike GL-16). Because the trail to the lake closely follows the stream, you may encounter some boggy places in spring or early summer, but the tradeoff is a streamside environment for wildflowers and ferns (oh yes, and mosquitoes). If you like wildflowers—and who doesn't?—you'll enjoy this stretch.

After a visit to Smith Lake, return to the first-described trail junction. Unfortunately, one of the least visible parts of the trail down to County Road A-14 near Plumas Pines Estates begins at this point. Ferns and lush low-growing plants have obscured the trail for about the first 25 yards after the junction. Stay right, near the creek, and easily plow through the greenery. Quickly the trail becomes obvious and remains so for the rest of the hike, if you pay attention to the instructions on where to make the creek crossings. The topo map doesn't show these multiple crossings correctly, but, in spite of the heavy tree cover, my GPS picked up good satellite coverage overhead, so I think I describe the route properly.

The trail closely follows Smith Creek for the next 2 miles, crossing it in several locations. The rather dense forest provides a delightful trail cover of soft pine and fir needles. To your right, the creek plunges downhill with gusto. When you're ¾ mile from the Smith Lake Trail intersection, a large cedar log lies across the path and, a few feet farther, an even larger blown-over lodgepole pine blocks your way. The pine had been growing on the stream bank, and, when it blew over, its massive root structure was pulled out of the ground, making quite a sight. Don't climb over. Turn right, and make your second crossing of the creek. If it is August or later, you can, with dexterity and luck, make this and all subsequent crossings with dry feet. In spring and early summer, what with the water volume from snowmelt, it's another matter, so bring along an old pair of sneakers to change into for each crossing.

After wading across (aided by my bamboo walking stick), I put my wet sneakers into a waterproof bag so that they don't get my daypack wet.

For the next ¾ mile, the soft trail parallels the creek on its eastern side. Then it suddenly makes a left turn (easy to miss, but if you do you'll notice within a few steps that you are no longer on the trail) and crosses the creek for the third time. Rock-hopping here worked fine, keeping my boots mostly dry. An orange strip tied to a tree on the western bank indicates the location of the trail. Very soon after this crossing, the whole scene changes—rocks on the trail, much shorter trees, and dry manzanita brush on either side of the path.

In about ½ mile, you encounter a Y in the trail with a signpost saying "Trail" leaning against a tree. On close inspection, the arrows point in both directions, so the sign isn't much help. A right turn will lead you to a newly built logging road and, in 150 yards, Smith Creek again. This, however, is the

Sunset from the Smith Creek Trail

route for Hike GL-22 and the turnaround location for the Alternative Hike out and back. To continue the one-way hike down to A-14, take the left fork at the Y.

Soon the trail intersects a new logging road and follows it for 300 yards, past an old sign nailed to a tree on the right, again saying merely "Trail." Keep on the road for another 200 yards, until you see a large cedar on your right with a blaze on it. The whole trail from top to bottom was marked years ago by chopping the blaze mark (two rectangles) out of the bark of trees along the route. This cedar has blazes on both sides, helping both uphill and downhill travelers find the path. At this point the trail leaves the road and angles off to the right.

In ¼ mile the fourth crossing of Smith Creek occurs. Here the stream flows over smooth rock conglomerate, which looks like it could be concrete poured there to aid in the crossing, although it is a natural formation. A short distance later you make the fifth creek crossing where a log across the water makes a nice bridge, if your balance is good.

The trail picks up a smooth logging road and continues downhill, bypassing another logging road that cuts back to the left. In several hundred yards little Claim Creek flows under the road through a large culvert.

Just beyond Claim Creek, you reach a Y in the road. The right fork, a nice level track, leads down to Mohawk along Smith Creek. This fork has been the trail for more than a century (it shows on Arthur W. Keddie's 1892 map of Plumas County), but, although the nice folks at Graeagle Land and Water Company have given written permission to put the portion that runs through their property in this book, another owner has refused permission to pass, has installed locked gates across the century-old road, and has put up "No Trespassing" signs. So, take the logging road forking left. It climbs uphill over the low ridge, bypasses several other logging roads on the left, and, ¼ mile beyond the ridgetop, meets a well-graded gravel road (22N44). Turn right on the road, and soon you'll hear on your left the traffic on A-14. A locked gate across the road with a sign "Road Closed" is a clue that car number one is parked just beyond the gate.

Note: A portion of this hike beginning near the fifth creek crossing is on Graeagle Land and Water Company property. I have received written permission from the company's owner to include this hike with the condition that such permission is for foot travel only. Approval for access is explicitly denied for cars, trucks, bicycles, motorcycles, horses, dogs and other domestic animals, ATVs, snowmobiles, and any other off-road vehicles. Absolutely no camping, campfires, or wood cutting is permitted. Please respect this privately owned property, and do not leave trash of any kind. If signs describe an owner other than Graeagle Land and Water Company, the property has obviously changed ownership, and the former owner's permission for right to pass is automatically terminated. In such case, please check with the new owner before hiking this portion of the trail.

Camping: None.

Winter Use: I have snowshoed the route from the intersection of 22N44 with A-14 up to the fifth creek crossing (in this description), but the track is too steep in places for cross-country skiing. These roads are all closed to snowmobiles.

GL-6 Smith Lake to the PCT and Long Lake Loop

Distance: 12¼-mile loop

Highest Point: 7,284 feet

Total Elevation Gain: 2,130 feet

Difficulty: Strenuous

Hiking Season: July through October

Directions to the Trailhead: See Hike GL-5.

Comments: This hike is classed as strenuous because of its length and elevation gain. Otherwise, it is a very doable trail with plenty of scenery and some likable lakes to visit. Because the middle section of this hike on the PCT is above 7,000 feet, in a heavy-snow year the trail may not be snow-free until early July. Even in light-snow years, you may still find snow on the trail at the higher elevations in early June. Dividing this into a two-day hike with an overnight campout may be appealing.

The Hike: The trail to Smith Lake leaves the

western edge of the parking area (several trails leave from this general area, so make sure to take the one signed "Smith Lake"). The first ½ mile is a steady uphill climb without much shade on a well-beaten trail. However, after a 240-foot elevation gain, the trail levels and leaves the sunny eastern slope. It's easy to forget this sweat-building first portion of the trail as you dip down to cross sparkling Smith Creek. Here, you find numerous varieties of wetlands-habitat wildflowers throughout the summer, but you are also greeted by a voracious colony of mosquitoes until August. Soon after you hop easily across the creek, the trail reaches a T junction. A right turn would lead you onto the Smith Creek Trail (Hike GL-5). Instead, take the left with a sign indicating "Smith Lake ¼ mile." The route parallels the pretty creek for several hundred yards, and then splits. Take the right fork, which continues along the creek a short distance to the eastern edge of Smith Lake. The lake, at a 6,079-foot elevation, cuddles serenely in its scenic basin. Skirting the southern edge of the lake, the roller coaster path finally crosses the lake's inlet creek, which flows down from tiny Upper Smith Lake (unnamed on the topo map).

As the route starts to climb out of the lower lake basin, be sure to look behind you for wonderful views of the lake. The trail levels, crosses a broad saddle, then drops 620 feet in the next mile, crossing into a corner of Plumas-Eureka State Park, and, finally, intersects with Little Jamison Creek Trail. On this downhill portion, the tree cover thins, allowing great views of Eureka Peak and Mount Elwell across the canyon. Turn left, and follow the Little Jamison Creek Trail past Grass Lake and the turnoffs to Jamison Lake and Wades Lake (for

details of this portion of the hike, see Hike GL-14). The trail ends 1 mile past the turnoff to Wades Lake, at a jeep road (22N99A). Turn left, and hike along this road for about ¼ mile. Watch closely for the "new" PCT, not shown on the topo map, as it angles left from the road. Surprisingly, no sign marks this junction. A large red fir has fallen across the path on the north side of the road, and it is not clear that the PCT continues on the other side of the log—until you look. A "No Jeeps" sign signals that this is the way, not along the road. For the next mile, the PCT parallels the road; then it begins to zigzag downhill, crossing and recrossing the boundary between Plumas and Sierra Counties (which also, along here, is the boundary between Plumas and Tahoe National Forests).

Your route leaves the PCT where the trail crosses the jeep road leading right to Four Hills Mine and left back into Lakes Basin. As you turn left, the road along which you are now walking is an old wagon road shown on the 1892 map drawn by Arthur W. Keddie, pioneer Plumas County surveyor. Below, to the north, is the beautiful basin in which Jamison and Rock Lakes are located. When you've gone ½ mile from the PCT, at a point where the road makes a sharp right turn, take a trail that cuts off to the left. It follows the ridge above Long Lake. In ½ mile, you come to a four-way intersec-

tion with the trail coming down from Mount Elwell. Continue straight, and soon the trail plunges steeply downhill on the scree-covered eastern slope of Mount Elwell above Long Lake. This trail is described in detail in Hike GL-16; it winds its way back to Gray Eagle Lodge and the trailhead parking area ¼ mile beyond the lodge. Although you may be sweaty and dirty, a nice end to this long hike is dinner in the attractive log dining room at the lodge. Plan ahead, because dinner reservations (530/836-2511) are suggested, particularly on weekends.

Camping: Only four lakes are open to camping within the Lakes Basin Recreation Area through which most of this hike passes, and all four are along the route. You get to Smith Lake a bit early in the hike (within an hour) for an overnight mid-hike campout. Grass Lake is a possibility, but, because it is less than one hour from the popular Jamison Mine trailhead, it gets fairly heavy weekend camping use. Just short of halfway around our loop, both Jamison and Wades Lakes have very nice backpack camping. Both lakes are reached by short side trails off the main route with good signs at the trail intersections.

Winter Use: None. Throughout the winter, Gold Lake Highway is plowed only a short distance. Snowmobiles regularly ply the unplowed road and the side road to Gray Eagle Lodge. In early spring, once Gold Lake Highway opens, providing access to the trailhead, the hike to Smith Lake is delightful. However, at that season it entails crossing several substantial snowbanks that slope steeply down into the Gray Eagle Creek Canyon. Good boots and caution should see you safely through, if a wintry view of Smith Lake sounds like fun, which it is.

An old cedar near Long Lake

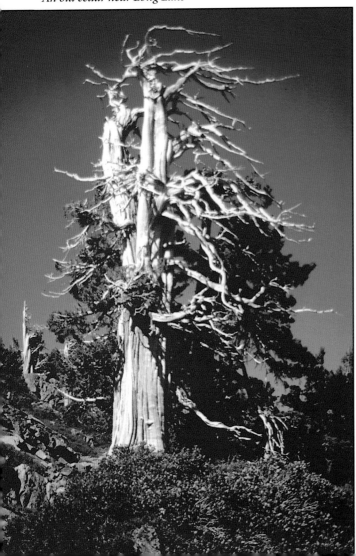

GL-7 Lakes Basin Rim Loop

Distance: 7¼-mile loop

Highest Point: 7,540 feet

Total Elevation Gain: 1,550 feet

Difficulty: Moderate/difficult

Hiking Season: July through October

Directions to the Trailhead: From Graeagle drive south on Highway 89 for 1.4 miles to Gold Lake Highway. Turn right, and drive 7.5 miles to a right turn into Gold Lake Lodge. There's also a sign on the highway saying "Round Lake Trailhead." This road immediately forks, with the right side going to the lodge and the left leading directly into the trailhead parking lot.

Comments: This ranks close to the top of my list of favorite hikes. It has it all: spectacular views in many directions, bunches of lakes, a challenging well-used trail, a huge variety of wildflowers, and easy access. What more can I say? This is one of the "long versions" of the several Lakes Basin hikes in this book; for a shorter version with some of the same attributes, try Hike GL-8.

The Hike: As you leave the far end of the parking lot, you see a posted Lakes Basin map of the trails in the area. To your right are some of the cute cabins of Gold Lake Lodge, across a meadow that is often packed with a showy display of wildflowers in summer. If you stop to gander at the flowers, make sure you have on plenty of insect repellent, because this area has one of the best collections of mosquitoes I've ever experienced. Soon, a Y in the trail signals the beginning and ending points of the loop. You can go left to do the loop the way I've written it, or go right and do it "backward."

In ¼ mile, a look to the right gives you a view of Big Bear Lake through the trees,

but don't get excited; there are lots more and better lake views awaiting you. Another ¼ mile down the trail, the first lake along the route appears. A quick check of the topo map tells you that this is such a piddly body of water, among many much more outstanding examples, that nobody has given it a name. So, after admiring the reflections in its often glassy surface, keep moving up the trail. Indeed, the trail becomes steeper and rockier underfoot. To your right appear views through the trees of Big Bear and Little Bear Lakes. In another ½ mile, you come to a signless Y; veer right on the more used trail, and wind around the hilltop, which once upon a time bore a weather station—well, a tin shack of some sort. It blew down years ago. Below, you see Round Lake and, closer on the hillside, the ruins of Round Lake Mine.

At this point, the trail splits, with one branch, marked "Silver Lake ¼," leading downhill to the lakeshore. Hike GL-8, a shorter loop, takes this branch, but our loop goes straight, following the sign "Pacific Crest Trail ¾." From here, the trail becomes less rocky, although it is steep in places. Good trail signs are a nice feature of the Lakes Basin Recreation Area, but, surprisingly, no trail direction signs appear at the T intersection with the PCT, only a sign describing the recreation area. Turn right on the PCT, to head northwesterly.

The next ½ mile provides some very spectacular views. To the east, the large lake below is Gold Lake. It is the only lake you'll see on this hike across

The Lakes Basin viewed from its western rim

which motorboats might be dashing. A bit farther up the trail, take a few steps to the left for a commanding view of the Pauley Creek drainage basin. Sierra Buttes are farther to the south, then Little Deer Lake, then Snake Lake and Oakland Pond directly below you. On a clear day, Mount Lassen can be seen in the distance. Farther along the PCT, your view to the right changes from Gold Lake to Silver Lake, Mud Lake, Long Lake, and almost the entire Lakes Basin. If, at this point, you're not saying "Wow!" there's something wrong with you.

With its predominantly northeastern exposure, this part of the trail, which follows the eastern edge of the ridge, might be impassable due to snow until well into midsummer. On several occasions in early summer I've had to turn back. If you can get through, within the next ½ mile the trail cuts over the ridge to travel on its western slope. Your views of the Lakes Basin end, but you'll find the next mile very enjoyable—a shady trail, nicely carpeted with pine needles, that gradually loses altitude.

Although you're sure you've gone too far and

missed the loop trail back, just keep walking; the intersection is well defined and well signed. The downhill trail to the right, which you want, says "Silver Lake ¼," as you leave the PCT. I should point out that the route of the PCT has been changed since the topo map was created. The route shown in this book is the current one. The next mile of downhill trail also rates as one of my favorites because it has a "Swiss Alps" feeling. You encounter a whole new cast of wildflowers, the ridge towers above you on your right, and various lakes, highlighted by Long Lake, appear in the basin to your left.

On the way down, you'll pass small Hellgramite Lake (there are two, but the map doesn't label them "upper" and "lower"). Neither is particularly attractive, lacking "blueness." However, Mount Elwell, towering behind them, is often reflected beautifully in their mirror surfaces, unless, of course, a breeze breaks up the effect. A short stretch of uphill surprises you just before pretty Silver Lake pops into view. If you bring your bathing suit along, Silver Lake is a great place to take a dip, although in early summer you may find it too chilly—heck, even in late summer it's far from warm. Just before you reach the lake, a trail branches to the left to Mount Elwell (see Hike GL-15), and, just after you pass the lake, a trail branches right to Round Lake (the back part of the loop of Hike GL-8). Turn left here, and crest a small rise to greet a close-up view of Long Lake. Keep walking toward the Bear Lakes—first

Cub, ¼ mile later Little Bear, and finally spectacular Big Bear.

Soon after Big Bear Lake, a trail to Elwell Lodge branches to the left, although the sign refers only to the "Long Lake Trailhead" in that direction. However, your car is parked near Gold Lake Lodge (which, as you can tell, is not near Gold Lake), so take the trail to the right. I hate to give you the bad news (well, it's not really that bad) but you will hit a short stretch of dusty uphill just before reaching the trail intersection where you began the loop. When you get there, you're close to your car. In the summer, the Gold Lake Lodge building around the corner from your car is open, so you can pop in to wet your whistle with a cold glass of whatever in nice surroundings and reminisce about what a swell day's hike you've had.

Camping: There is no trail camping at any of the lakes you've passed or seen on this hike with the exception of Snake Lake, well below the PCT in the Pauley Creek basin. Oakland Pond, which was also visible from the ridgetop, is campable but not at all attractive as bodies of water go. Car camping is available at the nice Lakes Basin Campground just north of Elwell Lodge or at Gold, Goose, and Haven Lakes off Gold Lake Highway. The USFS gets very uptight when backpackers are discovered camping at Long, Silver, Round, Mud, or any of the Bear Lakes.

Winter Use: None.

GL-8 Round Lake/Bear Lakes Loop

Distance: $4\frac{1}{4}$-mile loop (Alternative to Big Bear Lake only, 1 mile out and back)

Highest Point: 7,020 feet

Total Elevation Gain: 430 feet (Alternative, 125 feet)

Difficulty: Moderate (Alternative, easy)

Hiking Season: June through October

Directions to the Trailhead: See Hike GL-7.

Comments: I have done this loop at least a dozen times, more than about any other hike in this book. For maximum scenery with moderate effort this is "it." Hike GL-7 is a longer version, but this shorter loop is worth including separately because it is so perfect for a "middle-distance" hike. If time constraints or energy levels limit you to a much shorter trip, the Alternative hike out and back to just Big Bear Lake will fulfill your desire to visit a very scenic lake (without any big bears around, I hope).

The Hike: Follow the directions for Hike GL-7 as far as Round Lake. When you get to the Round Lake overlook by the mine, find a sign at a trail intersection pointing downhill to "Silver Lake ¼" and pointing straight ahead to "Pacific Crest Trail ¾." Take the downhill route, and, after a bit of a steep descent, you arrive at the eastern edge of Round Lake. The super view looks west across the lake to the ridge towering 825 feet above its surface. A trail leads both left and right around the lake; turn right, and head north along the shore. At this point a mini-peninsula going out into the lake makes a great location for a rest stop. In the shallow, clear water you can see a Model T Ford engine lying on the bottom. Perhaps it was used as part of the mine machinery, because it's difficult to imagine how a Model T could have driven to this spot, and there's no sign of the body, frame, or other parts.

To pick up the trail to Silver Lake at this mini-peninsula, walk to the right at the water's edge as the path follows the eastern shore of the lake. You can cross the outlet creek for the lake on large rocks,

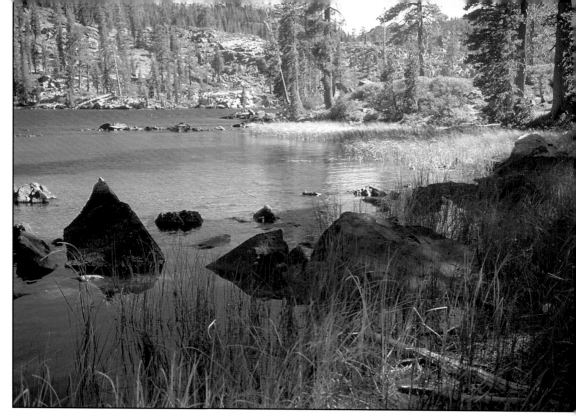

Big Bear Lake

and, after ¼ mile of easy hiking, you arrive at the eastern shore of Silver Lake. Its scenic beauty benefits from the high ridge to the west.

The route follows the eastern shore of the lake, and, after crossing its outlet creek, reaches a trail intersection. A sign tells you that Round Lake is ½ mile in the direction you just came from, the PCT and Mount Elwell are westward via the trail along the northern shore of the lake, and the Bear Lakes are ¾ mile in the northerly direction. So, go north.

At this point, you'll be back on the exact route to your car covered in Hike GL-7. Pick up the description there commencing where it leaves Silver Lake. You may notice a nice campsite on the northern edge of Silver Lake that looks like it has been used in recent years. No camping is allowed here, and the Forest Service folks tell me they have a dickens of a time with people who pay no attention to the "No Camping" sign. They plan to put up even larger and more noticeable "No Camping" signs so that backpackers will get the message.

Camping: Camping is forbidden at any of the Lakes Basin lakes. Backpackers need to hike up to the ridge (see Hike GL-7) for a waterless camp there or continue a little way down the other side to Oakland Pond or Snake Lake. For car campers, the USFS Lakes Basin Campground is less than ½ mile north of the trailhead via a trail heading by Elwell Lodge, or via the Gold Lake Highway from the trailhead.

Winter Use: None, although my wife and I had fun hiking this loop on an early spring day, which required tromping through lots of snow.

GL-9 Lakes Basin Long Loop
via Snake and Hawley Lakes

Distance: 11-mile loop

Highest Point: 7,440 feet

Total Elevation Gain: 2,135 feet

Difficulty: Strenuous

Hiking Season: July through October

Directions to the Trailhead: See Hike GL-7.

Comments: This monster hike can be done in one day if you get started very early and do not dilly-dally. As an alternative, plan one or two overnight campouts along the way. The hike covers some very scenic country and allows you to travel along historic pack trails that are seldom used today.

The Hike: Follow the directions in Hike GL-7 to the Round Lake overlook and up to a junction with the PCT. (The topo map doesn't show this

"new" PCT.) Turn right on the PCT, and go ¼ mile to a trail cutting back sharply to the left heading downhill. Leave the PCT for this side trail, which drops down to a jeep road just above Oakland Pond. The jeep road is the route of the "old" PCT before it was redone along the much prettier crest of the ridge. Turn right on the jeep road, and try not to be too disappointed by muddy Oakland Pond as you skirt its eastern and northern edges. Just after the pond, the barely visible "old" PCT branches off to the right. That's a hike for another day, however, so continue downhill on the jeep road (which does not show on the topo map) almost due west to the north shore of Snake Lake, approximately ¾ mile after leaving the PCT. When a friend and I got there, I liked Snake Lake—I suppose because, other than Round Lake, it was the first decent body of water I'd met on this hike. It'd be a good camping spot too.

Just past the lake, a trail cuts south to Little Deer Lake (see Hike GL-10). Pass it by, and continue on the jeep road another ⅓ mile to another trail on the left. Turn left onto it, and immediately cross over a new large culvert, through which the inlet creek to Snake Lake flows. The new bulldozer work surprised us on our hike, and ½ mile farther, we crossed another oversized new culvert. I hope all this activity doesn't signal some development of the area. It's just fine without making it accessible to more people (so cried the hikers in search of solitude). The track reaches a stream too wide to jump and devoid of stepping-stones. But a giant log spans the creek just north of the trail, making a perfect bridge, so crossing is a piece of cake.

A few minutes after the log-crossing you come to the tricky part of the hike. The topo map shows the track, now like a jeep road, fording another stream, after which a trail cuts off back uphill to Hawley Lake, your next destination. My hiking buddy and I could see no sign of this trail, so we followed the jeep road south for ½ mile into the upper end of Gold Valley just to make sure we hadn't missed it. We retraced our steps and searched again, to no avail. After recrossing the ford, we struck off cross-country hoping to find the trail. Lo and behold, within 300 yards, there it was! So, I guess you just have to experiment a bit, because its intersection with the jeep road has become obliterated. This seems even more surprising because the trail soon becomes a broad wagon road in quite good condition. The early miners who built this track certainly

did a fine job, because its stone surface is relatively smooth and looks as if it were completed yesterday instead of 100 or so years ago. Heading north, it climbs 600 feet on a steady grade to Hawley Lake, passing an old weather-beaten sign for the former camp for children at the lake. I particularly enjoyed this 1½-mile old wagon road, because I could envision horses and oxen struggling uphill carrying or pulling large loads bound for the mines. (See Hike GL-26 for information about the petroglyphs near Hawley Lake.)

My reverie was broken by the appearance of Hawley Lake, with Boy Scout Camp Nejedly on its shore. This camp complex was evidently once much larger and was a camp for physically challenged youth, before its Boy Scout days. The main building is a swell-looking cabin on the lakeshore. A sign informed us that, once upon a time, the cabin was open at all times as a refuge for anyone who might be lost but that careless people had left the facility open and much of the interior had been damaged by animals; hence, it is now locked up. The camp has road access from the north and is actively used by Boy Scouts during the summer. To travel on, take the dirt road that leaves the lake from its northern side. In 100 yards turn left at the next road junction. This route parallels the inlet creek of the lake, which is dry in late summer, and passes a nice-looking place to camp, albeit out of view of the lake.

When you're 1 mile north of the lake, the road intersects another jeep road near the Four Hills Mine. For more information on that mine and the Sierra Iron Mine, planned for but never opened in the area through which you just walked, see Hike GL-26. Road 22N99A, along which you have been walking, continues north to the A-Tree (see Hike GL-26), but you need to turn right and head back toward your far-off car. The road gradually makes its way up to the ridge on a crossing of the PCT, ½ mile from the last road intersection.

Continue on the same road, which, at this point,

is another old wagon road, shown as a main thoroughfare on surveyor Arthur W. Keddie's map of 1892. When you're ½ mile beyond the PCT crossing, a trail branches left to Mount Elwell. Walking another 200 yards, you finally leave the road on a trail to the left heading briskly downhill with fine views of the Lakes Basin, dominated by Long Lake 650 feet below. This next mile of trail to Hellgramite Lake is one of my favorite parts of the Feather River country. Wildflowers abound on the slope throughout most of the summer, and an amazing amount of water trickles down the hillside from the jagged ridge above, even in August and September. Just past small but pristine Hellgramite Lake (there are two of them, near one another, but the topo map is no help in giving them separate descriptions) the now-well-beaten trail approaches the north edge of Silver Lake. From this point, the distance back to the trailhead is described in Hike GL-8, past Cub, Little

Bear, and Big Bear Lakes. Wow, what a day, if you did this whole loop without an overnight!

Camping: No camping is allowed in the portion of the Lakes Basin through which this hike crosses, but the portion of the hike west of the ridge above the basin is OK for camping. Camping is allowed at lousy Oakland Pond or much nicer Snake Lake. You might enjoy taking a ¾-mile side trip to camp at Little Deer Lake; take the trail heading south along the west side of Snake Lake (see Hike GL-23). This ¾ mile is a rough-as-it-gets jeep road, but Little Deer Lake with its petite island is such a swell camp spot that the extra effort may be worth it. I bet you won't have to share the lake with any other people; cows, maybe, but no people. I have already warned you about Boy Scout summer activities at Hawley Lake.

Winter Use: None.

GL-10 Gold Lake Mine and Squaw Lake Trail

Distance: 3 miles out and back
Highest Point: 6,680 feet
Total Elevation Gain: 245 feet
Difficulty: Easy/moderate
Hiking Season: June through October
Directions to the Trailhead: See Hike GL-29.

Comments: As you can tell throughout this book, I like to visit old abandoned mines. I enjoy envisioning each mine in its heyday with sweating, cursing miners working like crazy to extract gold from their mountain. Few of their primitive living quarters are still visible, but the hardships the miners endured are easy to imagine. Some mines produced richly, and others hardly at all. A few have even been worked during the past 20 years, although none that I have visited is currently in operation. The Gold Lake Mine is one of the best examples I know of a Feather River country mining operation. (I have never seen this mine listed on any map, so I have named it Gold Lake Mine even though it probably had a different name.)

Most mineshafts have caved in over the years, and, quite often, no machinery or buildings remain. At Gold Lake Mine, the flattened remains of the buildings are still noticeable in their final stages of rotting away. The stamp mill site is evident, and the mineshaft itself is still a gaping hole in the mountainside. The squashed Model T Ford indicates that someone drove to the mine site but failed to drive out. I wondered why and pondered how the

Sundown in autumn at Squaw Lake

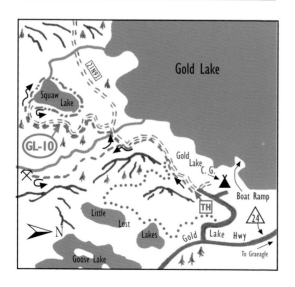

car became as flat as a pancake. You also will enjoy a visit to picturesque Squaw Lake for the second phase of this hike.

The Hike: From the trailhead, walk southwest along the jeep road, which, I'm sure you will agree, is for four-wheel-drive vehicles only. The road soon becomes quite rocky and tough on the feet if you are wearing thin-soled sneakers (so don't). To miss some of the rocky road, look for a stub road to the right, slightly less than ¼ mile from the trailhead, which has an unappealing campsite within view of the jeep road.

Directly across from this short side road, a trail leads off to the left. This short trail segment is used by the Gold Lake Stables as a horse trail, so it has samples of what horses do on the trail besides walking. Don't worry, in about 300 yards of curvy uphill walking, the trail reaches a T. Keep your eyes peeled for this intersection, because the trail to the right, which is the one you want, is much dimmer than the one to the left or the one you're on. Fortunately, the dimmer trail receives almost no horse traffic and, hence, lacks internally processed and expelled horse feed. The trail winds up a low ridge and, in less than ¼ mile, again meets the jeep road. (If you don't want to bother with this smoother and more scenic detour, just stay on the jeep road instead.)

Where the side trail meets it, the jeep road has veered away from the lake in order to ford a small unnamed stream at a better place. A scant 25 yards after the side trail joins the jeep road, another trail cuts off to the left and is almost hidden behind two large boulders. (The stream ford is only 200 yards farther, so, if you come to it without seeing this trail to the left, go back and look more carefully.)

This elusive trail is the way to Gold Lake Mine, although it is not shown on the topo map. It clearly was once a wagon road and not just a pack trail. Even though it gets no vehicle use and but a small amount of foot traffic, you can easily follow it. A little more than ¼ mile from the jeep road, you reach a small clearing and see the first of the fallen-down mine buildings on your left. Wander over to inspect these remains, and look a bit farther to the left to see the squashed Model T. Given the flat condition of the vehicle and its lack of engine and nameplate, how do I know it is an early 1920s Ford? Well, I'm just guessing, but I have been a Model T owner and member of the Model T Ford Club of America for many years.

Beyond this site, you can see a pile of boulders on the far side of the clearing at the bottom of the hillside. Climb on top of the pile. You will agree that this flat area once held the stamp mill used to crush the quartz ore prior to processing out its gold. One clue is the crushed culvert pipe that evidently supplied water power for the stamp mill. Clamber up to the next level above

to find a large cable drum in excellent condition.

The uppermost level contains the yawning mouth of the mine tunnel. For some reason, it hasn't caved in. Most other mine entrances, which are in dirt rather than solid rock, have. However, do not enter, because it poses extreme danger. Make sure any kids along don't try to show how brave they are by crawling into the opening. I want all of you to be ongoing readers of this book.

Back at the clearing, walk toward the bush-covered creek that adjoins the site. The squashed buildings here were probably living quarters, judging by the pile of tin cans almost rusted away near the rotting boards. Miners mostly didn't bother carrying their trash to a remote garbage pit; it seems they just threw the empty cans out of the window. What a rodent (or bear) attraction these empty cans must have been, unless the miners thoroughly washed them first, which I doubt.

Now, return to the jeep road, turn left, cross the creek, and walk another 20 yards until the trail to Squaw Lake cuts off to the left. The "Squaw Lake ½" sign is a few yards farther, but it is poorly situated, because the arrow points in the wrong direction.

This jeep trail is quite rocky in places and, like the main jeep road, is not drivable unless a vehicle has a high road clearance and four-wheel drive. Thus, it gets little use. The hike to the lake is more like ¾ mile than the ½ mile written on the sign. You'll like the lake—tranquil and probably free of people.

If you have an extra 20 minutes, I suggest walking around the lake. There isn't a beaten path, but enough of a way has been made by other people making the circle. Where this semi-trail is not obvious, it is easy to improvise and find your way. The views from the far end of the lake are terrific. The glacier-smoothed rock face of the mountain behind the lake, seen from this vantage point, creates a massive backdrop. But who the heck painted that huge white cross on the face of the mountain, and why?

On the hike back downhill you'll enjoy the views of Gold Lake that were all behind you on the way up. Once you reach the jeep road, you can either hike back to your car on it or return on part of the Gold Lake Lakeshore Trail (Hike GL-30), accessed by turning left on the jeep road and following it for ¼ mile to a point where it nears the lakeshore again. Leave the road, and walk toward the lake (which is visible through the trees) for about 100 yards. You will easily find the shore trail. Turn right, and follow it back to the boat ramp and campground. When the campground comes into sight, you will be in a campsite with a sign "No Camping Here." Turn right, and follow the well-outlined path to where you parked.

Camping: The sign along the entrance road says "Camp in Organized Campsites Only," thus ruling out camping at Squaw Lake. That's too bad, because there's a very nice site where the jeep trail ends at the lakeshore and an even better one to the right about 100 yards on the other side of the lake inlet creek.

Winter Use: None.

GL-11 Pauley Creek through Gold Valley Loop

Distance: 10¾-mile loop

Highest Point: 6,840 feet

Total Elevation Gain: 1,805 feet

Difficulty: Moderate/strenuous

Hiking Season: July through September (avoid weekends, when bike use is heaviest)

Directions to the Trailhead: See Hike SC-3.

Comments: I figured that I could polish off 10¾ miles in about 5 hours, but it took me considerably longer because of the ups and downs, the many views to stop and admire, and the several streams to cross without the aid of stepping-stones (bring an extra pair of old sneakers for wading across these ankle-deep creeks). The historic Pauley Creek Trail was an early pack trail between Downieville and Johnsville, and its route is shown on the Arthur W. Keddie map of Plumas County dated 1912. Gold Valley is wonderful, but I've read that it is a place to stay away from during hunting season in the fall. The creek is named after Ben Pauley, who mined the area in the 1850s and later operated a sawmill. The creek was originally given the awkward name East Fork of the North Fork of the North Yuba River.

Take this trail on a weekday. On weekends the first several miles along the Butcher Ranch Trail are heavily used by mountain bikes. They have fondly dubbed it the "Downieville Descent" because it goes downhill at a fairly steep grade from Forest Road 93 all the way to Downieville, so all a biker needs are a bike, good brakes, a helmet, and an I-don't-care-if-I-crash attitude. The track for this first stretch is well worn and dusty in places from heavy bike use.

The Hike: In less than ½ mile, the jeep road becomes a trail, even though the topo map shows it as a road. The track crosses an unnamed creek (the South Fork of Butcher Ranch Creek?) at a ford where the water spreads out, which may be great for mountain bikes but is lousy for hikers because there are no nice stepping-stones. Normally, you'd just

next creek crossing, ¼ mile farther, is much easier.

Continue on the main trail
downhill, bypassing several trails
to the right (one of which is Hike
SC-3). When you're 3 miles from
the trailhead, the Pauley Creek
Trail intersects on the right. However, before turning right, I suggest a short excursion farther
downhill on Butcher Ranch Trail.
In a few minutes, on your right,
you spy a pair of unused cabins
(not shown on the topo map)
owned, I guess, by the USFS. I
suggest walking down to them to
check out, not the cabins, but the
unique world's tallest outhouse.
It's a dandy. On the trail, just
above the cabins, a tree bears the
laughable sign "Bus Stop." After
enjoying the scene, retrace your
steps to the intersection with the
Pauley Creek Trail, and head
northerly along that route, pass-

walk upstream or down a bit looking for rocks on
which to cross, but here thick alder bushes form an
impenetrable barrier. (The mountain alders you are
encountering are unusual because they bear both
male and female flowers on the same plant.) However, if you backtrack a few steps you see a mostly
knocked down barbed wire fence running through
the hillside covered with yellow-flowered mule ears
on the north side of the trail. The barbed wire disappears into the alder bushes. Head for this fence
line, and follow it into the bushes. Use caution, because the barbed wire has fallen in a lot of places,
and you crisscross it several times, so it's easy to
become entangled. After feeling like you've been
through the jungles of Vietnam, you come out the
other side where you can easily jump the creek. The

ing a nice, albeit well-used, campsite complete with
picnic table, big fire ring, and log benches.

Just past the campsite, the path crosses over
Butcher Ranch Creek on a heavy-duty footbridge.
Take a peek at the underside of the bridge to admire its impressive construction. I would be interested to know how the bridge builders got those
huge steel I-beams into this boondocks location.

As you leave the bridge behind, you see immediately that, thank goodness, you're no longer on the
bikers' steep dusty Butcher Ranch Trail. Pauley
Creek Trail is just the opposite—mostly smooth
with a gradual ascent. Yes, this route is used by
mountain bikers, but nowhere near as much as the
trail you just left.

In many places, concrete pavers have been

placed in the path to prevent erosion, particularly on the steeper places where downhill bikers jam on their brakes and skid, a practice that wreaks havoc on loose-dirt trails. It seems odd, out here in the wilderness, to be walking on concrete pavers, but better that than a beat-up dusty trail. The pavers are heavy, so it is a wonder how they were carried in to this remote spot. When you're a mile from the start of the Pauley Creek Trail, you encounter a pretty good campsite on the eastern bank of the creek alongside the trail.

Soon you reach a footbridge over Pauley Creek—very nice to have in this spot. Perhaps the creek will have lost a little of its grandeur by late summer, but certainly in early summer you will be in awe of its force and flow as it leaps over and around boulders. I hope you have your camera along. The wildflower display on the far end of the bridge includes several varieties that grow on dry hillsides—yet 20 feet away, down in Pauley Creek's ravine, you can see a wide variety of wetland wildflowers.

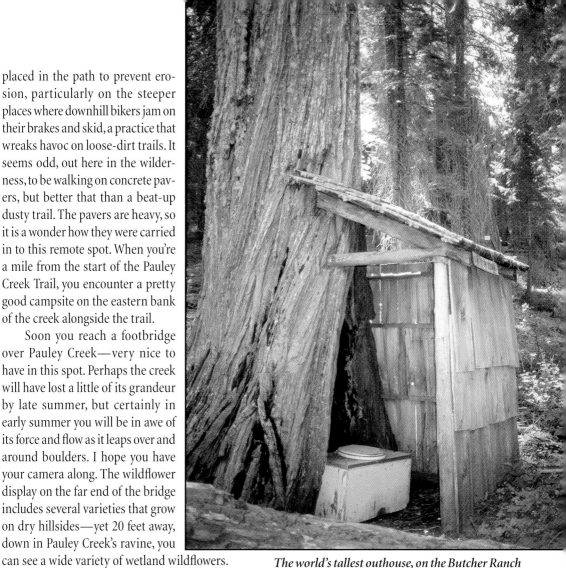

The world's tallest outhouse, on the Butcher Ranch Trail

The end of the Pauley Creek foot trail and the start of the Gold Valley jeep trail are signaled by the battered hulk of a 1938 Chevrolet two-door sedan (at least that's my guess—it was too beat up to allow positive identification, and all nameplates had been taken off long ago). The engine block still looked in OK shape, in case you care to carry it out.

Gold Valley is a wonderful place to walk through—level, quiet, full of flowers and scenery. How different this would be if the proposals for a major road through here had come to fruition. In 1860, and again in 1880, backers of a grand road tried to muster political support and funding. This route, claimed the proponents, would enable supplies to reach the mines near Johnsville more easily. It would also connect with the Mohawk Valley and points east, eventually reaching the booming silver mines of Virginia City, Nevada. The Donner Pass route (today's Interstate 80) was a treacherous undertaking for wagoners hauling freight to the Nevada mines over the 7,088-foot-high pass. Nobody had figured out how to build a wagon road up the North Yuba River, and the Gold Valley route, although longer, had the advantage of much lower elevations. Snow fell early and late on Donner, so the Gold Valley road could be used a full two months longer during the year, claimed the backers. Some survey work was actually done, and a suitable route was laid out on paper, but that was as far as it got.

The smooth jeep road at this point seems easily navigable by a modern-day sedan, but you'll see in a little while why a high-clearance, short-wheelbase, four-wheel-drive vehicle (a jeep) is required. A modern high-horsepower, shiny, four-wheel-drive SUV would certainly meet the same fate as the 1938 Chevy.

For the next crossing of Pauley Creek, a footbridge isn't needed because you can wade across—unless you forgot some "wading shoes." If so, the choice is a barefoot wade or a wet boot wade. About ¼ mile after the crossing, a jeep road cuts off to the left. (If you wish to do a multiple-day backpacking trip, that road connects in 1 mile with Hike GL-9, then GL-12, and so on, coming back to near the trailhead on GL-1.) However, today's loop turns right and does a couple of sharp turns before nearing the creek and a road to the right with a gate across it. A sign on the gate warns "High Explosives—Danger—No Trespassing." The road leads to Empire Mine, one of the area's biggest producers and one of the last to remain active. I had hoped to see what was cookin' at Empire, but I guess the owners don't want hikers nosing around whatever machinery they have there. I bet they don't leave explosives lying about. There weren't any recent tire tracks on the road to Empire, so nobody must be working it now.

My plan was to take the Empire Mine road until it connects with the old Gold Valley Trail leading back to the Butcher Ranch Trail to complete the loop. However, my book cannot direct hikers on a route marked "No Trespassing" even though my USFS detailed map shows this to be national forest land with the Empire Mine claim and private property south of the road. So, instead continue another ¾ mile to an intersection with the "main road," 93-3. A sign indicates that Gold Valley, Pauley Creek, and Smith Lake (a different Smith Lake from the one near Gray Eagle Lodge) are in the direction you just came from and that this is Road 93-3-7.

The remaining 2½ miles of the loop are easy. Turn right on well-graded and graveled 93-3, and don't mind the occasional vehicle that might pass you. The road is nearly level, making your end-of-the-day progress easier. After providing you with a nice view, ahead, of Sierra Buttes, the route turns easterly and makes a wide turn, crossing over Butcher Ranch Creek. The creek is much smaller here than where you crossed it on the footbridge at "the bottom" several hours earlier. Watch on your right for the old cabins of Robinson Cow Camp, adjoining the meadow at the bottom of the slope. Soon after spying the cabins, you arrive back at the trailhead. (For a visit to the Cow Camp, see Hike SC-3.)

Camping: Good backpacking campsites along the route include the one at the intersection of Butcher Ranch Trail and Pauley Creek Trail (bikers pass by, however), two along the Pauley Creek Trail, several in Gold Valley, and one at the Empire Mine gate. This hike would lend itself well to two days with an overnight at one of these campsites (or any other you may chose along the way).

Winter Use: I was surprised to see the snowmobile orange diamond markers nailed to an occasional tree way out in Gold Valley. Access to this area is one heck of a long snowmobile ride from Bassetts, and I'd sure hate to have my machine poop out that far away from civilization. The route is not accessible for cross-country skiers or snowshoers.

GL-12 Spencer Lakes Loop

Distance: Loop A, 7½ miles; Loop B, 5 miles; Route C, 4 miles out and back

Highest Point: 7,325 feet

Total Elevation Gain: Loop A, 1,725 feet; Loop B, 1,280 feet;
Route C, 845 feet

Difficulty: Loops A and B, strenuous; Route C, moderate

Hiking Season: July through October

Directions to the Trailhead: See Hike MF-1.

Comments: Loops A and B are for the experienced hiker who is in good shape and can cope with some challenging cross-country. Although the topo map shows a trail between Upper and Lower Spencer Lakes and from Lower Spencer Lake westerly along Spencer Creek to Lavezzola Creek, these two trail sections have been obliterated for many years. Zero trail maintenance and heavy growth of a wide variety of dense bushes make it impossible to follow what once was a lively trail route when the Four Hills Mine was active. Either loop is best taken in a clockwise direction so that the beating-through-the-bushes section is done downhill, where you can see ahead and better plan to avoid the worst of the almost impenetrable growth. If you like a challenge, this is your cup of tea. Although the total distance for Loop A doesn't look formidable, it is an all-day trip. For example, the most difficult part—the 1½ miles from Lower Spencer Lake to the intersection with the trail along Lavezzola Creek—took me and my hiking companion about two hours. Shorter Loop B is a good day's hike in itself and omits the difficult and largely trailless section between Upper and Lower Spencer Lakes. Route C, the out-and-back alternative, is for hikers who want a nice walk along the PCT that avoids all the bushwhacking required in Loops A and B. For either A or B, wearing long pants is a good idea for the bushwhacking 1½-mile stretch, to keep your legs unscratched. Boots rather than

running shoes are also a necessity, because this part involves stomping on plenty of heavy-duty bush branches.

The Hike: You can read about the A-Tree at Hike MF-1. Before you leave the A-Tree parking area, don't fail to get a good swig of spring water and fill your water bottle from the A-Tree spring. Walk to the west end of the parking area, where a jeep trail cuts off sharply downhill (on Loop A or B, you'll come back on this trail), and you'll see the clear cool water flowing out of a pipe. It's good at the start of a hike and especially good at the end, after the long pull up the trail that parallels Lavezzola Creek.

For all three routes, you leave the parking area on the PCT heading south. You can probably spy the small PCT marker, although it's not easy. The topo map shows the PCT following the road that leads off to the left as you drive into the parking area (22N99A), but a delightful "new" PCT route has been built since the map was published, so you don't need to hike down the dusty road, which is regularly used by four-wheel-drive vehicles.

The PCT winds around Hill 6825 and, just before turning south again, nearly meets the road that used to be the PCT. The new route follows along the contour south of the ridgetop, with nice views of the Spencer Creek Canyon in a southerly direction. About 1½ miles from the A-Tree, an unsigned trail cuts off to the right. Here is where you need to choose Loop B, if you're going to. For the big Loop A or the out-and-back Route C, stay straight on the PCT; if you're taking the smaller Loop B, turn right on this lightly used trail. The Loop B route heads almost straight downhill and, in ½ mile, reaches a junction with the Spencer Creek Trail, where it rejoins Loop A. You'll see Lower Spencer Lake from points along the B trail, and in spring to midsummer you'll encounter a great variety of wildflowers as you approach the lake.

Taking Loop A or out-and-back Route C, the trail begins to climb after the Loop B path cuts off, but you won't mind because the views to the south are so terrific. Lower Spencer Lake passes out of view and Upper Spencer can be seen against the massive rock outcropping rising steeply more than 600 feet above the lake surface. This rock has a large cleft in its face, which makes a particularly interesting photo, especially when the angle of the early-morning or late-afternoon sun puts the cleft in the shadow.

Ahead, on this rather treeless section of the PCT, you can spy the old PCT road (22N99A) winding up the crest of the ridge. This road might once have become an 1850s "superhighway." Various groups were working to establish a main route connecting Marysville in the Sacramento Valley with the gold-mining districts around Johnsville. Beyond Johnsville, the road was planned to travel to Sierra Valley east of what is now Portola and on to Virginia City, Nevada. Jim Beckwourth's Emigrant Trail, completed in 1851 (see Appendix D), was one proposed route, but other planners thought a better wagon road would run from Marysville to Downieville along the Yuba River, then northerly (along the final leg of this hike) to the A-Tree. What I call the "old PCT road" would have been the next section of the wagon road. The route was then planned to cross the ridge and drop down to Eureka Mine, Jamison City, and Johnsville along what is now the trail leading from the ridge past Wades and Grass Lakes to the Jamison Mine trailhead (most of which is described in Hike GL-13). The November 5, 1859, *Sierra Democrat* newspaper had two articles about this proposed route, calling it the "Jamison Road." Financial backing for the wagon road never materialized, although horses and mules transported freight along the route for many years. Arthur W. Keddie's survey map of 1892 shows the section of the road south of the A-Tree, so it was evidently in active use for many years without ever becoming the dreamed-of "main road."

In one article, the newspaper claimed, "The new trail from here [Downieville] to Beckwourth's will be completed next week, and then the Marysville, Downieville and Jamison route will be the most direct and best to the diggins [of Virginia City]." The fabulous silver mines at Virginia City, south of Reno, were, at that time, isolated from any points of supply. Hence, the best route for bringing in supplies was a top priority. (A *Sierra Democrat* article on April 2, 1860, described the atmosphere of Virginia City: "A great deal of wrangling is going on in regard to claims; and appearances indicate that blood will flow freely in the adjustment of existing difficulties. The pistol and the Bowie knife appear to be the great arbiters.")

The trail continues southerly, paralleling the road on the south side of the ridge in a treeless stretch, which is carpeted with wildflowers in midsummer. As you near the top of the ridge, a trail breaks off to the left with a sign to Wades Lake, Mount Washington, and Johnsville. Continue on the PCT, and, just after the top of the ridge, your trail

Flower-covered ridge on the PCT above Spencer Lakes

crosses 22N99A at an angle. A large red fir has fallen across the path on the north side of the road, and it is not clear that the PCT continues left on the other side of the log—until you look. A "No Jeeps" sign signals that this is the way, not along the road. The trail crosses over to the northern side of the slope. Soon thereafter, don't fail to walk to the edge of the ridge at the most obvious place and take in the view of Jamison Creek basin below. Wades, Jamison, and Grass are the three lakes you see plus Mount Elwell and Mount Washington.

If you are doing Route C, the out-and-back hike, this is a point of decision. Depending upon your time and energy, you can either turn back here, continue another mile or two on the "new" PCT before turning around, or follow the old PCT road for ¾ mile down to Four Hills Mine before turning back.

If you're continuing on Route C a bit farther before turning around, or if you're doing Loop A, stay on the PCT as it meanders through the forest and meets the road but doesn't cross it. A bit farther, however, the PCT encounters the road again, and the unsigned PCT angles left. Here, you need to begin walking on the road (still 22N99A), which soon brings you to the upper diggings of Four Hills Mine. The road then turns downhill to reach the lower portions of the mine.

Four Hills was a good gold producer for many years. A newspaper report dated June 21, 1883, related that the mine had yielded a chunk of ore with a record high gold content—a piece so heavy it took seven men to carry it. (True or false?) In 1896, a 30-foot-high dam was erected on Lower Spencer Lake and a powerhouse built downhill, 960 feet below the lake, to provide electricity for mine operations. I can find no evidence of such a dam today, although an article in the *Plumas County Historical Society Publication,* No. 9, dated July 15, 1962, describes it. By 1900, the complex was large enough to have its own post office, although that was closed in 1905. The mine operated sporadically until the 1920s, when it was abandoned. Another *Plumas County Historical Society Publication* article says that the Four Hills Mine was blown up. "The culprit, the youngest Brooks boy from the resort at Upper Salmon Lake, was tracked down because of his one heel track." (The article makes no mention of why he did this dastardly deed or what his fate was.)

More recently, in 1991, the mine's umpteenth owner proposed making it a monitored nuclear waste repository site. However, the good folks of Plumas and Sierra Counties vehemently disapproved, and the proposal was dropped, thank goodness.

What looks like the boiler part of a steam en-

gine sits at the scene of the lower mine, but, unfortunately, much of the area has modern-day litter—broken bottles and cans—thrown into the pits. Grrrrr.

Just beyond Four Hills Mine, the descending road reaches a T intersection with another jeep road. Turn right, and pass below the lower portions of the Four Hills Mine ruins. In 300 yards, you meet a jeep trail coming from Hawley Lake to the south (see Hike GL-26). Keep going straight in a westerly direction. The trail makes an S-curve and, ½ mile from the Hawley Lake jeep road, reaches an old campsite (without water) on the rim overlooking the Spencer Lakes basin with a view of Upper Spencer Lake. The trail takes off downhill from the northern edge of the campsite and drops toward the upper lake.

Now, the first phase of the tough part begins. Although the topo map shows the trail, it's a real challenge to follow, except that you can spy where bushes have been clipped to make room to pass. Stay above the northern edge of the lake, and don't hike all the way to the water. Just past the Upper Lake, the trail fades out at a rock outcrop. Because the northern edges of both Upper and Lower Spencer are choked with bushes, as is the creek between them, keep a high route even though you may not be on a trail. The going is easier higher up than nearer the water, although, when I say "easier," it's far from easy. Plenty of bushwhacking is necessary. Near Lower Spencer Lake the north shore has an area of less-dense foliage. What looks like a road can be seen crossing the clearing to the north of the lake, but, as you descend and arrive at the clearing, you discover it's merely an almost-straight dry creekbed. The trail doesn't go along the shoreline but instead stays 150 yards north of the lake. Continue past the creekbed through some pines on what is now a visible trail. Above the lake a trail coming down from the PCT intersects yours.

This is where hikers doing Loop B join those

who chose Loop A. (If, at this point, your time is slipping away more quickly than you'd anticipated or your energy level is less than you'd hoped, you might head up this side trail back to the PCT and then westerly back to your car, forgoing the strenuous remainder of the A or B loop.) To continue on the loop, head westerly from the intersection, and swing around the western end of Lower Spencer Lake, again staying on the hillside above the lake. Pass by the side trail that leads down to the outlet creek.

Now the fun begins! As the trail curves around the southern end of a rock outcropping, it disappears. Sure, it's shown on the map, but that doesn't mean a thing. For the next 1½ miles you will be virtually trailless and doing plenty of bushwhacking. This is not a good adventure for the novice hiker or for a person without the physical capabilities for plenty of punishment. Plan on almost two hours to traverse this 1½ miles. In two or three places my hiking buddy and I popped out of the heavy brush onto what looked like a trail only to have it disappear again within 50 yards or so. In one place, about midway, as we pushed our way through the omnipresent bushes, we were surprised to find a large pine tree with an old blaze on it, even though no trail was evident. In a couple of places our bushwhacking led us to the edge of Spencer Creek, but in general we tried to stay well above the creek on the hillside to the north. Look at the trail route shown on the topo map, and you may get a better idea of the general direction to follow. You won't get lost, because you can easily see the route of Spencer Creek below you as it courses through the bottom of the canyon on your left. I can't give you any better description of how to traverse this 1½-mile stretch; part of the fun of it is discovering your own route.

As you finally near the end of the horrendous 1½ miles, you can see ahead the canyon in which Lavezzola Creek flows south to join Spencer Creek.

The old wagon road along the eastern side of Lavezzola is visible, so make a beeline for it as you descend the steep canyon. Don't follow Spencer Creek when it makes a bend southward. The trail intersection is a welcome sight; it signals relief from bushwhacking. However, you'll still need to expend plenty of energy on your way back to the trailhead. Make a right turn at the signless trail junction, and head north along the eastern side of the Lavezzola Canyon.

For the next 1½ miles, go into "low gear" as you ascend steadily from 5,600 feet to the A-Tree trailhead at 6,560 feet. You can hear Lavezzola Creek rushing downhill on your left, but the path is far enough from the creek to make it difficult, although not impossible, to refresh your water supply from it. This steadily uphill wagon road must have been a real doozy for the pack animals and wagon-pulling horses or oxen, and going downhill in the other direction would have been an extreme test of wagon's brakes. Fortunately, loaded wagons went only uphill in the direction of the mines. In the days when this wagon road was in use, Lavezzola Creek was called the Middle Fork of the North Fork of the North Yuba River. No wonder it got renamed after the pioneer Lavezzola, who homesteaded a nearby ranch.

The last mile is, thankfully, shady and the old wagon road surface smooth and wide—a blessing after all the blasted bushes. The treat waiting for you at the end of the trail is another drink from the A-Tree's ice-cold delicious spring. Of course, taking off your boots will be a treat too, but your drink from the spring has priority.

Camping: The only water along the route is from the Spencer Lakes or Spencer Creek. Upper Spencer Lake is virtually uncampable due to lack of flat spots along the shore and choking shoreline brush. We camped at Lower Spencer on the south shore of the lake, reached by crossing over the outlet from the lake and looping back easterly on a visible path. There are several nice spots on this side of the lake and along the outlet creek. I expected to find a good campsite or two along Spencer Creek, and, indeed, at one of the two places we neared the creek an old campsite appeared. However, I bet most backpackers would just as soon finish the bush-whacking section rather than camp halfway through it. (I was in too big a hurry to check for potential camping spots downhill from the inter-section of the Spencer Creek Trail with the Lavezzola Creek Trail. The trail south crosses Lavezzola Creek ¼ mile from the intersection, and perhaps there's a decent campsite there.) For car camping, along the road to the trailhead is the A-Tree Road Camp-ground, which is without amenities but looks OK. Farther back on the Johnsville-La Porte Road is Ross Campground, also without amenities but lo-cated on a spectacular part of upper Jamison Creek.

Winter Use: None. These routes get snow up to your eyeballs.

GL-13 Little Jamison Creek Trail to Jamison, Rock, and Wades Lakes

Distance: 7½ miles out and back (with extension to Wades Lake, 8½ miles)

Highest Point: 6,300 feet (with extension, 6,549 feet)

Total Elevation Gain: 1,100 feet (with extension, 1,320 feet)

Difficulty: Moderate/strenuous

Hiking Season: June through October

Directions to the Trailhead: See Hike GL-14.

Comments: This is one of the most highly used trails in the area, because it leads to four beautiful lakes where camping is al-lowed, unlike the lakes within the Lakes Basin Rec-reation Area. Backpackers can choose an easy jaunt to Grass Lake or hike farther to Jamison or Wades Lake. Wades has the highest elevation of the four, and, hence, is the last to be snow-free in the spring. All four lakes can be visited in a nice one-day hike. If you do this hike in late spring or early summer, you might take along some wading shoes, especially if you plan to hike to Rock Lake from Jamison Lake, because you won't be able to cross the creek with-out getting your feet wet.

The Hike: The hike commences at the historic Jamison Mine. To learn a bit of the history of the mine and its buildings, which surround the trailhead, read Appendix C. Little Jamison Creek, which you follow up to Jamison Lake, joins (Big)

Jamison Creek a few hundred yards downstream from the mine buildings. The four lakes you'll visit on this hike were all owned by the Jamison Mine Company and valued as reliable water supplies for mine operations. Even so, in the rain-deficient years between 1910 and 1916, the mine operated for only a portion of each year, with 1914 being the worst year.

The well-beaten rocky trail starts uphill, and, in ¾ mile, reaches an intersection where the Smith Lake Trail branches off to the left. This initial part of the trip is not particularly beautiful, and the trail itself is not enticing, but it will get better and pret-tier soon, I guarantee. Continue on for ¼ mile be-yond the Smith Lake Trail to the signed trail on your right. Be sure to take this side trip, which leads you in just a few steps to a beautiful close-up view of Little Jamison Creek Falls. This 60-foot cascade is certainly worth a look and a photo.

Back on the main trail, you soon reach Grass Lake. Continue along the eastern shore of the lake rather than taking the trail to the right leading to its unattractive earthen dam. Throughout most of the hiking season, this part of the trail may be wet, as numerous rivulets trickle down the hillside into the lake, exploring the trail as they go. Be prepared to do a bit of stepping from rock to rock to keep your feet dry. Fortunately, the trail has a good rock surface here so you won't get muddy, I hope.

Grass Lake is close enough to the trailhead to attract fishing devotees, although on my last few trips I haven't seen any here. Perhaps the fishing isn't what it used to be. Fine photos of the lake with Mount Washington towering behind can be taken in numerous spots because the trail closely follows the shoreline. Why the lake was named Grass Lake is obvious, but I do laugh at the lack of creativity by the lake-namers of old: Just slightly more than 2 miles away is another Grass Lake. There's a third one on the same Gold Lake topo map south of Upper Salmon Lake and a fourth (sometimes referred to as Grassy Lake) just west of Gold Lake Highway. I bet every county in the Sierra has a few Grass Lakes.

The trail makes a loop to the west and, suddenly, you are at a crossing of Little Jamison Creek, which, at this point, isn't so little. On my most recent hike through here I found a somewhat precarious, but navigable, crossing spot with a combination of rocks and logs about 20 feet to the right of the trail. Having hiked this trail for the past 30 years, I realize that good crossing spots change, so if 20 feet to the right doesn't look possible, explore the creek bank farther, both upstream and down, to find a decent place to cross. A nice footbridge built by the Forest Service would be welcome here, but, given the ever-shrinking USFS budget, I'd say that's out of the question.

I've mentioned bringing footwear to change into for stream crossings, but I must admit that I prefer a precarious above-the-water crossing to a wade into the fast-flowing stream while trying to find footing on the slippery rock bottom. By late summer, the swiftness of the creek has subsided some and the crossing is easier.

Across the creek, the trail starts to climb and loops south to a well-signed intersection, where the trail on the right goes up to Wades Lake and the PCT, and the one on the left goes to Jamison Lake and Rock Lake. Although you want the left branch, take a detour on the right branch for about 300 yards beyond the junction, and keep an eye out on your right for the site of an old log cabin. Only the lowest level of logs remains, but 30 years ago, when I hiked this trail for the first time, the cabin was still standing. It is amazing to see how quickly the severe winters in this neck of the woods erase the wooden works of man.

From the detour, return the 300 yards to the trail junction. The next section of trail to Jamison Lake passes through some beautiful stands of aspens, whose white bark and shimmering light-green leaves add a lovely dimension to the conifer forest. Unfortunately, many crummy people have carved their names or initials in the soft bark, creating unsightly and permanent graffiti. After climbing steadily and encountering a few switchbacks, you pass by another intersection where the trail to the right leads steeply toward Wades Lake. In another ¼ mile you come to another Y, with the left fork leading to the Jamison Lake Dam and the right fork leading to the small peninsula that juts out into Jamison Lake. Try the latter, because, once you reach the shore, the view of the lake and Mount Elwell towering behind it is magnificent. The little island in the lake is just to your right. There are several small but nice camping sites here.

Trail in Little Jamison Creek Canyon

The topo map shows a trail leading north to the dam right along the shore. It actually is not at the shore but goes somewhat westerly behind a rock outcropping, and in less than ¼ mile cuts back to the dam. The rock dam is strange, because a big rectangular notch has been cut at the top, creating a spillway for the lake's discharge, which becomes Little Jamison Creek. Evidently, years ago, someone decided to lower the level of the lake, hence the notch. Just to the north of the dam are several nice specimens of western white pine, a species not found at lower elevations. It can be identified by its tufts of medium-length flexible needles and its cones, which are long and slender before they dry out and expand, leading to its common name, finger cone pine.

At the dam, a sign points easterly across the creek to the ¼-mile trail to beautiful Rock Lake. Here, too, no welcoming footbridge is available, no fallen trees span the creek, and no one-hop-apart boulders provide a passage across. So don your ex-

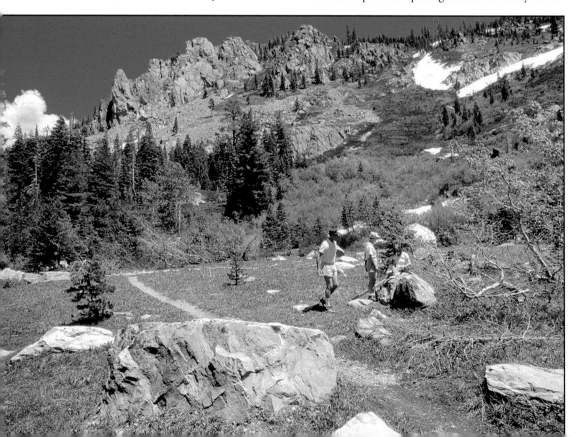

tra footwear, and wade across. The bit of extra effort is worth it, because the rocky shore, petite island, and backdrop of Mount Elwell ridge rising steeply 1,300 feet above the water make Rock Lake one of the prettiest in the Sierra.

Retracing your steps, you can extend your hike with a side trip to Wades Lake at the previously mentioned intersections with signs to it. In a recent late-winter year, by early July I still couldn't get to Wades because of the snowpack. In drier years, by mid-July I've gone for a chilly but tolerable swim in Wades on the way back from a hike up to the summit of Mount Washington (see Hike GL-14). Wades is nestled in its own glacier-formed, heavily forested basin, a unique, beautiful setting.

The all-downhill return trip is just as pleasurable as the trip up, and even the rocky final ½ mile doesn't seem so bad. If you are back in your car at nearly dinnertime and aren't too dirty and sweaty, when the dirt road from Jamison Mine hits the paved County Road A-14, turn left, and drive 1 mile into Johnsville for dinner at the Iron Door Restaurant, the town's only retail establishment. A reservation (530-836-2376) is usually necessary, especially on summer weekends, so you need to plan ahead. The restaurant's rustic bar and a decor highlighted by early artifacts and relics make the Iron Door a delightful find.

Camping: Backpack camping (without a campfire) is allowed at Grass, Jamison, and Wades Lakes. Grass Lake, being the closest to the trailhead, is the most popular. Its best camping spot is on the western shore, reached by crossing the dam at the northern end of the lake. An overused site at the south end of the lake has the easiest access. Jamison Lake has several nice separated campsites with good views on its western shore. My favorite, however, is Wades Lake. Its northern end has several lovely large camping places. Camping is not allowed along Little Jamison Creek.

Winter Use: The dirt road leading into Jamison Mine is one of the best cross-country ski trails in the area. A large paved and plowed parking area at a wide spot on the Graeagle-Johnsville Road (County Road A-14) accommodates half a dozen cars, although I have seldom discovered more than a handful of people skiing here. This ski trail goes all the way to the Jamison Mine trailhead parking lot. For a nice loop, at the upper right side of the snow-covered parking lot, take the ski trail across the new bridge over Little Jamison Creek and into the state park campground at campsite 54. Turn right, and follow the curvy campground roads to the entrance of the campground on the Johnsville-La Porte Road. Turn right, and ski the road back to the parking lot of the museum. From here, take off your skis, and walk back ½ mile to your car on Road A-14, which is paved and always plowed. Especially after a fresh snowfall, this trail is a heavenly experience on either skis or snowshoes.

GL-14 Mount Washington via Little Jamison Creek Trail

Distance: 10½ miles out and back
Highest Point: 7,369 feet
Total Elevation Gain: 2,089 feet
Difficulty: Strenuous
Hiking Season: Late June through October

Directions to the Trailhead: From Graeagle, head north on Highway 89 for .25 mile, then turn left at the Graeagle Frostee onto the Graeagle-Johnsville Road (County Road A-14). Continue for 4.6 miles to a dirt road leading off to the left with a sign "Jamison Mine." Take the dirt road for 1.3 miles (passing a spur road to the right saying "Camp Lisa") to the Jamison Mine complex of old buildings. Park in the parking area behind the buildings. (An alternative access to the trailhead is from Plumas-Eureka State Park Campground. A short trail leaves the campground to the left of campsite 54, crosses a new footbridge over the creek, and enters the trailhead parking lot.)

Comments: This is one of my favorite hikes, and Mount Washington is certainly my favorite peak to climb. The final 2 miles of the trail to the summit are fairly level and include some of the region's finest views. Likewise, it is pleasurable to achieve a summit that gives almost no indication that anyone else has preceded you to that spot. This trip is categorized as strenuous mainly because of its length, not because of unusual steepness or a lousy trail. The steep final 200 yards can be climbed fairly easily. However, anyone who does not like rock scrambling or is subject to vertigo may want to pass-up the final ascent to the summit.

The Hike: The hike starts at historic Jamison Mine. To learn a bit of the history of the mine and its buildings, which surround the trailhead, read Appendix C. For the first 3½ miles, follow the di-

rections for Hike GL-13. Then, after crossing Little Jamison Creek, climbing, and looping south, when you reach the well-signed trail intersection take the right fork toward Wades Lake. In ¾ mile, the short trail down to Wades Lake turns off to the left. Although the lake is only a few hundred yards away, you cannot see it from the main trail here. If you have time on the way back and the day is hot, take

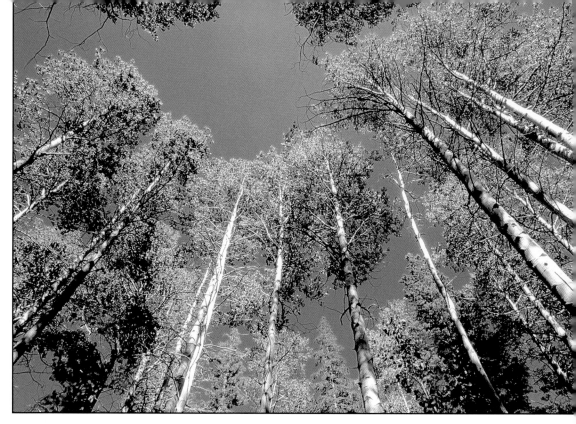

Aspen grove along Little Jamison Creek

this short trail down to the lake for a refreshing dip. It does get a few visitors, so skinny-dipping is risky. Wades is a good overnight stopping place if you want to make this hike a two-day affair.

However, you still have a good walk to the top in front of you, with an 820-foot altitude gain, so for now let's bypass Wades Lake and head uphill on the main trail. The country opens up for better vistas, and, although the trail gets rockier and steeper, you probably will not mind because the views to the east are terrific. If the spring rains were adequate, by midsummer this eastern slope has a lovely variety of wildflowers. Watch for the attractive solid-red snow plant (that's its common name), which is about the size of an empty roll of toilet paper. It appears when the snow has nearly finished melting, and it lasts through the spring and into early summer before shriveling and fading.

This portion of the trail, once upon a time, was proposed to become a major thoroughfare. For economic reasons, the city of Marysville, located in the Sacramento Valley, wished to be the western terminus of the main route into California, in competition with the Donner Pass route, which terminated in Sacramento. In 1860, and again in 1880, funds were appropriated and planning done for a major wagon road to be built from Marysville to Downieville, first along the North Fork of the Yuba River, then up through Gold Valley (see Hike GL-11), over the pass a mile from where you are now, and down to Jamison Lake. From the lake it would have gone north to Johnsville and continued downhill past today's town of Blairsden into Mohawk Valley. From Mohawk Valley, the road would have traveled easterly over Beckwourth Pass along the route of present-day Highway 70, and then south to Reno. Although longer than the Donner Pass road, it would have had the advantage of much lower altitudes, requiring less of a climb for the tired horses and oxen who pulled heavy wagons over the crest of the Sierra. It would also have had considerably less snow, allowing it to stay open much more of the year. Fortunately for today's hiker in search of solitude, once the new road had been completed from Marysville to Downieville, the road-builders figured out how to conquer the formidable Yuba Gap to the east. The final route followed the canyon of the North Fork of the Yuba River, later becoming today's scenic State Highway 49. How different this region would be today if the original plans had been carried out and the trail you are on had become a major highway.

Almost exactly ½ mile beyond the Wades Lake Trail intersection, keep a close watch on your right for the trail to Mount Washington. At this writing, no sign alerts you to make a sharp right turn onto the dim trail. Once there was a sign, but all that is left of it is a broken wooden signpost lying on the ground, so that is your clue to the start of the Mount Washington Trail. If you miss it, about 400 yards farther on the main trail you come to an intersection with a road running along the ridge. Retrace your steps, and look more closely for the elusive Mount Washington turnoff.

Unfortunately (or, perhaps, fortunately, for those of us who like unbeaten trails). from here to the summit, the trail is not maintained and does not show on the topo map (although it does show on the USFS map of Plumas National Forest). However, enough people use the route so that most hikers who have a good eye for the trail can easily pick it out. In a few stretches where the trail was not readily apparent, I continued walking straight ahead and in less than 100 yards again picked up the path. The dimmest sections are level and not heavily forested, so you can look for the route ahead without a lot of vegetation blocking your view. Surprisingly, the first ¼ mile of trail is the least clear, and, after that, the farther you go, the easier it is to spot the path. The route traces along the easterly side of the

ridge crest heading almost due north up to Mount Washington in a fairly straight line. The unobstructed views to the east are breathtaking. From here you can see Wades, Rock, and Jamison Lakes nestled below you, with imposing Mount Elwell towering behind them. It would be a callous hiker, indeed, who did not marvel at the vistas displayed during most of the first mile of the unimproved trail. A little more than 1 mile after turning off the main trail, you descend slightly to a shallow saddle and cross over to the western side of the ridge for the short ¼ mile remaining.

Along this last portion, you have an enticing view of the summit from several points. In places, the manzanita and other bushes obscure the trail, but you can easily push through the brush with an eye for the trail underneath. The route approaches the base of the summit from the south, and an eager-to-conquer-the-peak hiker may be tempted to strike off the trail at this point for the final ascent. Resist the urge, however, and hike for another five minutes along the trail as it skirts 100 feet below the top, on the western slope of the mountain. As the trail is about to leave the summit behind, keep an eye out on your right for the easy route to the peak. Although this last 100-foot elevation gain is trailless, you can find the best way up without difficulty. The rock strata here are almost vertical, and handholds are often the knife-sharp upper edges of rock. Fortunately, the rock is not very crumbly, and, as summit ascents go, this one is relatively easy and safe if you don't mind high places and a bit of a scramble. The 360° view from the top is worth the whole walk. You see all the other high peaks in the region plus the far-off communities of Blairsden and Graeagle.

A most welcome feature of the summit is its "freshness." No trampled-down place tells you that thousands before you have stood at the very top, no USGS brass benchmark plaque or weather station claims precedence, and certainly no log book records the names of other peak conquerors and their "nice view" superfluous comments.

With caution, you can scramble down from the top to the trail in a few minutes. Retrace your steps, which now, thankfully, are almost all downhill.

At the start of the hike at Jamison Mine you may have stopped to look at the sign map of the region's trails. Strangely, this map has no "You Are Here" label, and the first mile or so of the trail is beyond the boundary of the map. However, the map does show the unmaintained Mount Washington Trail as it leaves the main trail and heads for the summit. It also shows the trail continuing on from the summit in a zigzag fashion on the north slope of the mountain, leading down to Little Jamison Creek Trail just north of Grass Lake. "Ah," you say, "a nice loop route," and this north-side trail looks only half as long as the route just described. "I'll take the shorter trail back," you think. Don't, unless you enjoy heavy-duty cross-country hiking. A very short distance from the top, this north-side trail fades out completely. It is tempting to start downhill, figuring that you'll pick up the trail at some point. I have taken this route, both up from Grass Lake and down from the summit. Although I found the dim old trail in a few places, for most of the distance I was doing strenuous cross-country hiking, and about 60 percent of the route required beating my way through thick, tough manzanita and other scrub brush. Now it's true, I enjoy cross-country hiking—when I can hike. But here the going is slow, and if you are wearing shorts you will gather a good collection of scratches, scrapes, and cuts. From footprints in the short portions of discernible trail, I could see that only one other person had attempted this route from winter to early August. Naturally, with lack of use it will grow even dimmer as years pass, and another fun trail will sink into oblivion—well, I guess this portion already has.

Camping: See Hike GL-13

Winter Use: See Hike GL-13.

GL-15 Mount Elwell Loop from Jamison Mine

Distance: 12¼-mile loop

Highest Point: 7,818 feet

Total Elevation Gain: 3,103 feet

Difficulty: Strenuous

Hiking Season: June or July through October

Directions to the Trailhead: See Hike GL-14.

Comments: This is one of the best all-day hikes in the Feather River country. I recommend an early start because of the hike's length and elevation gain. Besides bringing you the marvelous 360° view from Mount Elwell, the hike offers visits to several sparkling lakes, a bit of the PCT as it traverses the ridge above Jamison Creek drainage basin, and a gazillion wildflowers in midsummer. Make sure you read Appendix C to learn the history of Jamison Mine before starting this hike.

The Hike: Follow the description of Hike GL-13 to the intersection where the left fork goes to Jamison and Rock Lakes and the right fork, the one you want, heading toward Wades Lake. In 1 mile a short trail on the left leads down to Wades, which is not visible from this junction. Follow the right fork uphill for another ¼ mile to an intersection with a jeep road (22N99A) that runs along the ridge. Turn left on the road, and hike for about ¼ mile. Watch closely for the "new" PCT, not shown on the topo map, as it angles across the road. Surprisingly, no sign marks this junction. A large red fir has fallen across the path on the left side of the road, and it is not clear that the PCT continues on the other side of the log—until you look. A "No Jeeps" sign signals that this is the way, not along the road. The trail crosses over to the northern side of the slope. Soon thereafter, don't fail to walk to the edge of the ridge at the most obvious place to take in the panorama of Jamison Creek basin below. Wades, Jamison, and Grass are the three lakes you see, plus Mount Elwell and Mount Washington.

The PCT meanders for ½ mile through the forest and meets the jeep road but doesn't cross it. A bit farther, however, just before the PCT encounters the road again, the trail angles left and zigzags downhill with more fine views of the basin through which you hiked two hours earlier. In ½ mile, at a junction, bear left along a road that continues to have fine overlooks of the basin. About ½ mile farther, take a trail that branches left toward Mount Elwell. It traverses a ridge, now with fine views below and eastward of Long Lake and much smaller Mud Lake. In another ½ mile you reach a four-way trail intersection where several signs give good directions. Turn left in the direction pointing to Mount Elwell and Smith Lake. The 800-foot elevation gain to Mount Elwell is made less onerous by the great views of Long Lake and much of the Lakes Basin to the east. See Hike GL-16 for a description of the views and of the best scramble route off the trail to the summit.

After enjoying the summit, continue along the trail heading north. This section of gradual downhill through marvelous forest is one of my favorite trail sections, even though it lacks sweeping vistas. After a 120° turn to the right, the path passes lonely Maiden Lake (unnamed on the topo map but identified by an old sign at lakeside) and several diminutive but scenic ponds. The route continues to meander downhill, finally reaching Smith Creek and, just beyond it, an intersection with the Smith Lake Trail. If you have your wildflower book along, you can probably

Red fir grove on the trail below Mount Elwell

identify several new varieties in this spot.

Follow the trail left to Smith Lake, less than ¼ mile away. The route crosses the outlet creek from the lake (Smith Creek, of course) and skirts the lake's southern shore in roller-coaster fashion. The inlet creek, coming down from much smaller Upper Smith Lake, is easy to hop over. You see a last view of Smith Lake as the trail climbs 260 feet out of the cozy basin in which the lake is tucked and up to a shallow saddle. From here it's all downhill to the car as the trail descends toward Little Jamison Creek and an intersection with the trail you started up many an hour earlier. Turn right, and in ¾ mile the trailhead and the Jamison Mine bunkhouse pop into view. Now, that was an all-time memorable day, wasn't it?

Camping: In addition to the sites described at Hike GL-14, camping is available at Smith Lake. The campsite I like best is on its southern shore, midway between its outlet and inlet creeks.

Winter Use: See Hike GL-14.

GL-16 Mount Elwell Loop from Gray Eagle Lodge

Distance: 12¼-mile loop (Alternative A to Smith Lake only, 2 miles out

and back; Alternative B to the summit only, 8 miles out and back)

Highest Point: 7,818 feet (Alternative A, 6,084 feet)

Total Elevation Gain: 1,949 feet (Alternative A, 281 feet)

Difficulty: Strenuous (Alternative A, moderate; Alternative B,

moderate/strenuous)

Hiking Season: June or July through October

Directions to the Trailhead: From Graeagle take Highway 89 south for 1.4 miles, and turn right on Gold Lake Highway. Drive for 5.0 miles to a road on the right with a fancy sign "Gray Eagle Lodge" and another sign "Smith Lake Trail ½, Gray Eagle Creek Trail ½." Take this road, which soon turns to dirt, for .4 mile, passing the Gray Eagle Creek Trailhead, and take a bumpy (but OK for cars) road on the right. Go about 150 yards, and park among the trees in one of the many available places.

Comments: This is one of my favorite hikes. It has it all: wildflowers aplenty, streams, numerous lakes close at hand and far away, smaller ponds, and one of the area's finest vistas, from atop Mount Elwell (whose height, 7,818 feet, is surpassed within the area only by Sierra Buttes, at 8,591 feet). The trailhead is easy to get to, and most of the route is smooth. The total uphill is almost 2,000 feet, but that's the "price" you pay for the fine views from the summit and the thrill of being "on top." For people who want a short but pleasant hike, Alternative A to Smith Lake only and back is a good one. Because this ascent of Mount Elwell is from the north, it may be too snowy to do until late spring or early summer. You can get an idea of how snowy it is on top by viewing the mountain from afar from Gold Lake Highway. Alternative B, to the mountain and back, instead of making a loop, shaves 4¼ miles off the distance.

William Elwell, for whom the peak was named,

came to California in May 1850 at the age of 29. He entered the mining business and for a number of years was superintendent of the 76 Mine, later called the Plumas-Eureka Mine, located on Eureka Peak. He was a veteran of the Mexican War and became a Royal Arch Mason.

The Hike: For the description of the initial part of the trail, to Smith Lake, see Hike GL-6. Once you reach Smith Lake, you have actually gone ¼ mile out of your way. Sorry, but I wanted you to see the lake. So, backtrack ¼ mile to the intersection with the Mount Elwell Trail. If you're doing Alternative A, retrace your steps to your car from here. If you're game for the full Elwell loop or Alternative B, turn right, and continue on the trail you would have been on a half-hour earlier if I hadn't lured you to Smith Lake.

You immediately encounter another crossing of Smith Creek, and, from here, the climb is almost continuously uphill for 3 miles, although it is steep in only a few places. The route passes a few ponds on the left, which are part of the Hidden Lakes group, and then Maiden Lake on the right with its old sign attached to a tree. The red fir forest surrounding you on this stretch includes some fine specimens. Don't forget to look up when directly

Overlooking Long Lake from below Mount Elwell

under some of the largest red firs in order to appreciate what "big" means in Mother Nature's dictionary.

After a 90° left turn, you pass above 7,000 feet and commence an almost beeline route to the crest of Mount Elwell. Even in midsummer you may have to cross a bit of snow just before the summit. However, you can hike over it fairly easily or cut around it to the left and pick up the trail above the snow. Mount Elwell's summit finally pops into view at close range as the trail curves around its southern exposure.

A side trip to the very top is recommended, unless you have fear of heights, vertigo, or an aversion to rock scrambling up and down. If you fit any of these categories, don't feel embarrassed—there are lots of people like you, and achieving the summit just isn't your "thing." The best route for the short distance to the top is just past the saddle, as the trail crosses below the peak's southern side. A route through the bushes is visible, and your own view of the top will direct you the rest of the way, as

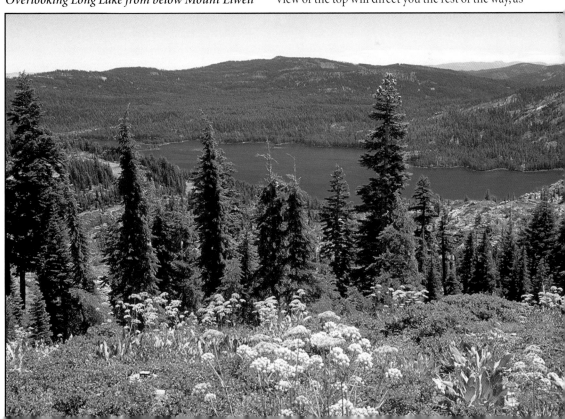

you clamber up the rocks. There's a nice flat spot on top, so you won't be perched on a precipice.

On the western edge of the peak, you'll have a spectacular view down into the Little Jamison Creek basin. Jamison Lake with its cute island near the far shore is directly below you. To its right is Rock Lake with its smaller island, and beyond Jamison is Wades Lake. Pointy Mount Washington rises behind Rock Lake, and, from here, it is apparent that you're looking down on its summit of "only" 7,369 feet. On a clear day, snow-capped Mount Lassen can be seen on the horizon to the southeast. Taking a few steps to the eastern side of the summit, you're rewarded with a view of Long Lake directly below and Silver and Round Lakes nearby, south of it. At an even greater distance, in the same direction, the largest body of water is Gold Lake, and the sliver of blue beyond it is Goose Lake.

Completing a visual sweep of the horizon in this direction gives you views of Mills Peak and, farther east, in the distance, Beckwourth Peak. Turning to your right, the southward view takes in the spires of Sierra Buttes and, on the far horizon many miles away, the tops of the "high Sierra" beyond Donner Pass.

On several occasions I've climbed to the top of Elwell with visitors who don't have time or energy for the full loop described here, and then done an about-face, choosing Alternative B. The out-and-back trip to the top is easier and a few miles shorter than the whole loop.

Scrambling down from the top isn't difficult, but it does require a bit of care. If you're game for the whole loop, picking up the trail again, you head southwesterly downhill with a few easy switchbacks. The tree cover isn't dense, so the trail down continues to have good views of the ridge to the south and the drainage basin from the ridge down to Long Lake. Mud Lake and Hellgramite Lake are now seen on the west side of Long Lake. The trail zigzags downhill to a point near Long Lake where you encounter a four-way intersection with a sign "Mount Elwell ¾" pointing back the way you came and, "Long Lake ¾, Gray Eagle Lodge 2½" pointing to the left. Naturally, the latter is the way you need to go.

This part of the trail, in the "old days," was a major north-south route. It shows on the 1892 map of Plumas County done by the county's prominent early-day engineer and surveyor, Arthur W. Keddie.

Terrific close-up views of Long Lake and its two small islands are sure-to-please photo opportunities. As the trail levels and parallels the shore 260 feet above the lake surface, the hillside you're walking on turns into a talus slope. Thank goodness the flat trail has been well established; otherwise, you'd have a very slippy-slidey time getting to the north end of the lake on this loose-rock section. You're treading on small rocks for more than ¼ mile of talus, and your feet may start objecting. Because the trail is not slanted sideways, it isn't scary, and slow careful going brings you eventually to the northern end of the talus slope. Your reward is the western shore of the lake. The sound of mini-waves lapping the shore in the afternoon breeze is welcome and refreshing. Across the lake in a cove on the western shore you can spy the Barker Cabin. Who the Barkers are and how they get supplies to this still-used cabin, I don't know.

For more than ¼ mile, the trail is almost at water level, but as you reach the northern end it veers northerly away from the lake. You get a few fleeting glimpses of the lake's dam (and an ugly dam it is, indeed). The outlet creek tumbles merrily downhill to your right supplying a new plethora of moisture-loving wildflowers. My favorite in this area is the Sierra lily (also called tiger lily) with its showy orange blossoms. Leaving the creek, the trail passes several beautiful dead trees with glossy white trunks and a wild array of branches. Some of the live trees are perched on rocks in a manner that makes you wonder how they ever could have grown that way.

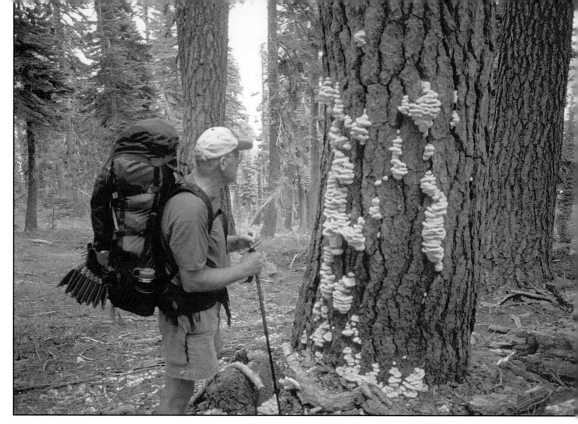

Sulfur-shelf mushrooms on the trail near Mount Elwell

A nameless pond appears on your right after you pass a dim trail cutting back sharply on your right, which is part of the Long Lake Loop Trail (Hike GL-21). A few hundred yards beyond the pond is another trail intersection, with two signs, one pointing back to Long Lake and Mount Elwell the way you came and to "Lakes Basin Campground ¾" to the right. The other sign says "Halsey Falls ¾, Gray Eagle Lodge 1¼." Continue straight, and ½ mile farther there's another cutoff trail on your right with a sign telling you that Halsey Falls are only ¼ mile away.

If you have the energy, the side trip to see the falls is worthwhile; or you may decide to do the falls another day (take Hike GL-27). On toward the car you trudge, with the beauty of the forest around you for comfort. One last trail fork is marked "Gray Eagle Lodge ¼" to the right (it also leads to Lily Lake) and, on a separate sign, "Smith Lake Trail ½" to the left, which is where your car is parked. If it's near

dinnertime and you've planned ahead by making a reservation (530-836-2511), a delightful end to the day is dinner in the dining room at Gray Eagle Lodge. This is one of my favorite places to bring guests for dinner. The lodge's wine list, although not extensive, is excellent; the owners carefully research the wineries of the Napa and Sonoma Valleys during the winter when the lodge is closed. Even if it isn't dinnertime, the short drive to the lodge from where your car is parked is worthwhile just to see its unique rustic interior made with massive logs.

Camping: No camping is allowed at most of the lakes or along the streams in the Lakes Basin Recreation Area, which includes all of the lakes you pass on this hike (except Smith Lake). Excellent car camping is nearby at the USFS Lakes Basin Campground (but it's often crowded).

Winter Use: None.

GL-17 Mount Washington Runoff Falls Trail

Distance: 2½ miles out and back

Highest Point: 5,440 feet

Total Elevation Gain: 175 feet

Difficulty: Moderate

Hiking Season: Late May through early July (the falls dry up by midsummer)

Directions to the Trailhead: From Graeagle, drive north on Highway 89 for .2 miles, and turn left onto the Graeagle-Johnsville Road (County Road A-14) at the Graeagle Frostee. After going 4 miles on A-14, turn left at the Plumas-Eureka State Park Museum onto the Johnsville-La Porte Road, which heads south from the museum parking lot. When you are 1 mile from the museum, park at a wide place in the paved road opposite the entrance to the state park campground.

Comments: WARNING: The vertical mineshaft at the end of the trail is **extremely dangerous,** and entry is strictly forbidden. Anyone who gets too close to the slippery edge and accidentally tumbles in will likely not live to tell the tale. This is a very hazardous spot for adults and particularly for kids who don't recognize the danger or who want to show off their daring by creeping up to the edge of the shaft. So, unless you have close control of your kids and teenagers, don't take them along. And, for goodness sake, don't let them do this hike without you! This trail and mineshaft are part of the state park but are not included in any of the park literature, because the rangers do not want to haul out dead or seriously injured people.

The Hike: Walk in to the campground entrance, bear right, cross the bridge over Jamison Creek, and wind through the campground maze until you find campsites 65 and 67. Proceed uphill between them, past a couple of cut logs lying parallel to the road, and soon you encounter a wide path of smooth white stones, looking much like a shallow streambed. Continue up it for 200 yards,

and, as it bends left (Hike GL-24), look for a track branching to the right at a sharp angle. It's easy to miss, so keep a close watch for it (the turnoff is almost in sight of campsite 65). Bushes narrow the path, and, in some places, they grow so close that you have to push through (unless some kind person has clipped off the offending branches since this was written).

As you approach the 1-mile point, a washout has made a small gully where the trail once crossed. Instead of climbing steeply down into this gully, go left about 15 yards to a place where you can scramble down more easily. Rock-hop down the streambed 15 yards back to an easy climb up to the continuation of the trail. Soon, mine tailings ahead

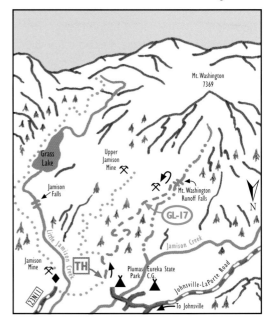

serve notice that the mineshaft is near, so grab your kids' hands, and proceed with caution. The pit is to the left of the trail, tucked in among some large rocks. Stay a safe distance back from the slippery edge of the plummeting shaft, even though you won't be able to see the bottom. Please don't try to lean over far enough to see how deep it is.

After carefully checking out the vertical shaft and wondering how in the world the old-time miners ever climbed safely down a ladder to the bottom, walk over to the edge of the tailings. From here, unobstructed by trees, you have a sweeping 180° panorama of much of the Jamison Creek Canyon. Massive Eureka Peak dominates the landscape beyond the creek. Glimpses of the creek itself, winding through the bottom of the canyon, add to the enjoyment of the scene. Nearby, up-canyon, you can hear the sound of a waterfall, and, sure enough, a few steps southwest from the tailings the falls come into view. The creek creating these falls arises from snowmelt on nearby 7,369-foot Mount Washington, so the stream disappears when all the snow has melted. To view the falls, do this hike in May, June, or early July. In a heavy-snow year, however, the trail may be impassable in May because of snow.

The path ends at the tailings, so you'll need to do a bit of cross-country scrambling to get a good view of the falls. Granted, these falls aren't high and free-falling, but their cascade is very pretty. You can clamber up higher for an even better falls view, but the hillside is steep, slippery, and full of loose rocks, so use caution as you climb. As in most steep trailless climbs, going down is even more treacherous than scrambling up, so take it easy. If this type of up and down isn't your forte, then merely enjoy the falls from the level of the tailings.

Return to your car by the same route. On the way back, when you reach the smooth white stone path, you may wish to add Hike GL-24 to your day's excursion, if time and stamina permit.

Camping: Because the terrain is nothing but hillside, no backpacking campsites are available, unless you camp on the level pile of tailings. However, the state park campground where the hike started has good car camping—and hot showers!

Winter Use: None. Hike GL-24, which starts from the same location, is more suitable for winter use. Also read the "Winter Use" section of Hike GL-19.

Mount Washington runoff falls

GL-18 Lily Lake Trail

Distance: ¾ mile out and back (with the loop around the lake, 1 mile)

Highest Point: 5,970 feet

Total Elevation Gain: 60 feet

Difficulty: Easy (with the lake loop, easy/moderate)

Hiking Season: May through October

Directions to the Trailhead: From Graeagle drive south on Highway 89 for 1.4 miles, turn right on Gold Lake Highway, and drive for another 5.6 miles. On the right, at a large turnout, is a sign "Lily Lake Trail." There is plenty of parking space.

Comments: To see a pretty lake in an alpine setting without a heavy-duty hike, this is the walk for you. Although the trail from the road down to the lakeshore is a bit steep, you can do it easily unless you're physically challenged. Put on insect repellent, and bring your camera.

The Hike: From the edge of the turnout, the smooth trail heads downhill, winding a bit, and, before you know it, reaches the northeast shore of the lake. On a recent visit, my friends and I watched a momma duck and a whole flock of ducklings paddle furiously away from us toward the safety of the middle of the lake. At the lakeshore, turn right, and hike around the north end of the lake. The trail is a bit rocky, so, if members of your party are unsteady on their feet, you can skip this part. However, if everyone is spry enough, the short walk to the western shore of the lake is rewarding, because you can see the huge-leafed water lilies close to shore there. In late July we were treated to the sight of yellow blooms on those near the western edge of the lake. The name given these lilies is yellow pond lily (is the pond yellow or the lily?) or cow lily (they certainly don't look anything like cows).

A side trail branches off from the lake leading to a trail that runs between Gray Eagle Lodge (only ½ mile from here) and Lakes Basin Campground.

This is the place to turn around and retrace your steps, unless you want to make the complete loop around the lake.

The trail for the rest of the complete loop is only slightly used, so be ready to encounter bushes to push through, boulders to climb over, and some detours from the shore in impassable areas. Follow the path along the lakeshore beyond the side trail intersection, and, in the first part of the remainder of the loop, you'll see beautiful foot-long pine cones on the trail, dropped by the sugar pines that grace the southern shore of the lake. While still green, the cones can weigh up to 4 pounds. Because they grow at the tops of trees 150 feet up, you certainly don't want to be walking underneath when a squirrel dislodges a green one. (Don't worry—squirrels don't like green cones.)

In early morning or late afternoon, the breeze usually dies, and the surface of the lake becomes mirrorlike, nicely reflecting the shapes of the conifers on the opposite shore. My photos of Lily Lake have been beautiful—I hope yours are too.

Camping: None. For car campers, the excellent Lakes Basin Campground is only 1 mile farther on Gold Lake Highway. By foot, it is 1¾ miles from Lily Lake via the side trail from the western shore.

Winter Use: None. Gold Lake Highway is not plowed this far in winter.

GL-19 Johnsville-La Porte Wagon Road to Gorges of the Jamison

Distance: 6¾ miles out and back

Highest Point: 6,178 feet

Total Elevation Gain: 953 feet

Difficulty: Moderate

Hiking Season: May through November

Directions to the Trailhead: See Hike GL-17.

Comments: This is one of the few hikes in this book that follows a dirt road on which you may encounter a few vehicles. However, the roadway is rocky, not dusty (I don't mind a few vehicles passing me, just so long as I don't have to eat their dust). Why walk the road when you can easily drive it? Well, the word *easily* is stretching it a bit; although the county occasionally does some maintenance, you'd never know it. What's more, driving the road you miss much of the scenery, the intimacy with nature, and the song of Jamison Creek. And I suppose I'm a history romantic, but I get a kick out of walking along a historic route that looks much as it did 135 years ago when cursing drivers whipped tired horses and oxen to keep them pulling heavy wagonloads of materials bound for the mines.

The first third of the hike is within the boundary of Plumas-Eureka State Park so please obey the park rules. To learn the history of the Plumas-Eureka Mine, read Appendix B. On your drive to the trailhead, I suggest a stop at the park museum. It explains much of the history of the area and displays stuffed animals and birds similar to the live examples you may spy along the route of this hike.

The Hike: Here, as in various parts of the Sierra, many wagon roads were built not by the county or state but by private entrepreneurs, who operated them as toll roads. The old wagon road this hike follows is one of the few in this neck of the woods that is still in use today. Wagon roads were of great importance for transporting supplies from San Francisco and the Sacramento Valley to the mines of Plumas County. Bringing in supplies on the backs of horses and mules along a trail was often prohibitively costly because such a limited weight could be carried that way. Many low-producing mines couldn't afford the prices charged by the men who hauled in goods by animal pack train. Wagon roads on which larger and heavier loads could be transported became profitable ventures.

In July 1862, the Marysville and Beckwourth Turnpike Road Company was formed with $30,000 of stock at $50 per share. Construction of the

Johnsville-La Porte wagon road began in May 1863 and was completed in 1864. It had moderate grades, allowing freight wagons to be loaded more heavily than they could on steeper roads. I have been unable to find out how long the road operated as a toll road before being taken over by the county.

From the trailhead, the pavement continues only another 200 yards. After ⅓ mile, the road becomes narrower and hugs the side of the mountain. At this point, Eureka Peak is only slightly more than ½ mile away to the northwest, yet the crest is 2,070 feet higher than the road.

The road parallels Jamison Creek for the entire walk. However, because the stream is sufficiently

far from the road and 100 or more feet below road level, this cannot be considered a creekside walk. In several places, short side roads cut off left down to the stream bank, affording picnickers and fishing enthusiasts access to the creek. When you've gone 3 miles from the trailhead, a side road turns left into Ross Campground, situated on a flat above the creek. This site has been used for more than a century as a stopping place along the wagon road, because it is one of the few level pieces of ground between McRae Meadow and Johnsville. The campground has no restrooms or piped water.

Renes Falls, announced by an old sign at the roadside, is the next point of interest along the route. Hike down to the creek, and enjoy the beautiful cascade. These falls are not high and mighty, but seldom will you find a prettier spot.

The hike's turnaround is at the highlight of the walk, the Gorges of the Jamison, less than ¼ mile beyond the side road to Renes Falls. When you hear the roar of the creek, scramble downhill 100 yards from the road to it. Here the stream rushes and tumbles through a gorge cut into the bedrock. Naturally, snowmelt makes the sight even more spectacular in spring. One nice feature of the gorges is easily accessed viewing plateaus on large flat rocks above the stream. Use caution with rambunctious little kids. Although the distance from the plateaus down to the water is not far, the gushing force of the stream is powerful, so a fall would not be a good idea. This is a wonderful spot for lunch. Photographs can hardly do justice to the beauty of the gorges, but with each visit I cannot help but take a few more in hopes of capturing the fine spectacle of the site on film.

Camping: I don't envision a backpack trip along this route because I think most folks like to backpack along wilderness trails, not roads used daily by vehicles. Free car camping is allowed at Ross Campground, and I have encountered people camping just off the road at the gorges. The excellent Plumas-Eureka State Park Campground, whose entrance is at the trailhead, affords nice RV and tent camping, complete with hot showers, flush toilets (hurray), and an RV holding tank dump location. A fee is charged.

Winter Use: One of the area's best cross-country ski routes commences at the plowed parking lot at the state park museum. It follows the road and turns left into the campground, which is closed to camping in winter. At campsite 54 the route leaves the campground, crosses a new bridge over Little Jamison Creek, and enters the open area next to the boarded-up Jamison Mine Bunkhouse. From here, the ski trail continues downhill, following the route of the Jamison Mine road, to the Graeagle-Johnsville Road (A-14). Here, you take off your skis, make a left turn on the road (which is always plowed), and return on foot to the museum. If this large loop is too much skiing, you can either make a U-turn when you get to the campground entrance or continue up the Johnsville-La Porte Road a bit farther before turning around. The ski trail from the museum sometimes suffers problems with washouts (caused by snowmelt and run-off from Eureka Peak) and avalanches. Some years, at a point several hundred yards before the turn into the campground, park rangers in midwinter occa-

Jamison Creek Gorge

sionally post a sign warning of avalanches from Eureka Peak.

GL-20 Lower Salmon Lake Trail

Distance: 2 miles out and back

Highest Point: 6,550 feet

Total Elevation Gain: 170 feet

Difficulty: Easy

Hiking Season: June through October

Directions to the Trailhead: From Graeagle, drive south on Highway 89 for 1.4 miles, and turn right on Gold Lake Highway. Drive for 12.7 miles, and turn right on a paved road with a sign saying "Salmon Lake 1.5." In .5 mile, turn left into a parking area. Beyond the parking area, a large steel-pipe gate blocks the road to through traffic.

Comments: This is a perfect hike if you want to go only a short distance on an easy trail that isn't too steep and experience a serene, secluded mountain lake. It is also an excellent choice for a light-duty backpack experience with small kids. Everyone will enjoy visiting the old mine on the far side of the lake. A warning penciled by someone on the sign attached to the steel gate at the parking area says "Dense Mosquito Population." During the middle of the day I didn't have a problem, but, due to the marshy edges of the lake, I imagine evening really brings 'em out. So, bring along mosquito repellent if you'll be near the lake in the evening or overnight.

The Hike: The sign on the gate advises that access to this lake is only for people hiking, fishing, and canoeing (do they expect someone to carry a canoe 1 mile to the lake?). Another sign advises that no motor-driven boats are allowed. The jeep trail down to the lake has a few rocks, but all in all it isn't too tough on hikers.

You won't have a view of the lake until the trail is almost at the water's edge. A 300-yard-long trail, of sorts, skirts the northern corner of the lake, pass-

ing several campsites before ending in a bog. However, if you're just day-hiking and want to see the mine, turn right at the edge of the lake, slip past another heavy-duty gate, and follow the tracks around the western end of the lake.

I took this hike in a wet year, and the path around the western end was quite boggy in places. My guess is that it would not be as sloppy in a drier year, because the old jeep track showed no signs of tire ruts; if a vehicle had used the path the year I visited, its tires would have sunk into the soft wet soil. The jeep track crosses two easy-to-ford creeks that flow into the lake, the first being the outflow creek from Upper Salmon Lake. Soon after crossing the second creek, the dim road branches in three directions. Rather than continuing on the track nearest the water or the one curving uphill to the right, choose the center one. Almost immediately, an even dimmer road slices left, but stay on the more pronounced route, which heads slightly uphill. In a bit more than 100 yards, the path turns a corner, and there's the mine.

It is one of the best-preserved mines in the Feather River country, and it looks newer than most. A cute narrow-gauge railroad track, in pretty good condition, curves around the hill and under the heavy locked door that blocks the entrance to the mine. The small size of the track would indicate that hand-pushed ore cars were used on it. There are no signs telling the name of the mine, nor does the map give it a name. Walk to the far end of the flat area in front of the mine entrance. Just below, you'll see a bunch of ore-processing equipment, still standing and in pretty good shape. A cable hung between two large pine trees has, however, almost disappeared because bark has grown over much of the lengths looped around the trunks, indicating that it wasn't strung yesterday. Scramble down the embankment to inspect the processing equipment at closer range. Then walk back in the direction you came, now on the lower road along the shore of the lake.

In about 50 yards, you come to a flat area with heavy iron plate lying round. Keep looking to your left to see the other mine entrance. This lower tunnel has no door, but the front of it has caved in so entrance is not possible. The flat area here appealed to me as a great camping spot, although there's no sign of a fire ring or previous use for camping. A grassy "lawn" (well, a lawnlike area—who ever heard of a lawn out in nature?) spreads down to the edge of the lake, and I could envision this as a swell place for tiny backpackers to play. Here, the water is quite shallow near the shore, as it is on most of Lower Salmon Lake, thus little tykes can splash and wade. The only problem is that the bottom near shore has a lot of settled sediment. Walking in the water stirs it up and makes the clear lake look cloudy, but what's a little crud on kids' feet? It won't hurt 'em. Don't drink the water, however, without filtering, boiling, or treating it.

Walk back the short distance to the three-way intersection on the lower road, at which point take the rocky road winding uphill. In 200 yards, you find the miner's camp, with his shack, cook stove with nice chimney, and other junk, including an old tub with Pepsi-Cola embossed on the side. (Sad to say, I revisited the site a year later and discovered that the cabin had burned to the ground. The surrounding trees were badly singed, but, miraculously, a major forest fire was somehow avoided.) Evidently the miner decided not to live right next to the mine itself and chose this spot, a short walk away. The second creek entering the lake runs not far behind the shack, so fresh water was close at hand and the nice gurgle of the creek made good company. Please don't disturb any of the property.

The road stops here, so, after viewing the meager camp, return around the western edge of the lake to the spot where the road down from the parking lot reaches the lake. From here, it's uphill back to your car, but it's not a long distance, so even your small fry can make it.

Camping: As I mentioned, this is as nice a spot as you'll find for backpacking only a short distance. As for fishing, I've seen cars parked in the parking area on weekends, so perhaps fishermen, fisherwomen, and fisherkids make the trek to the lake to try their luck. However, the shallow water makes shore fishing tough. I suppose an inflatable raft could be carried in. No camping is allowed farther up the main road at Upper Salmon Lake.

Winter Use: None.

The author inspecting the Lower Salmon Lake Mine

GL-21 Long Lake Loop from Lakes Basin Campground

Distance: 5-mile loop (Alternative Hike, 1¼ miles out and back)

Highest Point: 7,020 feet

Total Elevation Gain: 845 feet (Alternative Hike, 300 feet)

Difficulty: Moderate/strenuous (Alternative Hike, easy/moderate)

Hiking Season: June through October

Directions to the Trailhead: From Graeagle head south on Highway 89 for 1.4 miles to Gold Lake Highway. Go right, and drive for 6.6 miles to a sign pointing right to Lakes Basin Campground. Drive .9 mile on this narrow paved road, past a sign that points to Elwell Lodge and past the entrance to Lakes Basin Campground, until you reach the trailhead parking lot.

Comments: This is one of the finest hikes in the region. Although the trail circles the lake, some of the route is out of sight of the water. However, the rest of the scenery makes up for not having a water view for the whole loop. For most of the summer, a fine variety of wild flowers can be enjoyed along the trail. Lots of people do only the 1¼-mile Alternative Hike to the lake and back to the parking lot.

The Hike: From the trailhead parking lot, two trails lead off. The one whose sign says "Bear Lake" and "Silver Lake" will get you to Long Lake but adds ¾ mile to the loop. So, take the trail saying "Long Lake," which is on the right of the road leading into the parking lot. I believe the sign is a bit off on distance, because I calculate the distance to the lake to be a scant ¾ mile. Almost immediately the trail crosses the unnamed outlet creek from Big Bear Lake, which flows through a double culvert under the trail. Even though the trail is very well used, it isn't particularly smooth and is strewn with rocks as you head uphill. The elevation gain from the trailhead to Long Lake is about 300 feet, so, even if

you choose the Alternative Hike, you still have to expend a bit of effort.

In ½ mile, the trail splits, with the left fork sign saying "Silver Lake ½, Bear Lake ½." (There is no "Bear Lake;" the three Bear Lakes are Cub, Little Bear, and Big Bear. There is no "Goldilocks" either.) The trail you want is straight ahead with the erroneous sign "Long Lake ¼" (true) and "Long Lake Trailhead ½" (false—there's no such trailhead). Now, keep a close lookout for the unsigned loop trail branching off to your right. It's dim and easy to miss. A large pyramid-shaped rock just to the right of the intersection is a good clue. If you miss it, no problem, because 200 yards beyond the intersection

Tilted rock stratum on Long Lake

you'll see Long Lake, the little Elwell Lodge boat-house, and a miscellaneous collection of fishing boats pulled up on shore. (This is the turnaround spot for the alternate 1¼ mile out and back hike without the loop.) If you glimpse these, retrace your steps and look more closely for your turnoff. This portion of the loop trail is shown on the old topo maps, but it's not shown on the newer topo maps or other maps, including the big USFS map posted at the trailhead. That's why not many people take this section of the loop leading to the dam. Very soon after you make the turnoff, the trail makes a Y at a big rock. Take the right fork. In several hundred yards, the trail crosses a dry pond, which may be wet in spring. If so, go around it to the left.

This part of the hike has no lake views, but don't worry—you'll have some nice ones soon. In another couple of hundred yards, another pond pops into view on your right, followed by a third a

bit farther along the lightly used trail. As promised, Long Lake finally can be seen through the low bushes on your left. About ¾ mile from where you commenced this loop trail, it climbs a rock outcropping. However, it is easily followed because recent trail maintenance has provided rock borders and carins (some people call them *ducks* but I prefer the more classic *carin*—several rocks piled on top of one another) to help guide the way.

On the outcropping you can see evidence of the path of the glacier that covered this region 10,000 years ago. The surface of the rock was smoothed and polished, as the receding glacier moved down the valley. Long furrows were gouged into the smooth surface by small stones dragged along under the glacier's massive weight.

The route heads around to the top left of the rock outcropping, with the lake seen on your left. The trail heads downhill, makes a switchback on the far side of the rock outcropping, then switches back down to the lake level, and crosses the dam.

On the far side of the dam, clamber up the bank, bypass the nice-looking campsite (at which no camping is allowed), and keep heading away from the dam, paralleling the outflow creek from the dam. When you're 150 yards from the dam, the trail will meet the much more defined and well-used trail coming south from Gray Eagle Lodge. At this signless intersection, cut back sharply left and head toward the lake.

You are now on a more heavily traveled trail that winds next to the water, but in many places bushes prevent you from actually reaching the shore. You have, by now, left the trees behind and are experiencing the rock-strewn lower slope of Mount Elwell whose peak rises 1,300 feet above the lake level. The cute islands in Long Lake are visible ahead, close to the shore. The nice level trail skirting the lake suddenly cuts steeply uphill away from the water and encounters a talus slope. For the next ½ mile you have to tread on rocks that have slid down from the eastern face of Mount Elwell. Fortunately, the trail-makers and -maintainers have put a lot of effort into this section. As you traverse the steep slope of loose rock, be thankful that you can walk without slipping and cascading down into the lake. It's not hugely scary—just a little bit—and once you've completed it, you'll say to yourself, "Aha, I did it!"

Finally the talus slope gives way to good old dirt, and, as the trail continues to climb, you encounter trailside wildflowers again. About ½ mile after the talus section ends, you come to a trail intersection. To your right, a route leads to the top of Mount Elwell (part of Hike GL-16). The straight-ahead route leads to the PCT on top of the ridge. You want the route going left, with the sign pointing to "Hellgramite Lake 1¼, Silver Lake 1½, Lakes Basin Campground 2½." For the next ½ mile, the trail heads downhill through lovely terrain, including nice views of Long Lake and, ahead, Mud Lake. Eventually it reaches Mud Lake, although it stays

some distance from the shoreline. This lake doesn't deserve its name, as I'm sure you'll agree upon viewing its beautiful blue water and mudless shoreline. A partially buried iron pipe follows along the path for some distance, going to and coming from who knows where.

From Mud Lake, the trail starts uphill. You probably thought that all the uphill was behind you, but this part isn't long or very steep. You make an easy stream crossing, and soon the trail parallels another creek. Immediately after the trail passes the northern edge of Hellgramite Lake (there are actually two of them), it ends at a T with a trail (part of Hike GL-7) that comes down from the ridge and the PCT. Turn left, following the sign to Silver Lake, which comes into view in about ¼ mile. Silver Lake has always looked more blue than silver to me, but I suppose the person who named it was there at dusk when it had a silvery tinge. Just before reaching its outlet creek, you come to your umpteenth trail intersection, but, unlike most others in this area, it bears no nice sign telling you which way is which (unless one has been installed since I wrote this). Turn left, away from Silver Lake, heading north to the umpteenth-plus-one intersection 200 yards away. A sign on the trail to the right advises that Lakes Basin Campground is 1¼ miles in that direction, as well as Cub and Bear Lakes. A sign on the trail to the left also directs you to "Lakes Basin Campground ¾." Either route will get you there, but I suspect you've had enough walking for the day, so turn left. The trail runs above the southeastern shore of Long Lake, offering occasional views of the water with Mount Elwell towering behind it. The afternoon sun prevents you from getting a good photo of this, however. If you do the loop in the other direction, so that you're here in the morning with the sun at your back, you might get a great shot. As you march along this part of the trail, views of the lake are fleeting because trees and hillside are in the way.

You pass your last view of Long Lake as the trail cuts easterly away from the lake and reaches the very first trail junction you encountered on your way in, several hours earlier. A right turn puts you on the path back to the trailhead, ½ mile away.

Camping: The nice Lakes Basin Campground operated by the USFS near the trailhead parking lot has good car camping. It fills up on long weekends such as Fourth of July and Labor Day. No backpack camping is allowed anywhere in the vicinity of any of the lakes or streams encountered on this hike.

Winter Use: None.

GL-22 Smith Creek and Gray Eagle Creek Loop

Distance: 6½-mile loop

Highest Point: 6,230 feet

Total Elevation Gain: 1,260 feet

Difficulty: Moderate/strenuous

Hiking Season: May through October

Directions to the Trailhead: See Hike GL-16.

Comments: This loop is one of my favorites. It combines several out-and-back trails described elsewhere in this book into one longer loop. Like any loop, it can be hiked in either direction. I'm not sure why, but I usually hike it in a clockwise direction. If you choose to do it counterclockwise, just read the hike description backward.

The Hike: See the first paragraph of Hike GL-5 for the first ¾ mile of this hike. Immediately after crossing Smith Creek, at the T intersection turn right onto the Smith Creek Trail (unless you'd like to take the ½-mile out-and-back detour to Smith Lake, as described in Hike GL-5).

From the T, the Smith Creek Trail description for Hike GL-5 gives you all the details of the hike to the point where the trail forks, approximately 1¼ miles from the T. This junction used to have a sign saying "Trail" (pointing in both directions), and, indeed, the old sign may still be lying on the ground or leaning against a bush. Here, however, you want to take the right fork, leaving the route of Hike GL-5 to County Road A-14 and merging with a loggers' road, which drops down to sparkling Smith Creek,

only 200 yards distant. By now, you have crossed Smith Creek three times, but this fourth crossing requires a bit of dexterous rock-hopping—except at the end of summer, when the flow of the creek has abated. This crossing is one of many fine stopping places for lunch (I should say "napping" places to make this sentence more melodic and more descriptive of what I often do for a few minutes after lunch on the trail).

For the next 1⅓ miles of the loop, you have a carefree stroll along Logging Spur Section 20 Trail, described in Hike J-11. Few trails in this book gain only 120 feet in elevation over a distance of 1⅓ miles. The Logging Spur ends where it intersects the dirt road that leads left back to Graeagle and right to Gray Eagle Creek Dam. This intersection has a worn but readable sign indicating these directions. Turn right on the road, and pick up the description of the Gray Eagle Dam Trail, Hike J-8. The road soon becomes impassable to vehicles except for those whose owners don't mind having both sides thoroughly scraped by encroaching bushes. This nice walk up to the dam again gains only 120

feet in a distance this time of 1½ miles, so you won't be huffing and puffing on this portion of the loop either.

As I said in the J-8 write-up, don't expect too much of the dam itself. It's merely a diversion dam to direct water into the penstock (conduit pipe) to the powerhouse downstream on Gray Eagle Creek. At the point where the road cuts left downhill to the dam, you'll see a sign pointing straight ahead to Gray Eagle Creek Trail. Pick up this well-defined trail, and walk south, paralleling Gray Eagle Creek. In ⅓ mile, a trail from the left joins the Gray Eagle Creek Trail (it's easy to miss, however). A left turn at this intersection leads you down to the creek, about 100 yards away. It is worth taking this short side trip to visit the sturdy bridge and marvel at the creek as it leaps playfully downhill under the bridge.

Fern garden along the Smith Creek Trail

Retrace your steps to the Gray Eagle Creek Trail, and turn left on it, continuing the route of the loop. Hike GL-3 gives the detailed description of this next segment. Although the loop is a bit steeper here, the climb is still fairly gradual. Arriving at the trailhead parking lot, you will probably need to turn to the right to find your car, because the Gray Eagle Creek Trail reaches the parking lot west of where the Smith Lake Trail leaves it. This was a nice loop—agreed?

A fine after-loop treat is dinner in Gray Eagle Lodge's log dining room, near the trailhead. It is open to the public and has excellent food and a good wine list. A prior reservation (530/836-2511) is recommended.

Camping: None. Well, that's not exactly correct; if you took the suggested ½-mile out-and-back trip to Smith Lake, camping is allowed at that lake (one of only four lakes open to camping in the Lakes Basin Recreation Area). However, because it is only about a mile from the trailhead, it doesn't work particularly well for a backpack camp location in the middle of this loop. I haven't spied any campsites along Smith Creek, itself, or on Gray Eagle Creek—which, I believe, is off-limits to camping anyhow. For car camping, the USFS Lakes Basin Campground is good. It is only about 2 miles south of where the side road to the trailhead turns off Gold Lake Highway. The campground becomes full on summer weekends, so plan ahead.

Winter Use: Gold Lake Highway is not plowed in the winter, so the only access to the trailhead is via snowmobile.

GL-23 From Packer Saddle North on the PCT

Distance: 13 miles out and back including a loop at the north end

Highest Point: 7,400 feet

Total Elevation Gain: 1,035 feet

Difficulty: Moderate/strenuous

Hiking Season: June through October

Directions to the Trailhead: Follow the directions for Hike SC-3, but, when you reach Packer Saddle at the top of the very steep part of Forest Road 91, park at the saddle where there is plenty of room.

Comments: The northern end of this hike includes a delightful loop that visits pretty Little Deer Lake and Snake Lake (I saw no little deer or snakes) as well as less delightful Summit Lake and Oakland Pond. From the PCT, nice views are plentiful, including panoramas overlooking (Big) Deer Lake and Packer Lake. In this part of the PCT, like most others described in this book, the trail has been re-routed from that shown on the topo maps. This hike takes longer than you might think, so please allow sufficient time to complete it or plan a mid-hike overnight campout.

The Hike: The PCT crosses over Packer Saddle in a north-south direction and is easily confused with the jeep road that also heads north from the saddle. Fortunately, there is a PCT sign directing you north to the right of the jeep road. The trail begins a gradual ascent and, in ½ mile, passes a short side trail down to the abandoned Wallis Mine (described in Hike GL-1, which follows this part of the PCT in the opposite direction). Thereafter, you make several easy switchbacks on the way to the top of the ridge, about 385 feet above the trailhead. After this initial climb, the lovely trail traverses the western side of the ridge, near its top, with great vistas of the Pauley Creek drainage basin to the west. Along here, the red firs are broken off because loggers cut all but a few trees. Those remaining were left exposed to the gales that occasionally roar in from the west. With no close neighbors to protect them from the wind blast, their trunks snapped in two, leaving a devastated forest, as useless as if the loggers had clear-cut the area. A bit farther, the jeep road crisscrosses the trail several times, and, because both road and trail closely parallel each other, it takes a bit of luck to tell which is which. Now, views to the east occur, highlighted by Deer Lake in the basin below.

For the next 2 miles, the PCT stays on the eastern side of the ridge near its top, passing two side trails to the right leading down to Deer Lake. Finally, the trail leaves this eastern side and heads westerly, reaching another junction with the jeep road and a slew of signs that may help jeepers but aren't of much value to hikers. At this point, to see Summit Lake, leave the PCT and hike south 200 yards on the jeep trail. The lake wasn't very appealing to me, but, in spring and early summer, it is indeed appealing to a bunch of hungry mosquitoes.

Back on the PCT headed north, you need to pay attention to how far you've hiked beyond Summit Lake, because the start of the loop (which I think you'll enjoy) does not connect with the PCT. Along this stretch, the jeep road runs parallel to the trail and only 100 to 200 yards away to the west, albeit out of sight. About ½ mile beyond Summit Lake more or less, you need to make a 90° left turn from the PCT and hike the 100 to 200 yards cross-country to the jeep road (this is easy, because the two are so close).

Turn right on the jeep road, and watch for an intersecting jeep road to the left. (If you made the 90° turn too far north, as did I, you will miss this turn. When you've hiked for ¼ mile on the jeep road without seeing the junction, you'll know you have to backtrack to find it.) This side jeep road heads almost due west and, in places, can hardly be called a road, particularly as it bends north, after ½ mile. But who cares—you're on foot, not trying to drive this route. Soon charming Little Deer Lake pops into view. Do leave the road and mosey the few steps down to the lakeshore for a close-up of the lake and its petite island.

The next ½ mile of road north of Little Deer Lake would be a severe test for any jeep. The boulder-covered road (not rocks, boulders) winds up at the western shore of attractive Snake Lake and, just north of the lake, intersects with a bit better east-west jeep road. Turn right along the north shore of

Little Deer Lake at sunrise

Snake Lake, and hike this smoother road to Oakland Pond (a better name would be Mud Pond or Ugly Pond). At the northeast corner of the pond, the old route of the PCT can be dimly seen, heading north.

At this point you need to head back to the trailhead, so loop to the right around the northeast corner of the pond, and pick up the route to the south. In ¼ mile, it brings you back to the top of the ridge and a meeting with the new PCT. Gold Lake and part of the Lakes Basin stretch below this ridge crest to the east.

About ¾ mile later, you will find the place where you made the 90° turn off the PCT to commence the loop. The views along the PCT on the way back to your car are just as nice as the views you had several hours earlier.

Camping: There are campsites at Summit Lake, but, because the lake is less than wonderful, and because it is easily accessed by the jeep-SUV crowd, I suggest pushing on to Little Deer Lake. I have thoroughly enjoyed camping there, far from the jeepers (and just about everybody else). Snake Lake is OK too, and Oakland Pond would do in a pinch.

Winter Use: None.

GL-24 Upper Jamison Mine Trail

Distance: 3½ miles out and back

Highest Point: 6,160 feet

Total Elevation Gain: 895 feet

Difficulty: Moderate/strenuous

Hiking Season: June through October

(the falls shrink to a dribble by midsummer)

Directions to the Trailhead: See Hike GL-17.

Comments: WARNING: Entering the open Upper Jamison Mine shaft is strictly forbidden. It is **extremely dangerous!** Although, a person can scramble into the entrance of the horizontal shaft, it is far too hazardous to attempt. Kids with lots of bravado may try to show off by attempting an entry; they risk great injury or even death. Please keep kids, teenagers, and adults (who should know better) on the trail. And, for goodness sakes, do not allow your kids or teenagers to come up here alone! The state park does not put this trail in any of its literature because it is considered too

dangerous for the general public.

Enjoy reading about the history of Jamison Mine in Appendix C before beginning this hike.

The Hike: The trail leaves the campground loop road between campsites 65 and 67 heading uphill near some large cut logs. The start looks more like a shallow stony streambed than a trail. However, in a short distance it develops into a nice path made of smooth white stones. The path curves left about 200 yards from campsite 67 (here, the route of Hike GL-17 cuts sharply to the right). Another 300 yards of hiking brings you to an antique stone cabin, abandoned for many years but still standing, probably due to its massive stone walls. As you peer in the door, the wall caved in on the left will, I hope, convince you not to enter. It is far too dangerous, and you can easily see all there is to see from the doorway. Please make sure curious kids and teenagers stay outside, and don't let them try this trail without adult supervision.

Continuing on the path, you pass a large water tank on your left and, as the trail bends right, rusting old mine junk and machinery. Walk to the edge of the tailings pile, and look down toward Jamison Creek, where you can see old mill foundations, a long-gone part of the Jamison Mine complex. The nice white rock trail continues uphill, making a wide sweeping loop to the right. About ¼ mile from the stone cabin, the trail opens into a flat clearing, making you pause to wonder which way to exit. First, I

Old rock cabin on the Upper Jamison Mine Trail

suggest a visit to the mineshaft, so continue ahead and slightly to the right. This level side trail, paralleling the canyon, leads, in short order, to the upper shaft of Jamison Mine.

This horizontal shaft should not be entered under any circumstances! From the outside, you can hear water inside dripping from the ceiling into pools on the floor—an ominous and spooky "kerplink, kerplink."

Returning to the clearing, you can easily see that the main trail exits to the left of where you originally entered. The next mile will include a few switchbacks, plenty of bitter cherry and serviceberry bushes reaching onto the trail to scratch your legs (if you unwisely wore short pants, as I did), logs across the trail to clamber over, dead branches to tread on, and washed out places to cross. (I hope, by the time you read this, some thoughtful person will have clipped the worst branches and removed dead limbs from the unmaintained trail.)

Along this upper section of the route, the views to the north are magnificent. Ahead, the upper Jamison Creek Canyon stretches into the distance, with towering Mount Washington forming the south canyon wall. Behind you, the lower canyon of the creek can be seen extending past the rooftops of the village of Johnsville. Directly across from the trail, beyond the winding course of Jamison Creek, is the hulk of Eureka Peak rising 2,130 feet above the floor of the valley. Bring your camera and plenty of film for photographing this marvelous vista.

The trail now becomes significantly narrower and at long last ends. In mid-June I have tromped through plenty of snow on this final section of the route, which is above 6,000 feet in elevation. Snow here means that snowmelt is still occurring on nearby Mount Washington, which means you'll find a roaring cascade at the end of the trail. This delight may be partly hidden by snow cover until midsummer, but snow or no snow, it's a beautiful sight. When the snow above is gone, the cascade mostly dries up. The trail ends before reaching the falls; for a closer view, scramble cross-country a bit to come to the edge of the water.

The way back to the campground is all downhill, so you can coast along, assuming the bushes will let you coast.

Camping: None for backpackers. The state park where this hike began offers excellent car camping, including showers with hot water and (hurray) flush toilets. That's what I call deluxe camping!

Winter Use: The road from the state park museum to the trailhead is a designated cross-country ski route. Most winters, park rangers place a sign near the campground warning of avalanche danger from the slope of Eureka Peak. A ski loop is also possible—see the "Winter Use" section of Hike GL-19. I have snowshoed from the museum (the museum parking lot is plowed in the winter) to the campground, through the campground, then up the trail past the stone cabin partway to the upper mineshaft. The winter views from up there were wonderful.

GL-25 Trail to Frazier Creek and Cross-Country Extension to Frazier Falls

Distance: 3 miles out and back (with extension to Frazier Falls, 4 miles out and back)

Highest Point: 6,018 feet

Total Elevation Gain: 298 feet (with extension, 596 feet)

Difficulty: Moderate (with extension, strenuous)

Hiking Season: May through October

Directions to the Trailhead: From Graeagle drive south on Highway 89 for 1.4 miles to Gold Lake Highway. Turn right, and drive 2.9 miles to a road on the left with a sign "Frazier Falls 4." Go 2.7 miles on the paved, but narrow, Frazier Falls Road until you reach a big knobby cedar tree on the right of the road. The dim unsigned trailhead is on the left. Make a U-turn, and park just past the trailhead, where there is plenty of room off the pavement.

Comments: This old trail isn't on the topo map, but it does show on some USFS maps, although in the wrong place. Because the trail is only lightly used and is not maintained by the USFS, it had almost slipped into oblivion. I decided it was worth keeping around, so I spent several days clipping overgrown bushes, cleaning forest debris off the path, and adding markings. The trail is fairly well defined at the start, because it was blazed many years ago; still visible on big pines are a large rectangle below a smaller rectangle, chopped into the tree trunks. Long ago, the USFS put an end to the practice of marking trees in this manner, but it still promotes the ultimate desecration of the trees—logging. Indeed, the blazed trail disappears after about ½ mile because all subsequent blazed trees, being of good size, were cut down and hauled to the mill. The trail markings to follow when the trail gets less pronounced are colored strips fastened to trees along the route, cairns (several rocks piled on one another—some on big stumps), and rocks outlining the path. My trail rehab work progressed as far as the creek; beyond that you need the ability to do some aggressive cross-country hiking to the falls itself. Perhaps, some summer, I will find the time to finish a trail all the way to the falls. However, please don't reject this hike because it goes only to the creek. It passes through beautiful country, and if nobody uses the trail it will again deteriorate. If you do the hike in the spring or early summer, I guess I'd better warn you to wear long pants and a long-sleeved shirt—not to keep off the sun or brambles but to keep off the mosquitoes. Cover any skin left showing with a liberal dose of insect repellent. In late summer and fall, the mosquitoes are gone.

The Hike: Upon leaving the road, you immediately find an old campsite in the path, and, just beyond that, a pond appears on your right (by late summer it may have dried up). The trail skirts the edge of the pond, and then takes off in earnest for Frazier Creek. After 250 yards, you pass another pond on your left. In early morning or late afternoon when the wind isn't blowing, the mirror surface of this pond reflects the stately pines, firs, and cedars behind it, making a good photo opportunity.

About ¾ mile from the road, two large trees have fallen down the hillside across the trail. You can scramble over them or cut uphill a bit and go around their root ends. Perhaps by the time you take this hike, I will have carried my chain saw in and opened the path again. Thereafter, the trail does a short switchback and crosses a couple of intermittent creeks. You need to stay alert to notice the trail markers. The crossing of one dry creekbed filled with large rocks and boulders might be a bit confusing: you need to walk up the creekbed about 30 yards to pick up the marked trail on the far side.

The well-pruned trail (I hope my pruning lasts a long time) winds up at the edge of a cliff overlooking Frazier Creek. Your ears will have caught the roar of the creek for some time prior to reaching this spot. It sounds like the main falls but isn't, just the water cascading through its gorge—nonetheless a sight worth hiking here to see. At the overlook is an old campsite.

At this point, if you like to hike only on trails, retrace your steps back to your car. However, if you are game for some challenging cross-country, extend the hike by striking out upstream along the western bank, first making sure you note where to pick up the trail on your way back (I leave a "marker" of some sort). Your route should follow the stream fairly closely as the going gets steeper. At some point, crossing to the eastern side of the stream may make the climb a bit easier. Although the distance from the stream overlook to the falls is less than ½ mile, thick brush and a good deal of climbing make the pace slow. Your reward for the heavy-duty cross-country hiking is a spectacular view from the bottom of the 176-foot waterfall, one of the highest in California. Naturally, by late summer the falls, although still falling, are not as spectacular as during the spring snowmelt runoff.

Return to your car by the same route.

Camping: The creek-overlook campsite at the end of the trail looks nice, and it is located in an area where camping is not restricted. (No camping is permitted in the Lakes Basin Recreation Area.) Hence, for a backpack trip that isn't too long or strenuous, this site might be just the place. The only drawback is the lack of easy access to Frazier Creek for water. I didn't scope out a way down, but I'm sure there is one if you don't mind a bit of scrambling.

Winter Use: None. However, I have enjoyed some excellent snowshoeing along the Frazier Falls Road, starting where it branches off Gold Lake Highway. The winter view from the road where it runs along the top of the western edge of the canyon is wonderful. Mills Peak, which dominates the landscape to the east, makes the scene even more attractive.

GL-26 Hawley Lake, Hawley Meadow, and Petroglyphs Trail

Distance: 11 miles out and back

Highest Point: 7,305 feet

Total Elevation Gain: 1,348 feet

Difficulty: Moderate/Strenuous

Hiking Season: July through October (the best wildflowers begin in mid-July)

Directions to the Trailhead: See Hike MF-1.

Comments: About half of this hike is on the superb PCT. The other half is along a jeep road (22N99A) that a variety of four-wheel-drive vehicles can handle—hence, you may encounter a vehicle or two along this second portion. The road is sufficiently rough to discourage the Mercedes-Benz four-wheel-drive crowd. By August, the wildflower display will dazzle you, so don't take this hike too early in the year. The petroglyphs, whose location I had taken great pains to determine, turned out to be disappointing because of the large number of names, initials, and dates newcomers have carved on the site—not just a few, but dozens. I debated whether to include the description of how to visit the petroglyphs. However, I sincerely hope the readers of this book are all good conservationists and will not further ruin the site. Please look at the Indian markings, but don't add your own.

The Hike: For the first half of the way to Hawley Lake, please follow the description of Loop A in Hike GL-12 until you're at the lower portions of Four Hills Mine. Where the road divides there, and Hike GL-12 takes the right fork, you now take the left fork, and hike the rocky road down to Hawley Lake. The last portion of the road follows the little inlet creek, and wildflowers flourish along this stretch. You pass the proposed site of the Sierra Iron Mine. A large iron ore deposit near here caused a company of Boston capitalists, in 1874, to plan a massive undertaking, including a narrow-gauge

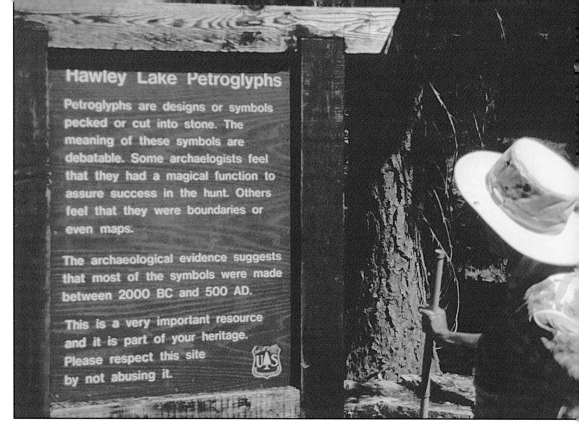

Hawley Lake Petroglyphs

Petroglyphs are designs or symbols pecked or cut into stone. The meaning of these symbols are debatable. Some archaelogists feel that they had a magical function to assure success in the hunt. Others feel that they were boundaries or even maps.

The archaeological evidence suggests that most of the symbols were made between 2000 BC and 500 AD.

This is a very important resource and it is part of your heritage. Please respect this site by not abusing it.

USFS sign near the Hawley Lake petroglyphs

railroad for hauling the ore out and a major road system. After much study and expense, their ambitious plans were scrapped when the iron ore deposits turned out to be smaller than anticipated. How different this area would be today if the huge mine had become a reality!

Near the lake, a sign tells you that continuing straight will bring you to Gold Lake. Turn right, however, and in 150 yards you arrive at Hawley Lake and Boy Scout Camp Nejedly. This eastern shore of the lake is carpeted with wildflowers. The snazzy Boy Scout cabin is usually in use during the summer, although I found it closed and locked on one September visit to the lake. A sign advises that the cabin used to remain open with food stocked for use by anyone in an emergency, but now it is locked because of being trashed. Too bad!

Follow the road above the cabin, and, when you reach the uppermost little storage building, walk to the left of it to pick up a rocky trail. In ¼ mile, after

the trail crests and begins heading downhill, watch for a dim trail to the left, where you see a large Jeffrey pine on your left and a small sloping clearing just ahead. Follow this semi-trail for 200 yards down to a large magnetite gray rock outcropping. Here a USFS sign describes some of the history of the petroglyph site. As I said, the rock face has been ruined with many initials, names, and dates carved by thoughtless people. The Indian markings are much dimmer than the more recent graffiti but can be made out nonetheless. Swirls, chevrons, and animal figures are part of the ancient display. Be careful not to walk on any of the Indian markings. The magnetite is soft and subject to erosion, so please tread softly.

Return by the same route to the upper storage shed, and, on its other side, take a rocky jeep road leading uphill. Follow it for ½ mile to beautiful

Hawley Meadow. The road cuts through the middle of the meadow and ends at a well-built unoccupied little cabin. Several months after I did this hike, an old-timer told me that an elderly woman lives in the cabin most of the year, even in the winter. I didn't see anyone around, but then I didn't snoop either. A herd of cows with tinkling bells grazed at the far edge of the meadow, lending a feeling of being in the Swiss Alps. The cabin is the turnaround place for the hike. The same route, minus the petroglyphs side trip, can be taken back to the A-Tree trailhead. Oh yes, don't forget to get a drink of delicious ice-cold water from the A-Tree spring located just to the right of the parking area, 20 yards downhill from the big tree in the center.

Camping: With Boy Scouts "doing their thing" at Hawley Lake, you probably don't want to spend the night there. However, I once encountered people who were camped at a delightful little meadow ⅓ mile uphill from the lake where the inlet creek crosses the road. A creek runs through Hawley Meadow, and I'm sure there are some good camp-sites along the edge of the meadow. The cowbells will cease clanging at dark, but they may provide an early wake-up call and, perhaps, some unwanted visitors.

Winter Use: None. Winter access is by helicopter or parachute only.

GL-27 East Side of Lakes Basin Loop

Distance: 6-mile loop (with side trip to Halsey Falls, 6½ miles)

Highest Point: 6,472 feet

Total Elevation Gain: 722 feet

Difficulty: Moderate

Hiking Season: May through October

Directions to the Trailhead: Follow the directions for Hike GL-16, but, instead of turning right off Gold Lake Highway onto the dirt road toward Gray Eagle Lodge, turn left at that intersection, and park just off Gold Lake Highway on the side road.

Comments: This nice loop adds variety to the commonly used trails in the Lakes Basin Recreation Area. The first third of the hike provides some great vistas not seen on other local trails. Later in the loop you can visit two pretty waterfalls.

The Hike: From the trailhead, start up the jeep trail opposite the road into Gray Eagle Lodge. This unused road climbs gradually and provides some marvelous views of the Gray Eagle Creek Canyon and far-off Mohawk Valley. In the days before Gold Lake Highway was built, the old road from Bassetts to Graeagle took a different route, and one of its sections is today's Frazier Falls Road. Years ago, in order to get to Gray Eagle Lodge, a visitor had to turn off the old Gold Lake Road and bump across the ridge on the road you are now hiking. (Imagine the dickens of a ride this road must have been in a Model T Ford.)

When you've gone ½ mile from the car, watch for a side trail to the right. It is easy to be so preoccupied with the splendid views to your left that you miss this nondescript trail intersection. To help you recognize the spot, look for a big dead tree on your right and a pile of stones marker. Don't fret if you miss this trail; you can continue walking on the jeep road as it swings to the right and eventually meets the paved Frazier Falls Road. However, the last ½

mile of the jeep road is not particularly pretty, and the cutoff trail is much more enjoyable. As the trail reaches a crest, you see a collapsed wooden structure on the left. It's too small for a cabin and has no noticeable water source, so your guess is as good as mine about what it once was.

The seldom used trail is easy to follow as it gradually swings right and heads south. The only place where you might get confused is near the end of the trail, where it enters a little clearing with a big rotting tree stump (broken off—not sawed) in the center. The path leaves the clearing on the left, next to a large leaning ponderosa pine tree, and soon joins the paved Frazier Falls Road. Turn right and walk uphill on the road, which goes almost straight for the next ½ mile. You're probably not a big fan of hiking on paved road—I'm not either— and, what's worse, this one has a bit of traffic going to the Frazier Falls Trail (see Hike GL-4); but this section is only ½ mile, so just bear with it.

Your exit from the pavement is on a dirt road that angles off to the right. Elwell Lodge had the same problem as Gray Eagle Lodge in the days before the modern highway was built, and this jeep road was the way visitors got there in the old days. As the unused jeep road crests, Lakes Basin appears below, with Mount Elwell rising majestically behind it. Other trails have basin views looking easterly, but this is one of the few with a westerly view.

After 1 mile of hiking on the "old Elwell Lodge Road," you reach the modern Gold Lake Highway. Cross directly over the highway, and walk down the paved road toward Lakes Basin Campground. In a short distance, turn right past the usually locked gate into the group campground, then loop left at the group parking lot. Keep an eye out for numerous stone foundations on both sides of the road exiting the parking lot. Between group campsites 11 and 12 make sure to read the plaque telling about these ruins and the long-gone Lake Center Lodge constructed in 1912. Exit the campground on the Grassy Lake Trail, which heads westerly between campsites 15 and 6A. The trail soon crosses a footbridge over the East Fork of Gray Eagle Creek. If you brought your bathing suit, try the dandy swimming hole just downstream from the bridge. On a hot day this midway-through-the-hike spot is perfect for a refreshing dip. Skinny-dipping is out because of the proximity to the campground.

Grassy Lake Trail is well used and passes the lake in ¼ mile. If you didn't know there was a lake off the trail to your left, you might just miss it. The best lake view is found by turning off the trail and walking cross-country to the edge of the lake. Actually, because the lake is quite shallow and full of willows (and long grass, naturally) on this side, you cannot get to the shore. A bit later along the main trail, a spur trail cuts to the left toward the western shore of the lake, but the spot I just described makes for a better photo. The topo map calls this Grass Lake but the USFS trail signs call it Grassy Lake— so, take your pick.

Soon, to the left of the trail, you can see a pond with lily pads, followed by a marsh. Then, ¼ mile farther, the trail enters a stream habitat, and the wildflowers change from those of dry hillsides to those that like wetlands. A short distance beyond the marsh, the trail approaches the creek and, darn it, continues on the other side. I took off my shoes and, using my walking stick as a third leg, easily waded across; only then did I notice an old log downstream that might have made an OK bridge.

Once on the other side, leave the trail and walk to the right to get a close-hand look at Tumbly Falls. The smooth rock face is not too tricky to descend for a view of the falls from near the bottom. The falls in Lakes Basin can't compare with those in Yosemite, but you're not standing elbow to elbow with a bunch of gawking tourists either. Back on the trail headed north, if you love the color green you will enjoy the next ½ mile, as ferns and other lush growth crowd the path.

Do take the side trail to the right whose sign says "Halsey Falls ¼." Cute but not breathtaking is how I'd describe the falls. As you approach Halsey, an old sign points left across the creek saying "Fern Falls." I don't recommend the uphill trailless scramble through the brush to see the lower part of Fern Falls. (Hike GL-28 gives you a good view of Fern Falls with much less uphill bushwhacking.)

After enjoying Halsey, retrace your steps to the

main trail, and continue hiking north toward Gray Eagle Lodge. At the next trail intersection you have your choice of several routes for the ¾ mile back to the trailhead. Staying on the trail straight leads you to the parking area for the Smith Lake Trail, at which point a right turn leads you to the gravel road running between the lodge and Gold Lake Highway. Go left on that road for ¼ mile, crossing over Gray Eagle Creek, to the highway and your car. Choice number two is to turn right, and follow the signs first to the lodge and then back to your car. Choice number three is to turn right and, when the trail divides, take another right to Lily Lake. Just beyond the lake, this route intersects with Gold Lake Highway. You turn left onto the highway, and a walk on pavement for ½ mile back to your car. I'll admit, the whole loop seems like a lot more than 6 miles, with another ½ mile if you make the side trip to Halsey Falls, but I measured it several times by different map-measuring methods, and each time I got the same distance.

Camping: Camping is prohibited anywhere along this route except in the nice USFS Lakes Basin Campground.

Winter Use: Gold Lake Highway is not plowed in winter, so snowmobiles enjoy zooming along it. I have tolerated the snowmobile noise while snowshoeing in to Elwell Lodge, which is closed from fall to spring. The snowmobilers stayed on the highway, so I had the side road to the lodge all to myself.

Aspens in autumn at the start of the East Side of Lakes Basin Loop

GL-28 Fern Falls Trail

Distance: 1¼ miles out and back (with extension up to the falls, 2¼ miles)

Highest Point: 6,160 feet

Total Elevation Gain: 160 feet (with extension, 335 feet)

Difficulty: Easy/moderate (with extension, strenuous)

Hiking Season: May through October

Directions to the Trailhead: Follow the directions for Hike GL-16, but don't turn off at the Gray Eagle Lodge intersection. Instead, drive for another 1.1 miles, and park at a wide parking area on the right of Gold Lake Highway with a sign saying "Fern Falls Picnic Area & Vista Trail."

Comments: Most hikers can easily do this scenic short hike, without the tougher extra hike to the side of the falls. The lone picnic table is a lovely spot for lunch (or picnic breakfast, or early picnic dinner in the late light of summer). However, the view of the falls is from quite a distance. The unimproved trail from the picnic table to the side of the falls is fun if you don't mind a bit of bushwhacking and finding your way. Someday I plan to spend a day improving this last section by clipping bushes and making the trail more recognizable. Check it out— perhaps by the time you try this hike I will have

accomplished my trail work, and the second part will be moderate in difficulty too. None of this hike is shown on the topo map.

The Hike: The fairly well-used trail starts down from the parking area, and then crosses a footbridge over the East Fork of Gray Eagle Creek, before turning north paralleling the creek. You pass a spur trail used by fishing enthusiasts to cut down to the creek, which at that point is only 100 yards from Gold Lake Highway. The trail makes a hairpin turn, begins to climb, and then switches back twice. At the top of the rise, a picnic table sits serenely by itself overlooking the vista mentioned in the trailhead sign. This is the turnaround place for those not wanting to extend the hike a tougher ½ mile to the side of the falls.

If you don't mind a bit of heavier going, I recommend the extension. Start downhill on the slightly traveled trail just beyond the picnic table. In a couple of hundred yards the path flattens out and makes a fork that is hardly recognizable. The trail straight ahead is a bit longer than the right fork, but I think you'll enjoy the views from the former. If you go straight, the route gradually curves right and more or less disappears where a large rock outcropping, smoothed by a glacier 10,000 years ago, appears on your right. You can ascend this smooth rock surface without difficulty, and the vista from its highest point beats the view from the picnic table. In addition to the splendor of Mount Elwell to the southwest, you will enjoy good old Peak 6509 due south of your vantage point. (If a peak doesn't have a name, trail books merely give it the name of its elevation. Old 6509 may be nameless, but it's a handsome piece of rock.)

From here, there's no exit trail, but you can see the trail you want by looking down in the little valley in the direction of Fern Falls. No problem— make your way down the eastern face of the promontory on which you've been standing, and meander in the general direction of the trail you spied from the top. The terrain is open, so you can hike without difficulty even though there isn't a trail. When you get to the trail you saw from above, you will be a bit disappointed to discover that the wide-open nice gravel path you spied poops out in another 100 yards. It enters a bushy thicket, and from here (until I get time to go clipping) remains kind of a mystery. Nonetheless, you can hear the roar of Fern Falls ahead of you, so do a bit of pathfinding on your own. In about 300 yards you will be standing at the side of beautiful Fern Falls. The falls actually occur in several leaps rather than one majestic free fall. It is difficult to get a perspective of the entire falls, but several vantage points provide views of different sections of the plunging water. Sitting next to the cascade is a delightful place for lunch.

For the return to the picnic table, I suggest you take the low route rather than reclimb the glaciated rock outcropping. You first walk up a wash in the direction of the picnic table. A talus slope of loose rock appears on your left. Don't hike up to it; instead, stay on the dry streambed, clamber up a few boulders, and head across the bushless and treeless gradual slope

to the dim split in the trail where you went straight coming over. Turn left, and in a few hops, skips, and jumps you are back at the picnic table. From there, the walk back to the trailhead is a piece of cake.

Think you missed the ferns that gave the falls their name? I didn't see but a couple of small ferns either.

Camping: None.
Winter Use: None.

Fern Falls

GL-29 Two Little Lost Lakes Loop near Gold Lake

Distance: 2-mile loop

Highest Point: 6,648 feet

Total Elevation Gain: 173 feet

Difficulty: Easy

Hiking Season: June through October

Directions to the Trailhead: From Graeagle drive south on Highway 89 for 1.4 miles, and turn right onto Gold Lake Highway. Drive 9.7 miles, until you see a sign "Gold Lake Boat Ramp ½" pointing to the right. This new paved road to the ramp is not shown on the topo map. It replaces a very rough road, which, I'm sure, was a terror for people who hauled in boats. Drive .5 mile from the highway, past the main campground entrance, until you see a sign "Squaw Lake 1, Jeep Campground 1¼, Little Gold Lake 2, and Summit Lake 3½." There is plenty of room to park.

Comments: This is a nice, easy, fairly level walk that goes by two picturesque, seldom visited, unnamed lakes. The downside of this hike is that much of the trail is sometimes used by horses from the Gold Lake Pack Station. The horses don't seem to suffer one bit from constipation. Actually, it's not that bad. I have hiked this trail several times, and I never had to step over any fresh smelly poop piles—some old ones, yes, but no "ripe" ones. Horse trails also often get dusty because the horses' hooves tend to chew up the trail, but the ground is firm enough on most of this loop so that, even late in the season, dust isn't a problem.

The Hike: From the trailhead, backtrack along the paved road on which you drove in. Just before it makes a loop and intersects Gold Lake Highway, keep an eye out on the right for the trail as it crosses the road at an angle. There is no sign, but, if you are attentive, you should easily spy the crossing. The trail parallels the out-of-sight highway for ¼ mile, and then veers south to the edge of the first lake.

Dead fir trees with barkless white trunks standing starkly on the far shore make a dandy picture on a calm day as they are reflected in the smooth surface of the lake.

The trail winds southerly through some pleasant forest and, ¼ mile later, nears the shore of the second unnamed lake. Here you need to leave the trail and plow through some low-growing brush for a better view from the lakeshore. Back on the trail, you zigzag up a low ridge, then drop downhill back toward Gold Lake. Keep your eye out for the flattened remains of an old cabin on your left.

When you are ¼ mile past the second lake, watch for a T intersection in the trail. A right turn would quickly put you back on the jeep road that adjoins Gold Lake. However, I suggest you continue straight on the trail on which you've been hiking. This next section is seldom used by horses, hence it is not as beaten down or studded with fertilizer as the part you've been on. In less than ¼ mile, the trail intersects the jeep road, which now has veered away from the lake. The easy way back is to take a right on the rocky jeep road and follow it ¼ mile back to the car.

You will easily see why it is called a jeep road. I noted several large boulders in the middle crowned with oil spots. Evidently someone's jeep wasn't high enough off the road and mashed its oil pan on them. No Winnebagos are seen along here, for sure, although it can be driven, albeit slowly, in a four-wheel-drive SUV.

If you want to bypass a bit of the rocky road, wander northwesterly toward Gold Lake; you will arrive at the shore in two minutes. The trail along the lakeshore back to your car is sometimes there and sometimes not (see Hike GL-30), but you can easily find your way, and the views across the lake are nice.

Camping: There are no backpack campsites on this short loop but the newly refurbished Gold Lake Campground near the trailhead is dandy for car camping.

Winter Use: None. Gold Lake Highway is not plowed in winter, so there's no access to this trailhead. However, the snowy highway is a favorite route for snowmobilers coming north from Bassetts or south from where the snowplows quit plowing.

Autumn evening at one of the Little Lost Lakes

GL-30 Gold Lake Lakeshore Trail

Distance: 4½ miles out and back (with extension to the ridge, 5½ miles)

Highest Point: 6,723 feet

Total Elevation Gain: 316 feet (with extension, 770 feet)

Difficulty: Moderate

Hiking Season: June through October

Directions to the Trailhead: See Hike GL-29.

Comments: Gold Lake is the largest of the Lakes Basin lakes and allows jet skis, speed boats, water skis, kayaks, canoes, fishing boats, and plastic floats for swimming kids. The trail follows along the southern shore of the lake. In places, the path disappears; it is not an officially maintained trail, merely the most common route of people who have walked the lakeshore. This disappearing act shouldn't be a concern, however. You keep going in the same direction parallel to the shoreline, and the beaten path will soon reappear if you keep watching for it. Once you reach the western end of the lake, a short trek up the jeep road toward Summit Lake provides you with not only marvelous lake views but also a chance to visit the remains of "Uncle Bob's" cabin and the gold mine of no gold.

The Hike: The trailhead is where the nicely paved Gold Lake Boat Ramp access road turns into a jeep road filled with large rocks. At a few places along the hike, the trail nears this jeep road. However, the road gets such infrequent traffic that close encounters should not disturb your wilderness experience. What will separate this hike from the wilderness are the sound of boat motors on the lake and the frequent unofficial campsites at the edge of the water. Sad to say, thoughtless campers have left a few sites cluttered with garbage. Just walk through these, and pretend not to notice.

If you parked near the end of the pavement, walk along the short dirt section of a loop road that heads northerly toward the lake. After 100 yards,

where the loop turns right, continue straight, and pick up a trail, in places outlined with rocks, leading to the lakeshore. If you don't see this trail right away, no problem—just walk without benefit of a trail toward the lake, and, in an easy 200 yards, you are there.

The boat ramp is only 50 yards to the east, and, in midsummer, you will spy campers and boat trailers on your right. This short trail to the edge of the lake ends at a big log and campsite. Here the shoreline trail begins to the left, although its starting point is a bit nebulous. Merely walk near the water in a westerly direction, and in a few steps you will spot the favored route.

As you proceed, two parallel paths occasionally appear. They soon become one again, so chose either one. This multi-trail situation arises because some hikers like one way, perhaps the higher one with less foliage to plow through, while others like another, perhaps the one alongside the water.

Especially on holiday weekends in the summer, you may encounter campers using some of the sites along the way. These are accessed only by the jeep road, so you won't find motor homes and station wagons. I usually try to detour slightly around any camps in use instead of tromping right through and disturbing the occupants. You may encounter an occupied campsite with no vehicle, a sign that the campers got to it by boat. I think it would be fun to kayak in to one of the less frequently used sites for a campout someday.

After about a mile of meandering along the lakeshore with its ins and outs around little coves, you have to detour around a large rock promontory angling out into the lake. With care, you might choose to clamber up the face of the rock rather than detouring. If you prefer the easier detour route, be sure to walk out onto the top of the rock from the detour to enjoy a nice view of the lake.

About 1½ miles from the trailhead, the jeep road and trail merge where the road approaches the edge of the water, so begin walking on the road as it loops around the western end of the lake. Where the road fords a little creek, you'll find an easy crossing on closely spaced rocks just to the left of the ford. A short distance farther, a similar small creek crossing is easily (I hope) accomplished on a log without incurring wet feet.

By now you have passed the nice sign telling you that the state and the USFS have teamed up to provide and maintain the end-of-the-road jeep camps—a team concept unique in the Feather River country. Likewise, you have walked past the jeep road that turns off to Little Gold Lake. Finally, a Y in the road appears with a chain across the seldom used right fork. The left fork is obviously used by the jeep folks—and you. (Throughout this description, I repeatedly call it a jeep road, and it appeared to me to be so strewn with boulders that only jeeps could navigate it. Not so. To my surprise, I encountered a few Ford Explorers, small Toyota pickup trucks, and other four-wheel-drive vehicles along the way.) The road leaves the lakeshore and heads uphill toward the ridge crest and Summit Lake.

Approximately ¼ mile from the Y, a less-well-used road branches off on the left. Take it, and soon a nicely kept sturdy cabin comes into view. Just before you reach the cabin (it is privately owned and used by "the family" during the summer, so please do not go up to it or disturb anything), turn right onto a very dim unused road that climbs uphill and loops around above the cabin.

In about 250 yards this road reaches the charred remains of "Uncle Bob's" cabin, which burned in 1958. (The cabin you just passed replaced it several years later.) "Uncle Bob" was murdered in Grass Valley many years ago, and his ashes were scattered on the mountainside above his much-loved burned cabin. (This bit of history was related by "Uncle Bob's" nephew Jim, whom I met while exploring the mine site above the charred cabin. Jim had spent many summers here as a cowboy when the family raised cattle at this location, but his visit on the day I met him was his first return to the site in 24 years, he said.)

The dim road passes the old cabin remains and angles uphill for another 200 yards to the mine site. I refer to it as the no-gold gold mine, because the lack of tailings, tunnel, or mineshaft indicate that its operators gave up without accomplishing much. Just beyond here the views of the lake are outstanding. A very tall red fir that snuggles against two white firs is beautifully silhouetted against the now more distant lake. This is where I've elected to have this hike turn around and retrace the route to the trailhead.

If you wish to extend the hike, however, return past the nice cabin to the jeep road, then follow its rocky route up to the ridge. On top, the PCT crosses the road (see Hike GL-23). Continue straight on the road for 200 yards beyond the trail crossing, to a jeep road intersection. The jeep road to the left, in another 200 yards, brings you to unspectacular Summit Lake. Turn around here, and retrace your steps to your car.

Another alternative on the return hike from "Uncle Bob's" cabin is to walk the jeep road back to the trailhead rather than taking the lakeside trail. The road is decidedly quicker but rather rocky, harder on the feet, and much less scenic. Take your choice. Unfortunately, a loop clear around the lake is not possible because much of the northern side is privately owned, and hikers are not welcome.

Camping: There are scads of nice lakeside campsites, albeit somewhat overused, on the southern shore of Gold Lake. For a pleasant overnight backpacking trip, camp at less-than-perfect Summit Lake or go even farther north via the PCT to Snake Lake or Little Deer Lake (see Hike GL-23). Good car camping (no hookups) is available in the vicinity of the trailhead near the boat ramp.

Winter Use: Gold Lake Highway is not plowed in winter, so only snowmobiles make it to Gold Lake during the snowy months.

Gold Lake Shoreline Trail follows the jagged shoreline starting on the lake's far end

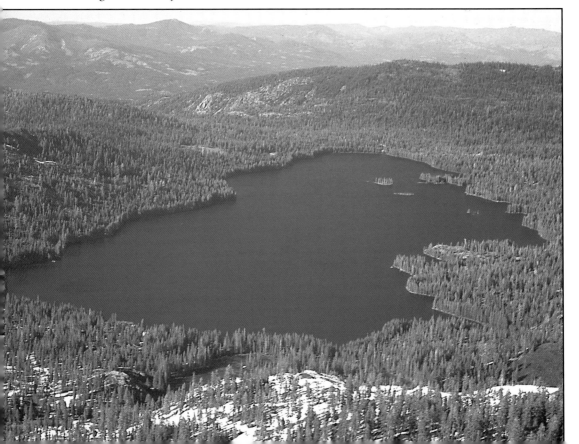

Chapter 8

Clio Topo

C-1 Haskell Peak Trail

Distance: 4 miles out and back
Highest Point: 8,107 feet
Total Elevation Gain: 1,167 feet
Difficulty: Moderate
Hiking Season: July through October

Directions to the Trailhead: Follow the directions for Hike C-2, but continue on the good gravel Haskell Peak Road (Forest Road 09) another 5.1 miles past Howard Creek, until you see a sign saying "Haskell Peak Trail." There are plenty of places to park.

Comments: This is probably the easiest and nicest mountain peak hike described in this book. The trail is well trod, but not to the point where it's dusty. Until the final ¼ mile, the grade is moderate. Several nice meadows contribute fields of wildflowers, and flowers abound all along the trail in mid-summer. Hikers suffering from vertigo will enjoy attaining the summit because there are no cliffy places. On top are magnificent views from this second-highest peak in the region (only the 8,591-foot Sierra Buttes summit is higher). The summit is a great place for lunch.

The Hike: The trail starts at a sign "Haskell Peak 2" on the northern edge of the road. Although you start hiking uphill immediately, the grade isn't bad, and the trail is delightfully smooth. After passing through a very lovely fern forest, you encounter a couple of mini-meadows with a variety of wildflowers, including some nice groups of corn lilies (large leaves and a spray of small white flowers on a 3-foot stalk).

The trail crosses a tiny creek, which was still trickling in late July but may be dry by fall. The pitch begins to get steeper so the route zigzags to lessen the grade. To my surprise, I found a large snow bank across the path, even though August was only a few

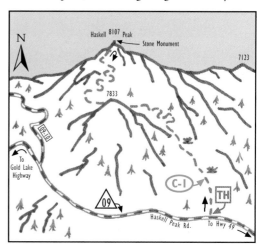

days away. It looked 8 feet deep, so September may arrive before the darn thing melts completely. I easily detoured to the right and picked up the obvious trail on the other side.

When you reach a saddle, the route changes direction to the northeast. More zigzags follow, and, just as the path starts to head westerly, the crest pops into view on your right. The USFS map shows the trail missing the top by about ¼ mile, and the topo map doesn't show this well-used trail at all, even though it has been in existence for years (it has tree blazes and silver diamond markers nailed to trees along the route—practices discontinued many years ago). Actually, the trail leads right up to the rock-strewn base of the peak, about 100 yards from the very top.

A bent and battered Jeffrey pine and a similarly twisted and gnarled western white pine at the end of the trail attest to the heavy snow that accumulates at this 8,000-foot elevation for at least five months of the year. Although the trail ends, you'll easily find the best route to the top through the rock talus. Climbing the last 100 yards to the top can be accomplished by just about everyone. The way

Corn lilys on Haskell Peak Trail

isn't steep, and there are no scary cliffs.

The top has plenty of room for wandering around to admire the view in various directions. Three large rock cairns have obviously entertained their builders for many hours, but I admit I prefer a mountain peak unadorned by human creations. A nice variety of wildflowers have found a foothold in this rocky environ.

Snow-capped Mount Lassen, many miles away, can be seen to the northwest on a clear day. To the northeast, below, you can identify distant Smith Peak with its occupied lookout tower (most fire lookouts are no longer staffed), and a sliver of Lake Davis. The Mohawk-Chapman Road can be seen snaking around below in the northerly direction, and the spur roads off Forest Road 09 that you drove by earlier seem amazingly close to the summit on which you are standing.

After clambering down from the top, you'll notice a rocky knoll in front of you. Walk up it for a better view of the terrain to the west, including Mount Elwell and Eureka Peak. Then enjoy the all-downhill walk back to the car. The sound of cowbells some distance to the east added a Swiss flavor to my return hike.

For an interesting alternative drive back, continue easterly on Haskell Peak Road for 1 mile to Chapman Saddle and a four-way intersection with the Mohawk-Chapman Road. A left turn returns you to Graeagle via the less-than-smooth Mohawk-Chapman Road (it becomes paved about halfway to town). If you go straight at the intersection, the road winds downhill to Highway 89 near Calpine. A right turn at the intersection keeps you on well-maintained Forest Road 09; after a few curvy miles, you intersect Highway 49 about midway between Bassetts and the spot where 49 meets Highway 89.

Camping: None.

Winter Use: None (although Haskell Peak Road has little orange diamonds nailed to trees, indicating it is a snowmobile route).

C-2 Howard Creek and Old Wagon Road Trail

Distance: 4 miles out and back

Highest Point: 6,847 feet

Total Elevation Gain: 655 feet

Difflculty: Moderate

Hiking Season: June through October

Directions to the Trailhead: From Graeagle take Highway 89 south for 1.4 miles to the Gold Lake Highway. Turn right, and drive 11.6 miles. Turn left on the well-graded gravel of Haskell Peak Road (Forest Road 09), whose sign says "Howard Creek 4, Chapman Saddle 10." In 3.1 miles turn right at a dirt road about .25 mile before you reach Howard Creek itself. At this intersection there is adequate room for parking.

Comments: This trail is the historic old wagon road that ran from the Yuba River north to Gold Lake. Although it hasn't been used as a road for a long time, it was built well enough so that it hasn't completely disappeared over time. The trail provides a creek view only occasionally but the musical burble of the creek can be heard all along the hike.

I had hoped to hike the trail from south to north by starting at Bassetts and following the creek uphill to the trailhead I describe here, and then back downhill. Unfortunately, where the trail commences at Bassetts on a dirt road, half a dozen signs shout out "No Trespassing," "Private Property—Keep Out!" So, the hike starts high and goes downhill. Even though the uphill part is all on the way back after lunch, it's not steep enough to be a problem. You'll enjoy seeing the extensive Westall Diggins mining area near your car at the end of this walk.

The Hike: First, I want to let you in on a bit of the trail's history. It was originally built in the 1850s as a pack trail. In 1886 it was widened into a wagon road and connected the Yuba River Wagon Road at Howard's Ranch (the name later changed to

Bassetts) with Lusk Meadow near the Salmon Lakes. In those days the wagon track was called the Hayes-Steelman Road after its builders, Phillip Hayes and Richard Steelman. These two men operated a mine east of Gold Lake near Lusk Meadows. In 1886 Hayes and Steelman found several large gold nuggets, and, as word of their find spread, other miners flocked to the area and opened new mines.

The next bit of history that impacts the hike is the extensive Westall Diggins on Howard Creek, immediately east of the trailhead. At the end of the hike, you'll be routed through the tailings and rock piles left by this hard-on-the-environment mining. Evidently lots of gold was extracted by hydraulic mining, sluicing, and tearing up the streambed and hillsides. Mother Nature often does a good job, eventually, of covering up human messes, but she'll be a long time repairing the damage done by the Westall Diggins miners.

Start the hike by taking the dirt road south from the trailhead. In 200 yards you reach a Y, with the more-traveled road forking left and a dimmer road heading to the right. The old wagon road is the dim one. Take it, and enjoy the cool shade and level forest track. You cross an intermittent creek and shortly thereafter spot a cabin ahead. As you get nearer, you discover that it's actually more of an old storehouse than a rustic cabin. It does, however, have a cute, not-in-service, outhouse. A rusting Chevy truck is parked alongside; its license plate expired July 1981. There's other junk lying about—but junk it is, not historic relics.

The trail skirts to the left of the building and shortly pops into a lovely meadow, except that the center of the meadow is decorated with a flattened 1959 (plus or minus a few years) Chevy. Your guess

is as good as mine about how it got there in a thoroughly squashed condition. The meadow is boggy in the middle, so stay to the left, skirting the edge near the creek. The plant life in the meadow is very fragile, and tramping through it would cause damage, so the edge route is a good move environmentally.

Next, the road leaves the woods and enters a flat area paved (by nature) with small smooth stones and graced by a few conifers. At this point the route of the wagon road isn't well defined. However, by walking more or less straight and keeping a sharp eye out, you can easily pick up the trail in about 100 yards. Soon after the flat area, the route disappears into a 3-foot-deep washout, which you can easily navigate by descending into it and walking its length. As you approach a small creek, cross it, and clamber up its embankment, at which point you'll find yourself on the trail. Only ¼ mile farther you're suddenly in very different surroundings.

The shady, friendly forest becomes an area nearly clear-cut by loggers. An occasional tree was left standing, so "technically" it isn't clear-cut, but darn near. Natural regrowth is slowly occurring, but it takes a long time to grow mature trees. The cutting was all on the hillside above you, so stay on the

Along the Howard Creek Trail

lower edge of the cut area, and keep paralleling the creek. The trail is a bit brushy underfoot (someone cut some of the brush a few years ago to make an easier way through) but, no problem, just go a bit slower. The route gets slightly steeper as it continues downhill.

At this point, the topo map does not show the old road going any farther, but we know that the old wagon road ran the whole distance between Bassetts and Gold Lake. Sure enough, it continues along, but you need to look carefully to find where it crosses the creek. Exactly where the logged-over area uphill from you ends and the full forest starts, watch on your left for the crossing spot. The trail runs close to the creek here. Ahead, the logging road continues, and 100 yards farther it begins to flatten out and looks invitingly smooth (naturally, now that you are going to turn off it). On your left are a clump of ferns and a patch of narrow-leaved lotus, which has very attractive multicolored small flowers with leaves somewhat like those of a sweet pea. Tramp through this vegetation, cutting back sharply down to the creek. On the far side of the creek it is apparent where the old wagon road continues. On the near side, some rotting boards indicate a once-upon-a-time bridge. Several big rocks are close enough together so that you can cross without wetting your feet, unless it's spring and there's a high runoff.

As the trail starts up the other side, a sign appears on a tree saying "Warning—This Is a Protected Property. Northern Mining Council— Downieville. All strange vehicles in the vicinity of this sign will have their license numbers taken and turned in to the Sheriff's Department." This is a laugh, because no vehicle has been in the vicinity for a very long time, nor has anyone been around to take down a license number. Anyhow, it doesn't say, "No Trespassing"—so continue downstream on the old wagon road, now on the eastern bank of Howard Creek. The track is still in OK shape, except for the numerous trees that have fallen across it. Stepping over, going around, or walking on top of branches slows your pace, but it's fun to think of the bit of history that this old road presents.

Knowing that I couldn't use the far end of the trail at Bassetts because of the "No Trespassing" signs there, I turned around after ½ mile of negotiating the fallen forest in my path.

On the way back, about ¼ mile before you reach the trailhead, a road cuts off to the right, downhill. Take this "detour" to see at close hand the awesome tailings and piles of rock created by the miners of the Westall Diggins. The amount of work needed to move all those rocks without modern mechanized equipment boggles the mind. I suspect that some powered equipment was available at the time, because piling all this rock by hand would have been nearly impossible.

Two gold-mining techniques have left their mark. One was hydraulic mining, in which high-pressure hoses squirted water at the stream banks, washing the soil into sluices. In the sluices, the sandy water ran through, while the heavier gold particles were washed to the bottom. Ridges on the bottom of the sluice caught the gold. When the sand on top was all washed away, the miners removed gold lodged in the bottom.

The other mining method was to pull up rocks and boulders from the streambed and sift through the sand in the cavity where they had been. Over the centuries, the natural flow of the creek washed down gold-laden sand. As the gold particles hit a rock, they sometimes sank to the bottom, being heavier than the sand, rather than washing around the rock. Thus, bits of gold would become imbedded in the sand under the rock.

You'll also see hundreds of uprooted tree stumps piled in a pit surrounded by tailings. I can only guess that the trees were cut for wood by the miners and the stumps, roots and all, were washed out of the hillside by the hydraulic mining.

To return to your car, follow a road that you encounter in the tailings, leading left, back up the hill.

Camping: None, although I suppose you could camp along Howard Creek in a few level places.

Winter Use: Although Bassetts is open all year, no trail access is available. The road to the trailhead at the north end is not plowed in winter.

C-3 Red Fir Nature Trail and Mills Peak

Distance: ½-mile loop (if you walk, instead of drive, to the peak, 2½ miles)

Highest Point: 7,342 feet

Total Elevation Gain: 20 feet (if you walk to the peak, 260 feet)

Difficulty: Easy (if you walk to the peak, moderate)

Hiking Season: June through October

(the wildflowers are best in June and July)

Directions to the Trailhead: From Graeagle go south on Highway 89 for 1.4 miles to a right turn onto the Gold Lake Highway. Drive 8.7 miles on Gold Lake Highway to a dirt road on the left with a sign "Red Fir Nature Trail 2, Mills Peak 3." Several roads lead off this main road, but keep driving until you see another sign, at a left turn, for the nature trail and the peak. Drive 1 mile on this bumpy (but OK-for-cars) road to a sign on the right "Red Fir Nature Trail" and a parking area on the left. After parking and taking the loop trail, drive 1 mile farther on the same road, past an orange sign on a tree saying "Warning—Cliff Area Ahead." There's a bit of rough road on this last stretch, but, with careful driving, I think a non-four-wheel-drive vehicle can make it. If you're wondering about the cliff, this road is used in winter by snowmobiles (that's what those orange arrows on trees along the road are all about). The cliff isn't scary for cars or hikers but a snowmobile at full speed may not recognize that a quick turn is necessary to avoid hurling off into the void. There's plenty of parking space at the lookout.

Comments: As educational nature trails go, this one is pretty light on education but well endowed with nice trees. At least you'll never mix up red fir and white fir after taking the loop. The grove of red firs wears an attractive mantle of light-green moss. The view from the closed-up lookout on Mills Peak is spectacular and well worth the extra drive (or hike, if you decided to walk it) beyond the Red Fir loop.

The Hike: From the Red Fir parking area on the west side of the road, walk across the road and pick up the trail at the sign "Red Fir Nature Trail." After 100 yards the trail splits. Although you can go either way around the loop (naturally), I guess automobile driving habits are deep seated, so I always go right (counterclockwise). Unfortunately, at the time of this writing, many of the explanation signs have been sufficiently mutilated by vandals (that's what we'd call them in the city) to render them unreadable. However, I hope that the important signs identifying the red fir and white fir are still intact when you do this loop. The walk is made more interesting by the many firs bent into weird shapes by the heavy snow load in this area and the marvelous frosting of pale-green moss on the firs. If you were lost in this area, you'd have a heck of a time finding north by the old adage "Moss grows on the north side of trees." The moss here isn't picky about which side of the tree it grows on.

This trail is conducive to sauntering, not rapid hiking. When you return to the split where the loop began, turn right, assuming you went counterclockwise, and return to your car for the 1-mile drive up to Mills Peak. Or, if you feel like more exercise, leave the car and walk that mile—the road to the peak isn't particularly steep. Whichever way you get there, you will enjoy the 360° view from the lookout. Satellite surveillance has helped make many USFS staffed fire lookouts obsolete, and Mills Peak is no exception. The sign on the building lists visiting hours, but the lookout was thoroughly locked when I visited during the posted hours on a weekday in early August. I remember visiting the lookout with my family 30 years ago when it was still in full operation. The

Mills Peak Lookout

ranger on duty gave us a pleasant reception and tower tour as well as a patient explanation of how fire spotting was accomplished. We were interested to see his cramped, confining, lonely quarters. However, I'm sure the USFS can't afford to have personnel on hand just to explain how fire spotting is done for the small number of visitors who come to the site each summer.

Camping: None.

Winter Use: Snowmobiles only.

C-4 Chapman Creek Trail

Distance: 3½ miles out and back

Highest Point: 6,645 feet

Total Elevation Gain: 575 feet

Difficulty: Moderate

Hiking Season: June through October

Directions to the Trailhead: From Graeagle drive 1.4 miles south on Highway 89, and turn right onto the Gold Lake Highway. In 14 miles the highway reaches Highway 49 at Bassetts. Turn left on 49 and drive 3.0 miles to a left turn with a sign "Chapman Creek Campground." If it's midsummer, park near the entrance along the campground loop road but not in a campsite spot. If it's "low season" and there are plenty of open campsites, then drive around the loop and park at a site. (Site 10 is usually open because it adjoins the two outhouses with their banging doors and less-than-wonderful aroma.)

Comments: If you want a very nice trail for only a couple of hours of easy walking, this is a winner. Unlike many creek hikes, Chapman Creek Trail never gets very far from the water. The stream banks have some elder bushes but far less brush than most creeks in this region.

The Hike: The trail leaves from the campground between campsites 9 and 11. A prominent sign announces "Chapman Creek Trail," and the path starts gradually uphill through a lovely red fir forest, with other conifers scattered throughout. The path has a gradual incline, without any steep parts, although, like all creekside trails, it's all uphill one way and downhill the other. The topo map shows another trail joining this one within 200 yards of the trailhead, but it is evidently wiped out because

no sign of it is apparent. Chapman Creek Trail must be an old one, because many of the large tree trunks along the way have old blazes. In some cases, the tree (usually a red fir) has tried to heal the wound by filling it in with bark. In several cases, I noted that the original cut was about 3 inches below the outer bark, signifying that the tree had grown "outward" by that much since the blaze was cut.

Less than ¼ mile from the start, the trail crosses three tiny creeks. They must be spring fed, because they were still flowing in mid-October. In about ½ mile, the trail climbs 100 feet above the creek, but soon the creek "catches up" and you find yourself at creekside again. Underfoot, the trail surface is perfect: firm, but not hard, with plenty of pine needles (actually fir needles in this case— funny how all needles get the name "pine" whether they are or not) and no dust. The trail doesn't seem very heavily used, which is a bit of a surprise because summer visitors abound in the area. The campground from which the trail leaves is popular, and, within 2 miles of the trailhead, along Highway 49 are three summer home tracts, Clark, Haskell, and Carvin, with sizable groups of unwinterized rustic cabins, on land leased from the USFS.

When you are ¾ mile from the start, you reach a larger unnamed creek. A log was placed across it, obviously to aid hikers in keeping their feet dry. The red firs along the trail sport a colorful cloak of yellow-green moss, adding an extra touch of beauty to the surroundings. After going ¼ mile farther, you reach another unnamed creek flowing into Chapman Creek, this one easily crossed on stepping-stones. Creek crossings seem to come at ¼-mile intervals, the next one being across Chapman Creek itself. By now you're on the upper part of the creek, and its volume is substantially less than farther downstream where it received inflow from the various small side creeks you've been crossing.

As the trail continues its gradual ascent, you encounter bog logs. Trail maintenance folks have laid a walkway of cut logs so that hikers don't have to wallow through mud in this boggy place. In several parts of the bog, four logs of about 6-inch diameter are laid side by side, parallel to the direction of the trail, forming an easily traversed log road. At the final crossing, where the trail turns right from dry land onto the logs, an old tree has fallen on the left of the trail. As it fell it left a jagged stump and a portion of the lower trunk broke off in a big "slice," which lies alongside the trail. This 3-foot-long section of trunk contains an old blaze, placed there by some trail scouter more than a century ago, I bet. I wanted to pick up this bit of history, carry it back to the car, and nail it up next to our front door. However, if I'd done that, it wouldn't be there waiting for your inspection and enjoyment.

On the western bank of the creek, you come to a pile of rocks next to the trail, obviously placed there by someone. I wondered what it signified, and backtracking a few steps I discovered what looked like a flume coming down the hill. Perhaps some mining activity occurred near here years ago. The maps don't show any mines or prospects, but I didn't explore farther off the trail to find out. The surface of the trail becomes sandy, but not so soft as to make walking difficult. It crosses Chapman Creek again and suddenly, there ahead of you, the trail ends at a dirt road. About 30 yards before the road, a sign nailed to a tree announces this as the Chapman Creek Trail, as if you didn't know. Whoever nailed up that sign sure didn't care whether anyone on the road noticed it, because you have to know where to look to see it from the road.

I suggest making a U turn here and retracing your steps rather than taking a left on the road and hiking ¼ mile to the not-worth-seeing bridge over Chapman Creek. (If you do add on the ¼ mile to the bridge, return to the trail by following a ¼-mile dim track that closely follows the eastern bank of the creek.)

On the way back, I was struck by how much the noise of the water increases as the creek loses altitude and gains tributaries. Somehow, on the way up the creek I didn't notice as the burble of the water faded with altitude gain. When I got back to my car, just-arrived campers were setting up their tents and opening their first beer of the afternoon. I silently urged them to take the Chapman Creek Trail, because it's a dandy.

Camping: The Chapman Creek Campground at the trailhead is good for car camping. Backpackers will find an old campsite just downstream from where the road reaches the bridge. It's near the stream, set in a grove of firs, with level grassy ground and an old fire ring. I hope some of the litter left by thoughtless prior campers will have been cleaned up by the time you plan a backpack campout there.

Winter Use: Because the access to year-round Highway 49 from Graeagle is a roundabout route via Highway 89, I have never tried a winter snowshoe of the Chapman Creek Trail, but it might be worth doing. Even with the trail obscured by snow, its proximity to the creek might make winter route-finding not too difficult.

C-5 Kelly Cabins and Locke Mine Trail

Distance: 3¼ miles out and back

Highest Point: 7,100 feet

Total Elevation Gain: 70 feet

Difficulty: Easy/moderate

Hiking Season: July through October

Directions to the Trailhead: From Graeagle drive south on Highway 89 for 1.4 miles, and turn right on Gold Lake Highway. After 8.7 miles turn left on a dirt road marked "Mills Peak" and "Red Fir Trail." Drive east on this good dirt road (called Church Creek Road, although no signs identify it as such), continuing past the turn-off to the peak, until you reach an intersection, 1.2 miles from Gold Lake Highway, that has a sign "USFS 28 Begin." Continue 1.3 miles on 28, past the "Water Hole," to a left turn marked "Not Maintained." Take the left (28-2, or 21N31), and drive

about .3 mile, parking along the road wherever there is room.

Comments: Most of the backcountry log cabins built many years ago have vanished due to lack of maintenance and the punishment inflicted by severe winters. So it was a delight to visit the very cute old Kelly Cabins, although they are far from being in livable shape. The trail is virtually level all the way to Locke Mine and very easy on the feet. The last ½ mile has great views down into Mohawk Valley through stately red firs and bushier white firs. Yes, you probably could drive to the cabins—and farther—but why drive when you can walk in such lovely surroundings, soaking up nature and enjoying the solitude?

The Hike: Begin walking along the road where you parked (28-2, or 21N31), which crosses the hardly noticeable Mohawk Gap, bypasses several side roads, and, in less than ¼ mile, meets a road to the right labeled 21N31A. At this point you see the back of a road sign; the other side says "Gold Lake 4, Mills Peak 5" pointing in the direction you just came from. Turn right on 21N31A, and, soon after crossing 21N31B, veer right easterly, still on 21N31A. After ½ mile of easy walking, you reach a clearing and the two delightful Kelly Cabins. For some reason, their location does not show on the topo map. I hope they are still standing by the time you do this hike.

Please stay out of these rickety structures. To see inside you can easily look through the glassless windows. The larger cabin was obviously expanded once upon a time, because the front two-thirds is of log construction and the rear third of shake siding. The second story has nearly collapsed, but you can peer in a window of the lower floor to see the chipped porcelain double sink. Judging from the exposed pipes, it had running water. The smaller two-story log cabin is in pretty fair shape. Although it has only one room on each floor, the logs holding up the floor of the upper level are still in place. Its very steep stairway would have been tough on a sleepwalker in the upstairs bedroom.

In a little more than ¼ mile past the cabins along this seldom used road, you come to a Y in a small clearing used by loggers. Take the right fork, which is still 21N31A. The next ½ mile to Locke Mine is a delight because of the views to the north. Giant red firs here have been thinned by loggers, and those remaining are even more spectacular because you see them individually with few neighbors.

You reach Locke Mine as the trail ends on a large, treeless slope. An intermittent stream called Little Boulder Creek runs through it. Because they lack vegetation, the banks of this watercourse have been covered with an unsightly net matting to prevent erosion, or, I should say, prevent worse erosion. The mine itself is less than spectacular, although I had fun snooping around the odds and ends of mining stuff left lying around.

On the return trip, I took numerous side excursions into the forest looking for four other mines: Denmire, Woodchuck, Foss, and Hayes (often called Hayes and Steelman in the history books). Loggers' mess has covered up any indicators of access roads or trails to these mines, all located within the vicinity of the Kelly Cabins. Perhaps your search will be more successful than mine was—I found only partial remains of the Hayes Mine. "No problem," I said to myself. "It has been a wonderful hike without discovering all of the 'lost' mines."

Camping: None.

Winter Use: Most of the roads into the area have little orange markers nailed high on tree trunks, indicating snowmobile routes. Gold Lake Highway is not open in the winter, so access is via snowmobile only, precluding cross-country skiing or snowshoeing.

One of the Kelly Cabins

C-6 Three Meadows Trail

Distance: 6¼ miles out and back (with the Alternative Loop, 6½ miles)

Highest Point: 6,991 feet (with the Alternative Loop, 7,168 feet)

Total Elevation Gain: 296 feet (with the Alternative Loop, 473 feet)

Difficulty: Moderate (with the Alternative Loop, strenuous)

Hiking Season: May through October (best in June to early August)

Directions to the Trailhead: Follow the directions for Hike C-3 but, instead of turning left on the road going north to Mills Peak and Red Fir Nature Trail, stay on Forest Road 28 for another 100 yards, and turn right at a prominent intersection onto Church Meadows Road. Drive .3 mile south on this dirt road, and park at any wide place in the road.

Comments: From spring through July, the three meadows by which this trail passes are ablaze with yellow buttercups set against the lush green of the meadow grasses. A prettier sight you will seldom see. The route is fairly level and makes a good hike for folks who want super scenery without expending a lot of energy. Prior to August, you'll want to douse on plenty of high-DEET-rating mosquito lotion. The Alternative Loop includes some hiking

on a very dim old logging road and is best undertaken by those accustomed to finding their way without a well-defined track.

The Hike: Church Meadows are named after Isaac Church, a member of the pioneer family that settled at Churches' Corners (now known as the village of Sattley). These beautiful meadows are on the east side of the road on which you parked. Church Creek, with its many small tributaries in spring, meanders through the meadows. Walk back along Church Creek Road to its intersection with Forest Road 28. Are you wondering why I didn't just have you park at that intersection? The reason is, I wanted you to enjoy the splendor of Church Meadows while walking rather than merely viewing them from a car window.

When you reach Forest Road 28, turn right, and hike until you come to a sign saying "Water Hole." Adjoining it is a mini-pond (*mini-pond* sounds so much more attractive than merely *water hole,* but this one isn't particularly attractive). Just beyond the water hole, your route turns right off 28 onto a seldom used dirt road, which wanders through some nice forest of white fir, red fir, ponderosa pine, and Jeffrey pine. In ¾ mile, Freeman Meadow pops into view on the right. Signs say "Sensitive Area— Wet Meadow—Stay on Trail." This sign should be obeyed here, as at all meadows.

The little creek, which you follow for the next ½ mile, is Church Creek. Soon after the road crosses it, another road joins yours at a sharp angle on the right. Continue straight for 200 yards more, and you encounter another road on the right, coming from an area that looks heavily logged. This is the point at which the Alternative Loop (described later) diverges from the main hike. For the main hike, turn right here, and travel through the area that was nearly clear-cut. The loggers did leave a few nice red firs, but, alas, without the sheltering protection of their neighbors, most of those big trees were snapped off by a big windstorm. You soon pass by this human-induced devastation, and the seldom used road approaches the western edge of Howard Creek Meadows. (The maps all use the plural for both Church and Howard Meadows, so I suppose there must be several parts to both of them, although multiple sections were not apparent to me.) The expansive Howard Creek Meadows are a sight to behold with the steep hillside rising almost 1,000 feet behind them. At the top of the hillside, slightly to the south, you can see a building of some sort. To visit this building, if you have the time and inclination, you can add an extra side trip of 1½ miles to this hike by picking up the route of Hike C-7, the Howard Creek Meadows Dam, Mine, and Ghost Camp Loop, at a point I'll describe later.

After providing almost ½ mile of fine meadow views, the road gradually descends a hill and encounters a Y. Take the left branch, and, in 100 yards, you come to Howard Creek. To the right of the place where the road fords the creek is a heavy-duty wooden bridge that looks like it might have been built for a railroad. It is now at a jaunty angle and not in line with the road; I hope it doesn't wash away when the creek is flowing swiftly and high with snowmelt. The bridge marks the turnaround point for this hike. If you wish to tack

on the Hike C-7 loop as a side trip, it starts and ends at the heavy-duty bridge. Walkers turning back here have the doubled pleasure of viewing all three meadows again on the return trip.

Alternative Loop around Howard Creek Meadows: If you are game for a bit of cross-country scouting and don't mind finding your way where there is no "beaten path," try doing this alternative. At the road junction where the loggers' mess starts, continue straight instead of turning right onto the road that skirts the west side of Howard Creek Meadows. In about 300 yards, watch for a yellow USFS section marker nailed to a tree on your left. Shortly after that you reach a dim four-way road intersection. Turn right, and follow this never-used road for ¼ mile to Howard Creek. In spring and early summer, the creek flows too mightily to jump across, and there are no handy stepping-stones or logs on which to cross. Hence, you must either plow across getting your hiking shoes wet, or, as I did, bring along a pair of old don't-mind-getting-wet sneakers to change into for the crossing. Once you're on the south side of the creek, clamber up the bank and head upstream, paralleling the creek for about 200 yards before making a 90° right turn. I hope you'll pick out the yellow USFS signs marking the forest

Freeman Meadow in early summer

boundary and another yellow section marker sign. In their neighborhood is the old loggers' road heading south paralleling the eastern side of the meadow. Don't be too concerned if you miss this hard-to-find road. Strike out due south, paralleling the eastern side of the meadow but going about 240 feet above it along the hillside. You need to step over loggers' mess and blown-down trees. Angle somewhat uphill from where you left the creek. Keep an eye out for the track of the old loggers' road, because it makes for easier hiking than tromping through the dead limbs and logs. You shouldn't get lost if you keep the meadow on your right and walk parallel to it along the hillside. Then, ½ mile from the creek crossing, you should encounter a rough, unused dirt road angling steeply uphill in a northeasterly direction. If you were lucky enough to find the dim loggers' road earlier, it meets the rough road at a point where that one makes a sharp turn uphill.

Follow the rough road downhill. (Or, if you wish to do part of Hike C-7, which visits the ghost camp and mine, take it uphill instead.) As you near the creek level, two roads intersect at a sharp angle, but stay on the one you've been on until it crosses Howard Creek. At this crossing you see the heavy-duty bridge that is the turnaround place for hikers who skipped the Alternative Loop. Cross the creek, turn right, and follow the route northerly on the road along the western side of Howard Creek Meadows to the point where you started the Alternative Loop. I enjoyed the challenge of this loop. If you try it, I hope you do too.

Camping: None.

Winter Use: Forest Road 28 and Church Creek Road are suitable for snowmobiles, but, because Gold Lake Highway isn't plowed in winter, no cross-country skiing or snowshoeing is possible here.

C-7 Howard Creek Meadows Dam, Mine, and Ghost Camp Loop

Distance: 1½-mile loop

Highest Point: 7,300 feet

Total Elevation Gain: 460 feet

Difficulty: Moderate (if you take it easy on the steep uphill part)

Hiking Season: May through October

Directions to the Trailhead: Follow the directions for Hike C-2 but instead of parking to the right of Haskell Peak Road (Forest Road 09) drive 100 yards farther, and park on the left where a dirt road branches off with a sign "Road Not Maintained—823."

Comments: When the Westall Diggins were going full blast (see Hike C-2), they needed lots of water for the hydraulic mining. A sizable earthen dam was built across Howard Creek, flooding Howard Creek Meadows. A cut through

the dam now allows the creek to flow freely, restoring the meadow to its former grandeur. This hike first visits the dam site, and then climbs 460 feet to the motley collection of abandoned cabins that I've named the Howard Creek Meadows Ghost Camp. On the way back downhill, you see several abandoned mines adjoining the road, as well as lots of scrapped machinery and mining stuff.

Note: Please do not disturb or enter any of the cabins, because they may be privately owned, although they obviously haven't been occupied for many years.

The Hike: Walk north on Road 823 for 250 yards to a Y. Take the right fork, and immediately you see Howard Creek. The road fords the creek, but you have the luxury of a bridge crossing. To the right of the ford, a heavy-duty wooden bridge spans the creek. The bridge rests at a jaunty angle, indicating that one end has slipped from its original position. I hope the bridge is still there when you take this hike; most bridges of this nature have long since been swept away when the creeks became swollen with spring runoff.

After crossing the creek, follow the road until it forks three ways. At this point you leave the road, cutting left, back toward the creek. Although there is no trail to follow, the forest is not thick, and you can easily follow the route of the creek. In about 300 yards you come upon the old earthen dam and can easily climb to the top. The sluice gate mechanism

that regulated the flow of water through a pipe under the dam is still in place. It must have been no small feat to pile up all this earth and shore it up with big boulders. Sometime after the Westall Diggins closed, the dam was purposely cut, to drain the lake and allow the stream to flow freely again. Aside from that cut, the dam looks to be in pretty good shape.

Return to the road the same way you walked to the dam. Three forks head uphill. Take the middle rocky road, which, unfortunately, appears to be the steepest. In ¼ mile it makes a sharp right turn as a ditch runs across it. After the right turn, the rocky road continues uphill, and in 300 yards the ghost camp appears. It contains five old one-room cabins, each a modified A-frame. All of them have been given new (well, hardly new now, but newer than the cabins) corrugated steel siding. Three of the cabins overlook the Howard Creek drainage basin and, in the distance, majestic Sierra Buttes. The former occupants must have enjoyed evenings sitting on the now-rotted decks and looking at this marvelous view.

The door of one of the "view" cabins has fallen in, so you can peer into its cramped quarters. An old stove was still sitting to one side, and a loft above the single room might have been used for sleeping. Through a glassless window, a breeze blew, ruffling some decrepit mosquito netting suspended from the ceiling of the loft. Wow, what a ghostly scene in a very spooky place! Scattered around the cabins were odds and ends of junk, including a large, rusty flatbed truck and a flat-tired pickup truck whose license sticker was last renewed in 1988.

Now head downhill on the road, which passes all kinds of rusting compressors, engines, and other machinery. Adjoining a large flat area to the left of the road, you see what must have been an opening to a mineshaft running into the hill. As the road winds downhill, you spy on the right an old Caterpillar bulldozer partially covered by dirt, indicating that it hasn't been moved in a heck of a long time. I wonder why such expensive machinery was just left to rust.

The road downhill is so thoroughly washed out that it would take a pretty good jeep to make it up to the ghost camp. In another ¼ mile you reach a second mine, also with plenty of junk scattered around. This one looks "modern" (like from perhaps 20 years ago), but it obviously hasn't been worked for many a year. The mine tunnel entrance is covered by a jail-style gate of iron bars. A short distance farther downhill, two narrow-gauge rail spurs lead off onto wooden structures overhanging the canyon.

Finally you leave the junk behind and arrive at the three-way intersection from which you took the middle road up to the ghost camp. Head back across the heavy-duty bridge spanning Howard Creek and then back to the trailhead.

Camping: None.

Winter Use: None, although the road to the trailhead, Forest Road 09, has little orange diamonds nailed to trees to guide snowmobilers.

C-8 Bear Wallow and Mohawk-Chapman Loop

Distance: 8-mile loop (Alternative Loop, 1½ miles)

Highest Point: 6,329 feet

Total Elevation Gain: 779 feet

Difficulty: Moderate

Hiking Season: May through November (best fall color is in mid-October)

Directions to the Trailhead: From Graeagle drive south on Highway 89 for 1.4 miles to the gold Lake Highway. Turn right, and go 1.2 miles to an unsigned paved road on the left (Mohawk-Chapman road, 22N98). Drive 4 miles on this narrow road full of chuckholes to a dirt road branching off to the right. There once was a sign nailed to a tree here, but whatever was written on it has disappeared. Take this road for about 50 yards to a wide level place for parking.

Comments: If you are looking for a hike with maximum fall color, this is it. In mid-October, the loop is alive with brilliant yellow trees and shrubs (mountain maple, cottonwood, bitter cherry, tobacco bush, and thimbleberry) as well as a few red and orange ones (dogwood and currant). True, it isn't as grand as a New England autumn, but it's pretty darn fine for California. If you want only a small sampling of this easy-to-get-to trail, then do only the 1½-mile Alternative Loop. Either loop is also a nice spring or early summer hike.

Autumn foliage on the Mohawk-Chapman Loop

The Hike: Begin by walking up this seldom traveled dirt road. It makes a wide, ¼-mile-long curve, nearing little Mohawk Creek. For the next ¼ mile, the route parallels pretty Bear Wallow, a bushy meadow straddling the creek. (I have yet to encounter a bear wallowing.) The road peters out, but don't turn around. Keep walking parallel to Bear Wallow and directly uphill for about 150 yards. The last 50 yards of this short trailless section climb steeply to a road, which you can identify from below by its flat profile through the trees.

Once you reach the road, you have to decide whether to do the 1½-mile or the 8-mile loop. For the shorty Alternative Loop, make a left turn on the dirt road. In a little more than ¼ mile it intersects the paved Mohawk-Chapman Road. Turn left at this junction, and walk back to the trailhead, ¼ mile away.

For the 8-mile loop, turn right on the dirt road. In a few steps you hear the gurgle of Mohawk Creek, and soon you cross it as it flows under the road in a culvert. This lightly used road continues steadily uphill, but at a moderate grade. In ½ mile it makes a hairpin turn, changing from a westerly to an easterly heading. During the next 2 miles, two dead-end roads (21N55Y and 21N56Y) branch off to the right. Then you reach the highest point of the loop, making the rest of the way either level or downhill.

A road junction with a sign "Hwy 89–9" pointing back the way you came also says "Chapman Saddle 7, Hwy 49–13" pointing the other way.

However, it isn't clear whether these point to the left or the right fork. Well, both lead to the saddle and Highway 49, so it really doesn't matter, but the left fork (21N91) is the choice for our loop.

After 2 miles of nice hiking on 21N91, you're back at the Mohawk-Chapman Road (22N98), which is unpaved for most of the way back to the trailhead (and might be used by a car or two a day). Turn left to walk it, and enjoy the views of Mohawk Valley to the north. When you are ¼ mile from the trailhead, 21N55Y (the Alternative Loop route) joins Mohawk-Chapman where the pavement begins again.

Camping: None.

Winter Use: Gold Lake Highway is usually plowed beyond the Mohawk-Chapman Road intersection. So, although snowmobilers can park their trailers at Mohawk-Chapman, they usually bypass it and drive farther to the snowmobile parking lot. Fortunately, this leaves its snowy surface smooth for snowshoeing and cross-country skiing. It is one of my favorite winter outing sites. I admit that I have yet to snowshoe or ski the 4 miles to the start of the 8-mile loop, complete the 8 miles, then return the 4 miles to the car. Nonetheless, even a shorter distance provides excellent winter views of Mills Peak and Mohawk Valley.

C-9 Frazier Creek Trail

Distance: I mile out and back (with the trailless extension,
    2 miles out and back)

Highest Point: 4,961 feet (with extension, 5,023 feet)

Total Elevation Gain: 191 feet (with extension, 223 feet)

Difflculty: Moderate

Hiking Season: May through November

Directions to the Trailhead: From Graeagle go south on Highway 89 for 1.4 miles to Gold Lake Highway. Turn right, and drive for another 1.4 miles to an unsigned, not very prominent road (it looks more like a driveway) on the left, just after crossing the bridge over Frazier Creek. Park on this stubby side road 30 yards after leaving the highway.

Comments: Why this very nice trail, close to Graeagle, does not show up on any map is a mystery to me. It is a perfect trail for a quick hike with the close company of frolicking Frazier Creek. The 1-mile extension after the main trail peters out includes lots of fun boulder hopping, by, over, and through the creek. In October, the creek is still flowing, albeit with less

gusto than in spring and early summer, while the display of colorful autumn leaves adds to the beauty of the hike.

The Hike: Walk up the dim road to a steel gate across it, which is posted with a sign "Mining Claim." This does not mean "No Trespassing," merely "Don't mine here"—as if you had any intention to do so. So, walk around the gate, and follow the unused road as it parallels Frazier Creek. Here, the creek has no willows hiding it from view, and throughout the hiking season it has sufficient flow to be delightful company for your hike. In about 300 yards, the old road ends at a campsite overlooking the stream. Walk through the camp and angle slightly left as the road fades and the trail begins. The path passes the ruins of an old cabin, crosses over a tiny bridge of timbers spanning a small, dry watercourse, and continues to parallel Frazier Creek.

Lower Frazier Creek in winter

The trail climbs above the stream for a short distance, and then hugs the hillside above it. Again approaching the level of the creek, the route drops into a boulder-strewn dry streambed, which it criss- crosses several times before ending right at the side of the water. This last section of trail is not well de- fined because it has so little dirt and so many small boulders.

If you don't wish to spend the next half-hour boulder hopping, this is your turnaround spot. However, I highly recommend that you extend the hike for another ½ mile. In spring and early summer when the creek is high, the challenge of finding the right hopping route is greater than later in the year when the rocks and boulders are more exposed above the reduced flow. Seldom have I encountered such a wonderful selection of rocks and boulders. In places, I enjoyed "hiking" down the middle of the stream, jumping from one rock to the next without much danger of falling in. If your balance is not too good, plenty of easy hopping is available alongside the stream.

I crossed the creek to the western side where the trail ended and, except for my unrequired excursions down the middle of the creek, stayed on that side. The turnaround point of the extension can be just about anywhere when you get tired of boulder hopping. The hopping gets harder after about ½ mile.

Camping: Other than the backpack campsite 300 yards from the trailhead, there are no nice sites. When my kids were small, I thought that a short overnight backpack trip would give them a good first experience of camping away from the car. This site would be a good introductory one. The level location has plenty of room for kids' games; proximity to the pretty creek, however, requires parents to keep an eye on their offspring to prevent a mishap.

Winter Use: I have walked the first portion of this hike in winter without snowshoes, in a year without much snow. In a heavy-snow year, it could be done on snowshoes. In midwinter, the flow of the creek is much less than in spring or early summer, but the sight of snow on the round boulders in and along the creek is pretty.

Chapter 9

Johnsville Topo

J-1 Eureka Peak Partial-Loop Trail

Distance: 3½-mile round trip from Trailhead A; 6-mile round trip from Trailhead B

Highest Point: 7,447 feet

Total Elevation Gain: 1,227 feet from Trailhead A; 1,977 feet from Trailhead B

Difficulty: Moderate

Hiking Season: June through October

Directions to the Trailhead: From Graeagle, head north on Highway 89 for .25 mile, and turn left at the Graeagle Frostee onto the Graeagle-Johnsville Road (County Road A-14). Continue for 6 miles through the town of Johnsville and around a sharp hairpin turn to the Plumas Ski-Bowl parking lot, Trailhead A. If you don't like driving a non-paved road, you may wish to start the hike here. A rough 1.3-mile dirt road exits from the southeastern corner of the parking lot, curves uphill under the ski lifts, and ends at Eureka Lake Dam. I have driven this road, slowly, in a two-wheel-drive car, so it is doable, albeit not in your Ferrari Testarossa. However, the road is quite rocky, steep, and narrow (a single lane most of the way, requiring some expert maneuvering if you meet a vehicle coming the other way), so I leave the choice of trailheads to you. If you drive up to Trailhead B at the lake, you'll find plenty of parking at the end of the road.

Comments: If you have never attained the summit of a peak because the final climb is always too steep, "cliffy," or scary, then this is the hike on which you can reach your first summit. Almost everyone can make it to the 7,447-foot top of Eureka Peak South. If you decide not to climb to the top of Eureka Peak North, you will still love the view from just below the summit. On your way back, the western part of the loop includes one of the easiest-to-walk-on trails I have ever encountered due to its soft pine needle covering.

This trail is entirely within the boundaries of Plumas-Eureka State Park. No fee is required, but you need to follow the rules of the park. These include: no firearms, no dogs beyond the control of the owner, no picking wildflowers, and no feeding wildlife. (The latter three are actually no-noes for any trail in this book, right?)

The Hike: When viewed from Johnsville or Graeagle, Eureka Peak looks like it has two peaks separated by a ¼-mile ridge. The topo map calls the slightly higher southern one Eureka Peak, and attaches no name at all to the northern one. However, in this book, I have decided to call one Eureka Peak North and the other Eureka Peak South, to make the descriptions clearer. This hike allows you to climb to the top of both summits and experience their spectacular views.

If you parked at the ski-bowl parking lot, take the dirt road up the hill and under the ski lift cables. In 1¼ miles you come upon Eureka Lake and Trailhead B (you'll also find a pretty good flushless outhouse). The trail goes across the broad top of the dam (as unscary a dam as you will ever cross). At the western end of the dam, the trail makes a sharp left, dipping down into the overflow channel of the dam, and then continues uphill. In about 200 yards, you come to a trail intersection where the sign says merely "Trail," and an arrow points uphill directly in front of you; that's the way to go. (The sign does not say where the trail to the left goes, but it is the start of the around-the-lake loop described in Hike J-10.) Your well-maintained path climbs steeply and soon becomes rather rocky. Approximately ½ mile after leaving the dam, you encounter a fork with another sign saying "Trail" pointing to the left branch. This is the start of your loop, and you can actually take either fork. I usually take the left, only because that is the way the sign points and I like to follow directions. The topo map does not show this trail to the north peak, because the newest version is dated 1972 and the trail was built sometime later. In a few hundred yards, you encounter a 1942 surveyor's benchmark. Continue uphill, eventually passing to the west of the summit of Eureka Peak North. As the trail curls left below the summit, you have a wonderful overlook of Johnsville, Graeagle, and Mohawk Valley.

The climb to the summit of Eureka Peak North is not too difficult, but people not fond of cliffs, loose rock, and high places may wish to forgo it and wait for the much easier climb up Eureka Peak South. To climb the 7,286-foot north peak, retrace your steps 100 yards to find the easily identified beaten path to the top. If, instead, you start up from the view spot, you have to clamber over a false summit before attacking the actual summit.

On the peak, you are standing over 65 miles of gold mine tunnels that are part of the famous Plumas-Eureka Mine, which was the highest producer in the area. Appendix B relates the marvelous history of the mine and its surroundings. To continue the loop, return to the overlook spot, where you encounter a trail fork with no sign. Take the left branch, which looks like an extension of the trail on which you came up. At this point, the topo map commences showing the trail.

The next ½ mile to the south peak is a delight. It is fairly level, smooth, and endowed with great views to the east. Rarely will you find such an easy traverse between two peaks. Before you know it, the south peak appears, and you almost walk past it without realizing it is the summit, because it looks so "unpeaklike." Most people who do not like high places can accomplish this easy ascent via a dim signless trail that cuts north off the main trail through some bushes. The summit is less than 100 yards away, and, once on top, you find a flat area about the size of a walk-in closet on which to stand. People with vertigo can enjoy this mountaintop without feeling queasy. The fine view northwest includes 10,475-foot Mount Lassen in the distance, if the day is clear.

The trail continues around to the south of the summit. Be sure to stop and look southerly to take in the spectacular view of nearby Mount Washington and the more distant spires of Sierra Buttes. A few hundred yards after you begin descending from the summit, you'll be surprised as the trail becomes

Eureka Lake from Eureka Peak North

a smooth dirt road (you may well mumble about all this climbing on foot only to find out that nonhikers can drive almost to the top). The road crosses a level meadow carpeted with lupine and blue-eyed Mary; by August, the beautiful bloom they exhibit in late spring and early summer is over. At the western edge of the meadow, about ¼ mile from the summit of the south peak, you see the backs of some signs. Every hiker in the world will naturally bypass the closer sign saying "Trail," pointing to the right (which is the one you eventually want to take), and walk a few more steps along the road to see what is painted on the other side of the signs. (I am not telling; you just have to go see for yourself.) If you continued along this road you would wind up on the southern part of Eureka Ridge Road and on the route of Hike J-9. However, that is for another day, so backtrack up the road a few steps, and take the trail marked "Trail."

In about ¼ mile, you cross a burned area. Several large pines have been cut down, evidently by firefighters because no logging has been done in the area. Obviously, quick action prevented a much larger burn, because the blackened area is relatively small. (At this point I silently gave a word of thanks to firefighters everywhere who prevent forest fires from being worse disasters than they are.) The trail here, which is used less than the trail on which you came up, is covered with a generous soft layer of pine needles. This, coupled with wonderful views to the west, makes you feel like you could easily walk 25 miles a day if all trails were like this. Before you know it, you are back at the intersection where you began the loop up to Eureka Peak North. You simply skip along the final downhill ½ mile back to Eureka Lake (and the 1¼ miles of rough road back to the ski-bowl parking lot if you started from Trailhead A).

If you still have energy and time, you can do the quick swing around Eureka Lake (Hike J-10), a flat and scenic 1½-mile loop.

Camping: No camping is allowed in this part of the state park.

Winter Use: This trail is excellent for snowshoeing because the main road is usually plowed to the ski-bowl parking lot. A snowshoe trip is best planned for Monday through Thursday, because the ski-bowl is closed those days and your route traverses the ski runs. The entire loop makes for a lot of snowshoeing. If you make it only to Eureka Lake, however, you will still enjoy the view across the lake with snow-covered Eureka Peak North serving as a magnificent backdrop. The ski slope itself is too steep for my cross-country skiing ability. There are rumors that new cross-country ski trails are being planned near the ski-bowl, so they may be completed by the time you read this. I have also enjoyed snowshoeing and skiing many times along the route of the road that leads off from the hairpin turn just before you reach the ski-bowl parking lot.

J-2 Loop from Knickrem Mill around Big Hill

Distance: 6-mile loop (with the cutoff back, 5½ miles)

Highest Point: 5,650 feet

Total Elevation Gain: 690 feet

Difficulty: Moderate

Hiking Season: June through October (best before late summer)

Directions to the Trailhead: From Graeagle drive north on Highway 89 for 1 mile to Highway 70, and turn left. In 8 miles, at a sign "To Sloat," go left. After descending the hill, 2.1 miles from Highway 70 you find the Sloat Mill, which no longer operates as a sawmill. Turn right over the Union Pacific Railroad tracks, and cross the bridge over the Middle Fork of the Feather River (note your odometer reading here). At the far end of the bridge, turn right, and follow the good road (23N08), now gravel instead of pavement, toward Poplar Valley. Drive for 7 miles, passing through Poplar Valley and along Poplar Creek, which you cross several times. Check your odometer for 7.0 miles from the Feather River bridge, because the next intersection, where you need to go straight rather than taking the right fork, is unsigned. If you miss it, however, you'll know it: within 50 yards another intersection pops up as you cross an intermittent creek, with 23N08 going left and another unsigned road going right. Go back and find the unsigned fork you missed. After making the proper turn off 23N08, park immediately along the side of the road, just before reaching another intersection, where 23N36 goes to the left.

Comments: Perhaps, after doing this hike, you'll say, "Big Hill ain't no thrill." I agree, but the hike does have a few attributes that make it worthwhile. The views from the trail along the western slope of Big Hill are excellent. The experience of walking through two pine tree plantations, one old and not cared for, the other newer and well cared for, is interesting. I'll admit, the dusty road for the final third of the hike is less than wonderful, but, what the heck, cleaning off dust is easy. I also describe a shortcut back to the car that keeps you off the dusty last third of the big loop, if you so desire.

This whole loop is on roads seldom traveled or not traveled at all. The part of this route on the forest service road through the newer pine plantation is obviously through land owned or leased by the grower. Please stay on the road, and do not leave any trash on the property. Before beginning the hike you might be tempted to walk back "around the corner" to check out the site of Knickrem Mill, which is prominently shown on the topo map. I had expected to discover old foundations, the remains

of a millpond, and indications of a rail spur for a train to haul logs to the mill. I found nothing. I searched around the area, thinking perhaps the topo map was inaccurate about the actual location of the site—still nothing. Because little has been written about the history of old sawmills, I was unable to learn anything about this once-upon-a-time mill. Dozens of sawmills operated 100 to 150 years ago in the area covered by this book. Today, not one remains, and cut logs are hauled to the nearest mill in Quincy or Loyalton.

The Hike: From your car, walk the short distance to Road 23N36 (a typical brown USFS signpost tells you its number), and take the left fork. (You'll return on the right fork if you do the big loop. If you take the shortcut, you'll return on the same portion of 23N36 you started on.) Another sign says "Big Hill 2" in the proper direction and "Poplar Valley 4" back along the road on which you just drove in. In ½ mile, a road branches left with a sign "Dead End 1," so, obviously, pass by. From this point, the track levels, and then begins a gradual uphill to a saddle 1¼ miles from the trailhead. Here a jeep trail (23N35) continues straight, while you make a sharp right turn, staying on 23N36. In 50 yards, you encounter another intersection. To loop around Big Hill, turn left on what is still 23N36, identified by the brown USFS signpost.

This never-used road starts to climb Big Hill at a pleasant, gradual slope. The views to your left are outstanding; because trees are sparse, the vistas are mostly open. Below you, the canyon of Poplar Creek runs north and south. Behind it looms massive Eureka Ridge, whose 6-mile length has elevations as high as 6,957 feet, about 2,500 feet above Poplar Creek. At the south end of the ridge, Eureka Peak at 7,447 feet and Mount Washington at 7,369 feet are visible from this part of the trail. Along both sides of the trail grow dense greenleaf manzanita bushes with red bark and bitter cherry shrubs with white blossoms in spring and red-orange berries in late summer and fall (it is part of the rose family and has no relation to a cherry tree). The bitter cherry berry is, indeed, bitter if you bite into one. However, old Mr. or Ms. Bear doesn't seem to mind; some bear poop on the trail was evidence that he or she had been devouring the berries. Because no cars and few hikers use this road, tracks are easily seen in places, and, sure enough, bear paw prints were prominent. As I've said elsewhere, I've seen only one bear in all my hiking around the Feather River country, and the Big Hill loop was not where I saw it.

The trail levels and bends to the right around the western side of Big Hill, leaving behind your views of Eureka Ridge but allowing fleeting glimpses through the trees, ahead, of the Middle Fork of the Feather River Canyon with Mount Jackson, at 6,583 feet, behind. Suddenly, a dense forest of only Jeffrey pines closes in on the trail. The trees are all about the same size, with 12- to 16-inch-diameter trunks. The sensation of walking through this dense forest of similar-size trees, which crowd the road on both sides, is almost like walking through a tunnel. I noted a knocked-over signpost with a rusting yellow sign saying "Boundary—Planted Area N.E.—Corner No. 7," so obviously this was part of an old tree farm. A family of northern flickers swooped away with haste down the "tunnel."

As I turned a corner, a loud shrill shriek greeted me, and then another and another. Unfortunately, because of the denseness of the forest, I couldn't see the bird as it flew away above the trees still shrieking. However, several years ago I'd seen a bald eagle soaring near the Sloat Mill, less than 2 miles (as the eagle flies) from where I was now on Big Hill. My bird book describes the eagle's call as "a repeated piercing scream," hence I'm quite sure that what I heard, but couldn't see, was an eagle. The denseness of the forest also prevents getting a view of the top of Big Hill as the trail passes just south of the 5,693-foot summit.

On the right, as the forest becomes less dense, an old battered USFS sign pops into view. It says, "Big Hill Plantation—This area is part of the Nelson Creek burn caused by a careless camper in 1934. This National Forest was cleared of brush and planted with Jeffrey Pine seedlings. Reforestation will provide trees for lumber, improve wildlife habitat, reduce fire hazard and improve recreation for the future." I question whether it will reduce fire, because of the density of the forest, and I had to smile at the "future recreation" statement, because this area is seldom visited and I'm sure this hike won't be among the most popular in this book.

Later, I asked a forester why the trees in the plantation were all only about 20 feet high and 12 to 16 inches in diameter after approximately 60 years of growth (the sign said the fire was in 1934, and I assume the area was replanted soon thereafter). Mature Jeffreys in other parts of the Feather River country are two or three times this size. His reply was that this plantation was planted in the "early days" of forest conservation practices when little knowledge was available about how to grow trees effectively in a plantation. The seedlings were planted too close together, and no thinning had ever been done, hence each tree had to compete with its neighbors for light and nutrition. This resulted in the whole shebang being weak and stunted.

A short distance farther, the road was very effectively blocked by a huge pile of stumps and rotting tree trunks. I easily circumvented it on foot, and I had to appreciate whoever created the pile, because it left the road for hikers and kept out vehicles whose passage would have made the track dusty and rutted. Just beyond the pile a high dirt berm had been constructed across the road, and I began to wonder if some old Frenchman was attempting to keep out German panzer tanks. After these roadblocks, a road cuts off to the right. Here you need to make a decision. The road to the right loops around the south side of Big Hill, and intersects at the saddle with the road you were on previously. Take this "shortcut" back to the saddle, and then turn left on 23N36 if you want a quicker, less dusty return to your car.

My curiosity about what lay ahead in the bigger loop prompted me to continue on the road I was on, which had a 23N36 sign. I found two other broken and conflicting signs at this intersection, one calling this Poplar Valley Road with arrows in both directions. Who knows? Soon 23N36 grew dusty and was obviously used by vehicles. Another tree farm appeared on both sides of the road, this time with pines 15 to 20 feet tall and 8 to 10 inches in diameter. They were spread out, so that each tree had "elbow room." A dense manzanita growth underneath the trees had been chopped out, as had some smaller pines. I marveled at the amount of work needed to chop down the manzanita and other low growth in this extensive newer plantation. The forester I had spoken to explained to me that this treatment was the modern way of growing mature trees, giving them light and air and removing "competition." Their growth would be "twice as rapid" as in a forest not cared for, hence the expense of good forest management systems would be worth it. The pines that had been cut along with the manzanita were the weaker ones, explained the forester (I guess a pro can tell a weak pine from a strong one), and only the fittest were left to survive—until harvest time, that is. These two contrasting plantations vividly demonstrate how far we've come in the past 60 years in knowing how to grow one of our nation's most important products—trees.

The downside of the remainder of the hike on 23N36 back to the car is the dust on the road. True, dust doesn't hurt. My legs, feet, and socks needed only a good washing, and my boots, a good beating against one another. Nonetheless, there's something unpleasant about tromping through ½-inch-thick dust on a road, even if the road is used only a couple of times a day. At least you aren't swallowing dust clouds from passing cars, and you arrive back at your car with a clean—well, sort of clean—face.

Camping: There are no sources of water on this trail so camping is not appealing.

Winter Use: None. Access to the trailhead is not plowed in winter.

J-3 Madora Lake Loop

Distance: 1½-mile loop

Highest Point: 5,030 feet

Total Elevation Gain: 45 feet

Difficulty: Easy

Hiking Season: May through November (wildflowers are best in early summer to midsummer)

Directions to the Trailhead: From Graeagle take Highway 89 north for .25 mile to the intersection with the Graeagle-Johnsville Road (County Road A-14). Turn left at the Graeagle Frostee, and drive for 2.2 miles to a turnoff on the right with a sign saying "Madora Lake—Gate Open 8:00 AM to Sunset." About 100 yards from the turnoff is a large paved parking lot.

Comments: Madora Lake and its loop trail are located in the northernmost portion of Plumas-Eureka State Park. If you want an easy hike for an hour or so with views of a nice lake, this one should a thick forest of cedar, Douglas-fir, and ponderosa pine. About 200 yards from the trailhead, the path meets what might be mistaken for a small creek but actually is a constructed ditch, identified on the sign at the trailhead as Lundy Ditch, making it the one and only ditch I've encountered with a name. The trail goes along the ditch for another 200 yards, reaching a Y. A "Trail" sign points left to a small foot-bridge over the gurgling ditch. Actually, this is the start of the loop around the lake, so you can, if you wish, go right (counterclockwise around the lake) instead. You'll wind up back at this spot either way. For no reason other than habit, I have always obeyed the sign and taken the clockwise route on my initial loop of the lake.

fill the bill. The diminutive lake lacks a spectacular mountain backdrop, however, so it does not have the breathtaking beauty of many other Feather River country lakes.

The Hike: At the trailhead are a sign with a map of the lake and its loop trail, a picnic table, and a sturdy one-hole outhouse (clean but not odorless). The well-maintained trail immediately ducks into

For the first 200 yards of the loop, the lake is out of sight. It appears as the trail swings nearer the shore. Here a fine stand of cattails at the edge of the water enhances the lake view. When you're ½ mile from the Y, the trail reaches the north shore of the lake and its outlet creek, which flows through a culvert under the trail. At this point, another trail cuts left away from the loop. If you wish to extend your

Madora Lake in winter just before freezing over

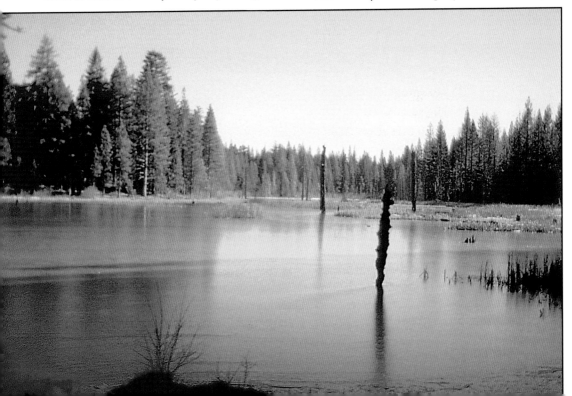

hike a bit, you can take this side trail. It leads to a T junction in about 50 yards, where you can go left to follow the route of an old wagon road (this is Hike J-14). Or you can take a prettier side trip by going right at the T. Here, the old wagon road parallels the eastern rim of Jamison Creek Canyon, 320 feet above the creek. You reach an open gate with a sign announcing the state park boundary. A level stroll of ½ mile from the T along the rim is worthwhile, but thereafter the route (Hike J-14) cuts easterly away from the canyon and drops rapidly downhill.

If you're sticking to the lake loop, start around the northern end of the lake, skirting a picnic table (a delightful spot for lunch beside the lake) and coming to another Y after 30 yards. The right fork is the lake loop route, which closely follows the eastern shore. A ½-mile stroll returns you to the start of the loop, and a left turn leads back to the car along Lundy Ditch. If I have the time, however, I often repeat the mile-long loop in the counterclockwise direction. It's amazing how different a trail seems going the opposite way.

Camping: None along the trail or at the lake. Plumas-Eureka State Park Campground, which is very nice for car or RV camping, is only 2½ miles away near Johnsville, 1 mile south of the park museum parking lot on the Johnsville-La Porte Road.

Winter Use: Snowshoeing the lake loop is delightful when the snow pack is sufficient. The trail is too narrow and twisty for cross-country skiing. The Graeagle-Johnsville Road is open all winter, although the driveway into the Madora Lake parking lot isn't plowed. Unless it is snowing (or has snowed recently so that a snowplow needs to scrape the roadside), parking is OK on the edge of the pavement.

J-4 Lower Jamison Creek Canyon Rim-to-Rim Trail

Distance: 6 miles out and back

Highest Point: 4,900 feet

Total Elevation Gain: 705 feet

Difficulty: Moderate

Hiking Season: April through October

Directions to the Trailhead: From Graeagle drive north on Highway 89 for .25 mile, then go left at the Graeagle Frostee onto the Graeagle-Johnsville Road (County Road A-14). Travel 1.7 miles on A-14 to a right turn into Plumas Pines Estates on Poplar Valley Road. Continue straight past Plumas Pines Country Club and Golf Course, after which the road makes a left turn and becomes gravel instead of pavement (23N37). From the clubhouse, the distance is 1.4 miles to the trailhead, where two dirt roads fork off to the right. There is plenty of parking off the road at this intersection.

Comments: The views of Lower Jamison Creek Canyon from both its eastern and its western rims are exquisite. A portion of the hike is on the good gravel road (23N37) that runs from Plumas Pines Estates to the summer cabin complex on Eureka Creek, so you might encounter a bit of light traffic. For this reason, I suggest doing this hike midweek (and not during a holiday week) when fewer vehicles will be traveling. The road is not very dusty, and any cars passing by will not be tearing along because the bumps and curves won't permit speed. The route crosses both Jamison and Eureka Creeks.

The Hike: From the trailhead, two roads fork

off 23N37. Take the right fork. Before striking out, notice the grade of an old railroad track, clearly evidenced by a flat-topped berm, between the left fork and 23N37. The ties and rails were torn up many years ago and sold for scrap, so only the level rail bed remains. Undoubtedly this was a logging spur used to haul logs out of the forest in the days before logging trucks were invented. It dead-ends in less than ¼ mile.

The right fork road is actually a very rutted jeep trail that gets little traffic, because it has no outlet. When you are ¾ mile from 23N37, the route abruptly ends in a small loop as it reaches the eastern rim of Lower Jamison Creek Canyon. The almost sheer drop to the creek 600 feet below is quite a sight. Down canyon, beyond the intersecting Feather River Middle Fork Canyon, Mount Jackson dominates the skyline.

Below, on the steep canyon side, are several interesting volcanic plugs, which look like giant thumbs pointing up. Each of these was formed

when lava came to the surface through a small vent not large enough to create a volcano. The lava solidified in the vent, and, over many years, the softer rock around it eroded away, leaving a column of lava exposed. You might wish to stroll for 100 yards or so along the rim to get some different views, although there is no beaten trail.

Return to 23N37 by the same rutted jeep trail, and, upon reaching it (and your car), turn right, and walk down the gradual hill for ½ mile to the bridge over Jamison Creek. Beyond the bridge is an old cabin (with a two-car carport, yet) and, beyond the cabin, a gravel pit. However, stay on the road as it heads uphill to the right of the cabin. You pass another, cuter cabin on the left as the road crosses Eureka Creek on a small bridge. Looking upstream from the bridge you can see Bear Creek, on the right, flowing into Eureka Creek.

When you've gone ½ mile beyond the Eureka Creek bridge, just past a road on your left that heads directly into a T, watch for a dim road branching off to the right that immediately curves farther right and then sharply left. Take this nice pine-needle-covered track; it has no traffic and, in ½ mile, ends at a promontory on the west rim of Jamison Creek Canyon. Along the rim are numerous excellent view spots looking across the canyon to where you were standing an hour or so ago. Mount Jackson and, farther east, Penman Peak (with its large, not very peaky, flat top) form a backdrop to the canyon below. The path narrows as it approaches the end of a peninsula that juts out between Jamison Creek Canyon and, on your left, the canyon through which Squirrel Creek runs. The two canyons join 500 feet directly below where you are standing at the end of the peninsula. Wow! This is a dandy lunch spot, and it certainly is worth a few photographs.

The only way back is the way you came, unless you brought your hang glider along.

Camping: I doubt if backpackers will care to do this trip, but there is a nice campsite on the west side of Eureka Creek, downstream from the bridge. Like so many unmaintained USFS campsites that are accessible by car, this one is, unfortunately, decorated with the most common name decorating such backcountry sites—Budweiser.

Winter Use: For cross-country skiing, 23N37 beyond the Plumas Pines Country Club is OK if there is enough snow cover, although snowmobiles may have roughed up the surface. With snowshoes you can make it to the east rim and, with a lot more effort, across to the west rim. One mild winter I was able to walk the entire route in December without snowshoes, and a couple of cars that passed me on icy 23N37 even had on snow tires or chains.

J-5 Mammoth Mill, Mammoth Mine, and Eureka Mills Ghost Town Trail

Distance: Alternative A, 2 miles out and back;

Alternative B, 4 miles out and back

Highest Point: Alternative A, 5,710 feet; Alternative B, 6,010 feet

Total Elevation Gain: Alternative A, 230 feet; Alternative B, 630 feet

Difficulty: Alternative A, easy/moderate; Alternative B, moderate/strenuous

Hiking Season: May through October

Directions to the Trailhead: Follow the directions for Hike J-1 to the ski-bowl parking lot.

Comments: Alternative A follows a well-cleared path to the Mammoth Mill ruins. Alternative B takes in the mill ruins as well as a hike up the old road, now overgrown with bushes, to the Eureka Mills ghost-town site and the Mammoth Mine site. A visit to the latter entails climbing up the edge of piles of tailings to mine tunnel entrances at two different levels. On the way to the mine site, the route passes through "downtown" and "suburban" Eureka Mills. You can see and inspect many old cabin sites along the road, littered with lots of discarded stuff, from old coffee pots, pails, and tin cans to broken china, pottery, and glass bottles. This entire hike is within the boundaries of Plumas-Eureka State Park, so no artifacts may be removed—look, but please leave everything where you found it.

Because the road patterns of the ghost town have become overgrown, finding your way in and out of the town isn't easy. Novice hikers who become uncomfortable when there isn't a clearly defined route should do Alternative A only. If you do Alternative B, I suggest wearing tough long pants to prevent your legs from becoming scratched by the bushes—they almost seem to reach out to damage bare legs. Before doing this hike, you might enjoy reading the history of the Plumas-Eureka Mine and Johnsville in Appendix B. You may see some trail signs along the way with different trail names. These are to identify ski trails in winter and are not applicable to this hike.

The Hike: Two dirt roads leave the southern end of the ski-bowl parking lot. Take the one on the left, which has a sign "Eureka Lake 1.3 mi." Hike around the first bend to the right, and, at the second bend right, 200 yards from your car, take a cleared dirt path branching left to a locked gate with a sign "Road Closed" (closed for cars but not for hikers). Beyond the gate, the road widens where state park people have cleared a swath of brush from the sides of the old road. In ¼ mile, you come to a wooden water tank used by Johnsville for its water supply.

I find it interesting to note how much the trees and bushes have grown in the ensuing 30 years. In those days, we walked right into the ghost "town"; today, you have to beat your way in through trees and brush for Alternative B. In the state park museum, photos from 100 years ago show that the entire hillside on which the town was built was treeless, because all the trees had been cut to provide lumber for cabins, railroad ties, and beams for tunnels in the mine. Today, the same area is solid forest with massive trees. Thank goodness 100

Remains of the explosives storage cave entrance near the Eureka Mills ghost town

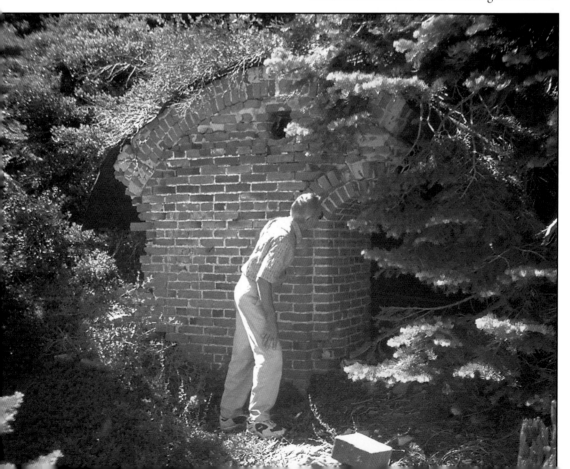

years have repaired the human devastation.

But I'm getting ahead of the hike. Soon after passing the water tank, the road forks. Go right, and follow the route recently cleared by the state park workers. Along this part of the route, check out some old cabin sites to the right identified by flat spots on the hillside.

At the next Y take the left branch to where the cleared path ends, and a huge square wooden beam can be seen on the right. Angle slightly to the right, and follow the trail for 50 yards to the Mammoth Mill site. This was a stamp mill, where gold ore was crushed prior to extracting the gold. The Mammoth Mill was built in two phases. The first phase was constructed in 1872 and included 40 stamps, costing between $111,500 and $130,000 (a huge sum in those days). This structure replaced an old mill at Eureka Lake that had collapsed. The location of Mammoth Mill was better than that of the mill at the lake because it was nearer the Upper and Lower Mammoth Tunnels, and it could be operated through some of the winter months. Later, another eight stamps were added. In conjunction with the mill, the owner of the mine constructed a new town on the hillside near the mill and named it Eureka Mills. It is now the ghost town you'll visit if you do Alternative B.

The mill was run by water power via a flume from Eureka Lake, although a steam-powered engine was installed and used when the lake ran dry in the late summer and all during the fall. Ore car tracks were laid from the mine to the mill. In April 1873, the new mill began operating. William Johns had just taken over as mine and mill manager. He created another whole new town farther down the hill, which bears his name, Johnsville (see Hike J-12). Johns's ambitious plans called for a second massive stamp mill farther downhill, called the Mohawk Mill. It still stands in partially restored condition uphill from the state park museum. The ruins of the Mammoth Mill include massive rock walls, some

huge anchor bolts, and a few machinery parts.

If you're doing only Alternative A, return to the trailhead by the same route you came in on. If you wish to do Alternative B, or at least part of it, return to the fork in the road just before reaching the water tank, and take the other branch. Although bushes and trees now encroach upon the trail, you can easily follow the route.

A trail intersects on the left, zigzagging down the hill to Johnsville, but you continue straight. A bit farther, several other obvious old roads intersect on the right, the first of which leads to a bunch of old cabin sites not far off the track. I cannot describe where each portion of Eureka Mills was located—you'll just have to explore. Most of the building sites were near the route you're on and can be identified by flat spots on the hillside, old rock walls, and rusting tin cans and other items discarded long ago. Naturally, in 100 years, the wooden structures have collapsed and rotted away. Some brick buildings were more durable, and their remains can be identified by a jumbled scattering of bricks.

After ½ mile, the old road ends at the bottom of a large pile of tailings. Circle to the right around the bottom of the tailings, and clamber up the hill to the next level, where you'll find another overgrown road. Go left on this road, and, if you've hit the right level, you soon stumble upon a flat spot at the top of the tailings pile with lots of unidentifiable steel machinery parts scattered about. The highlight of this spot is the still partly standing brick explosives cave built into the hillside. The dynamite used in the mine stayed cool and safe in this location.

Just south of the explosive cave in a clump of bushes is one of the main mineshaft entrances. The heavy supporting timbers have given out, and it is not possible to enter (as if anyone would be foolish enough to do so if they could). You'll see nice views of Mount Elwell from the edge of the tailings pile looking across the canyon of Jamison Creek.

If you want to explore more, and don't mind crashing through trees and bushes, the overgrown road heads south along the hillside. You come to another tailings pile, and a scramble up it puts you on a large flat area with huge boulders along the hillside. Another mine entrance was here, although cave-ins have obliterated it. A huge flywheel lies on the edge of the flat area. I wonder how in the world they managed to transport it up to this spot using only horse or mule power.

There are other mine entrances farther south, but the encroaching bushes have outdone themselves, and it would take a bulldozer to get through. So, turn around, and use your best judgment on how to return. If you don't follow the same route back (it's tough to retrace your steps exactly in this maze of trees and bushes) just head north along the hillside, dropping down to pick up the lower old road you were on earlier.

A few trails head north uphill but these lead to Eureka Lake and are clogged with tall dense bushes. If you come to a dead end, fall back and try a different route, always heading northerly along the hillside. It's fun to stumble across old cabin sites while negotiating your way back to the parking lot. Perhaps someday the state park will clip back the roads into Eureka Mills, as they have for the Mammoth Mill site, so that finding and exploring the ghost town will be easier.

Camping: There is no backpack camping; for car camping, the Plumas-Eureka State Park Campground, near Johnsville, 1 mile south of the park museum parking lot on the Johnsville-La Porte Road, cannot be beat.

Winter Use: My wife and I have snowshoed part of the Alternative A route. Why not all the way? Fresh large bear paw tracks in the snow made us think that some bear hadn't understood the notion of hibernating in winter. With other places nearby to snowshoe, we reasoned, why disturb a nonhibernating bear?

J-6 Mount Jackson Summit Cross-Country

Distance: 2½ miles out and back

Highest Point: 6,583 feet

Total Elevation Gain: 1,595 feet

Difficulty: Strenuous

Hiking Season: May through October (best before midsummer)

Directions to the Trailhead: From Graeagle drive north on Highway 89 for 1 mile to Highway 70, turn left, and continue for 6.3 miles to a turnoff to the right with a sign "Mt. Tomba Road." After exiting 70, immediately turn right. Go past the Jackson Creek Picnic Grounds and the closed campground. In .5 mile, just before crossing Jackson Creek, turn right on a dirt road with a sign "OHV61." Soon you see two large USFS signs on the right, one explaining that this is the "Layman Fir Plantation" (all the plantings I saw were ponderosa pines, not firs) and part of the "Penny Pines Project" (donors gave a penny for each new pine; "Dollar Pines Project" would be more realistic, although not as alliterative). The other sign advises that "In September 1989 a rotten tree broke off at ground level, fell into a power line and started a fire which destroyed 5,000 acres." The names of significant donors to the project are listed under the descriptions. After traveling 1.4 miles on well-graded OHV61, a crummier dirt road branches left, with a sign, partially hidden by a bush, saying it's USFS Road 23N49A. Park here, out of the way of traffic (of which there will be nil).

Comments: For the trailless climb to the top of Mount Jackson a hiker has to be in good shape and willing to tromp through brush, scramble up a long talus slope, and climb around boulders. No rope work or cliffs are involved, however. Avoid midday in the middle of summer, because the climb is shadeless, and wear long pants to prevent scratched legs. The tradeoff is that the top is always in view on the way up, so getting lost is not likely. Likewise, on the way down, you can easily determine the general locale where you left 23N49A. The view from the top is marvelous, so, if you're up to the challenge, give it a try.

The Hike: From the car, walk along 23N49A for ¼ mile to a point where the edge of the burned area commences and you see a tree to the right of the road with a yellow square. Here, turn right, and head uphill on a dim loggers' track. It takes you up the slope in the general direction of the ridge you want to follow to the top. Along this track, "penny pines" have been planted. They look healthy, but it will be many years before they grow to the size of the fine conifers that burned in the 1989 fire. As you gain altitude and gaze behind you, it is easy to understand how firefighters could not stop the progress of the fire before 5,000 acres had burned—the mountainside is just too rugged.

The ridge leading to the summit is obvious, and you want to stay along it, more or less. Bushes block your way every now and then, so, skirt them or tromp over and through them—whatever seems best. The route becomes steeper, and, as you look up at the 45° slope ahead, you think about how the coming climb will test your stamina. Many charred tree stumps are in evidence, but the brush that burned has all grown back afresh, so you won't get charcoal all over your clothes as you plow through the thickets.

About three-quarters of the way up, you encounter the talus slope. Loose talus rocks are apt to slip and slide as they are stepped on. However, to our pleasure, my hiking companion and I found that they weren't as slippy-slidey as we'd expected, so we progressed upward safely, albeit slowly and carefully. Once you negotiate the talus slope, you need to skirt a few boulders and plow through more brush

Now the top is close, so you pick up speed as the slope becomes more gradual and your expectation of arrival heightens. However, once on the summit, you gaze around and wonder where the heck the top really is, because all you can see is a flattish dome covered with manzanita in every direction. One prominent boulder peeks (or peaks) up above the manzanita, so wade through, and climb up to stand on the tip-top of Mount Jackson. Yes, I too had expected to find a sharp mountain peak (it looks like that, viewed from below). However, the views in every direction are terrific. Far below, Highway 70, the Union Pacific main line, and the Feather River can be seen winding through the canyon. Many neighboring mountain peaks are visible, and, on a clear day, snowcapped Mount Lassen is prominent on the skyline to the northwest.

To the east, the high ground behind Mount Jackson may make you wonder why this hike wasn't routed up the much easier "back way." Well, I suppose it could have been planned that way, but, darn it, the fun is in making it the tough way—not in doing an easy stroll up the back side.

Have fun going down. I had expected to slide and fall on my butt a bunch of times while descending the talus slope, but, to my amazement, adequate footing was fairly easy to find.

Camping: None.
Winter Use: None.

Trailless hiking on a talus slope below the summit of Mount Jackson looking down the Feather River Canyon

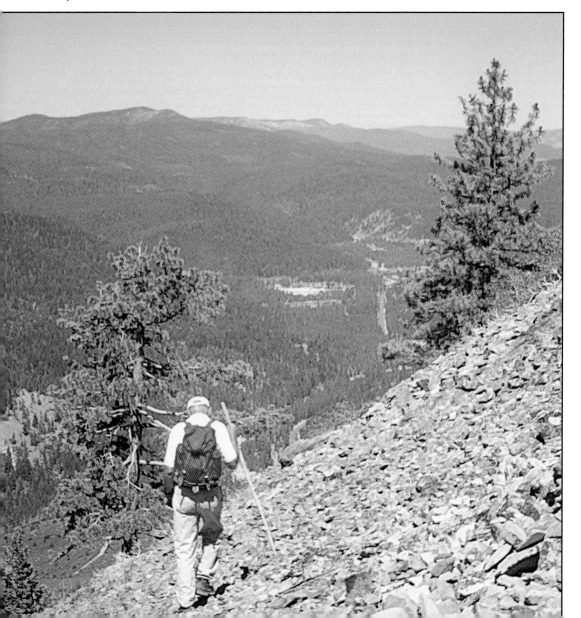

J-7 Gold Discovery Site Trail

Distance: 1 mile out and back from Trailhead A; 3½ miles out and back from Trailhead B

Highest Point: 6,406 feet

Total Elevation Gain: 209 feet from Trailhead A; 920 feet from Trailhead B

Difficulty: Easy/moderate from Trailhead A; moderate from Trailhead B

Hiking Season: June through October

Directions to the Trailhead: See Hike J-1.

Comments: This is one of the hikes Plumas-Eureka State Park volunteer guides lead several times each summer. It visits the site where gold was discovered on May 21, 1851, by two prospectors who were climbing up to the peak to make observations of the surrounding country. On their way up, by chance they came across a large quartz vein protruding from the rocky mountain slope, and, to their joy, the quartz contained a large sample of gold. This find set off a stampede of miners to the mountain, eventually resulting in four major mine companies (a mine company in those days was merely a group of miners who joined together to dig a mine, sharing ownership and profits, if any). To learn more about the fabulous mines on Eureka Peak (then called Gold Mountain), please read Appendix B.

The road from the ski-bowl parking lot (Trailhead B) to Trailhead A at Eureka Lake is poor and primarily suitable for four-wheel-drive vehicles, although I have seen conventional pickup trucks and even a Volvo two-wheel-drive station wagon parked at the lake. If your car is not suitable for maneuvering over big rocks in the road, park at the ski-bowl parking lot, and walk 1 ¼ miles up the road to the lake.

The Hike: The road to Eureka Lake leaves the ski-bowl parking lot at its far left corner. If you are walking to the lake, you need to stay on the rocky main road as it climbs the mountain, passing un-

der the ski lift cables. When you reach the lake, and Trailhead A, head left toward the little concrete-block outhouse. The old wagon trail starts there and gradually ascends the hillside above the eastern shore of the lake (Hike J-10, the lake loop trail, is nearer the lake and below the wagon trail). The path is all rocks, but they are so uniform and closely packed that you won't find walking on them too tough on your feet.

For much of the route you have nice views of

the lake, below, with Eureka Peak North jutting up sharply beyond the far side. Through the clear water, sawed-off tree stumps can be seen below the surface. How did the miners saw these trees below the water line? They didn't. The trees were cut before the level of the lake was raised by the dam built near the trailhead. The larger lake provided more water for turning the wheels that ran the ore-crushing stamp mills.

Where the trail reaches a point above the far end of the lake, look over the trail edge to see a level place near the lake that is strewn with rotting boards. These are the remains of the large boardinghouse where many of the miners stayed almost 150 years ago. After the lake view disappears, the wagon trail reaches the ridge crest, and you see evidence of an old building site on the left. Detour over to it, and enjoy the vista down into the Jamison Creek drainage basin. When you're back on the trail, it makes a right turn and heads directly for Eureka Peak North. An orangish streak of rock on the mountainside ahead is the discovery site you are seeking. You pass a partially buried ore car and, a few yards farther, can see another one down in the gully to the left of the trail. Here, turn right, and, at a Y a few yards beyond, go left uphill.

Now the discovery site is close at hand. A path starting at a gnarled old white pine tree leads up to it. You can easily make your way to the massive vein of white quartz that was undermined by prospectors long ago. It is even possible to climb down right to the crevice itself. Within the crevice, feel its cavelike coolness.

After exploring the vicinity, return to the lakeside by the same route.

On the day I first did this hike, lead by Walt, a state park volunteer guide, the other hikers included a mom and two kids. The enjoyment of visiting a historic site that set off a gold rush was summed up by eleven-year-old Alex, who said, "Wow, this has been the most fun hike I've ever been on." Perhaps you will agree.

Camping: None. Good car camping is available in the Plumas-Eureka State Park Campground near Johnsville, 1 mile south of the museum parking lot.

Winter Use: The road to the ski-bowl parking lot is plowed all winter. I have snowshoed up to Eureka Lake, and the rest of the route to the discovery site can easily be done on snowshoes. Avoid weekends when the ski hill is operating, because several ski runs intersect the road. The ski operations are closed Monday through Thursday.

J-8 Gray Eagle Creek Dam Trail

Distance: 3 miles out and back from Trailhead A; 4 miles out and back from Trailhead B; extension adds 2 to 4 miles

Highest Point: 5,150 feet

Total Elevation Gain: 605 feet from Trailhead A; 925 feet from Trailhead B

Difficulty: Easy/moderate from Trailhead A; moderate from Trailhead B

Hiking Season: May through November

Directions to the Trailhead: See Hike J-11.

Comments: This is an easy local hike on an almost-never-used dirt road. After the first ¼ mile beyond Trailhead A, the road is more like a trail, because overgrown bushes make it impassable for all but the most rugged four-wheel-drive vehicles whose owners do not mind having them scratched up. The turnaround point of the hike (unless you take the suggested hike extension) is at the petite diversion dam on Gray Eagle Creek. The dam is the water inlet for the penstock (conduit) pipe of the powerhouse. Just above the small pond behind the dam is a great place for a picnic.

The Hike: If you parked at Trailhead B, walk the bumpy road to Trailhead A. From Trailhead A, take the old road with the sign pointing to Gray Eagle Creek Trail. When you've gone ¼ mile from Trailhead A, an unused signless road intersects on the left. A quick side trip of 200 yards along this partially blocked side road leads you to the penstock pipe of the powerhouse. Walk to the edge of the canyon to see how the penstock makes a sharp downward bend and plunges almost straight downhill 360 feet to the powerhouse. Well, I suppose seeing a plunging penstock is not terribly exciting, but it is worth a five-minute detour. Retrace your steps to the old road, and continue south along it. The path narrows as bushes attempt to take over the road completely.

When you're 1 mile from Trailhead A, you come to a place where the Gray Eagle Creek Trail com-

mences to the right, and the old road heads left, downhill. Keep on the road, and soon the penstock reappears. In 200 yards, the tiny dam comes into view. When I say tiny, I mean really tiny, so please don't expect something elaborate or you'll be disappointed. Clamber up onto the dam, and note how it directs part of the flow of Gray Eagle Creek into the penstock.

My family's favorite picnic spot here is above the dam. To reach this spot, go back up the short stretch of road to where Gray Eagle Creek Trail cuts off. Take the trail left, and, in a few hundred yards, turn left onto a signless trail that drops back downhill to the creek. Even if it is not lunchtime, this is a delightfully tranquil spot for a rest.

Once you have climbed the short distance out of the ravine, the way back to your car is all downhill. Or, if you would like to extend your hike a bit farther, continue south along Gray Eagle Creek Trail for another mile or two. Although the trail parallels the creek, it is too far from the water for you to see it or even hear its babbling. Don't worry. The forest here is so beautiful that you'll enjoy plenty of nice scenery on this extension of the hike. Along the route of the extension, you'll encounter one side trail to the left that drops back down to the creek and the sturdy footbridge described in Hike GL-3. This five-minute detour down to the footbridge and back

is worthwhile to witness playful Gray Eagle Creek as it leaps and tumbles under the bridge. The turn-around spot for the extension hike is wherever you'd like it to be. Return on the same route to your car.

Camping: None.

Winter Use: Iroquois Trail is plowed all winter to the point where the pavement ends. Park where the plowing ends, and snowshoe the trail. The initial ½ mile is too steep for cross-country skiing, but you might be able to carry your skis until you're beyond where the Logging Spur Section 20 road cuts off and then ski the trail almost all the way to the dam. Most likely you will have the fun of breaking fresh trail for either skiing or snowshoeing this route.

Big-leafed woolly mule ears and lower-growing mountain pennyroyal on the trail to Gray Eagle dam

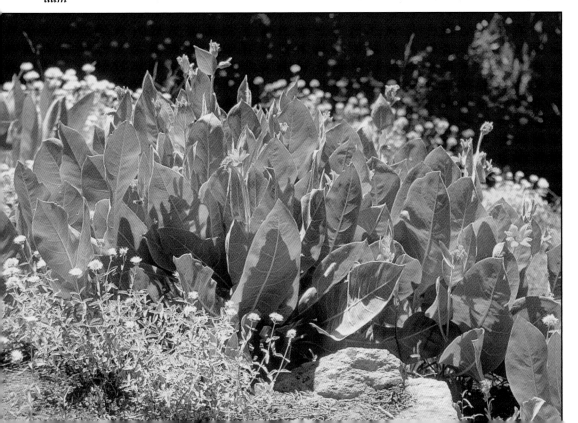

J-9 Eureka Peaks Back-Way Trail

Distance: 8 miles out and back

Highest Point: 7,447 feet

Total Elevation Gain: 1,073 feet

Difficulty: Moderate

Hiking Season: June through October

Directions to the Trailhead: You can take a long easy drive (47 minutes from Graeagle) or a shorter tougher drive. If you have a four-wheel-drive vehicle or a pickup truck, the shorter drive will be OK. Regular cars should take the longer route. For the longer drive, from Graeagle go north on Highway 89 for 1 mile to Highway 70. Turn left, and drive 9.1 miles to the Sloat turnoff to the left. Drive through Sloat, and, at the old Sloat Mill, turn right, bump over the railroad tracks, cross the bridge over the Feather River, and go left at the T just beyond the bridge. The road (23N08) now becomes well-graded gravel. Stay on the best-appearing road for 17.6 miles, bypassing several less-well-maintained roads branching off. Park at a four-way intersection with several signs pointing in various directions.

For the short route, follow the directions for Hike J-1, but, at the sharp hairpin turn, before you reach the ski-bowl parking, take the dirt road to the right. Continue on it, bypassing side roads to sum-

mer cabins, cross the bridge over Eureka Creek, and 1.9 miles from the hairpin take the left branch of a Y onto 23N37. At the next intersection, in .5 mile, bear left onto 23 N08. The next 2.5 miles to the trailhead are twisty-turny but on a nicely graded gravel surface.

Comments: Although most of the way to Eureka Peak South (called just Eureka Peak on the topo map) is via a seldom used dirt road, it is relatively smooth, isn't dusty, and is graced with many wild-flowers and various densities of forest. The climb up the south peak can be done by just about any-body, even those with vertigo, fear of heights, or an aversion to clambering up rocks. There is just enough room for four people on the very top, and there are no very steep cliffs. As good as the views are from the south peak, the views from Eureka Peak North (which the topo map does not even grace with a name) are even better. The north peak is a bit more difficult to climb, but, if you follow the route I describe, even if you have a fear of heights you might attain the summit. There is standing room for a bunch of people there, and the 360˚ views are awesome. (I know *awesome* may sound a bit trite, but I think when you get there you'll agree that's what it is.) Under Eureka Peaks are 65 miles of mine tunnels. Please read Appendix B to learn some of the history of the mines.

The Hike: From the trailhead, two of the four roads leave almost side-by-side in a southerly direction. Take the one on the left, which has a sign "Eureka Peak 2" (my calculations show it to be more like 3½ miles). Although you could navigate this road fairly easily in your car, why drive when you can walk? The seldom used road provides a lot of nice scenery and scads of wildflowers. In midsummer, mint-scented pennyroyal is the predominant species, and its aroma adds to your enjoyment of the hike.

When you are 2 miles from the trailhead, you encounter a Y in the road. A sign pointing left says "Eureka Peak 2" and "Don Meadow 2," and one pointing right says "Eureka Loop Spur." About ½ mile after taking the left, you reach another junc-

The trail just west of the summit of Eureka Peak South

tion, with the road ahead labeled 22N75Y. Turn left on the better road. Then, ½ mile later, the final road junction appears, with a sign pointing left to "Eureka Peak 1" (actually ½ mile) and right to "Don Meadow 1½." The road passes a great vista point on the left, overlooking the Deer Creek drainage basin. As you approach the south peak, the road traverses a dry meadow strewn with blue lupine and yellow mule ears early in the hiking season and with blue-eyed Mary (or, more correctly, Torrey's collinsia) later in the summer.

The road ends 300 yards from the south summit, but a trail continues, which passes to the right of the peak. There is no side trail for the 50-yard climb to the top, but you can spy where others have pushed their way through the brush and clambered up the boulders. On the crest you will be treated to a wide vista, from Mount Lassen in the far distance to the northwest all the way around to Sierra Buttes to the southeast. This is a dandy place for lunch.

Back on the trail, continue along it for the ½-

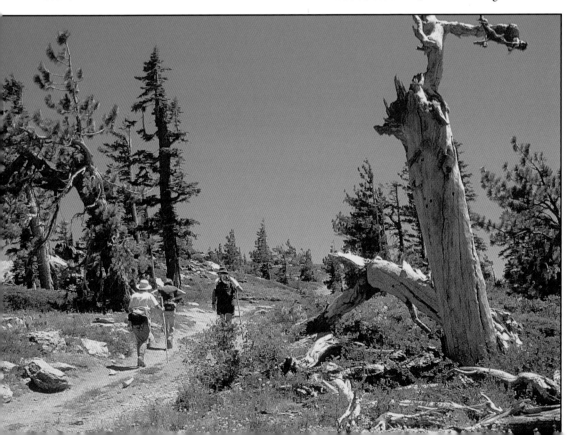

mile hike to the north peak, whose elevation of 7,286 feet is lower than the 7,447-foot south peak. Between the peaks the trail follows a ridge crest with nice views on both sides. The large amount of snow in this area crushes the poor little white firs, and most of them are twisted and bent into weird shapes. As you approach the north peak, peel off to the right for a good vista to the east and a nice stopping place for folks who don't want to make the climb to the summit.

To climb to the top, skip the path from here that heads toward the top. Instead, follow the main trail as it begins to wrap around the western side of the peak, and, in 100 yards, keep an eye out on your right for a beaten path up to the summit that avoids a climb over a false summit. The final 100 yards to the top are fairly easy for just about everybody to do. On the summit the view is 360°, and,

although some of the more distant peaks are not visible, the sight of Eureka Lake to the north and the roofs of Johnsville below to the east is terrific. You can pick out Graeagle, Sierra Valley, Portola, and Smith Peak, with its manned lookout tower, in the distance. An accommodating flat spot right on the crest allows viewing in all directions without vertigo. It also is a wonderful place for lunch. The north peak is the turnaround place for this hike. Although you won't have the fun of being surprised by the wonderful vistas you saw on the trip in, you'll still enjoy them a second time on the way out.

Camping: None.

Winter Use: When there is good snow cover, on the short route to the trailhead, starting at the hairpin near the ski-bowl, the road is excellent for snowshoeing, cross-country skiing, and even inner tube or saucer sliding for kids.

J-10 Loop around Eureka Lake

Distance: 1¼-mile loop from Trailhead A; 3¼-mile round trip from Trailhead B

Highest Point: 6,205 feet

Total Elevation Gain: 25 feet from Trailhead A; 790 feet from Trailhead B

Difficulty: Easy from Trailhead A; moderate from Trailhead B

Hiking Season: June through October

Directions to the Trailheads: See Hike J-1.

Comments: The drive from the ski-bowl parking lot (Trailhead B) to the parking lot at the lake (Trailhead A) isn't for everyone. The road is rough, with some rocks that may scrape the bottom of a low-slung car. However, I've seen normal cars at the parking lot at the lake; on my most recent visit, a two-wheel-drive Volvo station wagon and two Ford Windstar regular vans were there. The hike from the ski-bowl parking lot up to the lake is not especially pretty, and it's all on the same rutty road to the lake. The loop around the lake is pleasant and usually devoid of other people, because most visitors hang out

right at the dam and don't walk much.

Eureka Lake holds a prominent spot in the early mining history of the area. The original damless lake was a focal point for early processing of gold ore extracted from nearby Eureka and Mammoth Mines. Please read Appendix B for a history of the mines and the stamp mills for crushing gold ore that were built in 1855 and 1857 at Eureka Lake.

The Hike: For some unknown reason I always hike this loop counterclockwise, so that's the way I describe it here. From the eastern edge of the earthen dam, the trail traverses the top of the dam, which is so broad and has such a gradual slope that anyone with fear of heights need not be concerned about walking across. The water level of the lake is 20 feet below the top of the dam, and an outflow channel at the far end of the dam prevents the lake level from nearing the top. At the far end of the dam, the trail descends to this outflow channel, and then climbs, curving to the left. Almost immediately, you see a sign on your right with half the paint gone saying "Trail" and an arrow pointing straight ahead. This "trail" leads to the top of Eureka Peak (see Hike J-1). Take the left, and walk along a track that plunges into dense forest. The smooth path follows the western edge of the lake for about ¼ mile. Although the trail is always less than 100 yards from the shore, the thick tree cover between the trail and the lake blocks a view of the water. Along this stretch, a winter snow-gauging station, slightly off the trail, measures snow level and water content, enabling water engineers to determine the amount of water expected from the snowmelt.

As you approach the inlet creek to the lake (the creek dries up in summer), the trail fades due to erosion caused by heavy rains in January 1997 and the unusual "el niño" rain year of 1998. Even without 150 yards of defined trail, you should have no problem making your way, because the lake is nearby on your left and the upslope of the mountain commences less than 50 yards away on your right. Just stay on the level, and curve slightly to your left. Dead ahead, you'll see a very large boulder with a fallen tree lying on it. Go past this, but don't head down to the lakeshore quite yet. You pass another big boulder where people have obviously camped in years past. Continue on the level route another 100 yards, and you find yourself at the north shore of the lake. Here, a thick grove of new little pines separates you from the water's edge. Continue along the lake between the hillside, on your right, and the shore, on your left. Although this portion of the route has no definitive trail, none is necessary. From here until halfway around the lake, you can clearly see the lakeshore along which you need to walk to complete the loop back to the dam.

At this halfway point around the lake, you pass some tangled pieces of old mining equipment, reminders of the feverish mining activities that took place here so long ago. A bit farther, on a flat shelf 20 feet above the level of the lake are the flattened remains of the wooden bunkhouse that sheltered unmarried mine and mill workers (all male, naturally).

Beyond this point, as you can see, it was difficult to create a specific trail, due to the large number of small, smooth lakeside stones and the changing level of the lake as it recedes slightly during the summer. The view across the lake toward the dam is nice, and it gets even nicer the farther you go. As you reach the eastern shore, Eureka Peak North becomes a backdrop for the lake. (This mountain has two distinct peaks about ⅓ mile apart. The southerly one is a bit higher than the northerly one—7,447 feet versus 7,292 feet—and thus is named Eureka Peak. Although the northern one has a sharper, much prettier shape, and the view from it is much better, it has the ignominy of having no name. I call it Eureka Peak North and give the higher, but not as spectacular, summit the name Eureka Peak South.) The summit of Eureka Peak North is less than ½ mile, as the crow flies, from where you stand on the eastern shore of the lake, yet it towers 1,112 feet above the surface of the wa-

Eureka Peak North mirrored in Eureka Lake

ter. In the early morning, before the breeze stirs little ripples in the water, the mirror surface of the lake makes a perfect reflection of the peak. A photo opportunity this is, indeed.

As the route winds along the eastern lakeshore back to the car, you come to a talus slope with small rocks leading down to the water. Don't worry, because this stretch is easily navigated, although no definitive trail crosses it. Once you're past this section, more rocks on the lakeshore may make you grumble a bit that they're hard on the feet. They're smooth and rounded, though, and far easier to walk on than the sharp rocks you find on many mountain trails. At one point along the eastern shore, it looks like the path leads up a short but steep slope to a dirt road heading back to the parking area. It's OK to clamber up this slope and walk the road, particularly if your feet are objecting to walking on the rocks. However, I usually continue back along the

edge of the water for the short distance remaining. If, before you began this hike, you didn't check out the sturdy building that looks like an outhouse by the parking area, you may wish to do so. Yes, an outhouse it is. (I must confess I've never peeked inside to see how "accommodating" or clean it might be.) If you drove to the lake, your hike is over, but, if you walked up from Trailhead B, the remaining 1-mile hike back to the ski-bowl parking lot won't seem too bad. It's all downhill, and you'll have some attractive views of the forested Eureka Creek drainage basin and 6,583-foot Mount Jackson in the distance.

Camping: None. Car camping is available at the excellent Plumas-Eureka State Park Campground near Johnsville, 1 mile south of the museum parking lot on the Johnsville-La Porte Road.

Winter Use: See Hike J-1.

J-11 Logging Spur Section 20 to Smith Creek Trail

Distance: 2¾ miles out and back from Trailhead A; 3¾ miles out and back from Trailhead B; extension to Smith Creek Trail adds 2 miles

Highest Point: 4,960 feet

Total Elevation Gain: 120 feet from Trailhead A; 440 feet from Trailhead B

Difficulty: Easy from Trailhead A; moderate from Trailhead B

Hiking Season: April through November

Directions to the Trailhead: From "downtown" Graeagle on Highway 89, across from the Chevron station, take Iroquois Trail through the residential area. In .5 mile the pavement ends where Sioux Trail intersects on the right. (These "Trails" are paved or dirt streets, not trails.) Continue on Iroquois's good dirt road for .2 mile to a gate that is usually closed (even if it is open, a "No Trespassing" sign prevents you from going farther). This is Trailhead B, so, unless you elect to drive to Trailhead A, park here alongside the road where there is room. However, if you don't mind driving a bit of bumpy uphill dirt road (four-wheel drive is not needed), make a sharp right turn onto a one-

lane dirt road that's less well kept. It immediately makes a hairpin turn left and heads uphill. Continue for .5 mile to where a track intersects on the right with a sign "Logging Spur Section 20" pointing in the direction of the track and "Gray Eagle Creek Trail 1 Mi" pointing along the road. Park here at the wide spot in the road. This is Trailhead A.

Comments: This is one of my favorite hikes for visitors who don't like heavy-duty hiking (provided I can drive to Trailhead A) or for a short hike close to town. On this trail, grandparents and toddlers (and those in between) can sample nature without overdoing it. Because of the low elevation of the trail and its good drainage, it is excellent for an early spring hike when most other trails are muddy or covered with snow and trailheads are inaccessible due to soggy roads. Please read the note at the end of the hike description.

The Hike: From Trailhead A, take the route referred to as Logging Spur Section 20. Usually, logging spurs are not particularly good for hiking because they are hastily built for the sole purpose of hauling out cut trees in massive logging trucks. Proper drainage, good surfacing, attention to erosion control, and moderate grades are not attributes that the builders of logging roads care a hoot about. However, Logging Spur Section 20 is a definite exception, I suppose because the terrain is naturally level and pebbly. For those unfamiliar with map nomenclature and surveying, "Section 20" refers to a numbered grid of townships into which the

United States is divided. (The Governmental Survey System of rectangular grids was created by a committee headed by Thomas Jefferson and adopted by the Continental Congress in 1785.) There are 36 onr-mile-square sections, each containing 640 acres, in each township. On the topo maps, sections are shown with red lines with red section numbers.

Anyhow, this is a book about walking, not about spurs and sections, so let's get moving. One spring day, as I commenced this hike, a western gray squirrel was chasing another down a tall pine tree (male after female, I might guess, although my *Sierra Mammals* book says they mate in the winter), both squawking as loudly as they could. I had no idea squirrels could make such a racket. If I hadn't seen them in action, I'd have thought it was the Charge of the Light Brigade. I smiled to think how scary unusual forest noises can be unless you know the cause.

The trail starts out pleasantly level and pebbly underfoot, which makes walking easy. I try to notice and enjoy such trail portions, knowing that a steep rocky portion may lie ahead. However, no tougher parts occur on good old Logging Spur Section 20. The whole trail is a delight on which to tread.

Almost from the start, you see old rotting charred tree limbs lying on either side of the trail and some fire-scarred tree stumps. Obviously a forest fire passed through here many years ago. Much of the natural foliage has had time to regrow, and the fire's blemishing of the landscape has been nearly erased. The scene has no tall old conifers, however, or telltale signs of logging (sawed-off stumps), so fire probably removed the tall trees.

In 200 yards, you reach an opening on the right. This is the top of the Graeagle to Valley View Rock Loop (Hike J-16) with good views of Mohawk Valley below and Penman Peak across the valley. Logging Spur Section 20 straightens out and travels for almost ¼ mile without a bend, an unusual occurrence for Sierra trails. If you hike this part of the trail in the fall, you will enjoy seeing bitter cherry bushes loaded with berries (not cherries). I thus suspected this section to be a favorite for Mr. or Ms. Bruin, and one fine October day a few years ago, a pile of bear scat on the trail confirmed my suspicion. (If you're worried about a bear encounter, relax—for the past 30 years I have hiked hundreds of miles in the Feather River country doing research for this book and have seen only one bear. Sure, black bears are out there—the black bear is found in a variety of colors ranging from black to brown to yellowish to reddish cinnamon—but they are usually scared of humans and avoid any encounter if possible. The horror stories about bear maulings almost all involve grizzlies, and for many years there have been no grizzlies in California—except on the California state flag.)

About ½ mile from Trailhead A, an old jeep trail intersects your route on the right at a 90° angle. Two Douglas-fir trees (big Christmas trees) on either side of the road help you to identify this turn, and, in front, a fine view of Eureka Peak appears as the trees thin out. Here you have a choice. You can continue straight for another ¼ mile to where the Logging Spur dead-ends, then do a U-turn, and retrace your steps to the car. Or, if you are still peppy, take a right at this intersection and extend the hike a bit.

The extension has the same attributes as the logging spur—level (with a slight uphill toward the end), easy on the feet, and scenic. As more nice views of Eureka Peak appear before you, the sound of Smith Creek in the ravine on the right below is welcome on a warm day. When you've gone 1 mile from the logging spur, the trail takes its first noticeable right turn, and, in 100 yards, you encounter Smith Creek. This is a lovely picnic spot and the suggested turnaround spot for the hike extension. Retrace your steps to the car. Near the end, on your left you get more fine views of Penman Peak and Mohawk Valley.

Note: A portion of this hike is on land owned by Graeagle Land and Water Company. The company's owner has requested that people not use his property except for foot travel. Approval for access is explicitly denied for cars and trucks (other than for travel to the trailhead), bicycles, motorcycles, horses, dogs and other domestic animals, ATVs, snowmobiles, and any other off-road vehicles. Absolutely no camping, campfires, or wood

cutting is permitted. Please respect this privately owned property, and do not leave trash of any kind. If signs describe an owner other than Graeagle Land and Water Company, the property has obviously changed ownership. In such case, please check with the new owner before hiking this trail.

Camping: None.

Winter Use: Iroquois Trail is plowed to where the pavement ends. From there, you can snowshoe the route, or, if the snow isn't too deep, even walk it in boots.

J-12 Jamison Creek Mining Site Overlook and Johnsville Loop

> **Distance:** 1½-mile loop (with side trip down to the creek bluff, 2 miles)
>
> **Highest Point:** 5,155 feet
>
> **Total Elevation Gain:** 76 feet (255 feet with side trip)
>
> **Difficulty:** Easy (moderate/strenuous with side trip)
>
> **Hiking Season:** May through November

Directions to the Trailhead: From Graeagle, head north on Highway 89 for .25 mile, and turn left at the Graeagle Frostee onto the paved Graeagle-Johnsville Road (County Road A-14). Drive 5.5 miles to Johnsville, and travel through Johnsville past the last street on your right, Church Street. Continue about .2 mile to a dim road angling off to the right with a gate across it. Park on the shoulder of the paved road, which has plenty of room.

Comments: This hike is loaded with history. The town of Jamison City long ago passed into oblivion as floods on Jamison Creek wiped out every trace of it. The hike takes you to an overview of Jamison Creek, just upstream from the site of the ghost town, where, for more than 50 years commencing in the 1850s, mining activity was feverish. In the second part of the hike, you tour the historic town of Johnsville, which escaped the ghosts. You'll enjoy wandering through the Johnsville cemetery and noting the numerous nationalities listed on gravestones. For even more history of the Plumas-Eureka Mine and Johnsville than I relate here, please read Appendix B.

The Hike: The start and the end of the hike are within the boundary of Plumas-Eureka State Park, so please abide by park rules: dogs on leashes only, no firearms, no picking of wildflowers, and no feeding of animals. A gate across the path, visible from the main road, blocks vehicle traffic on the trail. A forest fire has blackened trees at the commencement of the route. However, the firefighting crew must have responded quickly, because the burned area is not extensive. The trail is mostly level and smooth. You see rusted junk scattered in places, but not so much that you feel you're walking through a dump.

This portion of the route is the long-gone historic wagon road between Johnsville and Jamison City. It was traveled daily by the miners who lived in Jamison City and worked on the mountain at the Plumas-Eureka Mine. In ¼ mile, the level part of the trail ends, and it pitches steeply downward, becoming rocky and strewn with tree limbs. If you are not keen on hiking this kind of trail, you can turn around here and backtrack as described later to continue the rest of the hike. Because the side trip down the hill returns to this same spot, hikers in a group who do not want to do the more-difficult next segment can wait here (perhaps 30 to 45 minutes), while others hike down the hill and return.

The downhill side trip is perhaps only ¼ mile long, but it requires careful footwork to avoid tripping on all the deadwood cluttering the route. When you reach the "bottom," it flattens out to a narrow, tree-covered bluff overlooking the creek. You need to keep a close eye on any kids, because a slip over the edge of the bluff would result in a nasty fall. The edge of the bluff may be crumbly, so stay back from it.

I used to walk down this trail with my wife and our two small kids 30 years ago. At that time, there was hardly any bluff. I'd walk right over to Jamison Creek and begin fishing, while the others would wander along the shore, sit on rocks beside the stream, chase butterflies, throw pebbles in the creek, or just sunbathe. I am amazed at how deep the gorge has become in just 30 years. I'd estimate that the level of the creek is 20 feet lower today than it was back then. It's easier to envision how the Grand Canyon was formed when I witness this rapid erosion process on Jamison Creek.

Nowadays, I suggest not scrambling down the bluff to the creek, because climbing back up is difficult. I had envisioned walking the western streambank all the way back to Johnsville, but 200 yards upstream the way is blocked by the bluff. By late summer it might be possible to wade around the bluff in the creek, but the creek here has lots of boulders, and the water is swift and dangerous, so I suggest staying at bluff level. (Hike J-17, Jamison Creek Lower Falls and Swimming Holes Trail, is a better bet for visiting the portion of the creek blocked by the bluff.)

Walk a few hundred yards along the bluff back toward Johnsville. The first thing you see is the remains of an old cabin and a sagging cable, attached to a tree, stretching all the way across the canyon to the bluff on the other side. When my family and I came here 30 years ago, the cabin was still standing, and an old hermit emerged to greet us. We assumed that he would run us off, but, to the contrary, he was friendly, welcomed us to his domain, and said he hoped that I would be successful fishing in "his creek." In those days, the cable stretched tautly across the creek. He used a sling seat and a pulley hanging from the cable to go from one side of the creek to the other without getting his feet wet.

On the bluff you find various relics of the mining days. When I say *relics,* I really mean just junk, because all of the "good stuff" has been taken by collectors years ago. As you gaze downstream, try to imagine the bustling town of Jamison City located around the bend out of sight and the feverish mining activities that took place on the shores of the creek below you.

Jamison City got its start in 1851 as a small tent village, which the miners named Washington. One of the first miners to locate there was a man named Jamison, and the creek running through Washington took on his name. Soon the number of miners had grown to 76, so the name of the town was changed to City of 76. However, as the town continued to grow and some of the original 76 drifted off, the name became inappropriate. Then, the name of the creek was given to the town, and it became Jamison City. On November 19, 1880, a fire com-

pletely destroyed the village, but, within two years, it was rebuilt, complete with hotel, post office, store, express office, and, of course, several saloons.

The banks of the creek below you thrived with mining activity in the latter part of the nineteenth century, but the principal activity was not panning for gold. Within a few years of the 1851 gold rush to the area, most of the easy-to-get-to streams had been panned out, and miners typically worked for one of the big mining companies after that. The main activity was removing gold from ore that was mined on the mountain.

The big chunks of gold-bearing quartz ore extracted from Plumas-Eureka Mine had to be pulverized before the gold could be removed. The best method of crushing the quartz in those days was a stamp mill with large hammers (stamps) to pound the rock into small pieces. However, a stamp mill

Tombstones in the old Johnsville Cemetery

was difficult and very expensive to build, so early crushing along Jamison Creek was done in less-expensive *arrastras* (from the Spanish verb meaning "to drag").

An arrastra was a circular enclosure with a vertical pole in the middle onto which a horizontal boom was tied. Outside the circle, a mule or donkey was tied to the outer end of the boom. Inside the circle, a large rock was attached to the inner end of the boom (chile wheels, introduced by miners from Chile, used a massive stone wheel instead of a rock). Mine workers fed ore into the enclosure, and, as the poor animal plodded around and around, the dragged rock or wheel crushed the ore. At the peak of activity in 1890, there were 27 arrastras operating along Jamison Creek in the 1-mile stretch between the bridge and Jamison City, a portion of which you are viewing. You might think that some of the circular enclosures or stone wheels could be found along here, but none is to be seen; probably they've been washed away by the floods that occasionally course down Jamison Creek Canyon.

In 1898, Johnsville miner and hotelman William Passetta contracted to process the leftover tailings from the Jamison Mine. He built a 2-mile-long flume from Jamison Mine to the site below you and operated several dozen arrastras in which the last bits of gold (reportedly at a yield of only $1 per ton) were extracted. That same year this portion of Jamison Creek saw the start of placer mining (washing away the hillsides with high-pressure water in order to get gold from the dirt runoff). These activities continued into 1921, and the ugly raw face of the cliffs across the creek from where you are standing is the result of this ecologically destructive method of mining.

As you walk along the bluff, you discover that it fades out into a steep hillside, and another shelf of the bluff appears above you. It's not worth the trouble to scramble up the steep slope to this higher shelf. You'll find only a short horizontal stretch and then more steep hillside, slippery with pine needles and loose dirt. Instead, I suggest you turn around and retrace your steps, past the site of the hermit's cabin and back up the branch-strewn trail to the top.

Once you're "on top," rejoin any of your group who waited for you here, and head back on the smooth track toward the trailhead. After about 200 yards, keep your eye out on the left for a rusting pile of unsightly large pipes. Soon after this pile, a trail branches off to the left (which you probably didn't even notice on your way in). Take this level smooth trail, and, after a few hundred yards, you can spy a hillside on your left leading down into a small ravine despoiled by one huge pile of junk. There are no relics here either, unless you really stretch the definition of a relic. (If, by chance, you do find any relics within the boundaries of the state park, they are not to be taken.) Passing the dump, you soon reach the back of the interesting Johnsville cemetery on the northern edge of town. The cemetery is worth a visit, but it is completely fenced, so you need to walk all the way around to the gate on the other side to get in.

Although most of the wooden grave markers have rotted away, numerous stone markers testify to the rich ethnic makeup of the mining community. Ireland, Italy, Spain, England, Switzerland, Austria, and Herzegovina (part of former Yugoslavia) are some of the native countries mentioned on the readable gravestones. One prominent gravestone contains the epitaph "John Redstreake, Native of Johnsville, Undefeated Longboard Snowshoe Champion." (Longboard snowshoes are actually old-time skis.)

After poking around the cemetery, you can do your own tour of the town's three principal streets, enjoying the quaint old houses (with a few new ones mixed in), the old hotel (now a private residence), and the restored firehouse. A 1911 photo of Johnsville, taken from the hillside on the other side of Jamison Creek, shows that all the trees in and around the town and all the way to the top of the ridge behind town had been cut down, with the exception of a few pines in the cemetery. I have to smile to think that the only first-growth trees remaining in the entire area are located in the cemetery. The cute white Saint John's Catholic Church (adjacent to the cemetery to the west) was built in 1901 but fell into disuse as the population of the town dwindled. It was condemned in the 1960s.

The 1911 photo also shows a few houses down the hill nearer Jamison Creek. A steep trail leaving from the southeast corner of the cemetery will lead you down the bluff to the site of these long-gone houses (see Hike J-17).

Johnsville was founded in 1876, 25 years after Jamison City, and became more popular, especially for families, because it was closer to the mines. One account says that Jamison City became the favored town of single men because of its tolerance for rowdy and raunchy behavior, while "family men" preferred more-sedate Johnsville. The 1882 *History of Plumas County,* however, relates that the second building erected in Johnsville (a store was the first) was a brewery owned by August Crazer. It was later destroyed by a landslide but was rebuilt.

Johnsville got its name from the popular superintendent of the Plumas-Eureka Mine, William Johns. At its peak, the town had three stores, two hotels, an I.O.O.F. lodge (the once-prominent Independent Order of Odd Fellows), two meat markets, and the "usual complement of saloons." The Johnsville (or, as it was then called, Johnstown) post office was established in 1882 and remained open until April 1953, when its operations were moved to Blairsden. When the mines gave out, the town drifted toward, but luckily did not fully sink into, ghost town status.

In the winter, Johnsville receives heavy snow, and in "big years" the snow is as deep as the eaves of the houses. An old (questionable) account of one particularly severe winter relates that residents dug tunnels under the snow from one house to another. A rancher who was driving a herd of cattle to Quincy (in the winter?) passed through Johnsville on the way; the cattle easily walked on top of the hard-packed snow until one cow had the misfortune of falling through into one of the tunnels between houses. There was no apparent means of hauling the cow alive to the surface, so the rancher slaughtered it on the spot and distributed the pieces to folks throughout the town.

In Johnsville, like all isolated mining communities, fire was the residents' greatest fear. As long as the mines were producing profitably and employment for the miners was available, the town could rebuild each time it burned—in 1884, 1892, and 1902. However, after the disastrous 1906 fire, mining output and employment were at such a low ebb that the town never fully rebuilt or recovered its previous vitality.

Well, that's enough about Johnsville. Although you could return on the "forest route" you came in on, I suggest walking back on the paved highway. In 5 minutes, you'll be at your starting place.

Camping: No backpack camping is available, but the excellent Plumas-Eureka State Park Campground for car and RV camping is near Johnsville, 1 mile south of the park museum's parking lot on the Johnsville-La Porte Road.

Winter Use: Johnsville's streets are plowed in winter, as is the road beyond Johnsville up to the ski-bowl. That road makes a sharp left turn ½ mile from town at which there is parking for several cars. Excellent cross-country skiing, snowshoeing, and sledding/saucer-sliding are available on the snowy road leading northerly from this parking spot. The ski-bowl lodge has recently been renovated, and, by the time you read this, new chairlifts, now in the planning stage, may be operating.

J-13 Cromberg/Sloat History Walk Loop

Distance: 6-mile loop (Alternative A, Cromberg Walk only, 1¼ miles
out and back; Alternative B, Sloat Walk only, 2 miles out and back)

Highest Point: 4,320 feet

Total Elevation Gain: 30 feet

Difficulty: Moderate (Alternatives A and B, easy/moderate)

Hiking Season: All year

Directions to the Trailhead: For the loop or Alternative A (Cromberg Walk only), from Graeagle go north on Highway 89 for 1 mile to Highway 70, turn left on 70, and drive 6.6 miles to a turnoff on the left at a sign "Old Cromberg Road." Drive .1 mile on this side road, and park well off the pavement, so that traffic can easily pass. To drive to Alternative B (Sloat Walk only) from the Alternative A trailhead, go back to Highway 70, turn left, drive 1.4 miles, turn left on Sloat Road, drive .5 mile, and park along the side of the road.

Comments: If a town is defined as a place having some stores and residences, be prepared not to find Cromberg or Sloat; as towns, they are both history. Yet neither of them is considered a ghost town because a ranch here or a house there shows that the area never completely died. The Twenty Mile House, one of the sights on this walk, was established as a stage stop

in 1854, making it the earliest permanent vestige of civilization in the area. Cromberg and Sloat are both rich in history, and either the full loop walk or the two out-and-back alternatives allow you to savor the growth of these communities during the last half of the nineteenth century and early twentieth

TH *	TH for loop or Cromberg Walk
TA *	Turnaround for Cromberg Walk
TH **	TH for Sloat Walk
TA **	Turnaround for Sloat Walk

Historic Haddick Ranch near Cromberg

century. I call this excursion a walk rather than a hike because 80 percent of the loop is on paved roads.

The Walk: If you feel up to it, the full 6-mile loop gives you the best flavor of the area. However, I begin the description with Alternative A, the Cromberg Walk (the "out" portion of which is the first leg of the loop). At the point where Alternative A turns around, I continue with the description of the loop. At the place where the loop meets the turnaround point of Alternative B, the Sloat Walk, I describe both the loop and the Sloat Walk's return leg. Alternative B ends on Sloat Road, ½ mile before it reaches Highway 70. I then describe the remaining part of the loop walk to Highway 70 and back to the car. Got it?

For the loop and Alternative A, before beginning to walk southwesterly along Old Cromberg Road, cross the road from your parking spot to look over the fence and across the pasture. The ranch you see just beyond the pasture is one of the oldest and best-established "spreads" in the area. It was originally known as the Tefft Ranch, built in 1879 by E. C. Ross. Old E. C. never got to enjoy the fruits of his labor, because one year later he was murdered in Cromberg, by whom and why I have never been able to uncover. In 1880, the ranch was purchased by Leandor Van Ness Tefft, who reportedly paid $625 for it at a sheriff's auction. Mr. Tefft expanded the ranch by constructing a 10-room house, barns, and outbuildings. Chinese laborers helped clear the land. The ranch became a stage stop in the late 1880s. Mr. Tefft sold the property in 1917, shortly before his death, and eventually it wound up in the possession of Mr. and Mrs. Haddick; she was the granddaughter of Mr. Tefft's second wife. Mr. Haddick died at age 31, and for many years the ranch was run by Mrs. Haddick, proving that some of those old western movies depicting a hardworking tough woman running a spread by herself have an element of truth.

Beyond the Haddick Ranch building is the site of the Nibley-Stoddard Sawmill. Henry Stoddard moved to Cromberg from Santa Cruz, purchased the mill site from Mrs. Haddick, and began operations in 1923. A unique feature of Stoddard's mill was that it utilized a 1¼-mile-long hoist to raise and lower a railroad locomotive and logging cars on a steep slope from around Mount Jackson (north of present-day Highway 70) where logging was being conducted. A 1⅝-inch-diameter cable was used to lift the 65-ton locomotive—evidently quite a sight. The sawmill burned in 1927, never to be rebuilt.

Far beyond the Haddick Ranch, easterly and on the other side of Highway 70, is Mount Tomba Inn, which fronts on the side road, not Highway 70. The inn was built in 1923 on land that was part of the original Haddick Ranch. The foundations seen next to the inn were once an apartment house, a duplex, and a garage. The housing was destroyed by fire, and the garage not only burned but also exploded, killing one man. The original inn remains, not as a place to stay but as a dinner restaurant with excellent food and a marvelous bar. (The current owners are John Wayne fans, and part of the place is decorated with all kinds of John Wayne memorabilia.)

Now, begin the loop or Alternative A by strolling down Old Cromberg Road away from Highway 70. This is the route of the old stage line, which wound down to the Feather River. On your right, in a partially logged pine woods, is the site of the Metcalf Sawmill, established by the Metcalf brothers in 1909 or 1910. In 1918, the mill was destroyed by the bane of many Plumas County sawmills, fire. This property is posted "No Trespassing," so I have never been able to walk onto the site to search for old foundations or piles of old sawdust.

The next point of interest along Old Cromberg Road is the Cromberg cemetery. A sign on the right announces the driveway. Walk the short distance in, and spend a few minutes exploring the grounds and inspecting the gravestones. The cemetery's first "customer" was buried in 1885. Gravestones with dates up to the present can be seen. Many of the markers for old graves have vanished or are unreadable. However, those that can be deciphered show that people born in seven countries and a dozen states are buried there.

Returning to Old Cromberg Road, walk the zigzags downhill toward the Middle Fork of the Feather River. At the bottom of the hill, just past some old cabins, sits Twenty Mile House, a magnificent old brick residence with several outbuildings. It has been lovingly restored and is, today, a delightful bed-and-breakfast inn. (I have never figured out where it is 20 miles from—possibly Quincy.) The house was originally a trading post for local miners and a stage stop. It included stables where the stage or freight wagons could change horses. Part of the main building became a post office in 1880, but the postal service, according to the story, didn't like the three-word name Twenty Mile House. To give the post office a one-word name, the postmaster selected Krumberg, his grandparents' name in northern Germany. (In German, *krumm* means "crooked" and *berg* "hill," hence, the name aptly described the curvy part of the old wagon road.) Krumberg was then Americanized to Cromberg. (I discovered, however, that the *History of Plumas County* published in 1882 states that the Twenty Mile House and Post Office was run by the Cromberg brothers; if true, this discredits the Krumberg story.) The post office closed in 1917, was reestablished in 1920, but closed for good 12 years later and was moved to another site. This is the turnaround point for the Cromberg Walk, so, if you're not doing the full loop, return to your car. You can then drive to the trailhead for Alternative B, and follow the description of that part of the walk in reverse order from end to beginning.

If the whole loop is in your plans, continue on the road beyond the Twenty Mile House. Old

Cromberg Road now parallels the Union Pacific Railroad tracks and the Feather River but at a somewhat higher elevation. The pavement ends, and the road becomes rutted and dusty. You might expect this part of the walk to be attractive, with the river so close at hand, but the water is out of view for most of the next mile. The old Quincy-Beckwourth stage line, established many years before completion of the railroad in 1909, followed the bank between the river and the route of today's railroad tracks. About a mile from Twenty Mile House, on the stage route, a store was built in 1910 and later destroyed by fire. I have been unable to determine its exact location.

The road finally flattens out and runs alongside the railroad tracks as you approach Sloat. The prevailing belief is that the community was named after Commander John Drake Sloat, who occupied Monterey in the Bear Flag Revolt of April 1846 against the Mexican government and took possession of it for California. The big deal in Sloat was its sawmill, although old-timers might insist that the Snake Ranch Tavern was a bigger deal. The mill, originally known as the Sloat Lumber Company, was built in 1912. Back then, the area was covered with heavy timber (you'd never know it today), so logging was easy. That first summer, the employees and their families lived in tents. After the first cut lumber had dried sufficiently, cabins and a boardinghouse were built, before the winter of 1913 set in. The sawmill was destroyed by fire in 1918 but was rebuilt in 1919. The mill changed hands several times until its final owners, Sierra Pacific Industries, closed it permanently and demolished most of the buildings several years ago. At the old main entrance, still used by the remaining occupant, the Sloat Mill Company (which sells livestock feed and supplies, not mill stuff), is a brass plaque placed there by Chapter 8 of E. Clampus Vitus, describing the rich history of the mill. (If you have never heard of E. Clampus Vitus, you may be surprised to learn that it was formed not as a prestigious historical society but rather as a joke and given its highfalutin' name to sound prestigious. It was originally dedicated to "frivolity and various forms of debauchery," but today it carries out admirable functions researching western history and placing commemorative bronze plaques.) The history of Plumas County is checkered with dozens of sawmills that bloomed, withered, and died (or burned). However, the Sloat Mill might hold the record for longevity.

As you approach the mill site and the pavement resumes, you find an interesting lineup of vintage machinery of various sorts set out for view. You have reached the turnaround point for Alternative B at the Sloat Mill site. Thus, the next mile is both the loop and the out-and-back Sloat Walk.

On the left, just after Sloat Road crosses Long Valley Creek, is the site of the Sloat Store and Post Office, opened in 1915 and closed in 1977. I don't know what happened to the building. The old wagon road then made a left turn and curved northerly up the hill on the same route followed by a paved side road today that connects with Highway 70. Our walk, however, now leaves the old wagon road route and continues along Sloat Road. On the left stood three important buildings in Sloat's history: first, the school (1921–1966); next, the community chapel, built with donated lumber and volunteer labor (1930); and last, the Snake Ranch Tavern. On the right, the community hall is still standing.

Just past the community hall, 4 miles from the start of the loop, is the attractive Sloat Ranch, which began operations in 1866. If you're doing Alternative B, your parked car signals the end of your excursion. The loop walk continues along Sloat Road for another ¾ mile to the intersection with Highway 70. The original 1906 one-room school was located several hundred yards north of today's Highway 70 on the other side of the highway. In 1910 it was moved to a spot across from what is now Long

Valley Resort. As Sloat grew, so did the need for schoolrooms, so in 1912 a new schoolhouse was built in front of the old building. It is interesting to note that seven of the eight listed schoolmarms were Miss, not Mrs.

Turn right on Highway 70, and walk southeasterly back toward Cromberg. On the left was Cedar Tavern. Just after 70 crosses over Little Long Valley Creek, you see the old firehouse, now modernized and re-sided. Beyond the firehouse is the site of Metcalf Sawmill, built in 1917 but destroyed in 1918 by (you guessed it) fire. Next on the south side of the highway is the Cromberg Ranch, built in 1923, overlooking the pasture through which Long Valley Creek flows.

Long Valley Resort, located 1 mile from where you joined Highway 70, was originally called Rainbow Auto Camp. Constructed in 1930, it consisted of a store, a service station, two cottages, and a garage, which lasted but a short time before they burned down, never to be rebuilt. A small hydroelectric plant on Long Valley Creek furnished the "camp" with electricity—albeit of the direct current variety, unlike today's universal alternating current. The successor enterprise, Long Valley Resort, is still operating, although ownership has changed several times. Only ½ mile from the resort, you find Old Cromberg Road and your car.

Camping: None.

Winter Use: Because these roads are used all winter (the dirt stretch from Twenty Mile House to Sloat isn't plowed), they can be walked without snowshoes and, naturally, are not suitable for cross-country skiing.

J-14 Plumas Pines Estates to Madora Lake Trail

Distance: 5½ miles out and back (with the short steep alternative back, 5 miles)

Highest Point: 5,580 feet

Total Elevation Gain: 644 feet

Difficulty: Easy/moderate

Hiking Season: May through October

Directions to the Trailhead: From Graeagle drive north on Highway 89 for .4 mile to the Graeagle Frostee, and turn left onto the Graeagle-Johnsville Road (County Road A-14). Travel 1.6 miles on A-14 to a right turn on Poplar Valley Road into Plumas Pines Estates. In .6 mile, turn left on Madora Lake Road, and in two blocks park off the road, beyond the last houses.

Comments: This is a very nice close-in hike on a good trail leading to picturesque Madora Lake. The route initially bypasses the lake and leads across Lundy Ditch to meet A-14. A little loop back to Madora Lake closely follows gurgling Lundy Ditch with its beautiful bouquet of wildflowers (by late summer most are gone). Mosquito repellent is a necessity early in the season.

The Hike: Walk west on Madora Lake Road, a dirt road, for 1 mile, passing two huge water tanks at the ½-mile point. Just before you reach a right turn and cross Madora Creek, a crummy road leads off to the left. If, later, you select the steep downhill loop route back, here is where you will complete the loop. I guarantee that you do not want to walk up that very steep alternative loop, so turn right, and cross over the watercourse. The trail cuts westerly again on the rim above Jamison Creek. For the next

¼ mile you occasionally get good views of Eureka Peak on the other side of Jamison Creek Canyon.

You can easily step over the gate you encounter at the northern boundary of Plumas-Eureka State Park. Soon after you enter the park property, a track cuts left down to the lake. However, that is your return route, so keep going straight, passing another short lake-access trail. From here to County Road A-14, the delightfully level path passes through quiet forest, making you wish this nice a trail would go on forever.

Although your daydream ends when A-14 comes into view, you definitely won't be disappointed by the ½-mile return to the lake along the trail paralleling Lundy Ditch. With A-14 just ahead, cross the watercourse, and immediately turn left onto the path. "And what is so darn special about a ditch?" you may ask. Well, you will see. I have not researched where the water comes from, but the ditch surprisingly has the same volume of rushing water at the end of summer as at the height of spring snowmelt.

The zigzag route along the ditch reaches an intersection where the trail from the Madora Lake parking lot comes in, and soon thereafter comes to another Y. The right fork loops around the east side of the lake, and the left fork bridges over Lundy Ditch and then loops around the lake's western shore. Take your pick—either one will get you to the other end of the lake. If you have time, you could do a circle clear around the lake (Hike J-3) and then repeat half of the loop to get to the outlet at the northern end. Near the outlet is a picnic table at the edge of the lake that is a delightful spot for lunch.

Once you are at the north end, choose either the short steep way back or the longer easy way back, which follows the route you took hiking up. The short steep way cuts off from the lake loop trail just east of the picnic table, where a sign saying "Trail" points right. Instead, go left, and after a level stroll of sev-

eral hundred yards, be prepared to head straight downhill on a steep path (you will see why I suggested not coming up this way). At the bottom, turn left, and in 100 yards you return to the route you were on over an hour ago. A right turn brings you back to the trailhead, 1 mile distant.

I usually prefer a loop route, because I like the experience of hiking a different path back, but in this hike I tend to choose the same way back as out. At the northern end of the lake, a short trail to the west leads you to the trail on which you hiked in. Turn right, and, after a longer but much easier downhill, you recross Madora Creek; 1 mile farther, you reach your car.

Camping: None. Camping within the state park is prohibited except in the excellent park campground near Johnsville, 1 mile south of the museum parking lot on the Johnsville-La Porte Road.

Winter Use: For the first mile past the trailhead, cross-country skiing is possible, but once you reach the uphill section you need snowshoes. I have snowshoed the loop around Madora Lake, and I am sure this long-way-in route is a dandy way to spend a few hours on "shoes."

J-15 Old Long Valley Creek Pack Trail

Distance: 4 miles out and back

Highest Point: 5,570 feet

Total Elevation Gain: 370 feet

Difficulty: Moderate

Hiking Season: June through October

Directions to the Trailhead: From Graeagle drive north on Highway 89 for 1 mile, and turn left onto Highway 70. After 5.8 miles on 70, turn right where a sign announces "Mt. Tomba Road." You immediately come to a T, with the left branch going to Mount Tomba Inn (a fun dinner house loaded with John Wayne memorabilia and one of the few restaurants in the area open most of the winter—but on weekends only then). Turn right, where a sign points to "Jackson Creek Campground, Happy Valley 7, Grizzly Ridge 10." The pavement soon ends, but the road is easily traversed in a normal car, aside from a bit of washboard and a few narrow spots. On your left, the Jackson Creek Campground has been permanently closed, and steel guardrails block the entrance. When you've gone 2.3 miles from the Highway 70 turnoff, you encounter a Y with a sign "Jackson Saddle 5, Penman Saddle 5" pointing right (23N48) and "Happy Valley 5, Ridge 8" left (23N11). Take the left fork for another 3.8 miles to a crossing of the South Fork of Long Valley Creek and a final intersection. The sign neglects to say where a right turn will take you, but you want to turn left anyhow, toward Missouri Gulch Creek and Bull Run Creek. Watch your odometer for a distance of .3 mile from the intersection, and park alongside the road near a sign on the left that announces "Long Valley Trail."

Comments: This hike is best if you want to walk an old historic trail that has partially disappeared due to lack of use. Thus, in many places you need a bit of pathfinding experience. I do not rec-

ommend this hike for people who are uncomfortable having to find their own way, every now and then. To help make the trail visible, I've clipped bushes, smoothed the trail, and put up rock borders, but, especially in the fern and meadow sections, I couldn't tear up plants to make the trail well defined. If you feel up to it, I highly recommend this very enjoyable hike.

The Hike: You may wonder, if you check this hike out on the topo map, why in the world I start the hike way up on 23N12 at the "top" rather than at the "bottom" where the trail reaches the little ½-mile-long side road off Highway 70. Well, what the map doesn't show is that new residences have been built on this side road, complete with an array of "Private Property—No Trespassing—Keep Out" signs.

The first time I attempted this hike from the top I gave up because the first ¼ mile of the trail had been obliterated by loggers. Loggers care about hauling out felled trees in any way they can, not about preserving an old historic trail. On my return visit I decided to create my own trail through the loggers' mess. I hope you will be able to follow my less-than-perfect efforts.

Instead of starting out at the "Long Valley Trail" sign, continue walking along the road for another 60 yards. Just before reaching a point where the road narrows a bit and a perfect white fir Christmas tree

Sulfur buckwheat on the old Long Valley Pack Trail

stands along the left side of the road, turn left at my stone marker, if it is still there. Do a bit of zigzagging downhill, and watch for a rock with a foot-long piece of rusty iron plate on top of it.

The first ¼ mile mostly follows a dim track in a downstream direction where loggers drove their bulldozers. Here, as on the entire rest of the trail, if you are not sure where the path is, look around a bit, improvise, and have fun doing so. Because the trail, after the first ¼ mile, closely follows the creek along its north bank, you cannot go too far wrong.

I am sure there will be places where you will not pick up my trail improvements, especially as time wears on and especially in the bits of meadows. As a rule, the proper route follows along the upper side of these mini-meadows. Watch for places where bushes have been clipped. A clipped bush is a giveaway that you're on the trail.

About halfway through the hike you'll find a steel post in the center of a mini-meadow with a small white triangle sign attached. The sign doesn't tell you anything except the names of two graffiti writers and the fact that it made a good target for someone with a gun. It is, however, one of the few pieces of evidence that human beings were here; the only others are a few old blazes on the tree trunks, the remains of the old dam near the turnaround place, and the trail itself.

Next you come to a small stream running perpendicular to the trail. I clipped a passageway through the bushes and willows so that you can easily find the place to cross on stepping-stones. This is Bull Run Creek, and the crossing place is only a few yards from where it joins Long Valley Creek. Especially on the way back, the entrance through the bushes to the creek crossing is not easily seen, so stay close to Long Valley Creek to find it.

The next section of trail has some boggy areas, which are fed by springs up the hill. However, they aren't so boggy that you'll necessarily get wet feet crossing them—just watch your step. You'll see the remains of an old rock dam, with the portion abutting the side of the creek along which you are hiking much better preserved than that on the other side of the creek. The center of the dam washed away long ago.

I decided it was time to stop doing trail improvements when I came to a section of trail that needed one heck of a lot of clipping to get through overgrown bushes. You can easily identify this turn-around spot by the large "mooning" boulder on the other side of the creek. You'll see why I named it that when you get there.

One feature of the return trip that I enjoyed occurred several hundred yards after passing the triangle sign. At a place where the trail is beside the stream bank and a large smooth boulder is next to the stream, the creek forms a nice swimming hole—not deep, but sizable enough to get "under" by kneeling on the sandy bottom. It was a hot day, so I tried it out. Very refreshing, I assure you, and no worries about skinny-dipping on this little-used trail.

The final ¼ mile of "trail" angles a bit uphill away from the creek, so just meander along, and hope to find my "improvements." Along here you can't get lost—the creek is on your right, and the road, paralleling the creek, is uphill a short distance on your left. If you overshoot the place where my re-built trail climbs up to the road, when you've gone less than ¼ mile beyond the trailhead you will encounter Missouri Gulch Creek crossing perpendicular to your route. The road is just uphill from there, so find it, and backtrack the short distance to your car.

Camping: You will come across five or six old fire rings along the route, showing that someone once camped there beside the stream. This certainly would be fun remote camping, and I bet you wouldn't be bothered by any other human beings—other things, maybe; people, no.

Winter Use: The road leading to the trailhead is not plowed in winter.

J-16 Graeagle to Valley View Rock Loop

Distance: 4-mile loop

Highest Point: 4,885 feet

Total Elevation Gain: 485 feet

Difficulty: Moderate

Hiking Season: May through November

Directions to the Trailhead: From "downtown" Graeagle on Highway 89, across from the Chevron Station, take Iroquois Trail west for 3 blocks to Navajo Trail. (These "Trails" are paved streets, not trails.) Turn right, and drive 1½ blocks to where the pavement ends, continuing on the good dirt road .1 mile. Park along the side of the road.

Comments: Although this easy-to-get-to trail is moderately steep, the climb is worthwhile because the extraordinary view from the top encompasses much of Mohawk Valley, including most of Graeagle, Mohawk, and Blairsden. The route lacks definition, because there are numerous trails leading in approximately the same direction, crisscrossing one another as they gain altitude. The trail redundancy occurs because the Graeagle Stables use this area for some of their trail rides, and they evidently wish to avoid having the horses beat a single overused path up the hill. Hence, my hike description doesn't follow a specific route and leaves it to you to determine which uphill path you will follow. I'm sure by now you can guess the only negative part of this hike: the habit of horses to fertilize the trail. (Aw, it's not that bad!)

The Trail: After seeking to decipher the proper route at the first few trail crossings I encountered, I gave up trying to make reason out of them. At each intersection I'd merely guess which route to take,

based on which one appeared to be heading uphill most expediently or which one seemed to be traveled the most. Because I haven't taken every possible path, I cannot guarantee that each one terminates at the same place on top, but I think that's the case. So, from your car, cross the road, and head uphill on whichever path is handy. As you approach the top, the trail crosses the ridge, so that your view westward across the Smith Creek drainage basin disappears, and a view easterly into the Gray Eagle Creek drainage basin appears. The route continues upward on what now seems one unified path. Behind, the views east and west merge, so that more of the broad sweep of Mohawk Valley is visible. In another 200 yards, the top becomes evident a short distance ahead, but a side track to the right beckons. In only 10 yards, you encounter a huge rock (Valley View Rock) sticking out from the hillside, with a short path leading to its top. You can climb it without a scramble. To the left, the view from the rock extends down the Feather River Canyon. Sweeping to the right, the panorama includes Mount Jackson, Bonta Ridge, and Penman Peak. Below Penman, the villages of Mohawk, Blairsden, and Graeagle are all discernible. To the right, a sliver of Highway 70 can be seen in the distance, and, on the far right, the distinctive profile of Beckwourth Peak emerges on the horizon. "Wow, what a place for a picnic," exclaimed my wife, upon visiting Valley View Rock for the first time—except we hadn't brought lunch along.

Views like this seldom show up as spectacularly on film as they look when you're there. I suppose that's just as well, because if we could garner the same awe from a photo as from an actual visit we might decide not to expend the energy to climb the hill for the full panorama. Returning the 10 yards from the rock to the trail, turn right. In hardly more than 100 yards, the path passes a stunted dead pine tree on the right, then fans out into a Y, and meets another trail. This is Logging Spur Section

Sunset looking toward Eureka Peaks near Graeagle

20. (If you wish, you can add a couple of very easy out-and-back miles to your outing by making a right turn on the logging spur—see Hike J-11.)

The loop route continues with a left turn on Logging Spur Section 20, which arrives, in a few hundred yards, at an intersection with the Gray Eagle Creek Dam Trail (Hike J-8). Turn left, passing the old trail sign, and pick up the seldom used dirt road. Walk down the hill to an intersection with Iroquois Trail. Here a gate on your right (sometimes locked) leads to the powerhouse, and a left turn brings you back to pavement and the residential part of Graeagle. Watch the street signs, and turn left off Iroquois Trail onto Navajo Trail. You drove to the trailhead on this street, and, sure enough, in ¼ mile, there's your car.

If you decided to turn around at Valley View Rock rather than doing the loop, the route back will seem just as confusing downhill as on the way up, as various horse trails meander in and out. Don't worry about picking the "right" one. Just head downhill, and choose the most beaten path at each intersection. You'll wind up on Navajo Trail near your car. I hope you agree that it was worth stepping over or around the few piles of horse pucky in order to see the spectacular view from the rock.

Camping: None.

Winter Use: Wearing waterproof boots, I have hiked this loop in early January, albeit in a light-snow year. In a heavy-snow year, it could be done wearing snowshoes. However, near the top the route narrows and the manzanita coverage thickens, so picking out the proper path may be a bit difficult. Once you reach Logging Spur Section 20, the rest of the loop back to your car needs no winter path-finding prowess.

J-17 Jamison Creek Lower Falls and Swimming Holes Trail

Distance: 1 mile out and back

Highest Point: 5,127 feet

Total Elevation Gain: 195 feet

Difficulty: Moderate

Hiking Season: May through October

Directions to the Trailhead: Follow the directions for Hike J-12, but turn right in Johnsville on the most northerly paved street that intersects Main Street. A sign saying "Cemetery, Church" is on the left side of the road but points to the right. After 1 block the road makes a loop around two large pine trees in the middle of it. Make a 90° left turn after passing the two trees, and take a single-lane gravel drive just to the right of a nice one-car garage with "99" on it. In 1 block, you arrive at the gate of the quaint Johnsville Cemetery (see Hike J-12 for a history of the town and cemetery). There is plenty of parking under the pines near the cemetery gate.

Comments: Why is a hike of only 1 mile classified as "moderate"? Well, the first ⅛ mile of the trail down into the canyon is rather steep. Although exposed roots and rocks act as stair steps, they must be trod upon with caution. There are no cliffy or scary parts on the path down to the creek, but on the bluff above the creek, cliffs requiring careful foot placement are numerous. Nonetheless, I bet you will consider this short hike well worthwhile once you take in the various waterfall views along the bluff. The bluff path cannot be done in a hurry, and you'll need many stops for sightseeing and photographing, so the hike takes far more time than you'd expect for a distance of only 1 mile. Oh yes, you might want to wear your bathing suit for sampling the swimming holes. (These refreshing pools get

enough visitors so that skinny-dipping is risky.)

The Hike: Follow the fence line to the right of the cemetery entrance gate. When you reach the corner, you will notice an unsigned trail angling right, which quickly starts downhill toward the creek. Clamber down the roots and rocks, and, in a few minutes, you reach a level open spot in the forest. Old pictures of Johnsville in its heyday show that the hillside you just negotiated was completely cleared of trees to furnish timber for houses, beams to shore up mineshafts, and railroad ties. This level spot, seen on the old photos, was the site of several miners' cabins, although no foundations or scraps of wood from the houses are in evidence today. Thus, Johnsville, commonly considered to have escaped ghost-town status because of its many occupied old residences, actually has a ghost-town section on this shelf just above the creek and below the inhabited part of town.

The trail cuts diagonally across the level area, and, at its edge nearest the creek, descends a rock retaining wall constructed by the builders of the cabins here nearly 150 years ago. On the lower side of the wall the trail divides. The right branch heads back uphill and terminates at the edge of the existing village where passage is blocked by a fence and a slew of "Private Property—No Trespassing" signs.

Instead, take the left fork. In a few steps, you arrive at the bluff above the river, overlooking swimming hole number one. (The numbering scheme is my own; there are no signs or map references.) Recent floods altered the falls above the swimming hole by transporting three large trees and stuffing them into the opening that had been the top of the waterfall. This blockage rerouted the creek, making the waterfall less spectacular but still darn pretty. The rerouting also ended the fun of floating in the pool directly under the falling water. The trees look pretty permanent, so swimming hole number one will have to survive without an overhead shower feature.

Climbing down the bluff to the edge of the swimming hole is a little tricky. You can see where others have managed to accomplish the feat in two places. I liked the one nearer the waterfall better, but, with use and erosion, the better way down might change over time. A swim on a hot day is delightful, but in spring the snowmelt runoff makes a dip in the creek mighty chilly.

Once back on top of the bluff, head downstream on the trail, which sometimes is a trail and sometimes isn't. There are many rock piles along the bluff, created by miners years ago in their search

for gold. The trail goes over or around these in ways that may not be obvious. If you suddenly seem to be without a trail, just keep walking downstream near the edge of the bluff, and a trail will soon reappear. Actually, because this is not a state-park-maintained trail, it has come into existence merely because people walking downstream beat down a path. In several places, multiple paths appear because different people chose different routes.

The next major waterfall downstream does not have good access to the creek, so viewing and photographing are best done from the bluff. To reach swimming hole number two, you need to loop away from the stream to detour around an impassable part of the bluff. However, the distance around is no more than 200 yards, and, at the end of the detour, you find yourself back overlooking the water. Below, you see swimming hole number two. It is even prettier than number one and, because it's more remote from Johnsville, has the special feeling of being your own private spa. Jamison Creek makes a wonderful show upstream as it cascades down between the steep banks of its ravine.

The trail beyond swimming hole number two is nonexistent, so, rather than beating your way through bushes to see a less-interesting stretch of the stream, I suggest turning around here. When you reach the place where the trail down from Johnsville meets the bluff trail, continue for another ⅛ mile upstream for more nice views, including one double waterfall, not as high as the others but still worth a look. As you start heading upstream toward it, note that the best beach for swimming hole number one is on the upper side of its falls.

You might think that it would be nice to walk along the bluff on the west side of the creek all the way to the bridge where the Graeagle-Johnsville Road crosses Jamison Creek and then double back on the road to the cemetery. Unfortunately, a slide area blocks the way well before the bridge comes into sight. On the other side of the creek you can see the sheer cliff with concrete barriers at the top separating it from the Graeagle-Johnsville Road. Doesn't it look like only a bit more erosion could easily cause a slide wiping out a good portion of the road? I'm sure the road engineers have thoroughly checked this out, but from the west side of the creek it looks mighty precarious. This ugly cliff was caused by hydraulic mining (high-pressure hoses washed gold-bearing dirt from the hillside) many years ago before environmentalists could get preventive laws passed.

Walk back the ⅛ mile to the trail coming down from the cemetery, and take your time going back up the steep parts to your car. If you haven't visited the cemetery, I suggest doing so either before or after the hike, and you can read about it in Hike J-12. One final thought: If you want a more elaborate excursion, combine this hike with Hike J-12 for a comprehensive tour of this historic area.

Camping: None. Good car camping is available in the Plumas-Eureka State Park Campground on the other side of Johnsville, 1 mile past the museum parking lot on the Johnsville-La Porte Road.

Winter Use: I have walked this trail in midwinter in waterproof boots, but, I will admit, it was a mild winter, so the snow wasn't too deep. In a heavy-snow year, this trip would not be possible, even with snowshoes, due to the steepness of the initial part of the trail.

Chapter 10

Blairsden Topo

B-1 Willow Creek and Two Toppled Trestles Trail

Distance: 2½ miles out and back
Highest Point: 4,793 feet
Total Elevation Gain: 243 feet
Difficulty: Moderate
Hiking Season: April through November

Directions to the Trailhead: From Graeagle, go south on Highway 89 for 2.7 miles. Turn left to Clio, crossing over the Feather River Middle Fork. You enter Clio on Lower Main Street; at the stop sign, turn right onto State 40A Road. In 1.6 miles the road passes under the spectacular Western Pacific Railroad Trestle A. Although the WPRR is now part of the Union Pacific, Trestle A is still usually referred to as the Western Pacific Trestle. Soon the pavement ends and the road becomes well-graded dirt. At 2.3 miles from Clio, State 40A makes a five-way intersection, with two roads branching to the right and one to the left. The trailhead is the road to the left with a cable across it. There's room to park without being on any roadway.

Comments: I enjoy hiking along the routes of long-gone railroads. This hike follows the Nevada, California, and Oregon (NCO) Railroad route, winding from the no-longer-there town of Clairville (see Hike B-2) to Clio. Railroad routes needed to stay fairly level because locomotives couldn't pull trains up steep grades. In very hilly country like the terrain of this hike, the men who planned the route (you can bet no women were employed in this profession in 1903) needed to follow contour lines and span creeks with trestles. To find out some of the history of the railroad along this route, read the "Comments" section of Hike B-2. And before starting this hike, you might read Appendix A, which has tips about how to hike an old railroad right-of-way.

The WPRR avoided the circuitous route chosen by the NCO by building the massive Trestle A high over Willow Creek. The much smaller NCO chose to build less-imposing, cheaper trestles but had to lay windier, more circuitous trackage. The remains of the NCO's two most prominent trestles are seen on this hike. The "famous" (well, it was in its day) Horseshoe Bend Trestle, which spanned Willow Creek, actually curved in the shape of a horseshoe and was quite an engineering feat for that time. The second, more conventional trestle (our turnaround point) crossed Betterton Creek just above the place where it flows into Willow Creek. Actually, the route of the NCO can easily be traced down to where it goes under Trestle A, with the NCO at almost the level of Willow Creek and the UPRR high overhead on its trestle. The NCO ceased operations in 1918, and by 1935 all of the rails had been removed and sold for scrap.

The Hike: Walk around the cable barrier on the road (see the "Note" at the end of this hike). The road follows the old railroad grade for slightly more than ½ mile, and soon Willow Creek can be seen and heard below. Where the road bends slightly to the left and starts downhill toward the creek, you angle right and climb a small embankment. At the top of the embankment, continue along the level path of the long-gone tracks. Old rotted ties lie scattered about, having been ripped up when the rails were removed. Plowing through some brush on the level grade, you suddenly come to a large washout where the railroad builders had filled a ravine, but

the dirt has now washed away. I crossed the gully by going to the right, carefully making my way down to its bottom and then up the other side to the level of the old rails.

You'll find the going a bit slow between this washout and the site of Horseshoe Bend Trestle because you have to step around ubiquitous bitterbrush and hop over fallen tree limbs. In a short time, the remains of the southern end of the Horseshoe Bend Trestle appear where Willow Creek flows westerly in the gully below. Alas, the whole trestle isn't there anymore, a victim, I suppose, of rot and occasional extraordinarily high water levels on the creek since the railroad was discontinued. I'm not sure whether going down the embankment to creek level is better to the left or to the right. I tried the right, was able to jump the creek without getting wet (although a dry crossing is probably not possible during spring runoff), and wound up in very deep grass with some boggy ground underfoot. Whichever side you choose, you can see where both ends of the trestle were, because both sides of the stream embankment are littered with large wooden timbers. Back up on the railroad grade, you immediately have to detour around a grove of cedars that has made the old route its home. Then the trail becomes easier. In midsummer, fine clumps of blue lupine grace the way. About ¼ mile after the Horseshoe Bend Trestle, the railroad grade passes through a place where rock was blasted out to cut a passage through. I have hiked many a mile of the Feather River country's long-gone railroad rights-of-way and this is the only place I've encountered where blasting through rock was necessary. I guess it was always easier to "go around" rather than "through" rock.

Before the rock cut, you may notice a faint road track cutting back down toward the creek on your left. This will be your route to a Willow Creek crossing on your way back; you won't have to backtrack to the Horseshoe Bend Trestle. For now, continue along the railroad grade, which follows Willow Creek downstream. Not many views of the diminutive creek are available, however; sight of the water is often blocked by—what else?—willows. Walking is easy, although in some places you need to zigzag around bitterbrush bushes rather than stepping over them. About ¼ mile from Horseshoe Bend Trestle, the path narrows where a landslide has reduced it from "standard gauge" to a narrow trail width. This portion is easily navigated, and, just around the bend, you reach the turnaround point at the remains of the trestle that spanned Betterton Creek.

Although you could easily scramble down the Betterton Creek ravine and up the other side to continue hiking the railroad grade, it's hardly worth doing, because in ¼ mile you'd encounter a rusting Volkswagon microbus, a well-stripped Mercedes Benz 220, a junk Subaru, a couple of rusting pickup trucks, and, as expected, a "No Trespassing" sign. The topo map (woefully out-of-date, with the most recent version dated 1972) shows a "jeep trail" for the remainder of the NCO railroad route paralleling close to Willow Creek, under Trestle A, and out to Road 40A near Clio. However, real estate development has taken over, and there are numerous homes and "Private—No Trespassing" signs along this once-upon-a-time jeep trail.

Anyhow, you've seen a good bit of the NCO route, and I hope you've enjoyed the walk along Willow Creek. On the way back, just after the rock cut, take the dim side road down to the creek. Here, too, crossing with dry feet is a matter of finding the best place, using your leaping and rock-balancing abilities, and trusting your luck. If you wish to wade across, the creek is not ferocious, and a sandy bottom with water only a foot deep can be found. My crossing was aided by a beaver dam in progress, but such dams seldom last for several years because they are easily washed away by fast-flowing spring runoff. I waited quietly for several minutes to see if

Mr. or Mrs. Beaver would emerge from a hiding place to continue the dam construction job. Finally I gave up (I've discovered that beaver sighting requires plenty of quiet patience). Remember how, on the way in, you climbed the small embankment rather than taking the road that angled downhill? Well, as soon as you have negotiated the crossing of Willow Creek, on the way back, you'll be at the bottom end of that road you didn't take earlier. About 200 yards up the road is the place where you went up the small embankment. From there, the route back to your car is an easy stroll.

Note: Near the start of the trail, you'll see a diamond-shaped sign saying "Private Forest Lands, No Dumping, Use Subject to Control of Owner—Civil Code Section 1008—Graeagle Land & Water Company." A portion of this hike is on Graeagle Land

Remains of the Horseshoe Bend Trestle over Willow Creek

and Water Company property. I have received written permission from the company's owner to include this hike with the condition that such permission is for foot travel only. Approval for access is explicitly denied for cars, trucks, bicycles, motorcycles, horses, dogs and other domestic animals, ATVs, snowmobiles, and any other off-road vehicles. Absolutely no camping, campfires, or wood cutting is permitted. Please respect this privately

owned property, and do not leave trash of any kind. If signs describe an owner other than Graeagle Land and Water Company, the property has obviously changed ownership, and the former owner's permission for right to pass is automatically terminated. In such case, please check with the new owner before hiking this trail.

Camping: None.
Winter Use: None.

B-2 Clairville Ghost Town Site and Old Railroad Trail

Distance: 4¼ miles out and back
Highest Point: 4,950 feet
Total Elevation Gain: 80 feet
Difficulty: Easy/moderate
Hiking Season: April through November
(prettiest in early summer to midsummer)

Directions to the Trailhead: Drive north on Highway 89 from Graeagle for 1.2 miles to Highway 70. Turn right on 70, and drive 5.6 miles, just past Chalet View Lodge. Take the road on your right with two signs: "Calpine Elks Lodge 2 & 32" and "Sembach's RV Repair & Fixit Shop." As you start up the dirt road, these two establishments are on your left. Within 200 yards, another sign points to a road leading left with a sign "D. Green." Take the right fork. You'll see some trailers and locked driveway gates along this part of the road. After signs of civilization disappear, and before crossing a small, intermittent creek bed, park wherever you can pull off the road.

Comments: This hike closely follows the old railroad grade of the Sierra Valley Railway (SVR). Before starting the hike, you might read Ap-

pendix A, which has tips about how to hike an old railroad right-of-way. By 1887, rails had been completed from Reno into Sierra Valley, with a targeted end at Quincy. A lack of funds stopped track-laying progress east of Beckwourth. In 1891, Henry A. Bowen of San Francisco took over the defunct railroad, renaming it the Sierra Valley Railway, and by June 1895 the line extended into Beckwourth. Finally, in June 1896 the end of the track reached the new town of Clairville, named after Bowen's daughter. (Some references spell it Claireville but my plot of the town dated 1897 spells it Clairville.) Clairville became a busy terminal point for passengers, mail, and freight, all of which were transferred from railcars into horse-drawn wagons and stagecoaches for travel to Quincy via the wagon road.

In March 1901, control of the SVR was acquired by the Nevada, California, and Oregon Railroad (NCO), a company that owned track from Beckwourth into Reno. The NCO extended a feeder line from Clairville to Clio, completing it in May 1903. This hike (like Hike B-1) follows the route of this feeder line. Eventually, in July 1916, the line was extended from Clio to the Davies Mill in what is now Graeagle, but the NCO never installed rail beyond Davies. In 1917, the Plumas County portion of the NCO was sold to the Western Pacific Railroad (now part of the Union Pacific), and on April 16, 1918, the Plumas portion was abandoned. By 1935 all of the rails had been taken up and sold for scrap.

The Hike: From the trailhead, hike south on the seldom traveled jeep road for a few hundred yards to a Y in the road. Take the right fork, and walk the smooth, fairly level, but crooked road for another ½ mile. Out of sight to your left only about 300 yards away, the Feather River, the current Union Pacific main line tracks, and the long-gone SVR tracks bend to the south. At this point the SVR ran parallel with, but about 15 feet above, the WPRR tracks. (On the day I tried following the SVR grade in the opposite direction, north into Humbug Valley, I came across a remote, well-kept storage building at the end of a dirt road with a sign saying "Notice: $500 Reward. All Saleable Items Have Been Stolen—Reward Paid for Any Trespasser Who Has

Been Shot Here." I hastily backtracked to the jeep road.)

About ½ mile from the trailhead, the SVR grade crosses the jeep road and runs parallel to it for several hundred yards. The exact point of this crossing is tough to see, but it's just before an area where loggers burned unwanted tree limbs. Keep your eyes peeled on the left side of the road for a couple of yellow USFS signs on pine trees saying "Bearing Tree" and a yellow section marker sign. At this point, let's do a bit of easy cross-country trailless hiking. From the road, make a 90° turn to your right, and strike out through the forest, which has been heavily logged. Only a few scattered ponderosa pines remain, marked with a white stripe around their trunks (USFS language for "Woodman, spare this tree").

Almost immediately you cross the old SVR grade, as evidenced by rotting wooden ties and a raised railroad bed running roughly parallel to the road, but angling slightly away from it. You could follow the railroad grade the remaining way into Clairville but it's mostly covered with brush (for some reason bitterbrush, also called antelope brush, loves the soil of old railroad right-of-ways), and logging activities have made the route difficult to discern at several points. Instead of following the exact course of the rail grade, just keep on a cross-country course perpendicular to the road.

As you leave the road, looking through the trees you can see an area that has no trees at all. Ahead, you see some trees with unusual painted markings: a white dot on top, a blue rectangular tag saying "Unit 2" under that, and two more white dots below. After walking about 180 yards from the road, you arrive at a beautiful, narrow, half-mile-long meadow. You also might spy another USFS yellow sign saying "Meadow—Vehicles & Skidding Equipment Prohibited Behind This Sign," warning loggers to keep off the pretty meadow. Please stop for a minute to soak up the view.

To your right, the meadow extends for several

hundred yards, and, to your left, it disappears in the distance. In summer it is lush with various grasses punctuated with delicate white brodiaea (a member of the lily family growing from a bulb, sometimes called white hyacinth). Turn left, and skirt the meadow in the same direction you were going on the road. To preserve the delicate meadow foliage, please walk along the edge instead of tromping right through the meadow. If you are as fond of meadows as I am, you will thoroughly enjoy the next 10 minutes as you traverse the remainder of its length.

Before it ends, a small, sandy gully starts in its center, running in the same direction as the meadow. As the meadow grasses and flowers start to disappear, keep going in the same direction, now walking along the sandy bottom of the gully. The route is easy and well defined by the gully. On the right you'll be annoyed at the sight of several large, ugly piles of limbs left by long-gone loggers. The sandy gully makes a little S-turn to the left, and— lo and behold!—in the middle of the S some rotted posts are sticking up from the side of the gully: the remains of a small trestle where the SVR crossed over it. Although the ghost-town site of Clairville is right around the corner, the railroad grade from the gully crossing into "town" is extraordinarily brushy, so I suggest you stay with the gully for another 200 yards (it's now becoming less like a gully and more like a meadow) to a point where it intersects a dirt road. Looking ahead at the intersection, you can see the eastern edge of the Clairville Flat Meadow. Turn right, and follow the road (22N23X) a short distance to Clairville. The trouble is, you won't know when you're in Clairville because it isn't there.

Clairville was founded in 1896 when the railroad tracks were completed to this point. Henry Bowen, the new owner of the railroad, laid out the town. A plot map dated March 1897, drawn by Plumas County's famous surveyor, Arthur W. Keddie, shows the layout of the streets. Bowen offered lots for sale at "$25.00 & Up." In 1897, the lo-

comotive engine house was built, and the community began to prosper. Between 1900 and 1912, Clairville was at its height and served as the base for railroad operations in the area. The town had a "wild and woolly" reputation with, according to one report, a murder or stabbing almost daily. In 1907, Mr. Perry, the grocery store owner, commented that there were only 2 "ladies" in town, his wife and daughter, but there were 20 other women (called "camp followers") scattered around the town's 16 saloons and other "houses."

When the WPRR construction was finished in 1913, the railroad workers all left, and the community became a ghost town almost overnight. Subsequently, all the buildings were removed or demolished. Today there's not so much as a foundation left to tell where the buildings once stood.

As you walk "into town" on 22N23X, you find a road (22N23XB) intersecting on your left. Continue straight for another 50 yards to another intersection, this one with State 40A Road (bigger, but just as dusty). You now are in "downtown" Clairville. To your right was the engine house, a large building where the SVR locomotives were repaired. To your left was the railway station, and, where you are standing was the most important street in town, Railroad Street, with the SVR tracks running along it.

I had assumed that the streets of town were laid out in the large Clairville Flat Meadow, behind you. However, my 1897 plot of the town shows that all the streets were north of where you are standing. Perhaps the meadow becomes too boggy in wet weather to support streets and buildings. In midsummer, it is in full bloom with mostly white flowers: yarrow, brewer's angelica, Gray's lovage, and yampa. Along the edges you may spy some lower-growing cute blue Bach's downingia.

Turn left on 40A, and walk "out of town" envisioning the sawmill, which was on your left. Two openings in the trees give you final views of the exquisite Clairville Flat Meadow as 40A curves left and heads for Clio. At this curve, you see a yellow USFS boundary survey marker nailed to a tree. Just beyond it, a dim dirt road cuts off at 90° to the right. Take it for a few steps, and note where it cuts through an embankment. This embankment was the route of the SVR out of town, headed for Clio. You might want to follow its obvious route for ½ mile or so, to see how fills and cuts made a level track while the 40A Road, a few hundred yards to your left, goes up hill and down. Much of the railbed, easily identified by its rotting ties, is covered with brush and trees, so walking is easier to the right, below the level of the fill, for some stretches.

Although you can follow the right-of-way almost to Clio, it lacks interest after a while. Turn around at any point and return along the former tracks to Clairville. Or turn to your left 90°, climb the hillside the short distance to 40A, and take the "easier on the feet" road. As you again approach the expanse of Clairville Flat Meadow, you may won-

der how towns in other parts of the world last for hundreds or even thousands of years but Clairville was born and disappeared in fewer than 20.

To return to the car from Clairville, I opted not to repeat the route to the jeep road that I'd taken on the way in. Instead, I stuck to 22N23X for ¼ mile, turning left at the four-way intersection of dirt roads. In ½ mile I saw the yellow marker where the gully/meadow/cross-country route turned off toward the meadow, and slightly more than ½ mile farther, I was back at my car.

To revisit Clairville, obviously you can drive right in from Highway 70 toward Clio on State 40A Road without having to walk. However, driving doesn't allow you to enjoy the meadow/gully route or the sense of railroad history as you explore the route of the SVR line.

Camping: None.

Winter Use: I guess this hike could be done on snowshoes or even cross-country skis, but I've never tried it in winter.

B-3 Gooseneck of the Feather River and Upper Gorge Trail

Distance: 3¼ miles out and back from Trailhead A;

2¼ miles out and back from Trailhead B

Highest Point: 4,845 feet

Total Elevation Gain: 110 feet from Trailhead A; 90 feet from Trailhead B

Difficulty: Moderate

Hiking Season: April through November (best in spring to midsummer)

Directions to the Trailhead: From Graeagle take Highway 89 south for 4.3 miles, passing Clio. Turn left on County Road A-15 toward Portola. In 5.2 miles, after passing the most easterly "Dancing Bear" entrance into Gold Mountain Estates, watch for a dirt road on the left with a not very prominent sign "O' Feather River" (written

only on the side of the sign facing east) and another sign "Dead End 1." Taking the road, you pass a couple of houses (is that car-chasing dog still there?) and in .2 mile enter Plumas National Forest. The road zigzags and, .5 mile farther, enters Humbug Meadow. If you do this hike in spring when the meadow is boggy, or if you have a low-slung car, you should park at Trailhead A. By midsummer the meadow is dry enough so that most conventional cars can carefully traverse it on the car ruts to Trailhead B, .5 mile farther, where the level road ends by circling a large pine tree. There is plenty of space to park at either A or B.

Comments: There aren't many places along the Middle Fork of the Feather River where a person can stroll along its bank, but the gooseneck section is one. A gooseneck is a stretch of river where the stream makes a sharp U-turn and doubles back on itself. At the narrowest point of this Feather River gooseneck, the part flowing easterly is less than 250 yards from the stretch that flows to the west.

The second feature of this hike is the uppermost gorge of the river. The lethargic Feather enters a steep-sided, boulder-filled gorge through which it roars with gusto. You can view the entrance to the canyon at water level, and then climb to the bluff above for a bird's-eye view of the gorge. My photographer friend, Woody, shot two full rolls of 36 exposures on this seldom visited but very scenic part of the Feather River country. Please read the note at the end of the hike description.

The Hike: If you parked at Trailhead A, merely follow the car track ruts for ½ mile to Trailhead B. Trailhead B is smack-dab on the riverbank at a beautiful spot where the water flows silently between grassy banks decorated with wildflowers and large, smooth boulders. Head downstream on the trail, which follows the edge of the river.

The trail soon fades out, but no problem! For the next mile, merely hike along the water's edge; where bushes or high grass block the way, walk up the low bluff above the river until you've passed the obstruction. This first mile, which includes the U-turn of the gooseneck, has easy walking and is a fun stroll, even though it's mostly trailless. There are several small sandy beaches—perfect for picnics. Just before beginning the U-turn, watch on the riverbank for the "Indian face" rock formation com-

plete with see-through eye. I couldn't tell whether this was a natural novelty or fashioned by humans. See what you think.

Across the river stretches Humbug Valley, with the main-line tracks of the Union Pacific Railroad running through it and Highway 70 beyond. When you reach the end of the river's U-turn, you'll probably be up on the riverbank and walking south along it, although you were going north only half an hour earlier. Make your way down to the edge of the river at your first opportunity, and continue downstream, with the boulder-sided gorge now in view, ahead.

I suggest walking as far as you can into this beautiful throat of the gorge, although you may later have to backtrack a bit. Nowhere else in the Feather River country can you experience the majesty of the large smooth boulders that line the banks as the river enters the main part of the gorge. When travel into the gorge becomes impossible, backtrack to where you can scramble up the steep eastern slope at the beginning of the gorge. Here you begin to pick up signs of an unmaintained trail headed in a downstream direction, where others have walked along the cliffs above the canyon, often cutting two parallel paths, several yards apart. If you're hiking with kids, be sure to prevent them from running wild—the sandy slopes leading down to rock ledges above the gorge are easy to slip on. The trails are safe enough, but carelessness or prank-playing could lead to a disastrous slip over the edge of the cliff. Likewise, the wonderful viewing rocks jutting out over the edge of the gorge can be dangerous if they're wet or if you don't climb them with care.

One gorge scene includes a view of the Union Pacific bridge spanning the river at the lower end of the canyon. When you have navigated the last cliff-hanging rock, walk back to the top of the bluff and pick up the trail heading back upstream. Several dirt roads lead down to the gorge edge and, as the trail reaches the most prominent one (about 350 yards from your last view spot), take it toward the other side of the gooseneck. In about 300 yards, the road will intersect another sandy road with the "jailhouse rock" on your right (a huge boulder completely surrounded by closely set pine trees looking like prison bars). Go left on the intersecting road. Two successive right turns later (about 100 yards apart) you're on the main dirt road running the length of the peninsula formed by the gooseneck.

This 120-year-old wagon road was the main route between Mohawk Valley and Sierra Valley and is shown on Keddie's 1892 map of Plumas County. Walk westerly along it for another 100 yards, and then turn left on a dusty road that heads

steeply downhill to Trailhead B, a short distance away. You can identify this last intersection easily by a large double-trunked juniper tree on the left (junipers are rather uncommon in the Feather River country).

The route from the gorge back to the car probably sounds a bit confusing. If you prefer a simpler, but somewhat longer way back, merely retrace your steps along the bluff above the gorge, going in the upstream direction. In less than ¼ mile, turn right, and walk cross-country across the peninsula for the 250 yards separating the south-flowing river from it's north-flowing stretch. Head down to the river's edge, turn right, and you're soon back at Trailhead B.

Late spring and early summer are the best times for gorge viewing, when the river is swollen with snow runoff. Conversely, the wildflowers along the first half of the hike are best from July on. So, take your choice—or try both times to experience their unique differences.

As a kayaker myself, I had to laugh imagining someone contemplating a peaceful paddle downstream from Trailhead B, not knowing that a mile later the quiet river suddenly becomes a roaring

The approach to the Upper Gorge of the Feather River

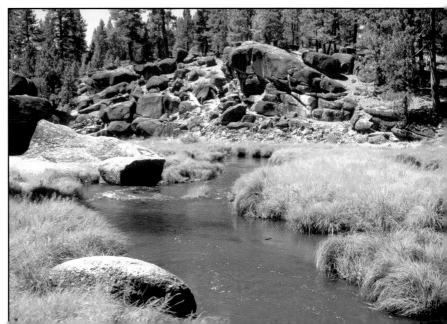

giant in a gorge through which few kayakers could make it in one piece. As you see from the top, the gorge is nigh impossible to traverse by kayak, canoe, or rubber raft.

Note: A portion of this hike is on land owned by Graeagle Land and Water Company. The company's owner has requested that people not use his property except for foot travel. Approval for access is explicitly denied for cars and trucks (other than for travel to the trailhead), bicycles, motorcycles, horses, dogs and other domestic animals, ATVs, snowmobiles, and any other off-road vehicles. Absolutely no camping, campfires, or wood cutting is permitted. Please respect this privately owned property, and do not leave trash of any kind. If signs describe an owner other than Graeagle Land and Water Company, the property has obviously

changed ownership. In such case, please check with the new owner before hiking this trail.

Camping: None. The US Department of the Interior has classified most of the Middle Fork of the Feather River a "National Wild and Scenic River," and its banks are therefore off-limits for camping. (One of the sandy beaches has an old rock fire ring, indicating that, prior to the Wild and Scenic designation, folks enjoyed a comfortable campsite on the bank there—except when the Union Pacific 2:00 AM fast freight thundered by on the other side of the river.)

Winter Use: A-15 is plowed all winter, so you can walk to Trailhead B on snowshoes and then do the loop. I must try it sometime. (If that ferocious dog at the last house is loose, be prepared to use some aggressive countermeasures.)

B-4 Graeagle Millpond Loop Walk

Distance: ½-mile loop

Highest Point: 4,362 feet

Total Elevation Gain: 2 feet (if the side trail down to the river is included, 20 feet)

Difficulty: Easy

Hiking Season: All year

Directions to the Trailhead: In "downtown" Graeagle drive through the parking lot adjoining the Graeagle Market. In 50 yards, park in a large gravel lot that fronts on the millpond.

Comments: This is a perfect short, flat, smooth, and scenic walk for the young, the old, and everyone in-between. If you want a bit of outdoor activity but don't have time for a "major" hike, or if you have guests who aren't keen on hiking or are physically unable to do so, try this loop walk. The millpond was created by the Davies Mill Company

as a holding pond for logs brought to the site first by the logging railroad of the mill and later by logging trucks. For more history on the mill and the town of Graeagle, see the first portion of Hike B-7. In fall, aspens on the pond's eastern shore add a blaze of yellow color to the walk.

The Walk: For some undefined reason, I usually do this walk in a counterclockwise direction. The path heads east along the lakeshore, and then crosses the pond's inlet and an underground culvert coming from Gray Eagle Creek. A left turn leads onto a dike constructed to separate the pond from

Graeagle Millpond

the ravine in which the creek flows. On the far side of the ravine are duplex condominium units that are part of the attractive Graeagle Meadows complex.

At the point where the path curves left around the eastern end of the pond, a dirt road angles right, downhill. If you wish to include a short extra trip, take this 200-yard side trail down to its end where Gray Eagle Creek flows into the Middle Fork of the Feather River. Although the beach at this point is rather stony and pebbly, it is a favorite spot for kids' river play. The river is not deep here, but it is swift, and the bottom is rocky and uneven. Hence, a competent adult should be supervising any youngsters who wish to splash in the water.

Returning to the pond loop path, follow it along the top of the earthen dam, on the northern edge of the pond. On your left, the top of the outlet gate sticks out of the water. This outlet regulates the pond so that its surface is always at the same level. The one exception happens when the pond is drained

for cleaning every few years, to prevent the bottom from becoming gooky. During the several weeks of draining and drying (usually in early spring), the pond loop walk loses its appeal—to say the least.

The path makes a sharp left turn at the northernmost end of the pond and, in 100 yards, fades into the community beach. During summer days, the beach is alive with activity, a focal point for kids of all ages and their families. The large grassy area adjoining the beach is maintained by the owner of the pond, the Graeagle Land and Water Company (current owner of the rest of the Graeagle commercial area). The company graciously allows free access to the pond, the beach, and the nice acre of grass. A pair of portable johns serve the potty needs of the summer throngs as well as pond loop walkers who can't wait for better facilities.

The beach is sand mixed with mud, but, what the heck, let's not be too picky about a free and scenic privately owned community park. Along the beach, the slope of the shore is gradual, so that even toddlers can enjoy splashing in the water, with adequate adult supervision. The bottom is relatively smooth and free of sharp rocks. During summer months, a snack shack adjoining the Graeagle Market parking lot rents paddle and float boats as well as selling snacks and even (can you believe it in Graeagle?) espressos and lattes.

Although I don't recall ever seeing a "No Fishing" sign, I've never seen anyone fishing the pond either, so it probably is fishless and purposely kept that way by the company.

Note: The peak activity at the millpond is the community's annual Fourth of July fireworks display (if the Fourth falls on a weekend, the fireworks may be another day). The shoot-'em-off area is on the grass, and the aerial bursts are directly over the pond. If you think that little old Graeagle's fireworks are mediocre, guess again. They are outstanding—no kidding.

Camping: None.

Winter Use: The loop certainly isn't plowed in the winter, but, unless the snow is deep, the pond can be circumnavigated without snowshoes all winter. Use plenty of caution, however, especially if icy conditions prevail. A cold snap will freeze much of the pond's surface, but ice-skating is too dangerous because the thickness of the ice is unpredictable.

B-5 West Branch of Humbug Creek Trail

Distance: 5½ miles out and back

Highest Point: 6,016 feet

Total Elevation Gain: 933 feet

Difficulty: Moderate

Hiking Season: May through October

Directions to the Trailhead: From Graeagle go north on Highway 89 for 1.2 miles to its intersection with Highway 70. Turn right on 70, and drive 5.8 miles to a left turn onto Willow Creek Road (24N12). After 1.1 miles, turn right at a Y onto a poorer-quality (but not bad) dirt road (23N17Y). Continue on 23N17Y over two cattle guards (detour to the right around the first one to avoid a bump), and, in 1.2 miles from the Y, you encounter another Y with 23N21. Take the right fork, continuing on 23N17Y, for another 1.0 mile, passing several rutty roads to the right, which lead into Delleker (a much shorter but much bumpier access). Branch left, still on 23N17Y (some nearby Delleker houses can be glimpsed on the right beyond the creek), drive another .7 mile, and park off the road. There is nothing remarkable about this trailhead location. The road ahead is a bit bumpy uphill so I figure this is as good a place as any to begin walking.

Comments: Although this trail is 100 percent back roads, these roads get so little traffic that you probably won't mind walking on them rather than a path. In late summer, tiny Humbug Creek West Branch seems to have about the same water flow as it does in spring, the result of being fed by springs rather than primarily by snowmelt. The English would call it a babbling brook, and, indeed, its babble can be heard in many places because it closely parallels the road for most of the hike. At the turnaround spot, you will enjoy the "dancing bear" and other volcanic formations. The trail lies within the State Game Refuge, hence no hunting or firearms are allowed.

The Hike: Head uphill on the relatively smooth and traffic-free road. The little creek flows downhill in the opposite direction, and its banks are clogged with bushes in only a few places (an unusual feature among Feather River country streams). Although you might pass by without noticing, within ¼ mile a side road (23N17YB), blocked with a steel barrier, leaves at a 90° angle to the right.

Almost all of the hike to the turnaround spot is uphill, but none of it is so steep that a hiker in average condition will have to huff and puff. The display of trees along the route is guaranteed to bring you enjoyment. Douglas-firs and white firs are prominent, with a few red firs thrown in. The pine family is well represented, with Jeffrey, sugar (with its foot-long cones), and ponderosa. There are some beautiful specimens of ponderosa along the way, with trunks almost bright orange. The conifer forest also includes many fine cedars, with their beautiful redwood-like trunks. I stopped to take a picture of a large boulder on the right side of the road whose left profile looked like George Washington (well, sort of) and whose right profile resembled a beast—I'll let you determine what kind.

Fleeting views of the top of Smith Peak can be seen directly ahead. A mile from the trailhead, water from nearby springs dampens the road. A road closed by a large berm goes straight while the main route angles right, crossing over the stream, which runs silently underneath in a culvert. A sign saying "Willow Creek 4, Smith Peak 6" points to the right. (My map shows Willow Creek to be closer than 4 miles—more like 2, I'd say.)

You go ½ mile beyond this fork, where 23N17YA intersects on the left but is blocked by a couple of well-placed boulders, and a few hundred yards farther you reach the first "major" intersection of the hike. Here, 23N84Y cuts back sharply to the right, eventually reaching Lake Davis. Whatever small amount of traffic passes this way seems to take this right turn, thus leaving your path ahead with few tire tracks. In 200 yards, the still-smooth route recrosses the creek and runs parallel to it on its western bank. By now, the stream is reduced to a big trickle, too small to babble anymore.

With less than ½ mile left to go to the hike's turnaround, the road makes a sharp left turn, and, for the first time, no longer parallels the creek. Another little spring on the right empties a small amount of water onto the road. Beyond the spring, the track gets steeper and a bit rocky in places. Good views off to the left encompass Peak 6826 (it is nice but nameless) and farther off the buildings in Graeagle. The top of the ridge nears as the tree cover thins.

The turnaround place is at the "dancing bear," a prominent lava outcropping to the left of the road. Clamber down from the road nearer to it and you'll see that I am not crazy: It does look like the silhouette of a bear in proper ballroom form. Other nearby volcanic outcroppings offer photo ops too, before you head downhill to your car. Or, if you want to see

the very upper part of Willow Creek as it flows off the south side of Smith Peak, you can reach it by continuing for another ½ mile beyond the turnaround place that I've selected.

Camping: Any number of levelish spots along the creek would do for a backpack campsite, but I did not see any signs of fire rings to indicate prior use by campers. The size of Humbug Creek West Branch is sufficient for drinking and cooking water, but the only part of your body you will be able to submerge in it is your feet.

Winter Use: None.

B-6 Mohawk Valley History Loop Walk

Distance: Loop A, 3½ miles; Loop B, 2 ¾ miles; Loop C, 5½ miles
Highest Point: 4,365 feet
Total Elevation Gain: 10 feet
Difficulty: Easy/Moderate
Hiking Season: All year

Directions to the Trailhead: All three loops commence in "downtown" Graeagle at the intersection of Highway 89 and Iroquois Trail (a paved street), across from the Chevron station. Parking is available behind the station or near the millpond. Please don't park next to the gas station or in the parking lot of Graeagle Market, both of which are reserved for customers.

Comments: I call this a walk, not a hike, because most of it is on paved roads. It's an excellent way to see and learn about some of the historic sites in Mohawk Valley. Loop C passes most of the sites in one long trek. Loops A and B are separate shorter walks, with A covering roughly the first half of Loop C and B following most of the remainder of C.

The earliest residents of Mohawk Valley were Native Americans. The Mountain Maidu people were the most recent tribe to live in the area, al-

though their small villages ranged far beyond the Mohawk Valley itself. In 1854, two brothers by the name of Penman were the first pioneers to settle in the valley. The Penman families established farms to supply fresh food to the gold miners in the mountains. It is believed that the name of the valley came from the Appalachia area of New York State from which some of the earliest settlers had migrated.

The Walk: Graeagle is a "newcomer" in comparison with the region's gold rush towns of the 1850s and railroad and lumbering towns of the 1890s. In 1917, Arthur Davies, a successful sawmill owner from Sardine Valley, closed his mill there and purchased a large tract of land from the Sierra Iron Company on which to establish a new sawmill. The site became known as Davies Mill. To provide workers' housing, Davies hired the Boca-Loyalton Railroad to haul company houses from the closed

Sardine Valley mill to his new mill town. Each house was sawed in half, loaded on a flat car, and transported to Beckwourth by rail. At Beckwourth, the 92 house halves were transferred to the Nevada, California, and Oregon Railroad and brought to Davies Mill. As you begin your walk, look to the right, down Main Street, and note that many of the company-owned houses, now occupied by various shops, have a seam down the middle where they were patched back together after the move.

In 1921 Davies sold the mill and town to the California Fruit Exchange, whose headquarters was in Sacramento. At that time the town was renamed Graeagle and the mill renamed Graeagle Lumber Company. Some fanciful controversy exists about how the name was chosen. My favorite of these tales contends that a name-the-town contest offered a $25 prize for the winning name. As the story goes, the company bookkeeper looked out the window of her office (a wing of what is now the Graeagle

Market) and saw a sign saying "Gray Eagle Creek." She put the words together, creating the winning name, Graeagle.

The reason a fruit company wanted to own a sawmill was to make its own wooden boxes for shipping Sacramento Valley produce. The new owners rebuilt the mill near the millpond and added a box factory, a moldings mill, a planing mill, dry kilns, and a huge boiler facility to generate steam. All of the buildings in town, including the houses, were heated by steam from those boilers. Employees joked that the steam heat, which was included in their $25 monthly house rent, provided two temperatures: too hot and too cold.

Davies had created a completely self-sufficient community by raising a herd of beef and dairy cows in the meadows back of the mill. A slaughterhouse and separate dairy were built. In 1956, after 40 years of operation, the California Fruit Exchange sold out. Soon thereafter the mill closed permanently be-

Loop A - - - -
Graeagle and
Mohawk Loop

Loop B - - - -
Greaeagle and
Blairsden
Loop

Loop C - - - -
Graeagle,
Mohawk, and
Blairsden
Big Loop

cause cardboard boxes for produce had made wooden boxes obsolete. Most of the buildings were dismantled or destroyed by fire. You will encounter the cute dairy building and the foundations of the old mill at the end of Loop B or Loop C.

Let's get started on Loops A and C, which follow the same route for several miles. From the Chevron station, cross Main Street (State Highway 89), and walk up Iroquois Trail. Although not visible today, several caves for cold storage of perishable fruits and vegetables were dug into the hillside facing Main Street at this point. Summer cooling was provided by chunks of ice packed in sawdust. Walking up the easy hill on Iroquois Trail, you see some of the old, but still used, company houses surrounding the athletic field. Supposedly most of these houses have a trapdoor in the bedroom under the bed. The story goes that, as a favor to its employees, in September each year, the California Fruit Exchange would send several carloads of grapes to town. When the grapes arrived, the mill whistle would alert the employees, and work would cease while they rushed to the railroad cars to get their "share." The art of making wine must have been learned from the mill's Italian employees. When prohibition arrived, the winemaking evidently continued, and the aforementioned trapdoors were installed for access into a secret shallow wine cellar. I doubt if there is any 1925 vintage still hidden.

On your left, at the crest of the hill, is the athletic field, originally built for the town's baseball diamond and boxing arena. The popular Sportsman's Association of Graeagle conducted monthly boxing matches in the now-long-gone 800-seat lit arena. These bouts attracted boxers from many parts of the western United States. Continue on Iroquois Trail for another two blocks, and turn right onto Navajo Trail. Follow the paved road past nice summer homes until the road turns to dirt and the houses are left behind.

Walk 200 yards on the dirt road, and then take a trail angling off to the left. It crosses a small, easily jumped, creeklet that is dry in summer and autumn. If you miss the trail, you'll soon come to where the road dead-ends at a fence line. Go back about 200 yards, and look for the trail. After crossing the creeklet, you encounter several horse paths crossing your route, and the trail becomes the old railroad right-of-way. Stay on the railroad grade, which is easily identifiable at this point. The tracks, which were ripped up many years ago and sold for scrap, ran through the forest on a flat course. The trail soon angles to the left, down from the berm and, in a few up-and-down steps, reaches a paved road cul-de-sac at the end of Gold Ridge Drive in the Goldridge Estates subdivision.

Bygone logging trains chugged along what is now Gold Ridge Drive, turning left onto today's Jamison Road. At the point where Jamison Road curves right, the rail spur curved left and headed up the south side of Smith Creek to Knickrem Sawmill, located ½ mile up the creek. No sign of the 1890s mill remains, although a few cabin remnants can be found in the forest nearby. The mill site is on private property, so please don't trespass. Follow Jamison Road for two blocks, past its curve to the right, to an intersection with the Graeagle-Johnsville Road (County Road A-14). Along this portion of Jamison Road, local residents have found Maidu arrowheads, and on the other side of Smith Creek is, reportedly, the site of an ancient Maidu village. Near the road intersection was the original location of the Mohawk Valley Post Office, which opened on July 24, 1870. In 1881 the building was moved farther west, and "valley" was dropped from its name. In 1929 the Mohawk Post Office was closed permanently.

Turn left on A-14, crossing over Smith Creek, which runs through a large culvert under the road. During the infamous New Year's Flood of 1997, the volume of water was so large that the creek overflowed the road. Just past Smith Creek is the once bustling village of Mohawk. On the left is Mohawk's "watering hole"—the old, and still fully functioning, Mohawk Tavern. If the day is warm (or even if it's not), the tavern is a good place to stop for "a cool one." Across the road are several dilapidated cabins, which were once rented out to tourists by the Mohawk Hotel. Next to the cabins is a large outdoor stone fireplace used for many years by the Mohawk Hotel for barbecues and under-the-stars cocktail parties. The long-unused swimming pool for the hotel is located near the fireplace. This is the site of the valley's first homestead, established in 1854 by pioneer Robert Penman and his family. His brother, George, built a log cabin across the river, where the Feather River Inn now is.

You cannot miss the closed Mohawk Hotel. The original was built in 1881 by John Sutton, who had purchased the Robert Penman homestead. When my wife and I first vacationed in Graeagle in the mid-1960s, the hotel had been closed but the dining room (the large room with big windows jutting out on the eastern side) served all-you-can-eat buf-

fet dinners. As I recall, they were long on quantity but a bit short on quality, although I always left in an overstuffed condition. The derelict hotel now sits quietly waiting for you to come along, purchase it (heck, the owner might even give it to you), and remodel it into a first-class bed-and-breakfast.

Behind the hotel is a more modern large square building with no windows. This is the Mohawk handball court. Why it was built, I'm not sure. Perhaps a once-upon-a-time owner of the Mohawk Tavern loved handball and wanted his own court, or perhaps someone thought it would establish Mohawk as a recreational center and thus cause a renaissance for the town. I've never seen anyone using it, so this may represent your opportunity to become a business owner in Mohawk if remodeling the hotel doesn't appeal to you.

Just past the hotel on the left is a private dirt road that follows Smith Creek westerly. This is the approximate route of one of the stagecoach roads

The old dairy building in Mohawk Valley

from the mining communities of Johnsville, Jamison City, and Eureka Mills down into the Mohawk Valley.

The unsigned Mohawk Highway Road turns right after the hotel, connecting Mohawk with Highway 70. At this point, you need to decide whether to turn right and do Loop C or turn around and head back on A-14 to complete Loop A. In either case, if you have plenty of energy left, you may wish to make a minor side trip and continue for another 300 yards along A-14 up the steep hill. Just before you reach the top, turn left onto the short steep road to Mohawk Cemetery, founded in 1867. It has been partially restored and is fun to visit if you like to wander around and look at old gravestones.

Back at the intersection, to complete Loop A, head back along A-14, and continue past the entrance to Feather River Park Resort. Just before you reach Olsen's Cabin Restaurant, you can see on the right a flat area several feet above the road. This was the site of the original Mohawk School, gone for many years. The one-room building was soon outgrown as the population increased in this part of Mohawk Valley.

Continue east on A-14 past the Community Church to the intersection with Highway 89. Across 89 is the two-story building that replaced the one-room schoolhouse. It was known as the Mann School, but many a year has passed since children trekked to the site. Old-timers remember how hard it was to keep "schoolmarms" because a large percentage of the mill workers and loggers were single males "lookin' for a wife." Turn right on Highway 89 (Main Street) and walk to your car past this part of the Graeagle commercial district, completing Loop A.

If you choose longer Loop C, take Mohawk Highway Road at the Café Mohawk, and head north toward Highway 70. On the left are the remains of the old Standard Oil gas station, probably with leaking underground tanks and a need for toxic waste

cleanup. A sawmill had been built on this site in 1855 by George Woodward, the Penmans' first neighbor.

Continue on Mohawk Highway Road across the "new" Feather River bridge. The "old" bridge was swept away by the flood of 1985. After the bridge, on your left, are the fourth and fifth holes of the Feather River Inn Golf Course, one of California's earliest, built in 1919. At Little Bear Road, just before reaching the USFS Mohawk Ranger Station, turn right and head east. Soon, on the bank high above to your left appears the main line of the Union Pacific Railroad. It was originally built by the Western Pacific Railroad (WPRR merged into the Union Pacific in the 1980s) as an alternative route to the tracks of the Southern Pacific Railroad over Donner Summit. The Feather River route, completed in 1910, became part of the transcontinental rail line over which heavy freight trains (but no Amtrak passenger trains) still pass. WPRR built a wagon road through the Feather River Canyon to serve the crews constructing the original tracks. The route of this old road became present-day Highway 70.

Continue on Little Bear Road as it winds through a very pretty part of Mohawk Valley with views of Penman Peak (yes, named for the pioneer Penman) on the left and of Eureka Peak on the right. Just before reaching an intersection with Highway 89, on the left you'll notice a large old barn. This is the site of the Lemm Ranch, one of the valley's most prosperous spreads. Once it had many buildings, but a 1928 fire destroyed some. The neighboring grain field became the impromptu "Valley Airport." The name "Blairsden" (no longer visible) written on the barn's roof alerted early pilots to the location of the unpaved landing field (Blairsden being the nearest town). In the late 1910s and early 1920s, whenever an airplane arrived, people came from all over the valley to see the new-fangled flying machine. The term "barnstorming" came from the practice of using barn signs like "Blairsden" before radios and other route-finding devices came into aviation service.

Where Little Bear Road crosses Highway 89 (and changes its name to Bonta Street), look left under the railroad overpass to see cars and trucks whizzing by on Highway 70, Plumas County's main route to Oroville and Reno. East of this point, 70 follows the old stage road that predated the railroad. Early efforts to build today's highway commenced in 1913 when area residents lobbied to make this route part of the Lincoln National Highway, the nation's first coast-to-coast highway. The effort failed, and road building did not start until 1928, when the state took it up with a crew of convict laborers. By 1930, the number of convict workers had swelled to 1,250, and a convict camp was established near Quincy. Construction slowed substantially in early 1930 due to the Great Depression. In all, 56 miles had been built "by hand" with convict labor. In 1935 steam shovels and bulldozers replaced the convicts, substantially speeding construction. By spring 1937, three tunnels had been completed, the road had been oiled (but not paved) from Oroville to Quincy, and the dangerous Keddie-Quincy "death stretch" had been improved. On August 14, 1937, Chief Winnemucca, last chief of the Paiute Indians, formally opened the $8.15 million Feather River Highway to traffic. The whole route was finally paved in 1942.

At this point, anyone walking Loop B from Graeagle along Highway 89 will turn right and join the route of Loop C on Bonta Street, which then enters Blairsden, the former site of the Bonta Ranch. Blairsden was named after James A. Blair, an early financier of the WPRR. The town was built by a subsidiary of the WPRR in 1910 to be a depot and a residence for the railroad construction workers. Many of the original buildings of Blairsden are still in use. Several had slot machines and gambling downstairs, and one reportedly had a house of ill repute upstairs.

When the Feather River Inn was constructed in 1914, Blairsden became the stop on the WPRR where people disembarked to stay at the inn. In those days, with car travel difficult, the train was the favored way to come to the Feather River country. The inn's reputation was so outstanding that many of the rich and famous passed through the Blairsden station on their way to a vacation at the inn.

As you approach the town, one of the first buildings on the left in the old days would have been the railroad station. No indication of its site remains, but the building itself lives on: It was moved a couple of hundred yards easterly and converted into a residence. During the First World War, a hobo camp came into being at the eastern end of town, with shacks made of tin and cardboard. Many of its residents were draft dodgers and deserters, so the sheriff occasionally visited the site.

Continue easterly along the road for ¼ mile to the one-lane bridge over the Feather River. As you walk across, stop midspan and look upstream. Where the river disappears from sight, the bit of green grass seen in the distance is part of the Graeagle Meadows Golf Course. This course was built by filling a large, soft, boggy swamp. I wonder how many birds, mammals, reptiles, insects, and other members of nature's domain lost their homes when the swamp became fairways, greens, and sand traps. On the other hand, it's a mighty nice golf course.

Much closer to the bridge, you'll notice some almost-rotted pilings sticking out of the water near both shores. They are the remains of the once famous (albeit only locally) Feather River Bridge, where the main wagon road from Beckwourth to Johnsville through the Mohawk Valley crossed the river. Compared to the Golden Gate Bridge, which was completed a mere 50 years later, it may not appear particularly spectacular. But to the early pioneers it must have been a heck of an improvement over fording the water in a wagon with a team of horses, especially in spring, when the river was full and fast.

Once across the one-lane bridge, you see the decidedly not historic trash recycling center on the right, demonstrating that modern Feather River country residents do indeed care about the environment. On the left is one of the pastures used by the mill company's dairy herd, and on the right is the cute stone dairy building with its adjoining corrals. Many people wonder about the emblem embossed in front of the building—an anchor bearing the name "Pacific Fruit Exchange." The Fruit Exchange helped make the mill town self-sufficient by operating its own dairy.

Just past the County Road Maintenance Facility, turn left onto Maricopa Trail, which makes a beeline for the millpond through the former site of the sawmill and its ancillary buildings. A few buildings remain, but old concrete foundations attest to the fact that, in days gone by, this was a much larger complex. Just before reaching the lot where your car is parked, note the large red building with a big truck door on the end. A closer look shows you that the door size was once much bigger. This was the mill's railroad car and locomotive repair shop. Tracks went right into the building so that a steam engine in need of repair could be run inside. The millpond was created to hold floating logs brought in from the neighboring forest by logging trains and later trucks. With log "storage" in the pond, a supply of logs to be milled was available into the winter when snow closed the rails and roads.

Loop B starts at the same place as Loops A and C but heads north on Highway 89 past the intersection with the Graeagle-Johnsville Road (County Road A-14) where the Mann School, mentioned in the Loop A description, is on the right. Continue on 89, crossing over the Middle Fork of the Feather River. When you're 1 mile from the start, 89 intersects Little Bear Road as it changes name to Bonta Street. You turn right onto Bonta Street and pick up the route of Loop C, described earlier.

Camping: RVs can camp at Little Bear or Movin' West RV parks. No other camping is available.

Winter Use: If the roads have been plowed (they all usually are plowed by the county soon after a snowstorm), any of the three loops can be walked most of the winter, watching out for icy spots. The only part that might be challenging is the railroad grade section through the forest between Navajo Trail and Goldridge Subdivision (Loops A and C). In winter, you can detour around this part by hiking Highway 89 north to the Graeagle-Johnsville Road, turning left, and continuing west past the one-room schoolhouse site to reunite with Loops A and C at Jamison Road.

Chapter 11

Sierra City and Haypress Valley Topos

SC-1 Tamarack Lakes Route to Sierra Buttes

Distance: 7½ miles out and back from Trailhead A; 5½ miles out and
back from Trailhead B

Highest Point: 8,591 feet

Total Elevation Gain: 2,436 feet from Trailhead A;
1,871 feet from Trailhead B

Difficulty: Strenuous

Hiking Season: June through October

Directions to the Trailhead: Follow the directions for Hike SC-3, but, once you're on Forest Road 93, do not drive all the way uphill to Packer Saddle; instead, drive .2 mile past the entrance road to Packer Lake Lodge, and turn right into a gravel parking area. This is Trailhead A. If you have a four-wheel-drive high-clearance vehicle and wish to drive to Trailhead B, turn left here, and drive the slow mile to Lower Tamarack Lake. Both trailheads have plenty of parking.

Comments: This hike takes the slightly more difficult, less-traveled route to the top of Sierra Buttes (it's an alternative to Hike SC-2). However, it's a lovely hike, and the view from the top is an "all-timer." If you don't have four-wheel drive, you'd best park at Trailhead A. This is no big penalty; it adds only 2 miles (round trip) and 565 feet of elevation gain. The jeep road to Tamarack Lakes is a nice hike from Trailhead A. If you have four-wheel drive and want to drive to Tamarack Lakes to start from Trailhead B, you will find the drive slow but doable. This is one of my favorite hikes, and I never tire of the views from the lookout on top of the buttes.

The Hike: From Trailhead A, cross 93, and head south on the jeep road toward Tamarack Lakes. You soon pass through an open gate and, in ¼ mile, reach a road junction at which you continue straight. Remember this junction in case you want to make a short enjoyable side trip on your way back—it's described at the end of the hike.

The jeep road to the buttes climbs some smooth rock outcroppings and zigzags slightly, following above the Tamarack Lakes outlet creek. Just before you reach the lower lake, a trail comes in from the left leading to the Sardine Lakes (Hike SC-4). Just beyond this trail intersection is Trailhead B, and there, through the trees, you can spy Lower Tamarack Lake close at hand. A great photo of Sierra Buttes rising majestically 1,890 feet above the surface of the lake can be shot from the lower lake's north shore.

If you stroll around the western side of Lower Tamarack Lake, you come to a jeep trail that cuts over to Upper Tamarack Lake. Here too, a camera buff will enjoy framing the rugged buttes behind the sparkling lake. Through spring and well into summer, snow still fills the crevices on the northern face of the buttes, enhancing the picture. You, however, need to tear yourself away from the great view and get back to the main trail. From the upper lake, you need not retrace your steps to the lower lake but can scramble cross-country directly uphill from the upper lake's western shore. A 100-foot climb puts you back on the trail, where you continue in a southerly direction toward the buttes. Up and up the trail climbs. In ¼ mile it reaches a jeep road that angles across it and heads down to the Tamarack Lakes inlet creek. I had hoped that I might reach a nice backpack campsite on the creek by taking this jeep road downhill. Unfortunately, the creek

there is so thickly choked with alder and willow bushes that the water is virtually inaccessible. The ground is boggy, so it's not even a very good side trip for a lunch beside the creek on your way up to the buttes lookout.

As the trail crosses the jeep road, make sure you pick up the trail heading uphill because, at this point, the jeep road looks more like a trail than the trail itself, and it is easy to get fooled. The nice trail continues to gain altitude at a rapid rate and, after a sharp turn right, circles left and reaches a T intersection with the PCT. Here, a sign on the trail you're on names it the "Tamarack Lakes Connection Trail" but no sign identifies the intersecting trail as the PCT. At this junction, turn left and continue up the steep route the remaining 1½ miles to the buttes lookout. You are now be on the same path as Hike SC-2, so please read the description in that hike of the route to the top.

I'll simply add that your views from here on are way above average (and average in this country is pretty high). I hope it is a clear day for your ascent. Along this portion of the hike, there are some marvelous spots for a lunch break with a tip-top view, so it's worthwhile starting early enough to lunch "on the mountain." The return hike is, naturally, all downhill. You'll remark that, indeed, you did a heck of a climb that morning because somehow the trail seems even steeper downhill than it did on the way up. I know, that isn't logical, but I think my anticipation of the lookout's grandeur always makes the trip up seem less steep than it really is.

If you happen to have leftover energy and time for a nice 1-mile-loop side trip, on your way back, at the junction you made note of earlier (about ¼ mile before you're back at the open gate near the start of the hike), take the road on your right. In 200 yards this side road forks, with the right branch blocked to traffic by a locked gate. If you walk past the gate for 300 yards, you encounter idyllic Dugan Pond. Surprisingly, when I took this side trip there were no "Keep Out" signs, so I walked to the pond and admired the Dugan cabin, located on the south shore. If you picture the perfect remote mountain cabin on the shore of a small lake with peaceful, beautiful surroundings, this is it. Of course, please don't molest the privately owned cabin or anything around it. Just admire from a distance, and keep walking around the south side of the pond. Just past the cabin is a private campground, well outfitted with all the wood-crafted comforts. Here, too, please, admire and skirt by without entering.

To finish this side trip, continue along a dim trail, which then reaches a better trail (Hike SC-6). Turn left, and loop back along the north side of the pond, crossing the outlet creek. The trail becomes a dim unused road, which comes, in a short dis-

Young America Lake and the Sardine Lakes viewed from the ridge just below the Sierra Buttes Lookout

tance, to a road junction. Here is where you turned right a while ago at the locked gate, so retrace your steps to the Tamarack Lakes jeep road, and head for your car on that road.

Camping: There is no camping on the buttes trail but both Tamarack Lakes have good camping. If your vehicle has the four-wheel drive needed to get to Trailhead B, you can car-camp at either the upper or the lower lake. On a backpacking trip along the PCT, I detoured down to Upper Tamarack Lake and camped on its south shore near the inlet creek. Several nice campsites are there, and, if you're lucky, no car campers will be on the other side of the lake, or if some are there, they won't be rowdy.

Winter Use: None.

SC-2 Easier Western Approach Trail to Sierra Buttes

Distance: 4½ miles out and back

Highest Point: 8,791 feet

Total Elevation Gain: 1,847 feet

Difficulty: Moderate/strenuous

Hiking Season: June through October

Directions to the Trailhead: Follow the directions for Hike SC-3, but, .4 mile after Packer Saddle, take the dirt road (93-02) off Forest Road 93 with a sign "Sierra Buttes L.O. 3." This gravel road is suitable for all cars. Don't park in the parking lot at this intersection; instead, continue on 93-02 for another .2 mile where you will find a parking lot on either side of the road. A sign on the road here says "Sierra Buttes OHV Trail 2¼ miles." Although a heavy-duty four-wheel drive can make it to the "upper" parking area, 93-02 is too tough for a normal SUV even if it has four-wheel drive, so, let's walk up the trail instead. (The PCT route shown on the topo map is completely different from reality today, so follow my directions instead.)

Comments: This trail to the lookout on top of Sierra Buttes is one of the heaviest used in the area, for good reason. Although it is uphill all the way, and steep in parts, the 1,800-foot-plus elevation gain can be done by taking it slow and easy. Spectacular views toward the Tamarack Lakes along the route are surpassed by even more spectacular views from the lookout on top. Folks with vertigo and aversion to heights may wish to forgo climbing the steel stairs up the rock to the lookout. The lookout building is closed, but the balcony around it gives unsurpassed 360° views of the region.

The Hike: The trail commences at a sign saying "Sierra Buttes Trail" on the eastern side of the road. Actually, the new route of the PCT follows this part of the trail as well as going along the road back

to Packer Saddle. You head uphill and continue uphill for most of the way to the lookout. (How else do you expect to gain 1,847 feet in only 2¼ miles?) The trail is a bit dusty and a bit rocky, but it's actually not too bad. In ¼ mile, you reach a Y with a wide trail to the right. Stay on the beaten path to the left. Hiking another ¼ mile, you encounter another wide trail going straight ahead (you see the backs of some signs, one above the other, on this false trail). Here your route makes a 90° right turn, and a row of rocks across the false trail helps you identify the proper path.

Lakes view from the balcony of the lookout tower on Sierra Buttes

The views are getting better by the minute as Upper and Lower Tamarack Lakes appear in the valley below. The trail follows along a dry slope that is covered with wildflowers in midsummer. Yellow sulfur buckwheat, yellow mule ears, white Mariposa lilies, red skyrocket gilia, red Indian paintbrush, and lavender pennyroyal all cluster to make a natural garden of which Mother Nature can be proud. About ¾ mile from the trailhead, the path levels, briefly, and a trail intersects on the left, with a sign saying "Tamarack Connection Trail" (see Hike SC-1).

The well-beaten Sierra Buttes Trail, however, is easy to follow and continues easterly uphill. Your rate of ascent will be slowed by numerous side trips to the left to take in nice views of the Tamarack Lakes almost 1,000 feet below. Inaccessible Young America Lake soon joins the view almost directly below the edge of the ridge on which you're standing. A photo opportunity this is, indeed, but there

are plenty more awaiting you on the route to the top. About 1½ miles from the start, you come to the parking area for the husky four-wheel-drive vehicles that braved the road up. This isn't a parking lot, but rather a jumble of dusty tracks all intersecting and going every which way. The trail is easy to follow through the maze, however, and now the final climb commences. A ½-mile steep ascent on a trail without scary cliffs brings you to the base of the lookout tower steps. On the way up you'll marvel at the views southerly across the North Yuba River basin.

Even if you don't ascend the steel stairs to the lookout tower on the summit, the Yuba views plus the views north toward Lakes Basin are reward enough. The large level area at the bottom of the stairs sports a metal plaque and a wooden sign. The plaque honors the five USFS employees who "with great difficulty made it possible for visitors to climb to the lookout with ease and safety." It explains that "they constructed the metal stairs, hand rails and platforms, attaching them to the rocky side of this peak in the summer of 1964." I have talked to people who made the ascent prior to 1964, and it entailed climbing a bunch of ladders. I'm glad the "famous five" did their deed, because I suspect I would not have accomplished a ladder ascent. The ladders were used for over 100 years, however, first by gutsy miners and then by adventuresome early-day tourists coming up from Sierra City.

The wooden sign tells how the buttes came into being 350 million years ago and describes some of the mining activity in the area 150 years ago. The climb up the steel stairs is easy but not for those with fear of heights or vertigo. The lookout station itself has been closed for many years, as have most other fire lookouts. The lookout building, however,

is surrounded with a balcony on which visitors can walk. The views are unsurpassed. The floor of the balcony is steel grating through which you can see. Much of the balcony hangs over the edge of the peak, so you look down between your feet a long way to the sharp rocks below. A bit unnerving? Yes, indeed.

The route back to the trailhead gives you a second chance to soak up the views. As you whiz back down, you will marvel (I hope) at how well you conquered the steep uphill trail on the way in. Guaranteed, when you show your photos, folks not familiar with the Feather River country will be highly impressed with the views from this hike.

Camping: None. Try the Tamarack Lakes (see Hike SC-1) for camping within hiking distance of the buttes.

Winter Use: None.

SC-3 Old Gold Valley Trail and Robinson Cow Camp Loop

Distance: 5½-mile loop

Highest Point: 6,820 feet

Total Elevation Gain: 902 feet

Difficulty: Moderate

Hiking Season: June through October

Directions to the Trailhead: From Graeagle, go south on Highway 89 for 1.4 miles to Gold Lake Highway, and turn right. After 14 miles, turn right toward Sardine and Packer Lakes. In a short distance, a paved road goes right at a 90° angle to Packer Lake and Sierra Buttes. Take it, drive past the entrance to Packer Lake Lodge, and continue up the very steep paved narrow road (at this point designated Forest Road 93) to Packer Saddle, a four-way road intersection. Turn left on 93, past the dirt road heading left to Sierra Buttes, and then make a right onto a gravel road (Forest

Road 93-3). After you go .7 mile on this well-graded road, a jeep trail cuts left downhill. Actually, this is the trailhead, but there's no place to park headed in this direction, so drive a bit farther to where you have room to turn around. There is a wide enough shoulder for parking along 93-3 at the trailhead in the opposite direction. (A husky four-wheel-drive jeep can actually do the first ¼ mile of the jeep road, but even SUVs should not venture down this steep hill.)

Comments: This hike starts on a jeep trail, branches onto a seldom used road (formerly the

Gold Valley Trail), reaches a gravel road that sees a few cars a day, and winds up at the historic Robinson Cow Camp. (Well, it's old, so it must be historic—anyhow, it's a ghost camp.) You'll need to cross Butcher Ranch Creek without a bridge or stepping-stones, so you might want to bring along an old pair of sneakers to change into for wading across (it's an easy wade). Change out of them into your regular hiking shoes once on the other side, wrap the soggy shoes in something waterproof, and pop them into your daypack. Or, if you don't mind hiking in wet boots, just plunge into the ankle-deep stream for the crossing, and squish along for a while until the boots dry out.

The Hike: From the trailhead, take the jeep road heading steeply downhill with the sign "Butcher Ranch OHV Trail." (You probably know that OHV means off-highway vehicle—or jeep.) The first mile of the hike is on the Butcher Ranch Creek Trail (also part of Hike GL-11), also known as the Downieville Descent by mountain bikers, who frequent this challenging downhill bike ride to Downieville. On weekends, you'll encounter more bikers than on weekdays, but it's only for the first

half-hour, so don't let the prospect of a few bikers whizzing by in a cloud of dust discourage you from taking this hike.

Before you reach the intersection of the Butcher Ranch Creek Trail and the old Gold Valley Trail, you need to cross the South Fork of Butcher Ranch Creek. Bikers naturally plow through the water, and you can too, if you plan to get your boots wet at the later crossing of the creek. However, here you have two other options: change into old sneakers to wade across, or backtrack 20 yards and watch on the north side of the road for a broken-down barbed wire fence line through the willows. Be very careful of the tangle of barbed wire underfoot. Keep following the steel fence posts through the thicket of bushes (there are nice wildflowers in the midst of the bushes to cheer you amid the branches and barbed wire), and try to avoid the muddiest spots. You emerge 30 yards later at a place where the creek has nice stepping-stones for an easy crossing (yes, this singular good crossing is accessed only by the barbed wire route).

When you're 1 mile from the trailhead, the old Gold Valley Trail branches off to the right with a sign saying "OHV Trail." This route is shown on Arthur W. Keddie's 1892 map of Plumas County as a major wagon road running from Sierra City north through Gold Valley, past the Empire Mine, the Sierra Iron Mine (which never produced any iron), and the successful Four Hills Mine. It then turned into a pack trail, crossing over the ridge, and descended to Johnsville via Jamison Creek (Hike GL-19). When it no longer was used as a wagon road, it became more like a trail than a road, but it has been resurrected into rough road status by the OHV crowd. I judge that not many jeeps use this route, however, because it is not very rutted or dusty.

Take the Gold Valley OHV Trail, which soon fords Butcher Ranch Creek. Here you need to exercise whichever creek-crossing technique you have selected. The route then strikes uphill and, in ¾ mile, begins to parallel the North Fork of Butcher

Ranch Creek. About 1 mile beyond the creek crossing, you reach a loggers' clearing, with a Y in the road at the far end of it. The OHV trail is the right fork, as an arrow sign nailed to a tree says. Because the old Gold Valley Trail was the left fork, I took that one and came to a dead end 1 mile later. Even the 1981 topo map shows the trail continuing north to the Empire Mine, but, alas, nature has erased its location. Even if the trail had been passable to Empire Mine, I'm sure I would have found "No Trespassing" signs (see Hike GL-11).

So, take the right fork at the loggers' clearing, and continue uphill as it slowly makes a big looping curve easterly. About 1 mile past the clearing, the jeep road intersects the well-graded gravel Forest Road 93-3. Turn right, and hike the road as it bends easterly and presents a fine view of Sierra Buttes, ahead. The road descends to a hairpin curve, under which Butcher Ranch Creek flows in a culvert. Because I enjoy walking along a stream rather than along a moderately used gravel road, I left the road and walked without benefit of a trail along the north side of the creek for ½ mile. I think you also will like this detour, because in midsummer the

banks had a plethora of wildflowers. The road eventually parallels the creek only a few yards away. When the two began to diverge, I climbed back up to the road and continued south on it.

As you trudge along, keep an eye out for an unsigned road on your right with a large neatly stacked pile of rotting logs that the loggers never took to the mill. Leave 93-3 via this side road, and, in ¼ mile, you arrive at Robinson Cow Camp. The cow camp was, I surmise, where the Robinson wranglers stayed while their herd chomped up the lush grass in the adjoining meadow. The larger cabin was obviously living quarters. Peeking in an open window, I thought it must have been many a year since a cowhand had stayed there—although I was surprised to see unopened cans of food on the shelf and soap by the deteriorating sink. The smaller building probably was a stable and supply shed; judging by the angle of the roof and walls, another year or so of heavy snow may collapse it.

The best feature of the cow camp is the marvelous meadow adjoining it. In midsummer it was

Yellow and blue lupine combined in a meadow along the old Gold Valley Trail

lush green and dotted with beautiful clumps of many different wildflowers. Across the meadow to the south, you can see a stream coming out of the hillside. To take a look at the gushing spring, I looped around the eastern side of the meadow, avoiding its soggy center. The spring is about the biggest I have encountered in the Feather River country. The cowhands must have enjoyed many a refreshing cold drink of water from its large concrete enclosure.

Back in the cow camp, a sign points left along a dim road announcing that Butcher Ranch Trail is in that direction. Several large trees have fallen across this exit road, preventing vehicle passage. In about 300 yards the blocked road intersects the trail. Turn left, climb the steep hill, and in less than ¼ mile you are back at your car.

Camping: The ghost camp is too spooky for camping (and too near the trailhead, anyhow). No other places look dandy for backpack camping, although at the loggers' clearing the creek was still running in August and would be an adequate water source for a camp.

Winter Use: None.

SC-4 Tamarack Lakes Trail

> **Distance:** 7 miles out and back (with extension to Sierra Buttes, 12½ miles)
>
> **Highest Point:** 7,060 feet (with extension, 8,591 feet)
>
> **Total Elevation Gain:** 1,591 feet (with extension, 3,424 feet)
>
> **Difficulty:** Moderate/strenuous (with extension, strenuous)
>
> **Hiking Season:** June through October

Directions to the Trailhead: From Graeagle, go south on Highway 89 for 1.4 miles to Gold Lake Highway, turn right, and drive 14 miles to a turnoff on the right pointing to Sardine and Packer Lakes. In a few hundred yards, at the first opportunity, turn left at a sign that says "Not a Maintained Road," and park; there's plenty of room. Alternatively, you can park along the paved road leading to the Sardine Lakes or even in the Sardine Campground 200 yards farther on the paved road.

Comments: You may have taken in many a spectacular view in the High Sierra or the Swiss Alps, but the view of Upper and Lower Sardine Lakes from this trail, with Sierra Buttes rising majestically in the immediate background, I bet will match any others you've seen. The northern exposure of the buttes, seen from many parts of this trip, is often partly covered with snow well into summer, adding to the splendor of the view. How's the trail? Well, a good bit of it is shadeless, uphill on rocks, so avoid this hike on the hottest days of summer unless you get an early start before the sun climbs too high. Boots instead of sneakers help the feet cope with the rocky trail. The views and the Tamarack Lakes certainly make the trip worth the effort. An extension of the hike leads you to the top of Sierra Buttes with its observation tower and unsurpassed 360° view.

The Hike: Near the parking spot on the "not maintained" road, on the north side is a sign saying "Tamarack Lake Connection Trail" and another "Sardine Lakes Overlook 2, Tamarack Lakes 3½, Packer Lake 4" (more like 5, I'd say). This first portion of the trail follows an old wagon road up to the Young America Mine. The trail no longer goes to the site of the mine, which is below the trail about a mile from the trailhead. The route starts uphill on small rocks, switches back and gets smoother, then passes a large concrete enclosure (probably over a spring) with 1966 embossed on it, and resumes going uphill on a rocky surface. Soon you start to get a glimpse of Lower Sardine Lake below, on the left, but don't start taking pictures yet; the view gets better the farther you go.

For a mile, there is precious little shade on this steep trail, and you will be glad that you wore a big hat, chose a cool shirt (unless it's a cool day in spring or fall), and brought along plenty of water. So far, your lake view has been of Lower Sardine Lake, but finally the upper lake comes into view too. It is even prettier than the lower lake, and the spires of Sierra Buttes rise steeply from its southern shore. Soon you hear the sound of the short creek between the upper and lower lakes below you even though the trail is now about 600 feet above the upper lake (it seems like a lot more than 600 feet).

A well-used trail branches off to the left with a sign "Sardine Lake Overlook Trail." Why this trail came into being, I'm not sure, and it is not, in my opinion, worth taking just to get a better view of the lakes. The view from where you are is just fine. Although the overlook trail is not exactly a dead end,

because it continues in a fashion all the way down to the upper lake, it has a lot of tough steep hillside, and rock slides have made the going very tricky in several places.

So, continue on the main trail a short distance beyond the trail intersection, and look over the edge. Here you can see some old rusty mining machinery and, a bit farther, a pile of tailings (obvious because they are buff-colored and without vegetation). The mine itself is just below the trail, but its entrance has caved in, and thick bushes now cover the area. What a view these miners had, though. The mine probably wasn't ever a big deal, because the tailings pile isn't enormous.

Just after the mine, the trail makes a sharp right turn. Here, to your delight, the rocks in your path disappear, and shady pine trees begin to appear, easing your progress along the few gentle switchbacks up to a saddle. The trail levels at its highest elevation (7,060 feet), and then commences gentle switchbacks downhill. Naturally, you've left the view of the Sardine Lakes behind, but to your left at one spot you can see your destination, one of the Tamarack Lakes. Shortly thereafter, off to the right, a quick glimpse of Packer Lake appears through the trees.

Dropping farther, on the right you see several shallow ponds with an interesting tapestry of round rocks on the bottom. (Perhaps by autumn these will have dried up.) No, these are not the Tamarack Lakes—keep going. Passing by some beautiful examples of glacier-smoothed granite fascia, you reach the Tamarack Lakes' outflow creek (in late summer, it may not be flowing). A few hundred yards farther, you intersect the jeep road that comes up from Packer Lake (see Hike SC-1). Yes, vehicles can reach the Tamarack Lakes on this four-wheel-drive road. Here you've hiked all the way in to these "secluded lakes," and a bunch of rowdy "jeep guys" are there having a whooping good time. The first time I hiked to these lakes several years ago, the jeep crowd was a bit noisy, but, on the visit I made to write this description and on subsequent trips, I found no vehicles there at all.

Lower Tamarack Lake is just to the left of the jeep road. The vista of Sierra Buttes rising sharply in the background is wonderful, viewed from the southern shore at either lake.

This hike does a turnaround at the lakes. If you have planned a monster trip continuing up to the top of the buttes and back, read Hike SC-1 for the remainder of the climb. The trip back to your car on the Tamarack Lakes Trail is dandy, because it's mostly downhill, and you again get to savor the views of Upper and Lower Sardine Lakes. Your return time will be extended slightly by the need to stop and drink in the scenery. Somehow, the rocks in the trail don't seem so bad on the way down.

In summer, there will be folks swimming and fishing in boats on the lakes. The shadeless part of the trail on the return leg makes a swim in the lake seem very inviting. You might throw a bathing suit into the car to change into upon your return and go for a quick dip in Sand Pond. It is located just downstream from Lower Sardine Lake, is open to the public, and has a good public parking lot only a few hundred yards from the Tamarack Lakes trailhead. Personally, I've never seen any sardines at any Sierra lake, but, years ago when lake names were being passed out, perhaps some prospectors were camped there and opened a can of sardines. Both upper and lower lakes have dams, so their levels are higher today than in the days when seekers of gold roamed these parts.

Camping: There are a couple of OK camping spots at Lower Tamarack Lake, but I think you'll prefer Upper Tamarack Lake for an overnight. It seems less grassy and more "alpine," somehow. There are also more campsites there. My favorite site is at the end of the upper lake (farthest from where jeepers might camp), because it feels most remote and is near where the inlet creek flows into the upper lake.

Winter Use: None.

SC-5 Saxonia Lake Trail

Distance: 2 miles out and back; with the partial loop extension,

2½ miles round trip

Highest Point: 6,545 feet

Total Elevation Gain: 436 feet

Difficulty: Moderate

Hiking Season: June through October

Directions to the Trailhead: See Hike GL-1.

Comments: Although this hike is not long, the pace is a bit slow because the trail goes up, down, and around about. Midway, you see the delightful log cabin on the far side of Dugan Pond with Sierra Buttes in the background. Saxonia Lake is a beauty, but it has steep brushy sides, so access to the water is difficult.

The Hike: From the trail parking area, walk through the campground, turning left into the camp's second section, and find campsite 12. If you're lucky, no campers will be occupying 12, because you need to walk through it to pick up the start of the trail—except that the trail doesn't actually start there. True, a trail out of campsite 12 drops down to the nearby South Fork of Packer Creek and follows close to the creek in a southerly direction. Go ahead and take it. However, in less than ¼ mile the trail peters out where the creek enters a little gorge. Climb up the bank on the west side of the creek, and find a seldom used trail that runs along the top above the creek. So, why not just start out on the top trail? Well, its first 150 yards above campsite 12 is not well defined. If you prefer to try this undefined route for the start of the hike nonetheless, merely stay to the left of the meadow, and, as the upper part of the meadow ends, you should find a discernible trail by wandering around a bit.

From here to Dugan Pond, the trail is a bit dim in places and not well maintained, but, by keeping an eye out for what is trail and what isn't, you should easily find your way. The trail more or less parallels the creek, so just keep the little ravine of the creek on your left (although a few trail detours around impassable parts of the ravine put you out of eye contact with the upper edge of the ravine).

It is only ½ mile from the campground to where Dugan Pond pops into view in front of you. Although I have never seen anyone at the cute cabin on the far end of the pond, it looks like it is used regularly (by the Dugans?). If you have ever pictured a cozy log cabin on a remote lake with a magnificent mountain peak in the background (oh, yes, and a large deck overlooking the lake), the Dugan Pond cabin is that picture. My wife dubbed it "the ideal mountain retreat."

Upon reaching the shore, the dim South Fork of Packer Creek Trail ends at a T with a more-traveled trail. Turn left, hike past an old campsite, and then walk over the easy-to-cross little rock dam. You will be much happier with this trail, which heads easterly uphill away from the pond. In ¼ mile, watch on your left for an overlook of Mud Lake, not far below you. On a scale of 1 to 10 (with 10 the best), I would give Mud Lake a 2, not for its muddiness (although there is some) but for its lack of redeeming features. In late summer, the shallow lake partially dries up, leaving a wide shore of dried mud.

There is no need to make your way down to a 2-rated lake for a closer view, so continue easterly on the trail for another ¼ mile. It terminates in a large jumble of rocks and boulders. Scrambling up these for 25 yards, you reach the top, and below you spreads pretty Saxonia Lake. To get a better lake view, you need to carefully rock-hop closer to the lake. Some huge flat slab boulders just to the right on the lakeshore make a fine lunch spot, although they are too high above the water for dipping in your feet.

I wanted to see the little lake above Saxonia (Upper Saxonia Lake?), so I rock-hopped and beat my way through brush around the north (left) side of Saxonia. I found some nice views of the lake, with Peak 7195 rising directly behind it (although the peak effectively blocks the view of Sierra Buttes behind). From here, Saxonia looks mighty deep in places; nonetheless, a small rocky island pops up at its eastern end, and huge boulders can be seen here and there lurking below the surface.

I will admit my disappointment upon seeing Upper Saxonia, a shallow nothing of a lake. It was hardly worth the trailless trip around to it. Its only virtue might be that, because it doesn't have the steep sides the big lake has, camping on the shore would be easier.

Return by the same route to Dugan Pond. After recrossing the tiny dam, you need to decide whether to do a loop back to the car or to turn right and retrace your steps on the trail following the South Fork of Packer Creek. If you don't mind going an extra ½ mile, the loop route back to the campground provides variety. Instead of turning right after the dam, continue along the north end of Dugan Pond on the nice trail. It soon becomes an unused road heading westerly. Less than ¼ mile from the dam, a road branches off sharply to the left with a locked gate to keep uninvited vehicles from driving to the Dugan cabin.

Quiet Dugan Pond and its hard-to-see little cabin on the trail to Saxonia Lake

Take the ungated branch to the right, which loops northerly and soon intersects the jeep road coming from Tamarack Lakes (see Hike SC-1). Turn right on the jeep road, and a short walk brings you to an intersection with paved Forest Road 93. Turn right, and, in 200 yards (just before you reach the turnoff to Packer Lake Lodge), branch to the right off 93 onto a rocky track that makes a beeline for the campground where you parked, less than ¼ mile away.

Camping: The campsite near tiny Dugan Pond dam looks great, but it bothers me to camp so near a cabin that is used now and then. I feel as if I'm encroaching on someone else's property, even though I saw no "No Camping" signs. Because the sides of Saxonia Lake are so steep and rocky, with an oversupply of brush, I could spy no good campsites.

Winter Use: None.

HV-1 1001 Mine Trail

Distance: 3 miles out and back

Highest Point: 6,504 feet

Total Elevation Gain: 464 feet

Difficulty: Moderate

Hiking Season: June through October

Directions to the Trailhead: From Graeagle go south on Highway 89 for 1.4 miles to Gold Lake Highway, turn right, and drive for 15.6 miles to the intersection with Highway 49 at Bassetts. Proceed directly across Highway 49 and onto Forest Road 54 and the one-lane concrete bridge over the North Yuba River. Road 54 is paved all the way to the trailhead, although it is mostly single lane with about a million well-executed patches. It is a pleasure to have such a good road to a boondocks trailhead. You need to be alert, however, for oncoming traffic (easily passed in most places). When you're 3.7 miles from Bassetts, take a dirt road proceeding straight while the paved road curves to the left, and park near 54, where there is plenty of room.

Comments: Many trails to old mines are dusty and not particularly attractive. The track to 1001 is definitely an exception. The first ¼ mile may show some tire tracks, but they disappear beyond the locked gate, and you'll appreciate the shady smooth route with nice views of Sierra Buttes. The mine itself is interesting, although not extensive.

The Hike: From the car, walk straight on the dirt road (ignore another dim road that leads to the right from the parking area). In about 300 yards, you see an old sign, hanging by a single nail and tilted at a jaunty angle. It points to "1001 Mine" in the direction you are headed. It's always nice to know that you're on the right path. A bit farther, the dirt road crosses an intermittent watercourse, and beyond it a locked gate bars the road with a sign

saying "Year Around Mining Claim. Respect Our Rights. Children & Dogs Present." Well, it doesn't say "No Trespassing," so you proceed, probably wondering how ferocious the children and dogs might be. Perhaps 250 yards beyond the gate the road enters a flat meadow. On the right is a fallen-down cabin; newish paint on its steel roof gives evidence that it received a dose of TLC before the poor thing was crushed by the heavy Sierra snow at this 6,000-foot altitude. There were no signs of habitation, although some yard chairs sitting around did not look old. Please don't disturb anything here.

The unused road leads away from the small meadow to the left. Pause here and feast your eyes on the view to the west—a full profile of Sierra Buttes as a backdrop to the meadow. This scene became my favorite choice for the cover of this book. The nice trail is well covered with soft pine needles, which make walking this somewhat downhill stretch very pleasurable. The presence of an old deteriorating semitrailer truck with 1001 written on it is a surprise, because apparently many years have passed since any vehicles drove along this road. Note the rusty iron Montgomery Ward Franklin heater wedged under the trailer. Too soon, you reach the end of the delightful trail as the main building ruins of 1001 Mine come into view across a gully. Keep an eye out to the right, where the trail ends, and pick up an overgrown path leading in 50 yards to an entrance into the mine. A sturdy door bars the way. (You wouldn't want to go in anyhow, would you?) Nearby is a small building that looks like it was the top of some sort of tramway or chute that took ore to the bottom of the ravine. However, no remains of an ore-processing building can be seen below.

Heavy water runoff in the gully has washed away whatever access road led to the large, partially collapsed wooden structure located on the far side.

Hence, getting to that building for a closer inspection is not possible. Indeed, this must have been a booming operation once upon a time. The old trail to the 1001 came from south of the mine, originating near Loves Falls on the North Yuba River, a route that is now part of the PCT. No sign of this early trail remains. Undoubtedly it fell into disuse when the easier trail on which you arrived and the trail that became Forest Road 54 were built.

On the way back to the car, do not fail to look over your left shoulder for glimpses of Sierra Buttes as their craggy profile plays peekaboo through the tall white firs. In trying to research the history of the 1001 Mine, I came across an excerpt from an old miner's diary that called the mine "The One Thousand and One." It's funny how today we call it the "One Oh Oh One"; naturally, either nomenclature is correct. And where were all those children and dogs the sign warned us about?

Remains of the 1001 Mine

Camping: None.

Winter Use: Nailed to trees along Forest Road 54 are small orange diamond signs with an arrow indicating a snowmobile route. Highway 49 is open all year, giving winter access to the beginning of Road 54. This would also make a good snowshoeing place, but the road is a bit too steep for my cross-country skiing prowess.

HV-2 Volcano Lake and Best Views of Sierra Buttes Trail

Distance: 6 miles out and back (with side trip to Volcano Lake, 6½ miles out and back)

Highest Point: 7,020 feet

Total Elevation Gain: 1,302 feet (with side trip, 1,578 feet)

Difficulty: Moderate/strenuous

Hiking Season: July through October

Directions to the Trailhead: From Graeagle drive south on Highway 89 for 1.4 miles, then turn right on Gold Lake Highway, and in 14 miles turn right toward Sardine and Packer Lakes. Drive .2 mile, and, at the intersection where the road to Packer Lakes goes to the right, turn left into an unpaved parking area.

Comments: This is one of the least accommodating trails to hike, because it is so full of rocks (don't wear thin-soled sneakers). However, the tradeoff is the views, particularly those during the last ¼ mile up to the turnaround point—some of the best in the Feather River country! The side trip to Volcano Lake rewards you with sight of a sparkling little lake highlighted by Sierra Buttes jutting up close behind it. Nice as that view is, the all-time great view still awaits you as the main trail makes a U-turn to the west, presenting a close full-face look at the buttes in all their majesty across the steep gorge of Flume Creek. The Mountain Mine at the end of the trail was started in the early 1880s by a man named Berger, who worked the mine until the early 1900s (he also was in charge of building the wagon road).

The Hike: From the trailhead, walk south along the jeep road, passing the back of Sardine Campground. Past this point, the road is blocked by a locked chain at the ford of Sardine Creek (although it had broken down on my most recent visit). The easy way to cross is to the right of the ford on the rocks piled across the creek adjoining a large log. Then cut back left, and pick up the jeep road.

Winter view of Sierra Buttes

The road seems OK for a while, but all too soon it becomes strewn with rocks. The uphill part commences and continues all the way to the end of the trail.

The views to the left look down on the North Yuba River basin, where you can see an occasional rooftop of a cabin near the river. A little more than 1 mile from the trailhead, a rocky road branches right, and the remains of a green gate signify that this is the road for the side trip up to Volcano Lake, if you're game. The road is similarly rough, but the ¼-mile hike up is worth the effort, to see the lake. Its beauty is magnified by the massiveness of Sierra Buttes, which serve as a backdrop to the scene. Volcano Lake is the only water source on this hike. It is a fine place for lunch before backtracking to the main trail and finishing the trek uphill to the mine.

Along the remaining 2 miles of the main trail, you will be in awe of the work the old-time road builders did constructing this wagon road to Mountain Mine. In several places, large parts of the mountainside had to be blasted away to create the level roadbed. In other places, rock walls were built on the slope below the road, to keep it from washing out. The fine engineering and construction work has kept the century-old road in one piece the whole way. At one point, two enormous steel girders shore up the outer edge of the road. How in the world were these heavy beams transported up to this place?

The trail makes a U-turn to the right ½ mile from the end, and the most splendid of all the views described in this book opens in front of you. I feel justified in making that grandiose statement, having photographed a gazillion nice views in the Feather River country during the past 30 years. Flume Creek can be seen in the canyon below, which separates the hillside on which you are standing from the east-facing jagged profile of Sierra Buttes. Small waterfalls and leaping cataracts of the tiny creek add to the splendor of the vista as well as contributing a delightful sound to the otherwise silent scene. Even in mid-August, this face of the buttes has deep patches of snow. I must visit this spot in spring, when much of the mountain is snow-covered, giving it, I expect, a Swiss Alps appearance.

The trail ends at the site of Mountain Mine. A tailings pile is all that remains of this one-time gold producer. It must have had great promise for the owner to spend the time and money to build such a magnificent wagon road to the site. At the apparent end of the trail, a continuation makes several switchbacks steeply up to a saddle, beyond which a much smoother but unused road heads downhill on the other side. This track is not shown on the map, and I had time to follow it for only about ¼ mile. Someday I will continue along it to see where it comes out—I can't imagine where. Upper Tamarack Lake is visible far below through the trees on the other side of the saddle. I was sad to turn around and head for the car, because the spectacular view was now behind me. I hope you enjoy the vista as much as I did.

Camping: There are no camping sites on the main trail. If you carry in all your water, an overnight somewhere along the final ¼ mile of the trail

would be neat—you'd see the sun setting behind the buttes in the evening and the first rays of sun spotlighting their jagged eastern face at sunrise. At Volcano Lake there is a campsite to the left of the level spot at the end of the trail down at the lakeshore. It has a picnic table and fire ring but precious little smooth flat ground for a tent. A sort of trail leads around the right side of the lake to the far shore, where the camping is better. However, in this location you miss the view of the buttes reflected in the early morning calm surface of Volcano Lake. Nice car camping is available in either Sardine Campground, which is at the trailhead, or Salmon Campground, which is just around the corner off Gold Lake Highway.

Winter Use: One December day in a light-snow year I navigated unplowed and icy Gold Lake Highway from Bassetts on Highway 49 to the trailhead using four-wheel drive. Snowshoeing the trail, my wife and I were rewarded with wonderful winter views of Sierra Buttes. In a heavy-snow year, when Gold Lake Highway cannot be driven, you have to snowshoe the extra 1½ miles from Bassetts to the trailhead.

HV-3 Williams Creek and Pride Mines Trail

> **Distance:** 4 miles out and back
> **Highest Point:** 6,360 feet
> **Total Elevation Gain:** 950 feet
> **Difficulty:** Moderate/strenuous
> **Hiking Season:** April through October

Directions to the Trailhead: From Graeagle drive south on Highway 89 for 1.4 miles to Gold Lake Highway. Turn right, and continue for 15.6 miles to the intersection with Highway 49 at Bassetts. Drive directly across 49 onto Greene Road, which becomes Forest Road 54. Cross the one-lane bridge over the North Yuba River, and

drive past the residential area called Greene Acres to a dirt road on the right, a distance of .25 mile from Bassetts. A white sign saying "Commercial Use Prohibited Without Permit" is visible from the trailhead farther up 54. There is plenty of room to park off the pavement out of the way of the logging trucks that come thundering downhill on 54.

Comments: This trailhead is easy to get to, and the hike gives you a taste of some beautiful country. In mid-July, at one place on the route, soon after crossing Williams Creek, my wife and I counted 14 different wildflowers in bloom within a few feet of where we were standing. We sketched drawings of four we couldn't identify and later, with the aid of wildflower books, learned that these were ginger leaf pyrola, mallow, Lewis' monkey flower, and monkshood. If you appreciate wildflowers (and who doesn't?) you will enjoy a few minutes in nature's "garden" at Williams Creek. The only difficult parts of the hike are several stream crossings that require clambering up and down steep banks (but none is scary). If I were the owner, I wouldn't take much pride in the Pride Mines, but they are historically interesting nonetheless.

The Hike: From the car, head downhill to the right off 54, and follow the loggers' road southerly toward the creek. In a few hundred yards, the road opens onto a large flat area, obviously once used by

loggers, who left behind ugly giant piles of tree scraps. A crushed trailer of some sort lies on one of the piles, making it even uglier, if that is possible. Walk by quickly—far better scenery is just ahead.

The road ends at the edge of Deer Creek and commences again on the other side. Evidently, miners and loggers once had a bridge here (a large steel post is embedded in the far bank), but it fell victim to the creek at flood stage years ago. At the former bridge site, the creek had a high bank and no good stepping-stones, so we clambered down to the water 30 yards downstream from the bridge site and walked on the rocks beside the creek to a spot that had nice stones for a crossing. This was just downstream from the confluence of Deer Creek and Williams Creek. A good stepping-stone crossing upstream on Deer Creek would have saved us one subsequent crossing of Williams Creek, but then we would have missed the aforementioned nature's garden. In spring or early summer the flow of the creeks may be too high for the stone crossing we accomplished with dry feet (and with the aid of our "third leg" bamboo walking sticks) in midsummer. Hence, if you take this hike in spring, I suggest bringing wading shoes to change into and a towel to dry off with (the crossing won't be more than knee deep). You should be able to make all subsequent stream crossings easily without changing shoes, even in spring, so just hide your wet ones on the opposite bank until the return crossing—you needn't lug wet shoes up to the Pride Mines and back (unless you think you might take the alternative route back, which is described later).

As you parallel Williams Creek, the treat of nature's garden commences. The ground is boggy, and I hope hikers don't beat up the garden too much by tromping through. It is a fragile area, so please tromp as little as possible and preserve the beauty for others. The garden is only 50 yards in length, and at its southern edge you need to scramble down the bank to cross smaller Williams Creek. On the other side, you are between Williams and Deer Creeks where the road continues from the former bridge site. It leads to a very flat, graveled clearing with crushed piles of quartz piled on its eastern edge.

The never-used road stays low along Williams Creek, but after about 100 yards you need to climb the bank on your left and pick up the "high road" on the bluff, which parallels the "low road" you've been on. We counted another five varieties of wildflowers along this drier stretch, bringing the total to 19 within the first ⅓ mile of the hike. The high road suddenly ends at a ravine through which Williams Creek flows, thus necessitating another crossing. This one requires a bit more dexterity because the sides are steeper. On the other side a pile of rocks marks the route.

The obvious path continues south and soon pops into a nice campsite originally used by the Pride Mines' workers. To your right you see lots of old machinery to explore and, beyond that, a pond used by the miners. As you return to the campsite you will notice an old cabin on the other side of the creek. Make another creek crossing here, an easy one because there is no ravine and a plank has been laid across the stream for a bridge. Once you are on

Part of nature's garden near Williams Creek

the other side, a left turn would lead back to the unused cabin, but we respected the "No Trespassing" signs and didn't snoop around.

Take the route to the right, which continues south, now on the eastern side of Williams Creek, along an old road. Bypass another road that branches left and curves back uphill, perhaps leading up to Forest Road 54. You pass an old shack with "Explosives" written on it, which was most likely used for storing dynamite for the mine. The road along the creek becomes grassy and dotted with wildflowers; major erosion has rendered it impassable to vehicles. The path then approaches Williams Creek again for your final crossing, this one the easiest of them all. After that, the road bends north and begins climbing steadily, with a couple of switchbacks. Just after the second switchback, you pass a road branching right and leading to an old abandoned truck trailer and other mining stuff. Farther on, you reach a Y. The right fork is the more prominent and, because it is flat, looks more enticing, while the left fork is narrow, almost overgrown with encroaching bushes, and covered with hard-to-walk-on small round rocks—not to mention that it heads steeply uphill. Naturally, the left fork is what you need to take. Ahead, you might hear traffic noise from Forest Road 54 (almost no cars but a few logging trucks) and can see a derelict yellow bulldozer up the hill. To get to what I call Pride Mine No. 2 (the maps don't give it a name, but the sign at the mine 1 mile back said "Pride Mine No. 1," so I concluded that there must be a No. 2), turn left at the next road fork, and walk down to the flat mine grounds.

No mineshaft is in evidence, and the entrances have evidently all caved in.

Naturally, odds and ends of rusty machinery are scattered about. This is the turnaround point for retracing your steps and stream crossings back to the car. If you prefer an easier but less-interesting route back, make your way up to the abandoned yellow bulldozer, which is parked just off 54, turn left on the narrow paved road, and walk it 2 miles back to your car. On the road you avoid all the stream crossings but you miss the fun of flowers, fords, and finding your way.

Camping: The campsite at Pride Mine No. 1 is quite nice, and my guess is that it hasn't been used much since the mine was abandoned.

Winter Use: Forest Road 54 would be fine for snowshoeing. The route of this hike is impossible in winter, however, due to the many stream crossings.

HV-4 Deadman Lake Trail

Distance: 2 miles out and back

Highest Point: 6,675 feet

Total Elevation Gain: 885 feet

Difficulty: Moderate/strenuous

Hiking Season: June through October

Directions to the Trailhead: From Graeagle take Highway 89 south for 1.4 miles to Gold Lake Highway. Turn right, and continue for 15.6 miles to Bassetts. Turn left on Highway 49, and drive for 2.8 miles. Just past a sign on your right saying "Campground ¼," the highway has a wide dirt shoulder. On the right are two roadside snow-marker poles so close together that a jeep couldn't be driven between them (most snow-marker poles are placed much farther apart—two this close together are a rarity). Park along this wide shoulder on Highway 49.

Comments: The person who designed this trail must have gone to the Swiss school of trail planning. Like many Swiss mountain trails, it heads straight uphill at a steep grade (so you just have to take it easy on the steep parts). Switchbacks to ease the grade are nonexistent but, true enough, the trail is made shorter by heading straight uphill. The forest you hike through is delightful and includes some massive sugar pines, which are not particularly common in this part of the Sierra. The view of

Deadman Lake with Deadman Peak rearing steeply behind it is super. I bet not many fishing enthusi-

Deadman Peak behind Deadman Lake

asts come to the lake, because maps don't show this trail. The North Yuba River crossing can be dangerous in spring or other times of high water runoff, so this hike is best in summer or fall.

The Hike: first, you cross the North Yuba River. Walk between the two snow-marker poles, and in a few steps you are at the spot where the trail makes the crossing. I use my river-crossing techniques here. At the trailhead I change into a pair of old sneakers, and, with my hiking stick to help my balance in the middle, I wade in and easily negotiate the crossing. Once on the other side, I dry my feet

with a small towel, change into socks and hiking shoes, stash my wet sneakers behind a tree, and take off on the hike with dry feet.

Once you're across, the trail turns right and parallels the river for about 150 yards. This is the only part of the trail that may be somewhat difficult to follow. Just walk along the south side of the river within a couple of dozen yards of it, and stay on the flat without starting uphill. There are a few cairns (small rocks piled on top of bigger rocks) along the 150 yards to help you find the path. When you come to an old campsite, turn left, and thereafter the trail is readily visible heading uphill. Except for its steep gradient, it's a delight—smooth, soft underfoot, and not dusty because it doesn't get that much use. Occasionally you have to step over a tree that has fallen across the trail, but all such barriers are easily negotiated.

Partway up, after passing a yellow USFS boundary marker nailed to a tree, keep an eye out for giant pine cones near the path, signaling that the huge trees you're walking under are sugar pines. Don't forget to look up as you pass one of these behemoths. Their size, looking up from the base, is spectacular. At this point, the forest floor is almost completely free of other vegetation, unlike most forested parts of the Yuba region.

The trail ends at a campsite. You have to look closely to the left through the trees to spy Deadman Lake, below. A dim trail heads down toward the lake, and on the way you encounter another campsite, on a shelf somewhat above the lake. Dropping closer to the lake, you reach a lower campsite, still 20 feet above the water level. To get to the water requires a bit of maneuvering through bushes and down over rocks. From what I could see, there's no easy access anywhere along the shore.

The view from this side of the lake is terrific. The top of Deadman Peak is less than ¼ mile from the lake but it towers 823 feet above the 6,675-foot elevation of the water. The 40-foot intervals of the contour lines on the topo map are about as close together as they can be above the lake's far shore. Climb down the boulders to the outlet stream (which is dry by midsummer) and back up the other side to a bouldery ledge above the lake for your best photo spot. As you can see from here, there's precious little room anywhere around the lake for a person fishing on shore to reach the wa-

ter. It's all too densely vegetated. This is a fine spot for lunch if it's that time of day and you brought one along. You will whiz back to your car on the straight-down-the-hill trail.

On your visit, I hope you didn't find "one" at the lake—or a dead woman either.

Camping: The several OK camping spots on three different levels at the lake are mentioned in the narrative. If you're backpacking to the lake, you'll do a bit of huffing and puffing on the steep trail, but, what the heck, it's only a mile long so you can take it easy. It's a good idea to bring along a collapsible gallon water container to fill from the lake. Scrambling down to the water to fill a canteen is a difficult task that you won't want to have to do often.

Winter Use: None.

HV-5 Sand Pond Interpretive Loop

Distance: 1-mile loop

Highest Point: 5,762 feet

Total Elevation Gain: 10 feet

Difficulty: Easy

Hiking Season: May through October

Directions to the Trailhead: From Graeagle take Highway 89 south for 1.4 miles to Gold Lake Highway, and turn right. Follow Gold Lake Highway for 12.8 miles to a turnoff to the right to Packer Lake and Sardine Lakes. Follow this paved road toward the Sardine Lakes for .7 mile, and turn left into the parking area that has a sign "Sand Pond—Picnic Ground & Beach." Park here.

Comments: This short trail is nice and easy as well as fun and instructive. It is a good hike for kids, because the various trail markers give descriptive information about the area, the flora, and the fauna. About a third of the hike is on a boardwalk over the marsh, which adds an interesting aspect to the loop. You're bound to learn some things from the interpretive markers that will enhance your ex-

perience of this unique part of California.

The Hike: The trail starts from the eastern end of the parking lot and is easily identified with a sign "Sand Pond Interpretive Trail." The path immediately curves right and runs behind the well-maintained USFS restroom buildings serving Sand Pond. At a point where the route is joined by a trail from the pond, a sign announces "Adopted August 1984 by Sacramento Boy Scout Troops 8, 11, 52, 53 & 313." Since 1984, I wonder how many of these troops have actually followed through with trail maintenance. I must say, the loop is fairly well maintained, but whether by the Boy Scouts, the USFS, or sheer luck I can't tell you.

The first marker is of particular interest because it explains that the sand at Sand Pond is actually tailings from the Young America Mine. The trail crosses a bridge over Sardine Creek and loops left. A marker explains that this portion of the trail is the route of the old wooden flume that brought water from Sardine Lakes to Sierra City for powering a stamp mill that crushed ore to extract gold from it. (Several miles away, Hike HV-9 also crosses this old flume. It must have been one of the longest flumes in the Sierra—4½ miles. An old-timer from Sierra City told me that he and a buddy used to float down the full length of the flume on inner tubes when they were boys in the early 1900s.) I won't list what is on each subsequent marker because that would take away from your enjoyment of the hike.

Once you reach the boardwalk, the route makes a left turn, keeping you above the swamp (or pond or marsh or whatever you want to call these bits of water). The final marker is also of particular interest because it tells why all the trees are dead. The last 100 yards of boardwalk parallel the back of well-used Sardine Campground. With this much nonflowing water, the mosquito "harvest" must be

The boardwalk trail through the swamp created by beaver dams; the swamp resulted in the demise of all those conifers.

awesome, and a stay at the campground must require lots of repellent. The trail ends at the paved road. You need to turn left and walk the road 200 yards back to the parking lot.

You might want to cap the trip with a swim at Sand Pond. The gently sloping sandy bottom is a treat for young kids (and adults who are squeamish about wading in muck). The damp sand also has a wonderful consistency for building castles and other fanciful projects.

Camping: No backpack camping is available, but car camping at the adjoining Sardine Campground is good.

Winter Use: None.

HV-6 Wild Plum Ridge and Loves Falls Loop

Distance: 5-mile loop

Highest Point: 5,560 feet

Total Elevation Gain: 1,205 feet

Difficulty: Moderate

Hiking Season: April or May through October

Directions to the Trailhead: Follow the directions for Hike HV-7, but, when you are .3 mile beyond the North Yuba River bridge, turn in on a dirt road intersecting on your left, and park just off the road. If Gold Lake Highway is still closed by snow when you plan this hike in spring, take Highway 89 to its junction with Highway 49, and then travel 49 west to the Wild Plum Road turn-off. (You can call the Mohawk USFS Ranger Station, 530-836-2575, to see if Gold Lake Highway is open.)

Comments: The ½-mile side trip down the PCT to the footbridge over the Yuba to see Loves Falls is a must-do. Because much of the route is through oaks, it is enjoyable in fall, and this portion of the trail is covered with a cushiony layer of oak leaves. Due to this loop's low elevation and good drainage, it is one of the first hikes you can take in spring after snowmelt.

The Hike: From the trailhead, you start up a rocky, steep jeep road. Quickly, you begin hoping that the rest of the trip isn't on a trail like this. Well, the rough rocky trail smooths out after about ¼ mile, but the route still has a few uphill sections. Soon the trail receives a coating of oak leaves, making walking very comfortable. Pass by a few spur roads that cut off to the left. As the sound of the Yuba River increases, you guess that Loves Falls is approaching. Just before the trail makes a sharp hairpin turn to the right, two tracks lead off to the left. For a short side trip, take the first one, a dim trail that soon crosses a flume dug by miners a century ago. A bit farther, this trail ends at a small un-

named creek, which leaps down the mountainside in majestic fashion (it may be dry by fall).

Back on the main road, just before the hairpin turn, a road leads uphill on your left, curving to the right. Follow it for a few hundred yards, and you discover Chipp's Mine. The mine entrance looks in good shape, but certainly don't venture in. I've been told by a fellow who had plans to reopen Chipp's that its tunnel goes 1,000 feet into the mountainside. There are no signs of mine buildings, although structures certainly existed in the late 1800s when the mine was operating.

Return to the main trail, and continue uphill around a couple of hairpin turns. Soon you reach a junction with the PCT. Here, do another short side trip by turning left on the PCT. Walk down its winding course ½ mile to the footbridge over the Yuba to see Loves Falls. My first visit to this spot was in late June, and a record snowmelt was still occurring. As the river coursed under the bridge, its awesome power could be felt, and the view both upstream and downstream of Loves Falls was spectacular.

Turn around at the footbridge, and retrace your steps on the PCT, passing the jeep trail you were on before and continuing southeasterly on the PCT. You soon come to several places where the trail traverses loose rock slides. However, the level trail is well maintained, and you need not be concerned about losing your footing and sliding downhill.

Wonderful views of the North Yuba River basin and an end view of Sierra Buttes appear on your

Springtime cascade near the North Yuba River

right. The tops of the buttes are only about 3 miles away, as the crow flies, but they are 3,700 feet higher than you are. The Yuba basin is a beautiful pattern of different greens, as deciduous trees mix with a variety of conifers. Incense cedar, sugar pine, ponderosa pine, Douglas-fir, black oak, alder, and dogwood combine randomly.

The PCT commences a series of switchbacks and reaches an intersection with the Wild Plum Loop Trail (see Hike HV-10). Continue on the PCT. In a short distance, a trail branches off on your left with a sign saying "Haypress Creek Trail." (This trail was originally slated for inclusion in this book, but it failed to make the "final cut" because it is not particularly interesting.) Follow the PCT downhill, and listen for the sound of Haypress Creek in the canyon below you. At one rock outcropping where the creek sound is loudest, walk to the edge of canyon to see below you the hard-to-reach Haypress Creek Falls. From here your falls view is somewhat blocked by bushes, but I could find no better or closer viewing spot on either side of the creek. Perhaps you can.

Continuing on the PCT, you finally reach the creek and cross it on a sturdy steel-girdered footbridge. At the south end of the bridge are a bunch of signs, one of which indicates that the PCT to Milton Creek turns left. The topo map at this point is confusing because it does not show this part of the PCT. However, here you leave the PCT and turn right, following the directions on another sign saying "Wild Plum Campground 1½, Sierra City 3." A third sign, placed by the PCT Association, merely points the way to both directions of the PCT. I had to chuckle at this sign, "PCT Trail," because, when you put words to the initials, it says, "Pacific Crest Trail Trail."

About ¼ mile after the bridge, the trail intersects a dusty road on which you turn right, and soon you cross a bridge over Hilda Creek. Follow the road downhill, and try not to be too annoyed that the lovely trail you've been on for the past two or three hours has turned into a dusty road without redeeming features. Big power lines overhead detract further from the scene, but they finally turn downhill to the small hydro powerhouse on Haypress Creek to your right. Typical of the smaller modern powerhouses, it is run remotely, and there is no person on site to mind the hydraulic turbine, generator, switchgear, or transformer. Heck, there isn't even a sign on the building to tell you whose powerhouse it is. I guess the response to that is, "So what?"

You may be wondering why the road you've been on has no traffic. A locked gate across it as you approach Wild Plum Campground tells you why. The USFS campground is a nice one, with lots of trees, fire pits, tables, and streamside sites overlooking Haypress Creek.

Soon after the campground, the dusty road crosses a bridge over Haypress Creek, and a trail sign on the right indicates the start of the Wild Plum Loop Trail (see Hike HV-10). A few steps farther down the road a locked gate appears on your right at a sign saying "USFS Residence ¼." (The topo map shows this residence road leading to the Wild Plum Forest Service Station but the station was closed several years ago, evidently a victim of USFS downsizing.) After another ½ mile on the dusty road you reach your car.

Camping: This stretch of the PCT doesn't offer any decent campsites suitable for backpackers. The Wild Plum Campground is nice for car camping but is decidedly not a wilderness experience.

Winter Use: None.

HV-7 Milton Creek Section of the PCT

Distance: 9 miles out and back (with extension to Henness Pass Ridge,
11½ miles out and back)

Highest Point: 5,895 feet (with extension, 6,480 feet)

Total Elevation Gain: 1,495 feet (with extension, 2,080 feet)

Difficulty: Moderate/strenuous (with extension, strenuous)

Hiking Season: June through October

Directions to the Trailhead: From Graeagle, travel south on Highway 89 for 1.4 miles to Gold Lake Highway. Turn right, and drive for 15.6 miles to Bassetts. Turn right on Highway 49, and travel west along the North Yuba River for 4.7 miles to Wild Plum Road (20N13) on the left. This paved road winds through a residential area and crosses the North Yuba on a single-lane bridge. Beyond the bridge it becomes well-graded gravel and in .6 mile passes a large parking lot with a sign "Wild Plum Trailhead." You can either park here or drive on another .2 mile and park off the road just before a road to the left labeled "USFS Residence ¼." (The topo map shows this residence road lead-

ing to the Wild Plum Forest Service Station but the station was closed several years ago.) The extra .2 mile of driving saves you a bit of uninteresting hiking on the dusty road.

Comments: This lovely section of the PCT is well maintained and, for a large portion of the trip, follows sparkling Milton Creek. You get to the trailhead by paved roads (except for the last .5 mile, so your clean car will get dusty). Although I encountered patches of snow at the far end of this trail at 6,400 feet in late June, the lower portions can usually be done in spring (the extension is higher). After the first bridge over Milton Creek, the PCT route shown on the topo map is completely erroneous, and the map shown in this book is close to being correct, corresponding to USFS survey markers and my own GPS plotting. The 9-mile round trip represents the best part of the hike. If you do the extension, for a total of 11½ miles, you reach the crest between the North Yuba and Middle Yuba basins after hiking a bunch of shadeless switchbacks to get there. However, the crest does have its attributes—read on.

The Hike: From the trailhead parking lot, walk ¼ mile on the road to the bridge over Haypress Creek. (If you parked .2 mile past the parking lot, then you're almost at the bridge.) Just before reach-

ing the bridge you have a choice of routes—trail or dusty road. Naturally, any happy hiker would choose scenic trail over dusty road, but in this case you add 2 miles to an already long trip. So, let's take the trail on the way out, while we're fresh, and the road on the way back, when we're tired and eager for a refreshing shower. The distances I've shown above are for that plan. You can shorten the trip by 1 mile if you stay with the road both out and back or lengthen it by 1 mile by taking the trail both ways.

A sign points off the road saying "Wild Plum Loop Trail, Pacific Crest Trail and Haypress Trail." So, off we go on the more-scenic longer route. This first part follows the route of Hike HV-10, so please follow that description until you reach the footbridge over Haypress Creek. At the far end of this very substantial footbridge, the trail forks. A right turn would bring you back to Wild Plum Campground and the completion of Hike HV-10; instead, turn left, and follow the sign "PCT Milton Creek." This short section of the PCT is not shown on the topo map. In a little distance it reaches the "dusty road." Turn left, and follow the road easterly for about 50 yards, and then, thankfully, the PCT cuts off in a southerly direction and so do you. Nice signing shows you the PCT route on this short road portion.

Now you can settle into some "above average" hiking (even if your "average" is pretty high). The trail follows along the western side of Milton Creek through incense cedar, white fir, ponderosa pine, sugar pine, Jeffrey pine, Douglas-fir, and black oak. You will even pass a few Pacific dogwood trees, whose white blossoms in spring add an extra attraction to the route. Soon you see a concrete water-gate structure on the left, just downstream from a small diversion dam. My guess is that this diverts water from Milton Creek into an underground penstock (large water pipe) that runs downhill to the little powerhouse you will pass on the "dusty road" going back. I stood on the concrete top of the gate structure and looked down into the water inside;

to my surprise, an 8-inch trout was swimming along, seemingly unconcerned that it was surrounded by concrete instead of streambed. I hope there was an "easy way out" so that it didn't go into the penstock (if indeed that's what this thingamabob led to) and get sucked into a turbine.

The trail continues lazily uphill along Milton Creek, passes through "the gateway" (a large boulder on one side of the trail and an unusual tree stump on the other side), and arrives at the first bridge over the creek. Just before crossing the bridge, notice the rock wall on your right. This was the beginning of an old trail leading south to Ahart Sheep Camp and the Middle Fork of the Yuba River. Typical of the unmaintained trails that show up on old maps, this route has been obliterated by rock slides and most likely has slipped permanently into oblivion. Maybe some people would respond, "So what?" but I, for one, am fond of old miners' trails. I can picture prospectors and mules trudging along on the way to strike it rich (well, maybe the miner, not the mule). From here on, the topo map becomes useless, because the route of the PCT has changed substantially since the map was drawn in 1981.

As you polish off a bunch of switchbacks, two trail markers appear, one saying "Downieville R.D." on one side and "Sierraville R.D." on the other side. Later, looking at the USFS Tahoe National Forest map, I discovered that this was the boundary between the Downieville Ranger District and the Sierraville Ranger District. Adjoining the two markers was the typical PCT signpost announcing that this was "Mile 26." I enjoy such signs because they are nice reminders that I am indeed on the right route. However, this is the last one you encounter as you continue several miles uphill; you may begin to wonder whether you missed a turn on the true PCT and whether the lovely trail you're on is something else. I suspect that, at the time the PCT was revised from the route shown on the topo, the National Historic Trails Association, whose logo is

on the other mile markers, never got around to reposting the new route. Anyhow, keep going; you're on the proper PCT, and there aren't any evident trails branching off.

The innumerable switchbacks that follow don't seem as unappealing as switchbacks normally do, because the PCT here is shaded, smooth, and not too steep. The two yellow USFS survey markers that you encounter nailed to pine trees do not bear the bullet holes that are the bane of such markers on routes frequented by gunslingers itching for yellow-sign target practice. These survey markers are useful, because a nail set in the marker by the surveyor tells you where you now are on the section grid of your topo map (unless bullets have obliterated the nail).

A few hundred yards after the survey markers, you come to a saddle. The trail levels and then commences downhill, the first downhill you've had in quite a while. This descent is short lived, however, and many more ascending switchbacks lie in store for you. Hence, this is where you turn around for the 9-mile round trip (unless you're game to extend your hike). To return, descend the same way until you're at the point where the trail intersects the dusty road, and walk the rest of the way back on that. Or, if you're still peppy, go an extra mile by taking the trail over the footbridge on Haypress Creek instead of the road.

I chose to forgo the extra mile of the trail back to the car and took the dusty road. Actually, I'm overemphasizing the word *dusty*, because this road, while not a joy to walk, is closed to traffic at Wild Plum Campground, so it's less dusty than the heavily traveled short section between the campground and your car. Along the road, you'll notice some high-voltage power lines overhead. Just before you reach the campground, the lines drop down to a little powerhouse on Haypress Creek. Continue walking the road through the campground, over the Haypress Creek bridge, and back to your car.

To extend the hike from the turnaround point on the saddle, continue on the PCT, and take on the next bunch of uphill switchbacks. On a hot summer day, those switchbacks, devoid of shade, have less appeal than the ones you did under the trees earlier in the day. finally, you reach the top of the divide and are treated to a fine view behind you of the Milton Creek watershed. The trail flattens out, so you pick up speed and pass a small unnamed pond. On the end-of-June day when I did this hike, there was still some snow to hike through on this ridge, so I elected not to take a dip in the pond.

I'll admit that one of the reasons I wanted to follow the PCT this far was so that I could look down the other side of the ridge into the basin of the Yuba River Middle Fork. Milton Reservoir and Jackson Meadows Reservoir should be part of that view, but, alas, the thick forest and lack of a promontory prevent a good view. Perhaps if you keep descending on the PCT toward the Yuba Middle Fork, a suitable view opens up. However, I elected to turn around, knowing that I still had a "fur piece" to hike back to my car.

Camping: There are nice campsites at each of the PCT bridges over Milton Creek, and the pond at the top of the ridge would be OK too. The Wild Plum Campground is good for car camping.

Winter Use: None.

HV-8 Loves Falls the Easy Way Trail

Distance: 1 mile out and back

Highest Point: 4,597 feet

Total Elevation Gain: 40 feet

Difficulty: Easy

Hiking Season: April through November

Directions to the Trailhead: From Graeagle, travel south on Highway 89 for 1.4 miles to Gold Lake Highway. Turn right, and drive for 15.6 miles to Bassetts. Turn right on Highway 49, and travel for 3.5 miles west of Bassetts to where a sign pointing right says "Pacific Crest Trail Trailhead." Turn in here, and park.

Comments: For a quick easy hike with a big payoff at the turnaround point, this is a dandy. Particularly in spring when the flow of the North Yuba River is at its maximum with snowmelt, Loves Falls are an awesome sight; the rest of the year they are just plain beautiful.

The Hike: From the PCT trailhead parking, cross Highway 49 to its south side, where the PCT leaves the road with a sign announcing "Jackson Meadows 11, Norden 41" (Norden is where the PCT crosses Interstate 80). Nowhere else in the region does a trail sign give target locations at such great distances. The trail turns left and parallels Highway 49 so closely that you can hear cars whooshing by—decidedly not a wilderness sound. At one point the trail almost abuts the highway, but finally it heads downhill a bit, and there in front of you are the North Yuba River and Loves Falls. Don't expect a 500-foot drop like that of Yosemite Falls. But what Loves lacks in height it makes up for in awesome power. The ground almost shakes beneath your feet as the water roars through the granite chasm. Just before you reach the bridge, a trail cuts downhill steeply to the side of the river below the falls. This short stretch is more of a gymnastic exercise than a trail and is only for the athletically inclined. Everyone else will want to bypass it and continue on the PCT another 50 easy yards to the footbridge. The lower part of the falls cascades under the bridge, so the upstream direction is your best photo op. Don't plan to hurry back to your car. This marvelous piece of nature is well worth spending a half-hour or more soaking up the immensity of the view.

This is a good place for a picnic. Because the trailhead is so accessible and the walk so short and easy, you could even take this hike in the early morning for a breakfast picnic or in the evening for a din-

Loves Falls on the North Yuba River thundering under the PCT footbridge

ner picnic. That would be fun—I must try it sometime.

One puzzling aspect of Loves Falls is where the maps locate it. The topo map shows the falls several hundred yards downstream from the bridge. I've checked, and, although the river tumbles downhill with gusto there, the term *falls* doesn't apply. The USFS map of Tahoe National Forest shows the falls several hundred yards upstream from the bridge. The terrain is too rugged to traverse upstream to check this out, so perhaps there is a falls section out of sight there. Anyhow, the falls right at the bridge are good enough for me.

Camping: None.

Winter Use: A short snowshoe trip on this stretch of the PCT to view the falls in midwinter would be nice. Maybe you won't even need snowshoes if the snow isn't too deep.

HV-9 Old Phoenix Mine Wagon Road Trail

Distance: 4 miles out and back

Highest Point: 5,870 feet

Total Elevation Gain: 1,270 feet

Difficulty: Moderate/strenuous

Hiking Season: April through June (Too hot during mid-summer)

Directions to the Trailhead: See Hike HV-8.

Comments: Wow, someone many years ago put a huge amount of effort into building this wagon road (now only a trail) up the southeast face of Sierra Buttes. Its even grade almost never varies in the entire 1,270-foot climb from the trailhead on Highway 49 to the upper mine. The rock surface, massive rock retaining walls, and numerous switchbacks have deteriorated very little during the past 100 years, although the route has had no maintenance for a long, long time. Bushes clog much of the trail, but you can find the way with no problem. You'll have to do plenty of pushing through the thicker growth, so wear tough long pants to prevent scraped legs, and wear boots rather than running shoes to cushion your feet from the rock surface of the trail. Because the route has little shade, from July through September choose a cool day to try this hike.

Note: Although I've not encountered a rattlesnake on this route, a fellow who has hiked the buttes southwest side more than I have told me that he's seen a few—so use caution.

The Hike: I noticed this old route on Arthur W. Keddie's 1892 map of Plumas County, and I thought, because it was called a wagon road, it might not have faded into oblivion as an unused trail would have (a wagon road usually is wider and has a more heavy-duty surface than a pack trail, so, even unmaintained and unused, it can often outlast a trail of similar age). To my delight it is still in darn good shape, except for the encroaching bushes—

primarily greenleaf manzanita, deerbrush, and serviceberry. During part of the summer these bushes have flowers, thus making their presence more tolerable.

From the car park, head north up the poorly paved road (the PCT, which you don't want, leaves from Highway 49 about 30 feet from the entrance to the parking lot, not from the lot itself). Fear not, the road surface soon changes from pavement to well-graded gravel. In less than ¼ mile the road curves right, past a bunch of junk dumped by crummy people who don't care about the environment, and comes to a no-longer-used gravel pit (misnamed on the map because it is actually two large flat areas, not a pit—but whoever heard of a "gravel flat"?). Try not to notice the continuing piles of junk, and hustle up to the higher flat. The trail starts at the west side of the flat, above a pile of dumped white PVC pipes.

Now the fun begins. In the first ¼ mile I counted 13 varieties of wildflowers, several of which I had never encountered before. (Late summer and fall hikers may miss much of this flower show.) Although you have to zigzag your way up the trail to avoid bushes growing in the path, the grade is so easy that you won't mind, except for a few places where you need to push through the growth.

The switchbacks commence with short ones and become longer as you gain altitude. In many places you will marvel at the 100-year-old retaining walls made of close-fitting rocks set artistically by the road builders to support the path. The old mine owners must have anticipated hitting a bonanza of gold to spend the time and effort to build such a first-class wagon road up the steep side of the mountain. After a ¾-mile climb on this dry hillside, an ice-cold spring gushing from a pipe just below the trail provides a welcome break and the only water source on the trip.

At the western end of the 12th switchback, a level path heads off from the higher end of the V, noticeable because it is the first bit of level you've encountered since leaving the gravel pit. Walk down this level stretch, and you see the tailings of Phoenix Mine directly ahead. The mineshaft has caved in, so there isn't much to look at except some old timbers and scrap.

Go back to the switchback V, and continue uphill on the upper leg of the switchback. At another corner, rotten boards lie strewn along another stretch of level path. This is what's left of the flume

Rotting timbers and stone walls on the route of the old Sierra Buttes flume

that carried water from Sardine Creek near today's Sardine Campground (elevation 5,938 feet) to the Sierra Buttes Mine (elevation 5,640 feet) 4½ miles away. Building this flume was an outstanding engineering feat—the water flowed gradually downhill in a wooden trough that clung to the steep side of Sierra Buttes. Awesome construction work prepared the level rock path on which the flume was built. An old-time resident of Sierra City told me that, as a preteenager, he and a buddy would get old inner tubes (all car tires in those days required inner tubes), pump them up, and float on them down the full 4½-mile length of the flume. It wasn't as wild a ride as you find at today's theme parks, but I bet it was great fun in 1908.

Hike westward along the route of the flume, making sure not to step on any rusty nails, of which there are plenty. In about ½ mile, a rock slide blocks the way, so turn around, and go back to the trail. As you do, the view ahead up the canyon of the North Yuba River and Haypress Creek is as spectacular as the westward view down the canyon. To add to your viewing pleasure, the rock crags of Sierra Buttes tower above, only slightly more than 1 mile away "as the crow flies" yet 2,500 feet higher in elevation.

Back at the trail, continue easterly uphill another ½ mile to where the wagon road ends at another mine, this one even less photogenic than Phoenix Mine. I had hoped that this was the Dottie Q Mine, but the maps don't prove conclusively whether it is or not, and, of course, there are no signs. Its tunnel caved in long ago, but its extensive pile of tailings indicates that it was once a mine of consequence—the tailings can be spotted from way down in the Yuba River canyon. No signs of buildings remain.

As I hiked back to the car, savoring the views in all directions, I was mighty glad to be a current-day hiking book writer rather than a miner or a builder of wagon roads or flumes a century ago.

Camping: None.

Winter Use: None.

HV-10 Wild Plum Valley Loop

Distance: 3¼-mile loop (with out-and-back side trip on the Haypress Creek Trail, 7¾ miles)

Highest Point: 4,920 feet (with side trip, 5,418 feet)

Total Elevation Gain: 517 feet (with side trip, 1,015 feet)

Difficulty: Moderate

Hiking Season: May through October

Directions to the Trailhead: See Hike HV-7.

Comments: This is a good hike in spring, because the snow in this area melts early. The only drawback is that the shortest route from Graeagle to Highway 49 is via Gold Lake Highway, which isn't plowed during the winter. Hence, unless you are staying along Highway 49 near or in Sierra City, in May or early June call the Mohawk USFS Ranger Station (530/836-2575) to see if Gold Lake Highway is open. If it is still closed, take Highway 89 south from Graeagle to its intersection with Highway 49, then go west on 49 to Wild Plum Road. The loop has some delightful views of Sierra Buttes and Haypress Creek Falls.

The Hike: I describe this loop in a clockwise direction, but after doing it that way several times I think perhaps a counterclockwise routing would be better. It would get the least pretty part of the hike on a rocky dirt road out of the way first, and the hike could end with the joy of downhill short switchbacks fresh in your mind. Take your choice. If you opt for counterclockwise, read the description from end to beginning.

For the clockwise version, from the parking lot, walk east along the road for 300 yards to the bridge over Haypress Creek. Just before the bridge, a sign on the left announces the beginning of the trail. For ¼ mile, the trail parallels the blocked-off road into the boarded-up Wild Plum Forest Ranger Station. Soon the trail begins a series of short, easy switchbacks climbing out of the basin. Because these switchbacks are not steep and are well shaded, you'll find them about the nicest bunch of switchbacks you've ever encountered. A little over a mile from the parking lot, the trail ends at the PCT, which has been relocated here, lower on the hill-

side from the route shown on the topo map. Turn right on the PCT, and head east. Don't fail to look behind you at the great views of Sierra Buttes seen end-on across the North Yuba River Valley.

Soon an unnamed creek intersects the trail. You can easily hop across on half a dozen well-spaced rocks. Your ears will lead you to the next point of interest, as the roar of Haypress Creek far below you intensifies. When the creek noise is loudest, turn off the trail a few steps to your right, and climb carefully to the edge of the cliff overlooking the creek. There below you are Haypress Creek Falls, not particularly high, but not bad either. The lower part of the falls is hidden from view by bushes. I have tried to find a good route down to the creek for a closer look, from both this side and the other, but I have yet to discover a decent one. Perhaps you can.

A bit farther along the PCT a rock pile on your left and an old sign announce that the Haypress Creek Trail is leaving the PCT. If you wish to extend your hike with a 4½-mile out-and-back side trip along the Haypress Creek Trail, turn left here. The turnaround point for this extra trip is at Great Eastern Ravine, where the trail crosses the creek. I cannot figure out how this canyon got its name, because it lies mostly in a north-south direction, is not at all "great," and is not particularly like a ravine (I picture a ravine as a small canyon with much steeper sides than this one has). The intersection of the trail and the creek is the site of Great Eastern Ravine Falls, which were mentioned somewhere as a "sight to see." I found them somewhat disappointing— more like a moderate cascade than a falls.

When you're back from the side trip, or if you skip it, the loop route continues along the PCT and begins to lose elevation, as it switches back several times, heading for Haypress Creek. Along this section of trail I saw some false Soloman's seal (I wonder who dreamed up that name) and death-camas (a member of the lily family that is toxic and has poisoned many a cow or sheep, says my wildflower book). The leaves of the camas look much

Spring snowmelt flooding on Haypress Creek

at which you turn right and leave the PCT, heading downstream above Haypress Creek. You don't see much of the creek on this next stretch, but you can hear its cascading presence. About ¼ mile beyond the bridge, the trail ends at a dirt road. Turn right on the road, and follow it to Wild Plum Campground and a locked gate across the road (which you slip past). The road bisects the campground and soon reaches the bridge where you commenced the loop trail several hours ago.

like onion leaves, and the flower is a cute spray of pointed small white flowers. It is also called white camas to differentiate it from the blue camas, which is not poisonous (and was actually eaten by Native Americans of the area, the wildflower book claims—woe to the colorblind Indian).

The nice footbridge high over Haypress Creek is a great spot for a photo of the creek as it rushes noisily to join the North Yuba River 1½ miles away. At the south end of the bridge is the trail junction

Camping: There are no backpack campsites on the loop, but the Wild Plum Campground is nice for car camping, with many sites right on the bank of swooshing (particularly in spring) Haypress Creek.

Winter Use: Cross-country skiing or snowshoeing on the road would probably be doable, but the trail would be mighty tough to follow when snow covers the ground.

HV-11 Hilda Mine Trail

Distance: 5 miles out and back
Highest Point: 5,920 feet
Total Elevation Gain: 1,480 feet
Difficulty: Moderate/strenuous
Hiking Season: May through October

Directions to the Trailhead: Follow the directions for Hike HV-7, but, instead of parking, keep driving along Wild Plum Road past the Wild Plum Trailhead parking lot. Cross the bridge over Haypress Creek, drive through Wild Plum Campground, and park at the far end by the locked gate across the road with the sign "Road Closed."

Comments: The Hilda Mine Trail was originally a pack trail for bringing supplies from

Haypress Valley up to the mine (and, for carrying gold out, the miners hoped). The route is all uphill, with a bunch of switchbacks. However, it's a smooth, even grade with loads of shade. Because the trail had become a bit dim (usage is light, and the USFS does no maintenance), I spent a day leveling, clearing, and clipping back bushes, so it is now in just about as good shape as it was in the old days. The mine itself isn't spectacular, but it has a cute still-standing cabin on stilts, and the site is certainly historic. When I explored the road leading away from the mine, I came across two USFS employees putting in new culverts. I asked why all the work on a road that goes only to the nonoperating Hilda Mine. They weren't sure, but one said that he'd heard the mine was going to be restored as a historic site. I doubt it, because of its boondocks location and lack of fine features.

The Hike: Bypass the locked gate and head up the road, past the powerhouse on your left. This

road shows on the 1892 Arthur W. Keddie map of the region, so it is old, indeed. The road parallels pretty Haypress Creek, named the South Fork of the North Fork of the Yuba River on Keddie's 1892 map. No wonder its name was changed. The name Haypress came from an old haypress used by one of the area's pioneering families.

The high-voltage line from the powerhouse closely follows the route of the dusty road, detracting from your enjoyment of the nice surrounding forest. A solid wooden one-lane bridge spans Hilda Creek, and 200 yards after the bridge, a sign says "Trail" and points left, where another sign says "Wild Plum Valley Loop" (Hike HV-10). However, keep walking on the road for another 250 yards, and watch for a wooden power pole on the right with the number 182 on it (there also is a large stump on the right with rocks piled on top). Go 20 yards beyond the pole, and clamber up the right side of the road bank back toward the power pole.

This initial part of the trail was wiped out by loggers, so I have reestablished its lower 100 yards by clipping bushes and clearing a path. Pass the heavy guy wire that helps support pole 182, then cut left, and veer back right, at which point the old trail becomes visible (here, you climb over the first of many logs across the trail). The remainder of the trail should be easy to follow. After six easy switchbacks, the trail climbs steadily and almost due south, following Hilda Creek, which can be heard gurgling downhill. At a talus slope the path becomes rougher, but it is still easy to follow. Soon after the talus ends, the trail intersects little Hilda Creek. In midsummer the place where the trail crosses was dry, although running water could be seen both 20 yards upstream and 20 yards downstream. There is no culvert, so the creek must be subterranean for this short distance. As you cross the creekbed, angle upstream slightly, and, upon reaching the far bank (and noting the blaze marks deeply embedded in the standing large cedars), turn sharply left, and clamber over a huge cedar log. After a few steps paralleling the creek (a nice lunch spot), the trail turns uphill.

Soon you begin a series of short switchbacks as you gain another 430 feet of elevation between the creek and the mine. The final 10 yards of the trail at the top fade out, but it is easy to scramble up the hillside to the road that leads to the mine. Before walking off to inspect the mine, note the silver diamond marker embedded in the tree at the top of your scramble. This was the type of trail marker used by the early trail planners. You probably saw several others on your way up the hill.

Turn right on the road, and enjoy the view of the cute cabin. (Who knows how much longer it will remain upright; it has big holes in the roof, and the snow loads on this ridge are heavy-duty.) The construction is interesting: one side is anchored to the hillside, and the other side is up on stilts. Farther up the road is the mine site. No tunnel entrances are visible, due to cave-ins. Plenty of junk machin-

The old cabin on half stilts at Hilda Mine

ery is lying around, which doesn't makes the environs look like a beautiful historic site. The road dead-ends at the mine.

Walking back on the road, if you continue past the tree with the diamond, the route leads gradually up the ridge and in ½ mile connects with another dirt road coming up from the Henness Pass Road. This extra ½ mile has no special features other than an old PCT sign, so I suggest that you clamber back down the embankment at the tree with the diamond and pick up the switchback trail downhill the way you came up.

Camping: In late July, a tiny creek was still flowing by the old cabin at the mine, and there is plenty of level space for putting up a tent, but an old mine site with junk machinery lying around isn't a very romantic backpack campsite.

Winter Use: None.

Chapter 12

Mount Fillmore and Blue Nose Mountain Topos

MF-1 A-Tree to McRae Ridge on the PCT

Distance: 5 miles out and back
Highest Point: 7,456 feet
Total Elevation Gain: 881 feet
Difficulty: Moderate
Hiking Season: July through October

Directions to the Trailhead: From Graeagle, drive north on Highway 89 for .2 miles, and turn left onto the Graeagle-Johnsville Road (County Road A-14) at the Graeagle Frostee. After going 4 miles on A-14, turn left at the Plumas-Eureka State Park Museum onto the Johnsville-La Porte Road, which heads south from the museum parking lot. When you are 1 mile from the museum, the paved road passes the entrance to the state park campground, and, shortly thereafter, the pavement ends. Although the next 3.3 miles of road are maintained by the county, you would never know it. With slow, careful driving, cars without four-wheel drive can navigate this portion without scraping bottom. The rough road ends at a signless T .3 mile beyond Ross Campground. Turn left at the T onto a better (but washboardy) road (23N08), and drive for 2 miles to a wide flat spot with roads forking off in several directions. This is the A-Tree trailhead, and there's plenty of off-road parking.

Comments: The road to the trailhead is one of the last in the area to become free of snow. Hence, delay taking this hike until late spring or early summer. It's fine throughout the summer and fall. This part of the PCT is scenic, with lots of wildflowers. The trail is fairly smooth and not too steep; it does have a few large logs across the path, but they are not too difficult to scramble over or skirt around. There are wonderful 360° views from the turn-around spot at 7,487 feet of elevation on an un-named hilltop that's easy to walk up.

The Hike: First, you need to check out the A-Tree. For years I'd seen this "landmark" listed on the topo map but never visited the spot. When I finally got to the trailhead, I looked around for a pair of trees that had grown together at the top with large limbs forming the center bar of the "A." No such tree formation was in sight, so I then guessed that the landmark had succumbed to old age or the logger's chainsaw. However, no telltale stumps were visible either, and the maps always said A-Tree, not A-Trees.

One of the ladies in our group walked a few steps on the road forking to the right and called for us to come see her discovery. There, on the far side of a large pine tree beside the road, carved deep into the bark, obviously many years ago, was a large "A"—hence, the A-Tree. This was a bit of a disappointment, because it wasn't the marvelous "natural wonder" I'd been expecting. Subsequently, I have learned that the "original A-Tree" has long since disappeared, and this one is a "replica." My research has not been able to uncover how the A-Tree originally came into prominence, other than the fact that this point was a trail junction for early pack trails. An article in the November 5, 1859, *Sierra Democrat* newspaper refers to "the A-Tree which is about four miles southwest of Johnsville and a gap on the ridge between Spencer Lakes on the south and Jamison, Rock and Wades Lakes on the north."

From the trailhead, the PCT crosses the road and starts steeply uphill in a westerly direction at a sharp right from the road on which you drove in. A small PCT sign can be seen on a tree up ahead. The outdated topo maps show the PCT routed along the road, but the "new PCT" you take no longer follows the road. The good-quality trail traverses along the side of the ridge above the headwaters of the West Fork of Lavezzola Creek. The wonderful minty aroma you smell along much of the trail comes from carpets of pennyroyals (dense whorls of pale pink flowers well exposed by short grayish leaves and slightly fuzzy stems). Break off a leaf, and sniff it to confirm the mintlike scent. Thimbleberry shrubs with large leaves somewhat like grape leaves line the trail, a delightful sight even when they're not in bloom or in berry. You may also spy the delicate orange columbine growing in wet spots and a few nice examples of Washington lilies sporting their Easter-lily-like white blooms, with petals curving back and yellow stamens sticking out.

In a little more than a mile, you come to a sharp right turn in the trail, followed in 300 yards by a sharp left turn, forming a larger-than-usual switchback. This puts you on the north side of the ridge and gives you a view of Eureka Peak and the Mohawk Valley in the distance. Less than ¼ mile from the end of the switchback, just after you cross an opening in the forest covered with pennyroyal, a dim unused road crosses the PCT at an angle. This is shown on the topo as a trail heading south to Cowell Mine and Sunnyside Meadow. Although I had hoped that this would make a nice loop route back to the A-Tree, our group tried it and had to turn back because we encountered a host of "No Trespassing—Private Property—Do Not Enter" signs about ¼ mile after leaving the PCT.

It's a shame owners feel the need to forbid hikers to traverse their land. This area is strictly boondocks; nobody would choose to camp here and cause a problem, and I can't think of anything hikers would do that might damage the property. (Oh, sure, a slip and fall on this section of trail might bring out an "ambulance chasing" lawyer—but that's why most folks carry liability insurance, and the chances of a "litigious event" by the kinds of people who hike this route are nil.) Indeed, private property owners have even disallowed some sections of the world-famous (well, at least, US-famous) PCT from traversing their precious property, so that extensive and expensive rerouting of the PCT had to be done to circumvent their holdings. In Europe, many of the well-marked GR series of trails cross miles (er, kilometers) of private property for which the landowners receive no recompense except the satisfaction that their woods or fields are bringing enjoyment to hikers from a host of nations. Ah well, the American lawyers win another round.

The northern part of this unused road that crosses the PCT leads down into the pretty valley in which the headwaters of Jamison Creek and McRae Meadow are located. Because this mile-long route drops more than 1,000 feet to an intersection with the road on which you drove in, we decided against trying it. However, you could complete a loop by taking it and making a right on the road back to the A-Tree.

Instead, for this hike continue on the PCT, which reaches a saddle, then heads gradually downhill for a stretch, makes a left turn, and begins plunging downhill in earnest in a series of switchbacks. Where the switchbacks begin, you'll see a tiny PCT marker on a tree and a dim unused road forking right. Take the dim road, leaving the PCT.

This dim, easily followed road heads uphill and soon reaches a Y. Take the left fork, and climb steadily for another ¼ mile to the top of the hill. Here's your turnaround point and a nice view-filled lunch spot. Due north, McRae Ridge disappears into the distance. Below, to the northeast, are McRae Meadow and the headwaters of Jamison and East Nelson Creeks. Looking west, you see some wild country with West Nelson Creek winding through it. In the far distance, the snow-capped top of Mount Lassen is visible on most days. To the east, Eureka Peak, Mount Washington, and Mount Elwell domi-

nate the horizon. Southward Sierra Buttes rise in the distance, and, southwesterly, the rugged country sports the promontories of Beartrap Mountain, Stafford Mountain, and Mount Etna. Not a bad view, I'd say, for a mere 7,487-foot "hilltop." From here, the trail back is just as interesting, because you witness the views from a different perspective, and the wildflowers are still wild.

Camping: Although this stretch of the PCT is used by through-hikers backpacking a longer section of the trail, it has no water sources, hence no good camping. Car camping is available at any of three unimproved USFS campgrounds: Ross (on the Johnsville-La Porte Road just before the T intersection); East Nelson Creek, 1 mile north of the T at the East Nelson Creek Crossing (see Hike BN-1); or A-Tree Road Campground, ½ mile south of the T.

Winter Use: None. The roads to the trailhead are not plowed until late spring, if then. Well, I suppose you could parachute in and snowshoe out.

Looking into Lavezzola Creek Canyon from McRae Ridge

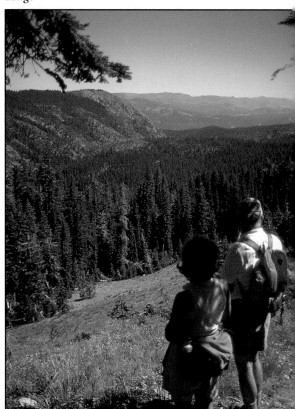

MF-2 Wildflower Pond Trail

Distance: 4 miles out and back

Highest Point: 6,770 feet

Total Elevation Gain: 485 feet

Difficulty: Moderate

Hiking Season: July through September

Directions to the Trailhead: See Hike MF-1.

Comments: My wife made a note of each wildflower variety we saw on this hike. She counted twenty-nine along the 2 miles of trail, and in early September, at that! Many other trails in this region have wildflowers in spring and into midsummer, but to find this huge a variety still in full bloom on Labor Day—wow! We couldn't get to the trailhead throughout June due to snow (granted, it was a late winter), so I suggest saving this hike for midsummer to late summer or early fall. If you like wildflowers, do this hike (and don't forget to bring your flower book along). The route you'll follow is shown on the Plumas National Forest map but it is missing from the woefully out-of-date topo map (the newest issue of which is dated 1951!).

The Hike: For a bit of information on the A-Tree, see the beginning of Hike MF-1. From the parking area where all the roads come together, take the jeep road farthest to the right, counting from the road on which you drove in. The PCT (Hike MF-1) is actually the first path on your right, but that's obviously a single-file trail, not a jeep trail. Don't take the dirt road to the left or the one on the right that commences very steeply downhill. The jeep trail you want is obviously seldom used. That's because, 2 miles from the trailhead, a locked gate across the trail blocks the way. Several "Keep Out—Private Property" signs are posted next to the gate.

A short distance from the trailhead a minor road branches to the left, but stay to the right and continue downhill on the jeep trail. Don't be worried that you'll have a long, steep uphill stretch on the way back; the downhill doesn't last long. Another road branches left but, again, take the right fork. In a few hundred yards, you cross a small creek. The topo map shows this as an intermittent creek, but it and another creek similarly marked ½ mile farther down the trail were still flowing on Labor Day weekend. Perhaps, since the 1951 topo map was issued, these creeks decided to flow year-round instead of stopping their fun in midsummer.

The trail follows the contour of McRae Ridge along its eastern side, approximately 300 to 400 feet below its top. The views to the east and south are outstanding as you look down into the verdant canyon toward the crest beyond. The creek flowing in the canyon is Lavezzola Creek, named, I guess, for the family that pioneered the Lavezzola Ranch, 7 miles south of you "as the crow flies." This is an improvement over the name the creek bears on the early maps: the Middle Fork of the North Fork of the North Yuba River.

You cross a pair of dry creekbeds, and, if you keep a close watch ahead and a bit downhill, you can spy the pond you're heading for, although the tree cover gives you only fleeting glimpses of it. As the trail curves downhill to the left, the pond pops into full view, close at hand. Even from here, you can see the carpet of flowers that surrounds most of it. Surprisingly, the topo map gives no indication of a pond at this location. Since there's no dam, it must be a naturally occurring body of water, and it's large enough to deserve a small blue circle on the map. So, how do I know its name if it isn't on any maps? Well, to be truthful, I made it up. I was going to call it Nirvana Pond, but my wife said that any pond with a pile of trash left on its shore by thoughtless campers can't be called Nirvana.

As the trail reaches the upper end of the pond, a jeep trail cuts left downhill to the water's edge. The wildflower display as you walk down this path is delightful. At the pond, there's a very nice campsite, except for the aforementioned pile of trash. Next time I do this trail, I'll bring a backpack so that I can carry the trash out, or maybe you'll beat me to it.

I was at the lower end of the pond, checking to see if there was any trail leading downhill away from the pond (there wasn't) and spied an old gasoline tank off in the bushes. On closer inspection I discovered that it was the back half of an old gasoline

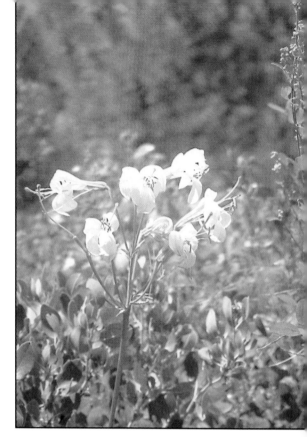

Washington lilies on the Wildflower Pond Trail

tanker truck, now without wheels. The faded letters on the side said "Richfield." Well, Richfield merged with Atlantic Oil Company to become Atlantic-Richfield several decades ago (later the name changed to the acronym ARCO), so the tank is at least that old. One of the top filler caps was open so I looked in. It didn't have any gasoline in it, but it still smelled of petroleum. How and why it came to be here is a mystery.

I recommend having lunch at the pond, because this is your turnaround spot. You'll enjoy being entertained by the butterflies and the humming bees as they too visit the wildflowers.

Once you've walked back up to the point where you branched down to the pond, you can see, just ahead on the main trail, the previously mentioned flimsy gate across the path with its unwelcoming "Keep Out—Private Property" sign. Darn. The map shows this route leading to Rattlesnake Peak, but, in order not to trespass, we returned to the car by the route we came in on, leaving the peak to the rattlesnakes, if there are any.

Camping: The campsite at the pond looks

ideal, and I bet you won't be bothered by other campers planning to use the same place. There are no facilities, however, and, I suppose, no lack of mosquitoes early in the season.

Winter Use: None.

MF-3 Peaks View Portion of the PCT

Distance: 6½ miles out and back (with the side trip to the mine,

7 miles out and back)

Highest Point: 7,011 feet

Total Elevation Gain: 976 feet

Difficulty: Moderate

Hiking Season: July through October

Directions to the Trailhead: Follow the directions for Hike MF-1, but, .3 mile past Ross Campground, when you come to the signless T, turn right, continuing on the well-graded gravel of the Johnsville-La Porte Road (23N08) for 1.2 miles to another intersection. Here 22N16 goes straight, and the road you want (22N12Y) goes left and immediately crosses East Nelson Creek. From this crossing, it is another 7.3 miles to where the PCT crosses the road (1.0 mile past the concrete bridge over the West Branch of Nelson Creek). It is easy to miss where the trail crosses the road, so

watch your odometer and keep an eye out for a small clearing with two large broken-off tree stumps on the left. Park alongside the road.

Comments: This hike violates my criterion for a trailhead no farther than a 45-minute drive from Graeagle. The Johnsville-La Porte Road looks good on the map, but it's slow going with many bumps from the Plumas-Eureka State Park Campground to the trailhead. The whole drive took me a little more than an hour, but the hike was so nice that I decided to include it in the book anyhow. The road is passable for all normal cars and trucks (with good tires and a driver who's not in a hurry). This part of the PCT has been rerouted from that shown on the topo map. The woefully out-of-date 1951 topo (yes, folks, that's the most recent issue) doesn't show a route for the PCT at all. The well-maintained trail provides great views of close-at-hand Stafford Mountain and Mount Etna and the more distant Blue Nose Mountain, Pilot Peak, and Mount Fillmore (still with some snow on it in mid-August). There are wildflowers galore and a mine to visit.

The Hike: The first thing you see as the trail leaves the road headed northwesterly is a large steel-plate sign with the following message carved into it: "Vehicle Traffic Prohibited on Trail." A short distance farther a map board shows the PCT route through the Plumas National Forest, but its scale is so small it is useless except as a curiosity. In ¼ mile you get some nice views of Stafford Mountain. As the trail reaches a saddle and crosses over to the northern slope of the mountain, those views disappear. On this hike, however, as one view is left behind, another one just as nice pops up. Now the vista is to the north, with big blunt Blue Nose Mountain the most prominent feature of the scene. I kept looking for a blue nose, but none is apparent from the vantage of the PCT.

The geology of the area is interesting. The main promontories on this hike are volcanic plugs (called *intrusions*)—solidified lava vents that thrust their way through the various layers of rock and sediment above them. Such promontories include part of Blue Nose Mountain, the lower eastern slope of Mount Fillmore, Mount Etna, Stafford Mountain, and Beartrap Mountain. The rock surrounding these intrusions was less resistant to erosion than the lava plugs so the plugs stand out as prominent hills or mountains. Some lava escaped in mudflow fashion and can be recognized by the fact that there is little or no forest on the areas it covered. In various places along this hike, you can see these treeless lava remains.

As the trail winds around the northern edge

of Stafford Mountain, you hardly know a sizable peak is above you on the left because of its dense forest cover. The trail continues gradually uphill as it passes between Stafford Mountain and Mount Etna. In midsummer, the wildflowers on this northern slope are numerous and various, although I saw none that were new to me. The route swings below the summit of Mount Etna and, 2½ miles from the trailhead, arrives at a flat spot where the PCT intersects a jeep road.

Here, I suggest you make a side trip from the PCT by taking the jeep road to the left for ¼ mile. A sign warning about "no mining" greets you as the forest disappears, and a humped ridge ahead leads to the peak of Mount Etna, now in full view. To the right you see Mount Fillmore in all its glory, although even better views of it are coming along the next stretch of the PCT.

You come to a pile of rock someone erected, and, as you stroll over to it, you notice four fallen steel pipes that once held barbed wire to keep visitors from falling into the pit. Sure enough, here is a vertical mineshaft whose bottom is way down there somewhere. I used the unscientific means of determining depth by tossing in a rock and seeing how long it took to "thunk" on the bottom. My guesstimate is a depth of 30 feet. Try it, and see what you think—but don't fall in, because you'd make a terrible "thunk."

I photographed in various directions and returned to the PCT. The trail now crosses over to the western side of the ridge, and the even better views of Mount Fillmore (as promised) appear to the south. Continue upward onto the west side of treeless Bunker Hill Ridge. Why not go on until I can see the other side, I reasoned, so I hiked up to the crest. At the top I was treated to a great view to the north, with 7,457-foot Pilot Peak the dominant landmark, crowned by a fire lookout tower at its summit.

This is the suggested turnaround point, approximately 3¼ miles from the trailhead. On the way back, as you approach the north side of Mount Etna, keep looking ahead to sight the two volcanic pinnacles on its eastern slope. They come into view, but not for long. When you're ¼ mile from the trailhead, your last treat will be nice views of tree-covered Beartrap Mountain directly to the south.

See, it was worth an hour's drive, wasn't it? But it's an hour back, too, naturally. Ah, well.

Camping: Because there is no water source along this route, I can't suggest any camping spots. Still, I passed two separate sole backpackers, late in the afternoon, who were heading north. I mentioned to each of them that there were no camp-sites with water ahead, and they both merely shrugged. The German had started his hike at South Lake Tahoe; the other fellow had started three months earlier at the Mexican border and hoped to get to the Canadian border before winter. Wow—now that guy is a hiker! I later learned that if I had hiked ¾ mile farther than the turnaround point and dropped 200 feet below the trail on the left, I would have found little Duck Soup Pond, which offers a campsite on a level spot (what hikers call a bench) between the pond and the trail.

Winter Use: None.

BN-1 East Nelson Creek and McRae Meadow Trail

Distance: 6½ miles out and back

Highest Point: 6,295 feet

Total Elevation Gain: 475 feet

Difficulty: Easy/moderate

Hiking Season: June through October (best in June and July)

Directions to the Trailhead: Follow the directions for Hike MF-1 but, after Ross Campground at the signless T, turn right instead of left. Continue on this well-graded gravel road another 1.2 miles to another intersection, where 22N16 goes straight and 22N12Y goes left. Turn left, crossing East Nelson Creek, and immediately watch for a jeep road on your right with a sign "Nelson Creek Trail" and, along the main road, a sign "West Nelson Creek 6, La Porte 25" (imagine 25 more miles of road like the one along Jamison Creek!). Park here; there's plenty of room.

Comments: In my opinion, this is one of the all-time best hikes in this book. True, getting to the trailhead is a bit arduous, but the trip is worth it. The hike has all the things I like: scenery, a level, easy trail, a cute creek running along the trail, meadows, a wide variety of trees, many kinds of wildflowers, and maybe some large wildlife you don't normally see. It probably even has a lot of history, although I'm not aware of it. The trail, however, is not well maintained, and in a few places it has faded out for 20 or 30 yards, but even there you'll have no problem, because the path follows the creek. Trees falling across the trail haven't been removed for several years, but you can easily skirt all of them. I know you'll like this hike. Good picnic locations are in plentiful supply along it.

The Hike: First turn and look behind you for a view of the southern part of McRae Meadow. If your favorite color is green, it can't get any greener than this. Jamison Creek commences at the south end of the meadow, flowing first southerly, then easterly, to Johnsville, and East Nelson Creek commences near where you parked and travels northerly and then westerly.

Follow the dirt (mud) road north. On it you see some nice car-camping sites far from the throngs at the state park campground. The tradeoff is that these sites have no piped water, no tables, and only a single outhouse in a sad state of repair. In about 300 yards, at a good-size campsite, the road ends at a barrier and becomes a trail. I was interested to see that the Blue Nose Mountain topo shows the remainder of this hike to be on a dirt road. Of course, the most recent version of that topo is dated 1951(!), albeit with a note saying that it was "Photo Inspected" in 1973. The trail shows no signs of being road width anywhere, and in numerous places huge boulders, trees, and bogs make anything but foot travel seem highly unlikely. I could see only one indication that motor vehicles once traveled this route: the presence of tires. In one place where the trail crosses a small creek, tires shore up the two

banks, and in another place an old truck tire is lying near some bushes. Who knows?

A short distance past the initial road barrier, a second barrier has been bent out of the way, obviously with means other than human muscle. Some moderate-size trees have fallen across the trail not too far after this, but none is so big that it cannot be climbed over. One big fallen tree nearer the trailhead had a trail-width section cut out to allow hikers (but not a car) to pass through. That is the sole effort the USFS has made to clear any of the trail.

Next, you reach a boggy stretch where springs on the left deposit water on the trail—even in autumn, I suspect. Slop through: You won't get too wet. Going up the bank to avoid the bog is not a choice because of dense bushes. In a little more than 1 mile you come to a grove of aspens, and thereafter aspens appear along your route in various places, adding to the rich variety of healthy conifers. Sadly, some of the larger aspens near the trail have been defaced by thoughtless people who have carved names, initials, and dates into the bark. All of the dates are more than 20 years old, so perhaps campaigns to make people more mindful of the ecology are paying off.

The trail continues along the western side of the creek, always within earshot and sometimes within view of the water, or more correctly, the willows at streamside that block your view of the water. Although McRae Meadow follows your route until near the turnaround spot, it is mostly on the other side of the creek, often hidden from view by trees and bushes. It gets narrow in spots, making it less meadowlike. About 2½ miles from the trailhead, another bunch of springs on the left side of the trail give you the opportunity to scout a path that will keep your feet dry.

Just before reaching the springs, my wife and I spied a pile of bear scat on the trail. Soon thereafter a "fresher" pile appeared, and, within ten yards, we encountered three more "recent" piles. My wife

McRae Meadow on East Nelson Creek

looked around anxiously and inquired if further passage was safe. As I said in chapter 5, in my 30 years of hiking the Feather River country, I have only once encountered a bear on any of the trails in this book, although I have seen lots of scat. There aren't any grizzlies, and the chances of an attack by a black bear (all California bears are black bears, even if their color is brown—weird, I know) are slim-to-none, so I told my wife "no problem" and indeed there was none. Due to the proximity of the springs to the four scat piles, she christened the locale "The Boggy, Buggy, Beary Place."

Less than ½ mile from the springs we encountered a campsite on the trail that obviously had been well used, once upon a time. A few yards farther, the trail disappeared, and we were unable to uncover it, due to thick bushes and twisted aspens. At this turnaround point, you will have hiked about 3 miles, and a 6-mile round-trip seems just about right. To the southwest, a nearby promontory of jagged rock rises 640 feet above you. It's part of the McRae Ridge you've been hiking below.

On your return trip, enjoy the blue forget-me-nots and the white puffy-flowered pussy-paws that adorn the trail. Back home, my wife and I agreed that the East Nelson Creek Trail was near the top of our list of favorite hikes. (We took it in mid-July of a "late-winter" year, and, although the elevation is only 6,295 feet at the trailhead, numerous good-size patches of snow crossed our path. I suspect this isn't a trip for springtime, even in dry years.)

Camping: In many places, a few steps off the trail bring you to the side of the creek and good-looking backpack campsites that probably have never been camped in before. However, if you're building a campfire, it's a nice ecological gesture to camp in a spot where a fire ring has already been used. Better yet, don't build a campfire at all. In particular, the campsite at the turnaround spot looks enticing, but prior to nightfall I'd certainly rig a bear bag to hang from a tree or bring bearproof containers to prevent a midnight food raid by Mr. or Mrs. Bruin.

Winter Use: None.

BN-2 Buckhorn Trail to the Feather River

Distance: 5 miles out and back from Trailhead A; 1 ½ miles out and
back from Trailhead B

Highest Point: 4,552 feet

Total Elevation Gain: 552 feet

Difficulty: Moderate/strenuous

Hiking Season: April through October

Directions to the Trailhead: From Graeagle, drive north on Highway 89 for 1 mile to Highway 70. Turn left, and travel 12.2 miles to Lee Summit. Just before reaching the highway maintenance building at the summit, turn left on a good gravel road (23N22). The next intersection is 1 mile distant, but stop on the way to read the interesting USFS signs about the Penny Pines Plantation, which resulted from the arson-caused Fells Fire in May 1984. At the intersection, turn right, staying on 23N22, and drive .7 mile to a Y in the road. This is Trailhead A. Park here if you wish to take the longer hike. If you prefer a shorter excursion, take the left fork, and drive the 1.7 miles to Trailhead B. This final stretch of dirt road is relatively level and smooth. (On my most recent visit, a little Toyota was parked at Trailhead B, proving that low horsepower and low ground clearance are OK on this road.) Both trailheads have plenty of off-road parking.

Comments: Before I took this hike I wasn't sure that I would want to put it in the book. I was very pleased to find it very book-worthy. I prefer Trailhead A because the hike to Trailhead B is pleasant, highlighted by excellent views of the Feather River Canyon. The road is only lightly used—several cars per week. When you arrive at Trailhead B, whether you walk or drive, the trail down to the river is full of great vistas. Once at the river you will enjoy hiking along its northern bank in this seldom visited area. However, you may be surprised upon

reaching the river to find modern-day gold mining in progress.

The Hike: My description assumes that you parked at Trailhead A. If you drive to Trailhead B, pick up the narrative at that point.

Less than ¼ mile from Trailhead A, the road crosses over the top of the Union Pacific Railroad Spring Garden Tunnel. This mile-long tunnel burrows through the mountain 500 feet below your path. I have always wanted to lie on the road with my ear to the ground and see if I could hear a rumble as a freight train roared through the tunnel. The trouble is, trains come along only about once an hour, and it hardly seems worth it to lie there with an ear to the ground for such a long time merely to hear a rumble. (Besides, I'd look pretty stupid lying with my ear to the ground if someone happened by.)

About 1 mile from Trailhead A, watch for a place where erosion has eaten a little gully out of the roadbed. Walk to the left edge of the road, and gaze down into the canyon. Way down by the river you'll see two metal rooftops on the Buckhorn Mine cabins. Only 10 feet below the road level, you can see a platform jutting out from the hillside. Although I couldn't initially determine what this was, I finally decided it was where building supplies had been attached to a cable and lowered down the hill to the riverbank. How else could they have gotten those metal roofs down there? Certainly not via the trail you will take from Trailhead B.

Continue along the road until it widens into a parking area on your right. This is Trailhead B. The start of the trail is to the left of the road just before the parking area. It's not obvious because it immediately heads downhill out of sight. In ½ mile, the trail drops 400 feet to the edge of the river. Near the river, the trail traverses a sandy hillside where it becomes narrow and slopes downhill (but it isn't scary), and a bit of careful hiking gets you to the other side of the slide area.

At the river, the good trail continues upstream along the north bank. The flow of the water alternates between white-water rapids and deep, slow-moving, murky stretches. Where the trail was directly across the river from the two shiny-roofed cabins, I saw a rope stretched across the river and a rubber boat tied up on the opposite shore. Evidently, the occupants of the cabins pull their boat across the river along the rope. Here the river is wide and

moves slowly so this method probably works well except when spring snowmelt swells the flow. The topo map shows that these two cabins adjoin the Buckhorn Mine, but from the north shore I could see no sign of the mine on the other side of the river.

If you hear a chug-chug, you undoubtedly will soon encounter modern-day miners plying the river in a manner never dreamed of by gold seekers a century ago. Today's fortune hunters tie a rubber float to the shore, sometimes using two ropes spanning the river with the float tied between them. Gasoline-driven pumps affixed to the float have large flexible hoses attached. The "miners," dressed in wet suits and scuba gear, dive down in the river with the suction end of the hose. They turn over rocks on the bottom and suck up sediment from under the rocks. Evidently, as gold and sand wash downstream, upon hitting a rock, the heavier gold sinks to the bottom and lodges under the rock. Even at today's 20-year low in gold prices, this process must be productive enough to make the miners' efforts pay off.

Looking up in the trees along the riverbank, I was impressed by the amount of debris 20 feet above the water level, undoubtedly left by the horrific New Year's flood of 1997. What an awesome flow the river had for a couple of days!

A little more than ¼ mile from where the trail reaches the river, you pass several nice sandy campsites among the trees. At this location, like many others along this stretch, the deep pools make marvelous swimming or fishing holes—that is, if scuba divers are absent. There are wonderful river views, both upstream and down. I turned around at the campground. A backpacker, whom I unwittingly awoke from a restful afternoon snooze, said that the trail fades out farther upstream due to a washout.

Upon arriving back at Trailhead B, rather than heading to the car, I took a detour and continued along the road for another ½ mile in the opposite direction from Trailhead A. The tire tracks ended at another parking area and another trail down to the river beckoned. This trail certainly fits the definition of the word *steep*—but steeper means shorter. At the river, another modern miner's float was moored in midstream, but no people were around. The trail continued downstream, so I followed it for a ways. Only about 100 yards from where the trail reached the river, I came across a dandy campsite, prettier and less well used than the one where I woke the napper. As I puffed back up the trail to the road, I wondered about my wisdom in trying this detour. On balance it was worth it, because the river at that spot was very pretty. You might give it a try.

Camping: Two locations are described in the hike. The downside is that, if modern miners are working the river, the put-put of their pumps is guaranteed to ruin your wilderness experience. If cars are parked at Trailhead B, scuba miners may be at the river, so you might opt for the site at the bottom of the steep trail.

Winter Use: Highway 70 is open all year, so the unplowed access roads may make good snowshoeing in from Lee Summit. The roads are so level that I'll bet cross-country skiing would work fine too. I must try it sometime.

BN-3 West Nelson Creek and Old Cabins Trail

Distance: 6¼ miles out and back

Highest Point: 5,644 feet

Total Elevation Gain: 694 feet

Difficulty: Moderate

Hiking Season: July through October

Directions to the Trailhead: Follow the directions for Hike MF-1, but, .3 mile past Ross Campground, when you come to the signless T, turn right, continuing on the well-graded gravel of the Johnsville-La Porte Road (23N08) for 1.2 miles to another intersection. Here 22N16 goes straight, and the road you want (22N12Y) goes left and immediately crosses East Nelson Creek. After the crossing, 22N12Y first climbs McRae Ridge, then makes a big loop, and zigzags above the drainage basin through which you will be hiking. The trailhead is at the intersection of 22N12Y (still called the Johnsville-La Porte Road) and a dirt road (22N41) that cuts back sharply to the right. The only sign at this junction is painted on a tree. The sign looks like a T and an arrow pointing right, with the shaft of the arrow being the crossbar atop the T. There is plenty of room to park along the main road.

Comments: Many years ago, West Nelson Creek was a beehive of activity, as men searched for gold in and around the creek. Miners piled up large mounds of round rocks after prying them from their resting spots, hoping to find bits of gold underneath. You can visit four old miners' cabins, none occupied for many years. Of course, please do not disturb anything at the cabins—look but don't touch. The first two-thirds of the hike is on a jeep road, which receives virtually no traffic during the week but may provide access for weekend modern-day miners. Yes, if you have a heavy-duty four-wheel-drive vehicle, you can drive 2 miles in, but why drive when the walk is so pleasant and scenic?

The Hike: For the entire length of the hike to the turnaround point, the route parallels the attractive West Branch of Nelson Creek. However, only at the end of the trail or one of the side trails will you actually reach creekside. The rest of the hike goes high above the creek on the steep hillside. Nonetheless, you'll have many creek views, and the sound of the water swishing over and around rocks below makes this hillside hiking a nice experience.

In a little more than ¾ mile from the trailhead, the road makes a rocky ford of Porter Ravine. This watercourse, like the others you cross on this hike, is spring fed and hence still flowing nicely throughout the summer and fall.

You ford an unnamed creek ½ mile after Porter Ravine, and soon thereafter you see the first of the four cabins to be visited down near the creek.

Giant red fir near West Nelson Creek

This tiny cabin is well preserved and so small it must have been used by a live-alone bachelor. You have to scramble down the hillside to see it at close hand because no trail leads to it. Along the side of the road here, the flattened remains of another cabin can be seen.

Along the way, several side roads turn off of the main road, all of which lead down to large level campsites near the creek.

The road continues gradually downhill for another ½ mile, and then arrives at the "big camp." I was surprised to find a large tent, dining fly, tables, chairs, and other camp stuff. Nobody was around, so I inspected the flattened remains of the 1920s car and some old cabin sites, without disturbing any gear. I surmised that the camp was occupied only on weekends by the modern miners. At the north end of the camping area is an old log cabin. The roof has caved in, and the walls have partially collapsed, but it is interesting, nonetheless.

A short distance beyond the log cabin, the road terminates, and a track on the left leads downhill. This is an interesting side trip of only 250 yards. At the bottom beside the creek are a mine and a bunch of metal indicating some sort of ore-processing facility.

Back where the road ends, the trail heads off in the downstream direction and immediately forms a Y, with the left branch leading to another campsite a few yards farther. Take the right branch. After one switchback, it crosses a watercourse called Frenchman Ravine. Along the next ¼ mile of trail you have some nice upstream views of West Nelson

Creek. Several small springs on the uphill side muddy the trail for short stretches.

When you're ¾ mile from the "big camp," the trail crosses Four Bits Creek. Just beyond the crossing, you can see another well-preserved cabin near the creek and can scramble downhill to visit it. Two whole rows of dusty empty Mason jars neatly line a shelf near the glassless window.

Less than ¼ mile farther, you see the final cabin below. A small cairn on the trail alerts you to the location. This green-sided one-room structure

is obviously much newer than the others, and its windows have glass—well, what remains of the glass. Peering in a window, you'll find that the insides look as rotten and shabby as those of the older cabins. The adjoining outhouse is interesting because it stands on stilts. I guess the drill was to place a bucket underneath, aim properly, and then discard the contents of the bucket in an ecologically appropriate place. Perhaps it was too difficult to dig a pit under the outhouse in this rocky ground—or perhaps the miners realized it was improper to deposit human waste so near a flowing stream (an unlikely scenario, given the lack of concern for the environment by the miners of a century ago).

Farther down the trail, a sign says "Rock Pile No. 2—No Mining." Here the path suddenly starts angling downhill toward the creek, where a nice campsite with a sandy beach is located. I was surprised to see a float tethered in midstream by a rope stretched across the creek between trees on the two banks. The float had a gasoline-driven pump and a bunch of flexible pipe for vacuuming up gold-laden sand from the creek bottom. I have seen scuba divers use these modern mining devices, manipulating the hose on the creek bottom. On the day I did this hike, nobody was around, perhaps because it was a weekday.

I had hoped that the trail might continue for another mile or so, but beyond this point it quickly fades out, and dense bushes completely cover where it once went. After enjoying lunch on the beach, I headed back.

Camping: There are several creekside camping places off the road, but they are all accessible by jeep, making them less desirable for backpackers. The campsite at the end of the trail is dandy unless the modern miners are operating their noisy vacuuming pump.

Winter Use: None.

On the PCT above Lakes Basin (Hike GL-7)

Chapter 13

Grizzly Valley, Mount Ingalls, and Spring Garden Topos

GV-1 Cow Creek Loop

Distance: 6½-mile loop
Highest Point: 6,302 feet
Total Elevation Gain: 405 feet
Difficulty: Easy/moderate
Hiking Season: May through October

Directions to the Trailhead: From Graeagle, go north on Highway 89 for 1 mile to Highway 70, and turn right to Portola, 10 miles away. In Portola, turn left on West Street where a sign points to "Lake Davis Recreation Area." Follow the paved road 5 miles to a Y where a sign points left to "Old Camp 5, Boat Ramp 2.5" and right to "Campgrounds, Boat Ramps 3." Take the left branch (24N10). A sign appears saying "Smith Peak Lookout 5, Genesee 24." In .2 mile the pavement ends, but the continuing gravel road is pretty good. When you are 4.5 miles from the Y, as 24N10 curves right, take a dirt road straight ahead posted 25N74Y. Drive only .1 mile, and park at a wide place on the road.

Comments: This loop is one of the easiest and prettiest I've encountered. In spring and early summer the meadows are verdant and sprinkled with wildflowers. The return part of the loop has many spectacular groves of aspens between the trail and the creek. Although I haven't taken this loop in the

fall, I aim to do so soon, because it must be a grand sight when the aspen leaves turn yellow. The entire loop is within the boundary of State Game Refuge 1-V, hence no hunting or firearms are permitted.

The Hike: Head south along the seldom traveled dirt road. In about a mile, to your right across the Cow Creek Valley, you have some fine views of jutting Threemile (all one word on the topo map) Rock, a rocky crag with an elevation of 6,442 feet. In a few places, the trail nears Cow Creek, and you can see the return trail of the loop on the other side of it. Several yellow USFS boundary markers are nailed to trees along the route. At approximately the 2½-mile point, the trail becomes a bit steeper, but not so steep as to cause much huffing and puffing. A huge log across the road has been sawed in sections, but for some reason the sections have never been moved, thus very effectively blocking the route to all traffic, even jeeps.

At about the 3-mile point, just before the trail

Cow Creek Meadow

---

loops back and crosses Cow Creek, I noticed that a section of the trail was sparkling in the noon sun. At close inspection I saw that the glinting was caused by gazillions of flakes of iron pyrite, or fool's gold. Fortunately, billowing cumulous clouds weren't covering the sun, or I would have missed this interesting sight. Just after crossing Cow Creek, the trail reaches an unsigned T intersection. The left fork goes I know not where, because neither the topo map nor the Plumas National Forest map shows it. I always hate to pass up exploring an enticing side trail, but the rest of the Cow Creek Loop beckoned.

I took the right branch, which is now a seldom used, gradual, smooth, downhill dirt road all the way back to 24N10. At this point the return route is called 24N55. In ¼ mile after the T, a side road cuts off to the left, leading to Threemile Valley. I had been wondering how Threemile Rock got its name; upon seeing the name of the 3-mile long valley on the map, I could guess. However, take the right fork, and continue north along the west side of Cow Creek. This return portion of the route closely follows the creek, so the cheery sound of rushing water accompanies you most of the way back.

For much of the return portion, marvelous

meadows spread down to the creek. For those whose favorite color is green, this is the place to be. In midsummer the brilliant green was punctuated with yellow buttercups. Near the creek in many places, groves of aspens grow, adding contrast with their white bark and shimmering leaves.

I always check out old signs, and a very faded yellow one on a tree partway down to the creek caught my eye. The lettering could still be seen: "Salt Ground Number 8" with a USFS logo at the bottom. Who knows what that means, but the forest service had some reason for putting it up many years ago. I looked around for an animal salt lick (salt licks I'd seen in my youth in Arizona were blocks of salt set on the ground by ranchers for cattle to lick), but I saw nothing to indicate what the sign meant. Ah well, another unsolved mystery of the Feather River county.

A mile before you reach 24N10, a bunch of USFS signs along ½ mile of the route announce "Boundary Partial Cut Unit—No Cutting Marked Trees Beyond This Sign." Sure enough, between the trail and the creek, forest service graffiti—a splotch of spray paint—was evident on every tree. I suppose this was necessary to protect streamside trees from the logger's saw, but the paint splotches sure ruined the natural beauty of the area.

When you've gone 2¼ miles after crossing Cow Creek, 24N55 ends at the main road, 24N10. Turn right, and walk the hard-on-the-feet gravel for ¾ mile back to 25N74Y and the trailhead. Although you may encounter some dusty car traffic on this ¾-mile finish of the loop, the meadow through which the route passes is so spectacular that you won't mind.

Camping: None.

Winter Use: None. Although the road to Lake Davis is plowed in winter, 24N10 is not, so the trailhead is inaccessible during the snow season.

GV-2 Beckwourth Emigrant Trail at Lake Davis

Distance: 4½ miles out and back

Highest Point: 5,815 feet

Total Elevation Gain: 20 feet

Difficulty: Easy/moderate

Hiking Season: May through October

Directions to the Trailhead: Follow the directions for Hike GV-1, but drive .3 mile beyond the turnoff onto 25N74Y. Just after crossing Cow Creek, turn right onto a less prominent dirt road (24N10B) that has a few ruts (in early spring with wet weather it might be pretty muddy) and a few big bumps. However, the trailhead is only 1 mile farther, and I think most cars can navigate it easily by taking the bumps slowly (low-slung sports cars and large RVs might have some trouble). The trailhead is where you can see on your left a vertical USFS brown sign with the logos meaning no jeeps, ATVs, or motorbikes. Just beyond the brown sign is a vertical white sign with the welcoming message "Beckwourth Trail Historic Route/Not a Through Trail/Oregon-

California Trails Association." There is plenty of parking space alongside the road. Lake Davis is directly ahead on 24N10B but the lakeshore at this point is muddy and less than beautiful.

Comments: This level trail is loaded with history. For hikers, it is the easiest part of Jim Beckwourth's famous trans-Sierra trail, which became popular among emigrants to California, particularly after the Donner Party disaster. Although it parallels the shore of Lake Davis, the lake itself is generally out of view from the trail. You cross several pretty meadows along the route. Unusual features of the trip are dealing with the fences around the spring and saying "hi" to the cow herd (if it's in residence at the time).

Note: If you would like a longer outing, you can combine this trip with Hike GV-4. The trailhead for GV-4 is at the same place as the turnaround for GV-2, so the two hikes are easy to connect—merely pick up the start of GV-4 instead of turning around. The GV-4 loop is 5½ miles, so the two combined make a 10-mile jaunt of virtually level hiking.

The Hike: First, if you're unfamiliar with the history of Jim Beckwourth and his wagon road, please read Appendix D. Most of the path is now a dim one-lane road that is not difficult to follow. Approximately ¼ mile from the trailhead, the route crosses a meadow, and the "beaten path" becomes more difficult to see as it curves slightly to the left through the clearing. Portions of dried and cracked mud flats here indicate that in early spring the trail may be quite boggy. Several cow paths leading down to the lakeshore cross the wagon road, and, in about ¾ mile, you can see Lake Davis in the distance to your right. The lake is named in memory of Assemblyman Lester Davis, who represented Plumas County in the state assembly for many years.

Several hundred yards farther, you encounter a barbed-wire-fence "obstacle course." The track approaches a dense, stubby Jeffrey pine standing alone in the meadow. On its far side, one of the white "Beckwourth Historic Trail" markers appears, giving you comfort that you're on the right route. However, dead ahead, a barbed wire fence blocks your path, so you need to circumvent it. The best way is to walk to the fence, turn left, and follow a cow path next to the fence a short distance to where the fence and the cow path make a right-angle turn. Follow the path another 100 yards to a place where a fence on your right intersects the fence you're following. At this point there is a wide barbed wire gate, which you need to climb over. This is actually easy, because the wire is strung so loosely at its center that it can be pushed away to let you carefully step over. An alternative is to slip the wire hasp off the top of the pole at the east end of the gate and open the gate slightly for passage. (This is tougher to do than it sounds; tilting the gate over at the middle is easier.) Once you're across, please prop the gate upright (or close it) again, so that it looks sturdy and can fool the cows.

You are now inside the passageway in which a cowhand can herd cows down to Freeman Creek for a drink or, by opening a gate on the far side, to pasture in the far meadow. Stepping-stones in the creek at this point allow easy crossing (unless springtime snowmelt has swollen the creek enough to put the stones under water). Once across, you have a choice.

One option is to walk around the end of the fence line on your right where it meets the creek (there's just enough room to get around the end post without getting your feet wet), and then walk away from the creek toward another fence line in the direction you were going when the first fence interrupted your hike. Here you will see a stile (steps up one side of the fence and down the other). Climb over this rickety stile, and cut back left through the sagebrush to the trail.

The other option, after crossing the creek, is to turn left, and walk toward another stile. This one has collapsed and is no longer safe to use, but you can merely walk a few steps beyond it to where the top row of barbed wire has sagged. Unless your legs are short, you should be able to step over this low section of fence. (My 5-foot-5-inch wife did it easily without ripping her pants on the top wire.) Once you accomplish this maneuver, walk back along the fence to the trail.

Near where either option rejoins the trail, a dirt road crosses the trail and curves northerly. You can pick out the Beckwourth Trail by looking ahead, where a white vertical marker for it can be seen. However, before continuing your walk, check out the marker on your right placed by Trails West, designating this as a point on Beckwourth's route. This unusual marker is a piece of railroad rail stuck into the ground with another short section of rail welded horizontally on top. A plaque on the top part has the inscription "Beckwourth Trail—Freeman Creek. Trail Route 1851 & Later. '. . . to a valley of good grass & water ten miles & camped beside a mountain stream; soil poor' —Joshua Variel, September 12, 1852." The quotation comes from Variel's emigrant diary.

Now that you've conquered the fence barriers and read the Trails West marker, head for the white Beckwourth marker ahead, and follow the trail. It is easy to follow until about ¾ mile after the fences, where it crosses a big meadow and dry creekbed (it may have water in spring). Just continue in the same general direction you've been going, skirt to the left of a clump of lodgepole pines, and watch for another of the friendly white markers on the little hillside ahead of you.

Soon thereafter, you encounter a Y at which you take the left fork. In a few hundred yards, you see the main road (24N10) ahead. Although this is your turnaround spot, walk to the road, and go left on it for about 30 yards. Look to your right, and you'll see Trails West Marker B-15 just past a few pine trees but closer to the road than to the edge of the meadow. Its inscription reads "Beckwourth Trail—Grizzly Valley. Trail Route 1851 & Later. 'Camped in Grizzly Valley called so for the abundance of grizzly bear found in this vicinity' —East Owen, August 28, 1852." It doesn't say if Mr. Owen encountered one or not, but you certainly won't, because grizzlies have not been seen in this area for about a century.

Now that you've mastered the fence-crossing maze, your trip back to the car should be easy. At least Jim Beckwourth and his emigrant companions didn't have to worry about fences—just grizzlies. I'll take fences any day.

Camping: There are no campsites on the trail, but some good campgrounds for car camping are located on the eastern side of Lake Davis.

Winter Use: None. The access road (24N10) is marked for use by snowmobiles.

GV-3 Oldhouse Meadow, Creek, and Ghost Camp Loop

Distance: 4-mile loop (with extension, 5-mile loop)

Highest Point: 5,940 feet (with extension, 6,080 feet)

Total Elevation Gain: 134 feet (with extension, 274 feet)

Difficulty: Moderate

Hiking Season: May through October (best in June and July)

Directions to the Trailhead: Follow the directions for Hike GV-1, but, instead of turning off 24N10 onto 25N74Y, continue on the main road for another 3.6 miles. Where it crosses the bridge over Big Grizzly Creek and intersects with the Beckwourth-Genesee Road (County Road 112), turn right, cross over Oldhouse Creek 100 yards farther, and then immediately turn left onto a dirt road heading north (24N76). Park here on the roadside.

Comments: This hike is best done in spring or early summer when the meadow is a lush green and filled with wildflowers. You will enjoy the ghost camp and the last mile of the hike along the route of the Beckwourth Emigrant Trail. If you want a bigger outing, the extension takes a longer loop along the upper part of playful Oldhouse Creek.

The Hike: Don't be discouraged as you head north along 24N76 treading a dusty, well-used dirt road. In little more than ¼ mile, the road narrows and becomes a lightly traveled track with little dust. A U-shaped murky pond appears on the right, and soon thereafter a dim road branches left with a "Road Closed" sign. Take this closed road, and walk parallel to beautiful Oldhouse Meadow into the ghost camp. The most recent topo map, dated 1972, shows 13 abandoned cabins at this spot. A few have now collapsed, but others are still standing, albeit barely. This complex of summer cabins, bordering on the meadow and surrounded by tall pines and aspens, must have been a delightful place to spend the summer many years ago. As you can see, none

of the derelict structures was very snazzy, and some look to be only one or two rooms. I didn't see any signs of electrical service or indoor bathrooms; those of us used to today's modern conveniences might not have liked the accommodations. Look closely to note that the foundations of a few of the structures seem to be wooden skids, perhaps so that the cabin could be dragged to a different spot each summer.

The dim old road fords an intermittent creek as it leaves the ghost camp and again joins the newer road (not shown on the topo map) that bypasses the camp. Keep bearing left on this newer road as it passes the turnoffs onto 24N75YA and 24N75YB.

The route again nears the meadow, then turns north, and follows diminutive Oldhouse Creek. In less than ¼ mile, the road, now dim, reaches a clearing used by loggers long ago. Here you need to decide whether to do the extension loop, described at the end of this hike.

To bypass the extension, turn left on the dirt road as it crosses Oldhouse Creek. Immediately af-

ter the crossing, turn left off the road onto a path leading to an old campsite. Continue through the campsite, and pick up the dim unmaintained trail that closely follows the west side of the creek.

In about ¼ mile the trail reaches a barbed wire fence and a yellow surveyor's corner section marker nailed to a tree. Follow the fence line toward the meadow. When the fence turns toward the center of the meadow beside some willows, make a 90° right turn, and head cross-country 100 yards to the road, which you can see. Go left on the road. It is used by loggers, who have been cutting down beautiful pines, firs, and cedars in the area. In a generous ½ mile, this more-traveled road ends at a T junction with the Beckwourth-Genesee Road. Turn

One of the ghost camp cabins on Oldhouse Meadow

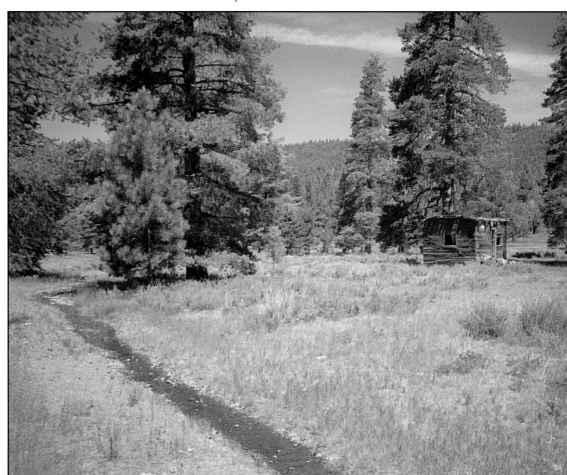

left, and walk along this main road for ¼ mile, until it crosses a meadow.

On the east side of the meadow take a lightly used dirt road that turns right toward a corral. Just before reaching the corral, turn left, and walk around it, picking up a trail that soon begins to parallel a barbed wire fence line separating the woods from the northern edge of the meadow through which Big Grizzly Creek meanders. A dim trail (well, sort of a trail) follows easterly along the fence line. This, I believe, is approximately the route of the 1851 Beckwourth Emigrant Trail (see Appendix D). Many parts of Beckwourth's trail have faded into oblivion; diaries kept by emigrants using the route are about all that history buffs have available for deciphering its approximate location. My research indicates that his trail followed this northern edge of the meadow, although a white trail marker farther along on the creek's south side asserts that the old trail was on that side of the creek. Due to boggy conditions on the south side, the north side seems the more logical choice. After paralleling the fence line for ¾ mile, you can spy the small bridge over Big Grizzly Creek that you drove across earlier. As you approach the bridge, the path is blocked by a fence running perpendicular to the one you've been following. No problem—turn left, and in 200 yards you encounter the main road. Turn right on it, cross a cattle guard, and there is your car ahead of you, just past the intersection.

If you choose to do the hike extension, at the loggers' clearing where you make the decision, continue north along the east side of the creek on a washed-out crummy path crisscrossed with fallen trees and scattered tree limbs left by loggers. To the right of this less-than-perfect trail an outcropping of lava in weird shapes adds a touch of enjoyment. In ¼ mile you leave behind the loggers' mess, and the walking becomes easier. In another ¼ mile you encounter another clearing, with several possible exits. Turn left, crossing the creek, and head back downhill on its west side along a never used road. As you come to a crossing of a side stream, the sight of a more-traveled road on the right greets you. A strange old sign at the intersection indicates that the road to the right dead-ends in ¼ mile, and the route over which you just came leads in 1 mile to "Cate Place." I backtracked to see if I could find Cate Place, to no avail, although I didn't know what I was looking for. Perhaps the ghost camp was Cate Place? The 1972 topo map lists a "Gate Place" site at the intersection where you parked. Daniel Cate, an early pioneer in the area, was elected the first treasurer of Plumas County in 1854. Perhaps he or one of his five children founded "Cate Place." Who knows? At any rate, turn left on this dirt road, and in ⅓ mile you reach a loggers' clearing. Turn left here too, and 200 yards farther, on your right, you find the path to an old campsite that the hikers who didn't take the extension reached soon after the decision point. From here, follow the route back to the car described in the main hike.

Camping: The old campground at the crossing of Oldhouse Creek would make a good backpack site. It's about halfway along the main hike (without the extension). Although the map shows the creek flowing all year, my guess is that it may well be dry by late summer.

Winter Use: None. However, 24N10 along the southwest side of Lake Davis to the trailhead is marked for snowmobiles.

GV-4 Grizzly Valley Loop
on the Beckwourth Trail Route

Distance: 5½-mile loop

Highest Point: 5,841 feet

Total Elevation Gain: 43 feet

Difficulty: Easy/moderate

Hiking Season: June through October

Directions to the Trailhead: Follow the directions for Hike GV-1, but, instead of turning off 24N10 onto 25N74Y, continue on 24N10 for another 3.3 miles. Just before reaching the bridge over Big Grizzly Creek, park just off the road.

Comments: This hike makes a loop traveling up the north side of the large meadow through which Big Grizzly Creek flows, and then crosses the creek on the 24N85Y bridge. This half of the hike follows the route of the historic Beckwourth Emigrant Trail, which explorer Jim Beckwourth pioneered in 1851. Appendix D gives a short interesting history of Mr. Beckwourth and his famous trail. The other half of the loop follows the southern side of the meadow. I have done this hike in early summer when the meadow is greenest and in late summer when it is not as pretty. The advantage of late summer is that the knee-high grass has been matted,

tromped, or chewed down, making hiking much easier. Yes, in early summer the trompers and chewers are cows. They aren't dangerous, but, if it makes you nervous to have a bunch of big animals moo and stare at you as you pass, then do this trip after mid-August. Along the return leg, in early summer, many rivulets flowing into Big Grizzly Creek cross your path, making boggy places around which you must skirt. (A hike going out on the north side of the creek and back on the Beckwourth-Genesee Road is a June alternative to avoid the meadow's boggy south side.)

Note: If you want to do a longer hike, combine this loop with Hike GV-2, a 4½-mile loop, for a total of 10 miles on fairly level trails. The turnaround point for GV-2 is at the same location as the trailhead for GV-4.

The Hike: Before leaving the trailhead area, walk down the bank of the road toward the meadow, about 200 yards south of the bridge, and look for the Beckwourth Trail marker placed there by Trails West. It is a steel railroad rail stuck into the ground with a shorter rail welded horizontally on top. A plaque on the horizontal rail says "Beckwourth Trail—Grizzly Valley. Trail Route 1851 & Later. 'Camped in Grizzly Valley called so for the abundance of grizzly bear found in this vicinity' —East Owen, August 28, 1852."

To begin the hike, walk north on the road for 200 yards past the bridge to an intersection with the Beckwourth-Genesee Road. Turn left, and cross the cattle guard that's only a few yards away, then double back 200 yards to the meadow and the fence line that runs between the forest and the meadow (this maneuver avoids having to climb over or crawl under the sturdy barbed wire fence that abuts the bridge). In ¾ mile the fence ends at a corral. Walk around it on the north side. (This first part of the hike is the same as the final ¾ mile of Hike GV-3.)

From here, you can choose your own route on this side of the meadow. Along much of the way, a well-beaten path will appear, making you think that scads of people must hike this part of Beckwourth's trail. Not so; the path was beaten by early summer cows who decorate it with an occasional cow-pie. In late summer, it is not as bad as you might imagine, because the pies are no longer fresh.

About ¼ mile past the corral, a spring feeds water into a round trough only a "stone's throw" from the road. This is the site of long-gone Midway House, a favorite tavern (and, according to some stories, a place where women of ill repute plied their trade upstairs) on the road to Walker Mine. Some 200 yards after the water trough, a dim road crosses the meadow and fords the creek. Just beyond this road, watch for the next railroad-rail Beckwourth marker, which says "Beckwourth Trail—Wagon Ruts. From behind this marker a trail trace may be followed across the meadow to the west. At a creek crossing, water flowing eastward along the trail has made a jog in the creek bed." Sure enough, you can

The 1851 Beckwourth Emigrant Trail in Grizzly Valley (the two parallel paths in the center of the photo)

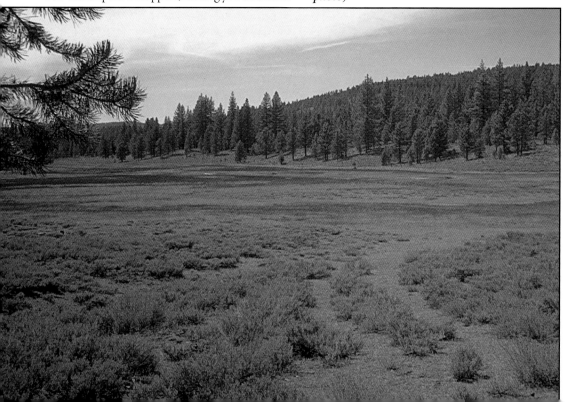

see tracks along the side of the meadow, but whether these are from emigrant wagons 150 years ago or cows two years ago, I can't say. Another cow path just within the shady forest is an alternative route at this point.

When you've gone ½ mile beyond the marker, a fence line blocks your way. On the return leg of the hike, on the other side of the meadow, I was able to step across the barbed wire at a low point. However, here I had to resort to crawling under the fence, naturally picking a place free of cow-pies. If this method doesn't appeal to you, merely turn right at the fence, walk 200 yards to where the fence meets the road at a cattle guard, cross it, and double back to the meadow. Your next impediment is two separate sections of the meadow that are fenced off in large squares. The left edges of the squares abut the creek, so you have to make a wet-foot crossing to get around them. A better alternative is to take a slight detour around them on their north side.

The creek branches, and you follow the left branch; within ¼ mile, you reach a good gravel road (24N85Y) that runs to Little Summit Lake and Blakeless Creek. Turn left on the road, and cross the bridge over Big Grizzly Creek. Once on the other side, turn left off the road and head back, now on the south side of the meadow. Cow paths meander along and allow you to meander also. On the way back, at two locations, the meadow narrows, and forest extends to the edge of the creek. These are easily traversed. In other places, the meadow widens to almost ¼ mile, requiring you to cut across it and stay in proximity to the creek.

Many people will recoil at my references in this hike to walking through the meadow, because most meadows are fragile, and hiking directly through them is a no-no. No problem, though, with tromping on Big Grizzly Creek Meadow. It is super-hardy, and the grazing cows scrunch it down much more than any bunch of hikers possibly could.

The way back also requires crossing the fence across the meadow. My long legs enabled me to step over at a low point in the barbed wire. Rolling under or hopping over—I will let you decide how best to reach the other side, since no handy cattle guard is available on this side of the creek.

As you see throughout this hike, the *big* in Big Grizzly Creek refers to the bear of many years ago, not the size of the creek. Because the meadow is so flat, the flow of the creek is mighty slow, and along most of the way there are no ripples and certainly no rapids. Nonetheless, the creek has a beauty all its own, different from that of the fast-flowing streams you encounter in most other parts of the Feather River country. In some places, lily pads add decoration. But, for all its slowness, it offers few dry-foot crossing places, and, if you try wading across shoeless, the bottom is so muddy that your feet will really be a sight when you climb out on the opposite bank.

As the hike ends at the trailhead, you may wonder, as do I, how emigrants using the Beckwourth Trail crossed the creek with their heavy wagons. Certainly, Beckwourth, who "built" the entire route from Reno to Marysville in one year, didn't construct bridges. Judging by the topography of the meadow and the location of the Trails West railroad-rail markers, his crossing point must have been somewhere near the starting point of this hike.

Camping: I didn't spy any backpack campsites in the forest adjoining the meadow, because both times I did this hike I walked mostly on the grass, not among the trees. However, there are undoubtedly a few good spots. I will admit that the parts of the forest I traversed had a good collection of cow-pies, and camping when the cows are present certainly wouldn't be enticing.

Winter Use: This would make a good cross-country ski route due to its flatness, but the access roads are not plowed in winter. Most of the access roads are marked with little orange diamond signs with arrows nailed to trees, indicating use by snow-mobiles.

GV-5 Happy Valley Loop

Distance: 4-mile loop (with side trip along Long Valley Creek, 7 miles)

Highest Point: 5,884 feet

Total Elevation Gain: 276 feet

Difficulty: Easy/moderate

Hiking Season: May through October (best in early summer or fall)

Directions to the Trailhead: Follow the directions for Hike J-15, but, at the intersection with the sign pointing left to Missouri Gulch Creek, turn right (onto 23N11). Drive 100 yards to a signless Y, and take the left fork. In .3 mile you reach another fork with a signpost on the left branch saying "61, 24N97." (The "61" is a new designation describing a route that's OK for snowmobiles and off-road vehicles.) In 50 yards along 24N97, you'll find a nice place for parking.

Comments: Sure, this whole loop is on back roads rather than wilderness trails, but don't let that dissuade you from doing this hike. In spring and into the summer the route crosses a bunch of green mini-meadows with all kinds of wildflowers. In October, deciduous trees and bushes in many places add beautiful bursts of fall color.

The Hike: Begin walking north on the smooth dirt road (24N97), which immediately crosses over Long Valley Creek. In ½ mile, you cross a tiny unnamed creek (North Branch of Long Valley Creek?)—so small that, if you aren't alert, you may miss it completely. Another ½ mile of hiking brings you to a third and soon a fourth small unnamed creek crossing, as the route loops around the north end of the valley.

By now you may be wondering, Where's the valley? So far, it has not been apparent that you've been happily hiking along the western edge of Happy Valley. The reason is that Happy Valley isn't very valleyish, and the tree cover is so dense that vistas into or across the valley are just about nonexistent. No matter—even without

a spectacular valley view, the hike is delightful.

At just about the halfway point around the loop, the more-traveled road (24N97) branches left, and you take a seldom used dirt road (23N45) that branches to the right around the eastern side of Happy Valley. You cross another unnamed branch of Long Valley Creek, and, 1 mile farther, you reach a road junction where 23N45 continues to the left and 23N46 branches to the right.

Here you are only 1 mile from the trailhead. If you would like to extend your hike a bit with a side trip, bear left on 23N45, which is now more heavily traveled than the stretch you've been on. For the next

1½ miles it closely follows sparkling Long Valley Creek, making this side trip a fun extra. After sampling the detour, make a U-turn, and return to the road junction, taking a left turn onto 23N46.

If you choose not to do the extension, at the junction take a right onto 23N46, which immediately crosses Long Valley Creek. This makes the sixth and final stream crossing in the 4-mile loop. In each case, the creek runs under the road in a culvert, allowing a dry-foot hike.

On the way back to the trailhead along the southern edge of the valley, 23N46 merges with well-used 23N11, and, soon after, a dirt road branches off to the right. The old maps showed an abandoned cabin site, Sheep Camp, in the center of the valley in the general direction of this side road. I had sufficient time left in the afternoon to satisfy my curiosity, so I hiked the ¼ mile to Sheep Camp. Unfortunately, some folks were camped there, and, because I didn't want to tromp through their camp, I backtracked to 23N11 without thoroughly snooping around the site. One of the campers was fishing in Long Valley Creek, which runs adjacent to the camp, so, perhaps the stream supports a fish population. However, if there are any trout in this diminutive creek, they're probably diminutive too.

Camping: Well, folks were car camping at Sheep Camp, but no good backpack camping sites were apparent anywhere along the loop.

Winter Use: Road 22N11 is marked with little orange diamonds nailed "above snow level" on trees, indicating that it is a snowmobile route, but the loop has no winter access for snowshoeing or cross-country skiing.

MI-1 Walker Mine and Ghost Town Loop

Distance: 1½-mile loop

Highest Point: 6,210 feet

Total Elevation Gain: 40 feet

Difficulty: Easy

Hiking Season: July through October

Directions to the Trailhead: From Graeagle take Highway 89 north for 1 mile to Highway 70, turn right, and drive through Portola. When you've gone 3 miles past Portola, turn left toward Lake Davis on Grizzly Road (County Road 175). Continue on 175 along the eastern and northern shores of the lake. The pavement ends, but the road is still smooth with a good gravel surface. Stay on the main road, passing Oldhouse Creek, the turnoffs left to Little Summit Lake, Blakeless Creek, and Lovejoy Creek (at this point the designation of the road is 24N10). The road parallels Little Grizzly Creek on the left, and then starts uphill, leaving the creek. On the left, through the trees, you can spy the Walker Mine Tailings Pond, a large, flat, treeless waste. As 24N10 levels out, you reach a junction where the left turn is the Walker Mine Road or, as it is now alternatively called, the Beckwourth-Taylorsville Road (25N05Y). The road ahead, 25N09, leads to Nye Meadows and Mount Ingalls, but there's no need to drive farther. This is the trailhead.

Comments: First, be aware that Walker Mine is private property, and, although no "Keep Out" or "No Trespassing" signs were posted at the time this was written, you need to take care during your visit. Please do not molest any of the abandoned equipment, and, above all, conduct your visit in a safe manner, staying well away from old walls and places where you could fall. Do not drink the water in Dolly or Little Grizzly Creeks even with the use of purifying tablets or filters. The tailings (or settling) pond is strictly off limits, and don't even think of taking a dip. Although you need to use prudent caution, you should enjoy seeing this ghost.

The Hike: Before you begin walking, here's a summary of Walker Mine's lengthy history. In 1904, explorer J. R. Walker and two brothers, G. L. Bemis and A. H. Bemis, went looking for an undiscovered ore deposit, because copper discoveries had been made within the "Plumas Copper Belt" during the previous 30 years. Indeed, they discovered what they thought might be a rich copper deposit. Finally, in 1909, the three hired a mining engineer to survey their find. The engineer enthusiastically reported that it would be worth mining, so Walker and the Bemis brothers staked a claim and, in 1911, formed the Walker Mining Company. The mine began operations later that year, and in 1916 a subsidiary of Anaconda Copper Mining Company purchased 51 percent of the company's stock.

The property consisted of 200 acres of claims and an additional 200 acres of USFS land; the combined holdings extended from the top of Mount Ingalls south to Little Grizzly Creek. The quartz veins of the mine contained between 7 and 12 percent copper plus small amounts of gold and silver. One historical report mentioned that, even though the amount of gold extracted was small, it was sufficient to pay for the basic mining operations. By the time the mine ceased all operations in 1941, it had 13 levels of tunnels. In total, the material removed was enough to make a layer 1 foot deep across more than 1,000 acres. Power was brought to the mine in 1917 from the newly constructed Lake Almanor powerhouse.

Ore dynamited from the tunnels was placed in electric railroad cars and transported to the surface. The ore chunks were reduced to finer particles through a series of rollers and crushers in the main mill buildings. The crushed copper ore was originally carried to Portola in ox-drawn wagons, and then loaded into Western Pacific Railroad (WPRR) cars, which carried it to Toole, Utah, for smelting. Milling refuse washed down the hillside and formed the tailings pond you passed on the way to the trailhead.

In 1920, a 9-mile aerial tramway was built from Walker Mine to Spring Garden, where the WPRR cars were loaded. The tramway had 60 ore buckets and operated so slowly that it took 3½ hours for a bucket to travel the 9 miles. During the winter when the roads to the mine were clogged with snow, the sole way in and out of the mining community was a 3½-hour tramway ride in a "passenger car"—an open box with no benches. (The path of the tramway can be seen on the topo map, but nothing remains of the line today.)

The company built four cabins along the tramway for use by the maintenance crew and by any unlucky winter passengers stuck midway due to a tramway breakdown (an 80-foot rope, kept in the passenger car, would allow a passenger to reach the ground). As truck transportation improved in the 1930s, the tramway was used only during the depths of winter; the rest of the year, trucks hauled the ore to Portola (along the route on which you came up).

Soon after the mine commenced operations in 1911, a small town began to form. In 1914 there were three privately owned homes and a bunkhouse. By 1940, at its peak, Walker Mine (sometimes spelled Walkermine) had 132 company-owned houses, 69 private homes, and 4 large bunkhouses, plus the necessary commercial buildings, including a grade school, a high school, a hospital, a post office, and even a movie theater. A ski lift was erected on the hill back of town for winter sport, and a baseball diamond was built on the tailings in front of the mine. When the mine closed, some of the houses were auctioned off and transported to Portola, where they are still occupied.

The mine was very productive in the 1920s, but the Great Depression adversely affected its operations. In 1930, the miners' workweek was reduced to five days in an effort to prevent laying off employees. By 1931 layoffs were necessary nonetheless, and by 1932 a crew of only 100 remained out of the original 420. In March 1932 the mine was forced to close completely, but it reopened in 1935, at which time 250 employees were rehired. By 1937, it was again California's largest producer of copper, and employment reached 450. Unfortunately, the "bottom fell out again," and by December 1937 only 80 miners remained on the payroll. (Most were married, because the mine owners gave preference to men with families.) One year later, things improved, and 450 employees were back mining. In mid-1940, a peak of 500 employees was reached, but soon thereafter the government froze the price of copper, and the mine's expenses were too huge for it to continue profitably. It closed for good in December 1941.

In 1942 Anaconda sold the mine. It was again sold at auction in 1945, and the purchasers, an investment group that included Robert R. Barry, planned to reopen the mine. It never happened. Over a period of several years Barry bought out the other investors. Litigation with one of the owners took years, but finally Barry owned it all by himself. (He would later rue the day this happened.) Barry was a Republican congressman from 1958 until 1964, and it was during those years that his Walker Mine troubles began.

I will try to make the very long Barry story short. Water pollution problems at the mine became apparent in the 1950s. Visitors to the area noticed that all the fish in Dolly Creek and Little Grizzly Creek had died because the streams had become polluted by mining operations. As underground water rose in the closed mineshafts, it came into contact with the exposed copper veins, creating copper sulfate and other contaminants. The embankments of the streams, as you will see at the end of your hike, became stained a brilliant turquoise blue by the copper pollutant.

In 1958, the state tried to get Barry to eliminate the cause of the water pollution, which had been going on since the mine opened. A massive legal battle ensued. Governmental dictums ordered Barry to conduct a cleanup and prevent further pollution, but nothing occurred, because the law evidently didn't have enough "teeth in it" to force the issue. Back and forth the orders and lawsuits flew, and various engineering solutions were presented. The state favored sealing off the mine, thus ending its life and preventing further seepage.

In 1987, some 29 years after the state first tried to get Barry to act, an appellate court finally ruled, "Do it—forty years of dead streams is enough." In November 1987, the regional water board, at long last, spent $280,000 for a concrete plug, and the mine was sealed, thus, we hope, ending further pollution. A final enforcement order was issued but not complied with, and the sordid tale ended for Barry when he died in June 1988, leaving his family and estate with the mess. In 1991 the Barry family wound up paying a $1.5 million settlement with the water board for cleanup operations. Even today, you can see that the tailings pond and some of the environment around the mine remain to be cleaned up. The reported cost to the American taxpayers in legal, engineering, and staff time during nearly four decades was almost $1 million. After completing your hike around Walker Mine you certainly won't be tempted to buy an old copper mine!

Note: Most of my information on Walker Mine's history came from Plumas County Historical Society Publication No. 38, *Plumas County's Newest "Ghost Town"* by Helen Lawry (1965) and Publication No. 61, *Competing Priorities: The Story*

of Walker Mine by Camille Barnes Leonhardt (June 1997). Copies of these excellent publications are available for purchase at the Plumas County Museum in Quincy.

So, let's get walking. From the car, head uphill on the road you parked on (25N09). On your right is the only whole building left standing from the mine. It is tucked away in the bushes, and its solid concrete construction with no windows suggests that it might have been a storage building for dynamite or blasting powder. Up the road from the concrete building some remains of wooden buildings are seen, but nothing recognizable is left of

The remains of the once prosperous Walker copper mine

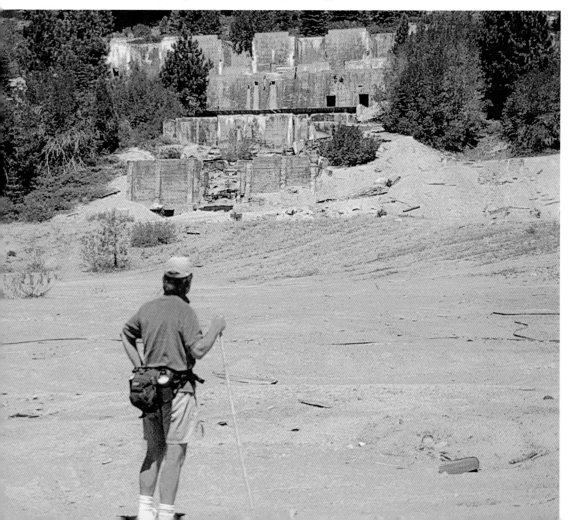

these, like all the other Walker Mine residential or commercial buildings from a community that flourished 60 years ago.

The road makes a sharp left turn, and then curves farther left as the elevation increases. Below you on the left you can see the remnants of other buildings and, of course, farther off, those of the main mine mill buildings. Dolly Creek's upper meadow appears on the left when you are about ¼ mile from the car. This probably is where the ski slope was located. At the far end of the meadow, you need to cut downhill, going cross-country and working your way toward the mine but avoiding the heavy bush cover. A few hundred yards of careful downhill in what was once part of the residential area brings you to the upper part of the mine, just to the east of the tunnel. When you reach an outcropping of dark tailings, a right turn leads you past the ore car depository. Here the old, very rusted, ore cars are gathered with no place to go and no future except to rust away in a few centuries.

From this spot, if you look downhill, you see the settling pond. To the left of the pond you may note what looks like a gravel path enclosed in a shallow, wooden trough leading down almost to the trailhead. If you wonder why I didn't vector you up this seemingly easier route, it's because this gravel trough is used to keep surface water from flowing across the mine property. The water containment measure is one of the minor (and weak) remedial efforts to prevent further pollution—so, let's not disturb it.

Walking westerly, you encounter some buildings with corrugated steel sides. A large locked door with rails running under it must have been one of the main mine entrances. Please do not enter any of the remaining structures, and watch your step as you cross planking that isn't quite all there. You can hear water running underneath; evidently,

Dolly Creek is subterranean at this point. Continuing farther around the loop, you come to a wide, level surface with the foundations of the main mill ahead. You pass a single ore car that looks like it was put there for display purposes. A few steps farther to the west you reach the hacked-off concrete walls of the mill. You don't want to fall inside the crumbling walls, so exercise utmost caution and stay well back from the edge.

The route continues on the easy level road, past the jagged foundations. From here you have a good view of the flat tailings area below. Many of the mill operation buildings were built on the periphery of this area; no sign of them remains. You come to a gate across the road, which you can easily walk around, and, beyond that, the road curves left and reaches a road intersection. Turn left, and follow the road back 250 yards to the trailhead. However, 100 yards before reaching your car, make a left turn, and jump the turquoise watercourse (*creek* and *stream* are words too dignified for this sad stretch of flowing water). Climb the hill of tailings to the flat below the mine. From here you have a good view looking up toward the old concrete foundation of the mill. Return to the road by the same route, and then turn left to walk the short distance to your car.

As you drive back on 24N10, when you're about 5.5 miles from Walker Mine, you pass, on your right, the site of Midway House. No sign commemorates this spot, but it figured prominently in the history of Walker Mine. One historical account of the mine relates that this was where illegal liquor was purchased (prohibition was in effect during part of the mine's tenure), and the upstairs was evidently occupied by the local house of prostitution. Well, the red light burns no longer.

Camping: None—don't even think about it in this polluted locale!

Winter Use: None.

SG-1 Greenhorn Creek Portion of Beckwourth's Emigrant Trail

Distance: 4½ miles out and back (with side trip to the mine, 5¾ miles out and back)

Highest Point: 4,365 feet (with side trip, 4,685 feet)

Total Elevation Gain: 425 feet (with side trip, 828 feet)

Difficulty: Moderate

Hiking Season: May through November

Directions to the Trailhead: From Graeagle go north on Highway 89 for 1 mile to Highway 70, turn left, and drive 14.4 miles, past Spring Garden, to an unsigned dirt road to the right. Just before this turn, Highway 70 makes a very large cut through a hill. If you miss the turn, the road up Squirrel Creek (25N18) is only 200 yards beyond; when you see that, turn around, and go back a short distance. There is plenty of easy parking on this side road.

Comments: This is one of the nicest streamside hikes in the book. The trail is fairly level (except for the climb to the ridge after leaving the creek, if you take the side trip to the mine). Unlike many Sierra streams, this one offers frequent views of the water, because for much of the way the banks are not completely clogged with willows and alder bushes. The side trip brings you to a seldom visited mine that must have been a decent producer of gold judging by the size of its tailings piles. The first half of this hike is very colorful in fall due to the large number of bigleaf maples, plus a few black oaks and Pacific dogwoods, mixed with the conifer forest. In summer, the leaf shapes and hues of green of those deciduous trees add a delightful variety of color and texture to the forest. Oh yes, you'll need to wade across the creek, so you might want to bring along some old sneakers or thongs to change into for the crossings and

a small towel to dry your feet. To learn more about Jim Beckwourth and his emigrant trail, which this hike follows, please read Appendix D. I'll admit that the less-than-definitive maps of his trail in this sector seem to indicate that it's actually in the next drainage basin to the east, not along Greenhorn Creek. I have explored the more eastern area extensively and find no evidence of the trail and no logical place for it. The route that I describe here does have evidence and logic. Am I right? Sure, but no guarantee.

The Hike: Before you begin, you might want to check out two historic features near the trailhead. The first lies directly on the other side of Highway

70 from where you parked; it's the unique Williams Loop of the Western Pacific Railroad. (Several years ago the WPRR became part of the Union Pacific Railroad.) Because locomotives cannot handle a very steep grade, the builders of the WPRR in 1909 could not gain the amount of altitude they needed by routing the tracks directly parallel to the Feather River. To solve this problem, the railroad designer (I suppose named Williams) came up with the idea of putting a 360° loop in the tracks. Thus, a train headed uphill crosses under the exiting track and makes a complete circle with a diameter of a little more than ¼ mile, twice bridging the Feather River and exiting the loop headed in the same direction as it entered but 40 feet higher in elevation. You can't see the whole circle today from Highway 70, but you can visualize it as the tracks curve sharply below you.

The other feature worth seeing is the site of the old sawmill just north of the trailhead. Recross Highway 70 after seeing part of the Williams Loop, and immediately take a left on a dim path. You soon come upon the foundations of the old sawmill, nearly overgrown with brush. Climb the embankment east of the crumbling remains, and gander at the sunken meadow below you. In days of old, the dam on which you are standing created the millpond, which was fed by Squirrel and Greenhorn Creeks. This spot was obviously teeming with activity when the mill was in operation. The 1950 Spring Garden topo map (yes, that's the most recent edition at the time this book was written!) shows the mill site and the millpond. Evidently a bunch of the outbuildings, now gone, were then still standing.

Your car is only about 100 yards away, so walk past it and up the road to a nearby Y. Take the dimmer right fork, and bypass the steep uphill track on your right under the overhead power lines. The road you're on isn't particularly attractive for the first 300 yards, and you pass some junk and an old hobo camp off to your left. However, this sad state of af-

fairs improves quickly as the road becomes free of tire tracks and reaches the side of Greenhorn Creek. Beyond this point, for the next 1½ miles, the road is more like a trail than a road. None of the route is shown on the 1950 topo map, so it must have been an unused thoroughfare even then. As you walk along the creek, its playful splashing and gurgling enhance your enjoyment of the fairly level, smooth trail. The oaks, bigleaf maples, and Pacific dogwoods in the forest add to the beauty in a fashion not seen in any other hike in this book.

After about 1½ miles, the trail seems to disappear, but it merely has taken a sharp left turn, jumped down to the creek, and crossed it. Just prior to this crossing, I left the trail to see that section of the creek at close hand. I discovered a camp that had been used fairly recently, judging by the unrusted cans and newer bottles left by careless campers. However, nearby under a bush I also found a shovel that was almost rusted away (the hardwood handle had rotted away completely), so this must have been an old camp too. It takes quite a few years for the forces of nature to accomplish that decay.

To cross the creek, you have to get your feet wet, because there aren't any handy stepping-stones and the logs spanning the creek are too small to act as a bridge. In midsummer, the stream was shallow enough and the bottom smooth enough so that crossing wasn't difficult. (Keep your soggy sneakers or thongs on, because there are a few more crossings in close succession.) The trail runs along the north side of the creek for a few hundred yards and then suddenly intersects a "beaten path" obviously used by horses. I suggest taking the path to the right, first. It immediately crosses Pine Creek (another foot-wetter). The junction of Pine Creek and Greenhorn Creek is just downstream from this point.

In a little less than ½ mile, the trail recrosses Greenhorn Creek and arrives at "the big picnic ground." Evidently, this old campsite is now used by the people who conduct the trail rides, because it is outfitted with a bunch of picnic tables, big barbecue grills, and even an old, but clean, portable potty (no toilet paper but plenty of paper seat covers). I imagined what a unique place this would be for a wedding reception.

Although a trail continues upstream along Greenhorn Creek from "the big picnic ground," and a dirt road reaches it from the other direction, retrace your steps to the Pine Creek crossing. At this intersection, you need to decide whether to make the side trip to the mine. If not, return to your car the way you came, on the trail along Greenhorn Creek.

If you prefer to hike up to the mine, turn right, and follow the well-trod and pooped-upon horse trail along Pine Creek (it's not as bad as I make it sound). Shortly, after coming to a small streamside meadow, the trail leaves the creek and turns left, heading uphill in a series of short, steep switchbacks.

Just before you reach the crest of the ridge, the surrounding forest largely disappears as a result of the lumberjacks' (are there now lumberjills?) chainsaws. The crest offers some nice, albeit not spectacular, views. The trail then dips downhill, and within ¼ mile you see the ruins of the mine. It is strange that this apparently once-productive mine doesn't show up on either the 1950 topo map (I'm sure the mine predates 1950) or the USFS Plumas National Forest map, although an old surveyors'

Springtime snow plants being visited by a swallowtail butterfly near Greenhorn Creek

map describes it as the Heath Quartz Mine. (They mined quartz because it contained gold, so this should more properly have been called the Heath Gold Mine, right?)

You can see one of the mine entrances if you scramble up the tailings pile. It is a hole big enough to crawl into (but don't, for goodness sake); I'm sure the original entrance was much larger, so a partial cave-in must have occurred. Piles of tailings farther up the hillside indicate the presence of mineshafts there too, but I could find no other openings.

It is hard to picture what the large wooden collapsed structure once was. Part of it may have been a small stamp mill for crushing the pieces of gold-bearing quartz extracted from the mine. However, stamp mills were typically powered by a water-wheel supplied by a flume from a water source farther uphill. I could see no signs of a flume or a large water pipe on the site, so who knows?

After "touring" the mine site, return by the same route to the trail intersection near the junction of Pine and Greenhorn Creeks. Here, turn right on the much less used trail along Greenhorn Creek that you came in on, and follow it back to your car.

If by now it's late afternoon, the sun at a low angle shines through the maple leaves so that they seem to be a translucent green. I have hiked this trail in October, and the variety of deciduous trees along the route makes it one of the most colorful autumn trails in the Feather River country.

Camping: You could try camping at a lot of places along the creek, but there's no permanent backpack campsite. The hobo campground near the trailhead stinks, literally.

Winter Use: When I hiked this trail I didn't think much about doing it on snowshoes in the winter. However, because Highway 70 is plowed all winter, access to the trailhead is available, so it should be a dandy snowshoe trail. The creek crossings present a challenge, of course, if you wish to snowshoe beyond them.

Chapter 14

Crocker Mountain, Portola, Calpine, and Reconnaissance Peak Topos

CM-I Crocker Meadow and Old Railroad Grade Trail

Distance: 5 miles out and back

Highest Point: 5,706 feet

Total Elevation Gain: 120 feet

Difficulty: Easy/moderate

Hiking Season: May through October (best in May through July)

Directions to the Trailhead: From Graeagle take Highway 89 north for 1 mile to Highway 70. Turn right on 70, and drive for 14.5 miles, passing through Portola, to Beckwourth. Turn left on the Beckwourth-Genesee Road (Forest Road 177). Most of the next 6 miles to the trailhead are on pavement, but the last couple of miles are on well-maintained gravel. At a sign pointing left to Crocker Campground, turn left, cross the bridge, and park by the USFS notice board just before you get to the campground.

Comments: If you are a fan of meadows (who isn't?), this hike is for you. The almost flat trail follows alongside beautiful Crocker Meadow for its full 2-mile length. The second feature of the hike is the historic railroad route you follow easily to the turn-around point. Bear in mind that meadows don't have trees, so most of the hike will be shadeless; don't take this hike on the hottest day of the year, and do slop on the sunscreen. Before starting out,

you might read Appendix A, which has tips about how to hike an old railroad right-of-way and tells some of the history of railroads in the Feather River country.

The Hike: Before walking, turn around to see the cute cabin across the road, the former USFS Crocker Ranger Station. It was built in 1912, replacing the original log cabin station. The interior was remodeled in the 1930s by the Civilian Conservation Corps (CCC), a US government organization created by the Roosevelt administration to help alleviate severe unemployment during the Great Depression. Many campgrounds and trails throughout the Sierra were built by the CCC. The shower outbuilding at the ranger station was converted from a Clover Valley Lumber Company Railroad camp car. By the early 1980s, the cabin's usefulness had diminished, as had the USFS budget for maintaining outposts like this, so it was closed and boarded up.

The trail begins close to the barbed wire fence separating Crocker Meadow from the eastern edge of the campground. At this point, the route is a

Rotting railroad ties on the old railroad grade in Crocker Meadow

smooth dirt road heading due south along the western side of the meadow. In a few hundred yards, an old rusted iron pipeline lies across the trail. Evidently, once upon a time, it brought water to the campground and perhaps the ranger station. Soon the old rail bed becomes obvious, raised above the level of the meadow. Its rotting ties are still scattered around, but the rails and even the spikes used to attach them to the ties were removed many years ago.

You see a small, fairly well-preserved rail bridge over a tiny creeklet running into the meadow on your left. I kept an eye out for evidence of defunct rail spurs, and, about ½ mile into the hike, I saw what looked like an old railroad grade heading off to the right. This wasn't on the map, but, sure enough, I found rotting old ties indicating that this was once a spur line. It paralleled a small creek uphill, so I followed it for several hundred yards. There I came across the remains of an old cabin that had been built close to the tracks. A few hundred yards beyond the cabin site, the route disappeared. Most likely this spur had been built to bring out logs from this part of the forest. As the old ranger station shower car demonstrated, part of the early tracks in this area were put in by the Clover Valley Lumber Company Railroad.

Back on the trail, I noticed a small brown bird flitting in the pine trees lining the meadow. I couldn't identify it until I saw a similar bird clad in blue. Ah, of course, the brown one was a female mountain bluebird. As is typical of many bird species, the male is a brilliant color, while the female is dull (sorry, ladies—just be happy that humans seem to be the other way around).

Along some of the route, the rail bed was built up about 3 feet above meadow level. Silver sage seems to love the tops of these built-up sections and grows in clumps between the rotting ties. As a result, it is easier to walk down at meadow level.

The meadow is rich in flower varieties. Yellow California butterweed growing a foot tall and western bistort of similar height are profuse in some places. You come to a short rocky section, although the meadow still appears on the left. Then the meadow forms a Y, and the branch you're following to the right becomes narrower. Shortly before you reach a creeklet flowing into the meadow, you see "the dump" on your right. This eyesore is a sizable pile of rusty cans. Often old dumps include interesting tidbits, such as old coffeepots, rusted tin plates and cups, and empty (naturally) booze bottles. Perhaps relic collectors have already cleaned out this dump; it contains nothing but cans, hundreds of them, all too rusted to identify what was inside.

A bit farther down the trail, evidence of the railroad disappears, and the route becomes a row of what look like old plow furrows. These follow where the railroad tracks were laid, and the topo map shows the route as a dirt road, although no car tire marks are in evidence. The "plow road" still follows alongside the meadow, and you soon pass a new spring-fed watering trough, as well as the old wooden one it evidently replaced.

Finally, the meadow ends, and the "plow road" makes a curve easterly. In a couple of places, another plow road intersects the one you're on at right angles. This mysterious configuration almost looks like the preliminary layout of a housing subdivision. The plow road is carpeted with small ponderosa pine trees, thousands of them. Ten years from now when they have grown, you'll not be able to walk down the middle of that road. I counted about 20 seedlings in each foot of route length. The road continues in this manner for about a mile, so I did a quick calculation: 20 seedlings per foot times 5,280 feet per mile equals 105,600 ponderosas ready to become a forest. With this density, the trees would form an almost solid forest, so the trees will have to decide somehow which ones will grow tall and which fade away.

About 2½ miles from the trailhead, two large berms block the plow road. When I climbed over them I found, to my surprise, a beautiful road of level hard-packed sand on the other side. It looked unused, and no cars could cross these berms. This is the turnaround spot for your return to the trailhead along the same route.

Crocker Creek runs through the full length of the meadow, according to the map, but it must be mostly marsh because no flowing creek is in evidence. One thing this hike is certain to prove to you: There's no such thing as meadow overdose.

I had a good laugh, several days later, while scouting Hike P-4. The P-4 trail turned into a nice level wide road with dim tire tracks, and the double berm appeared ahead! I hadn't coordinated my Crocker Mountain and Portola topo maps to discover that the end of Hike CM-1 overlapped a bit of

Hike P-4. Now I know where that nice road leads.

Camping: There are no campsites along the trail, but the USFS campground at the trailhead isn't crowded and looks good for car camping unless you desire more deluxe accommodations.

Winter Use: None.

CM-2 Crocker Mountain Trail

Distance: 6 miles out and back

Highest Point: 7,499 feet

Total Elevation Gain: 1,300 feet

Difficulty: Moderate/strenuous

Hiking Season: June through October

Directions to the Trailhead: From Graeagle drive 1 mile north on Highway 89 to Highway 70. Turn right on 70, and drive 10 miles east to Portola. In Portola, turn left on West Street at the sign pointing to "Lake Davis Recreation Area." Follow this road, called Lake Davis Road, out of Portola to an intersection with a sign pointing left to "Old Camp 5, Boat Ramp 2½" and pointing right to "Campgrounds Boat Ramps 3." Take the right fork, a continuation of Lake Davis Road (23N06). In 2 miles, after crossing the Grizzly Valley Dam, you reach a T junction. Turn left onto Grizzly Road (County Road 175, sometimes, at this point, known as Beckwourth-Taylorsville Road), and drive .7 mile on the paved road past the entrance to Grizzly and Grasshopper Flat Campgrounds. Turn right onto an unsigned dirt road that is directly across from a road left bearing a sign "Honker Bay Boat Ramp." After .2 mile on this rough but passable road, you see a road branching right toward a large green water tank visible through the trees up on the hill. However, keep going straight to a place .8 mile from the Grizzly Road, where you encounter a too-rough-to-navigate crossing of a dry creek (perhaps wet in the spring). Park alongside the road

where a long section of discarded 8-inch drain culvert lies to the left of your car.

Comments: Sometimes a hike that looks formidable on the map turns out to be easier than expected. That's the case with the hike up Crocker Mountain. The 1972 topo map shows the trail ending just below the ridge, so you'd have to make a tough 1½-mile cross-country trek to the tallest peak. Luckily, logging roads have since been built leading to a spot only 200 yards from the top and about 100 feet below it. The cross-country portion is now short, and the splendid view from the top is within reach of hikers who don't mind a small

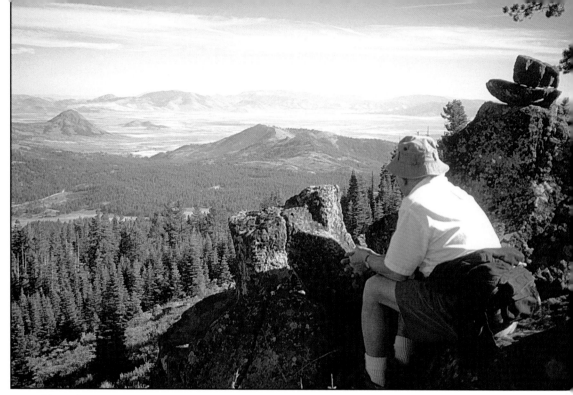

Sierra Valley from the top of Crocker Mountain

scramble to the summit. The 360° view from the 7,499-foot peak is particularly spectacular to the east, stretching from Red Clover Valley to Sierra Valley. While hundreds attain the more popular peaks, Mount Elwell and Eureka Peak in the Lakes Basin area, your climb to the top of Crocker Mountain will make you one of only a few people each year to achieve its summit.

The Hike: Head uphill on the jeep road, avoiding a road forking to the left in 100 yards, although it looks more heavily traveled. In another 100 yards of uphill hiking, you reach a second fork in the road. The left fork to the north is the correct path. This isn't the trail shown on the topo, but it's a better route. After ¼ mile, keep a lookout to the left for a very unusual large outcropping of lava rock near the trail. It's worth a few steps off the path to view this wonder of nature from different angles.

The route continues northerly uphill for the next mile in a fairly straight line. To your left, through the trees, you get some fine panoramic views of Lake Davis with Smith Peak behind it. The

road you're on hasn't been driven on for years, as shown by a large tree that has fallen across it. Erosion around the log indicates that it has been horizontal for a long time.

Finally, you reach a clearing used by loggers as a log marshaling yard. A big jumbled pile of old cut logs lies to your right in the flattish open area. Curve to the right around this pile to pick up the road on the far edge of the area. At this point, tire tracks are evident, and the road now aims for the ridge. About ¼ mile farther you come to a road intersection. The track you're on goes straight ahead but the road to the right heads up the side of the ridge that leads to the peak. On your right, just as you turn off onto this side road, a tree has two yellow USFS markers on it.

The side road you're on now also has had a minor amount of vehicle traffic. For some reason many midsize white fir trees have been cut but not limbed or stacked. They were left lying in profusion, many across the road, blocking it to traffic. Perhaps "thinning" was the reason for this seeming waste: midsize trees are eliminated so that the larger trees don't have to compete with them in the forest. There sure were a lot of great-looking still-green, cut Christmas trees lying helter-skelter in the vicinity. Who knows? Occasionally, you can see a juniper tree on this western slope of Crocker Ridge, although they are not common in this region. (The whole 2-mile-long ridge is called Crocker Mountain on the topo, but I prefer to refer to only the tallest peak on the ridge as Crocker Mountain.)

You pass another scattered log pile as the track, now heading south, gradually climbs parallel with the top of the ridge. In a bit more than a mile from the road intersection, you again encounter a pile of logs in a clearing, this one neatly stacked and made of healthy-looking good-size logs. Although they have evidently been piled there for a long time, judging by their gray bark deterioration, they look like they were all set, once upon a time, to be put on a logging track and whisked off to the mill. I am disappointed that loggers will kill nice-size healthy trees and then not even use them for lumber.

The old loggers' road ends here. Make a 90° left turn and scramble steeply uphill in the corridor left by the loggers when they dragged cut logs down to the clearing from higher up. After 100 yards, even this path fades. Now you commence the final ascent straight uphill without benefit of a trail. Fortunately, the ridge crest is only 100 yards away, and, although the climb is steep, the thinning forest allows you to make your way without beating through bushes. Along this trailless section are several rock cairns (or ducks, as some folks call them), strategically placed to help you find the way to the top. Ahead, you can spy the jagged rocky crest. Af-

ter easily climbing to it, you can drink in the grandeur of the view, particularly to the east.

Looking southward you discover that the topmost elevation is actually a few jagged rock outcroppings away from where you are. No problem. Merely climb down from the rocky crest, tramp south through and over some low-growing manzanita, and, within 100 yards, approach the highest point, crowned with a pile of rocks placed there by someone who wanted you to easily identify the tippy-top. Ascending this jumble of rocks is no big task, and you then stand at the top of Crocker Mountain. Here is an opportunity for taking spectacular photos in many directions. The jagged crest makes a good foreground in panoramic shots. Directly below your vista to the east, is Crocker Meadow (see Hike CM-1) and the Beckwourth-Genesee Road leading from Beckwourth up to the expansive Red Clover Valley. This road is shown on the Keddie survey map of 1892, so it's been there a while.

On the way back to the car, I heard a shrill high screech from up on the ridge. "Ah, an eagle," I exclaimed to my hiking companion. The bird flew into view and landed on top of a tall white fir not too far away. This "eagle" was, however, an osprey, easily identified by its white plumage and its wing pattern. It was fun to see, but I was disappointed that it wasn't an eagle.

Camping: Plenty of good car camping is available along the eastern shore of Lake Davis, particularly in the nearby USFS Grizzly and Grasshopper Flat Campgrounds. Because there's no water on this trail, backpacking is probably not a great idea.

Winter Use: I suppose a snowshoe walk up Crocker Mountain is possible, but somehow it wouldn't be high on my list of snowy trails to follow.

P-1 Beckwourth Peak Trail

Distance: 6½ miles out and back from Trailhead A (four-wheel-drive vehicle preferable but not mandatory); 9½ miles out and back from Trailhead B (accessible by two-wheel-drive and low-slung vehicles).

Highest Point: 7,250 feet

Total Elevation Gain: 1,610 feet from Trailhead A; 2,210 feet from Trailhead B

Difficulty: Strenuous

Hiking Season: April through June and September through October (July and August are rather hot)

Directions to the Trailhead: From Graeagle take Highway 89 north for 1 mile to Highway 70, turn right on 70, and drive 10 miles into Portola. Midway through Portola, turn right on South Gulling Street (County Road A-15), cross over the Feather River, turn right on First Avenue, then left on Colorado Street for 2 blocks, then right on Portola-McLears Road, which heads out of town with an A-15 sign. When you've driven .6 mile from Portola, take a road that intersects on the left. It immediately branches, with the left fork bearing a sign "Private Road—Keep Out" and the right fork bearing a USFS Road 22N55 marker. I have a dilemma in telling you exactly where on 22N55 the best trailhead is, because it depends on your car and your comfort level with driving a rough, dippy (but not steep) dirt road. Trailhead B should be a place beyond which you do not feel comfortable driving. In dry weather, even a non-four-wheel-drive vehicle can make it to Trailhead A, especially if the car isn't low to the ground and the driver is accustomed to back roads. A jeep can actually travel past Trailhead A all the way up to the locked gate described in the hike, but I chose a lower trailhead, to give myself a "nice climb." Trailhead A is 2.7 miles from Road A-15, at a large, flat clearing.

Comments: In this hike, like most hikes to mountain peaks, a bunch of continuous uphill

walking is to be expected, but, ah, the view from the top is worth it. You'll see a large portion of the upper valley of the Feather River Middle Fork, in which Portola is located, to the north, plus the wide expanse of Sierra Valley to the east. From near the radio/microwave towers, the westward views of Mount Elwell, Mount Washington, and Eureka Peak are outstanding, especially early in the season when they are snowcapped.

The Hike: It's simple: hike on 22N55, a semi-steep but fairly smooth dirt road all the way to the top saddle, and then hike cross-country to the very

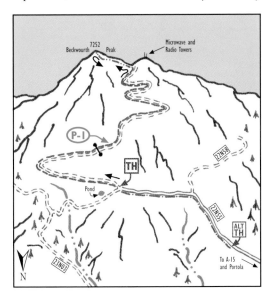

top. From Trailhead B, the jeep road gradually picks up altitude and travels more or less in a straight line through a ponderosa and Jeffrey pine forest to a large, flat clearing (where Trailhead A is located) with a road intersecting on the left (not shown on the topo map). You could follow this intersecting road all the way back downhill to Portola near the high school, thus making a giant loop if you feel inclined to do a "big one." I have tried most of this big loop and rejected putting it in the book because the best part is the summit, not the lower approach roads.

The only water along the route is found by taking a 300-yard detour on this side road to the left, just past the big clearing. A large water pipe comes out of the hillside and gushes water into a pond alongside the road. My guess is that this water comes from a spring, but, inviting as it appears, I'd still purify it. "Be safe, not sorry" is the advice of those of us who have been afflicted with the tough-to-get-rid-of protozoan giardia, which can lurk in even the purest-looking streams or water sources. After gathering and treating your water, return to 22N55.

Continue following the jeep road uphill. In slightly less than ½ mile, it makes a sharp right turn and begins an even steeper ascent. The views to your right of Portola and its surroundings are great, so you won't mind the steepness as much as you would otherwise. When you're ¼ mile past the sharp right turn, the largely treeless (hence shadeless) road is blocked by a locked gate. This obviously cuts off vehicle access to all but workers with gate keys who have business with the radio and microwave towers. Hikers can go around the gate and continue on the road.

Soon, you see a huge green edifice somewhat like a billboard. I thought it might be a giant sign lit up at night, saying "Portola High School" or some such message, but there's no electricity to it. Actually, I believe, it is used for microwave relaying. Once you know where to look, you can easily see it from Portola in the valley below. I've heard some talk that this less-than-beautiful edifice might be taken down, so don't be surprised if it's no longer there.

The road continues uphill to a sharp left turn, which the topo map indicates is the site of a radio

Summer afternoon cumulus clouds above Sierra Valley viewed from Beckwourth Peak

tower. The tower, however, is long gone, I suppose replaced by one in the tower complex higher on the mountain. Likewise, the dated topo shows the remainder of the route to the saddle as a trail, whereas it is now all jeep road. The road does two switchbacks and finally becomes level as it reaches the saddle.

Once you reach the place where the road flattens and just before it makes a sharp right turn heading directly toward the radio towers, keep an eye out on your left for the start of the dim trail heading to the peak, which is ¼ mile away. I had expected this part of the route to be 100 percent trailless cross-country, so this dim trail was a welcome sight. In midsummer the trail was so covered with low-growing Lobb's nama that I was forced to tread on the bluish-purple flowers. After a couple of hundred yards, this dim trail faded out in a grove of fir trees, and the way to the top seemed blocked by an impassable stand of brush. By experiment I found that going a bit left at the grove and tromping over some low brush brings you out on a shelf of large flat rocks. This provides easy walking to the rock pile just ahead that looks like the summit.

After scrambling up the boulders, you find that this is a false summit, and the highest point is down the other side, another 50 yards farther, and up the next rock pile. People not into boulder-scrambling up and down will want to pass on this portion of the trip, but there are no scary cliffs and, with care, the ascent can be safely made by anyone except little kids and folks who wouldn't make it up the steep jeep road anyhow. On top there are several nice level gravel spots to stand on, so don't be concerned if you suffer from vertigo.

The views to the north, east, and south are outstanding. Besides the upper valley of the Feather River Middle Fork and Portola, you can see Penman Peak, Grizzly Valley, Lake Davis, Smith Peak, and Mount Ingalls to the north plus almost the entire sweep of the extensive Sierra Valley to the east and southeast. The full vista to the west is blocked by the western portion of the mountaintop, thus depriving you of a 360° view. (I'm not complaining—the 260° view is plenty.) This is a fine place for lunch, especially because it has some level spots and is not all vertical rock.

Upon returning to the jeep trail, continue up its remaining 200 yards, and, just before it makes a right turn up to the radio tower complex, head off the road to the west, scrambling over rocks for a few yards to get a fine western view of Mount Elwell, Mount Washington, and Eureka Peak, which you couldn't see from the very top. I passed on trekking the final few yards up to the tower complex because some four-wheel-drive service trucks were there, and I thought they might consider their turf off-limits. A four-wheel-drive Sprint truck passed me on my way down, and the driver stopped to say "Hi." He told me that lightning from a severe thunderstorm the night before had caused a bunch of damage to some of the radio/microwave tower installations, hence the need for service workers—a rare sight there.

On the route back, I again enjoyed the magnificent views of the Portola area below. A large red-tailed hawk circled effortlessly above in the updraft created by the prevailing easterly wind rising on the southwestern face of the mountain. An old map, dated 1912, drawn by Arthur W. Keddie, Plumas County's famous surveyor, identifies the peak as Bogue Mountain. Whoever Bogue was, he eventually lost out to the more renowned Jim Beckwourth, whose name is also attached to a town, a pass over the Sierra, and the original emigrant wagon road through this part of Plumas County (see Appendix D).

Camping: None.
Winter Use: None.

P-2 Ross Ranch Meadow Loop

Distance: 3½-mile loop (with riverside detour, 4 miles)

Highest Point: 5,100 feet

Total Elevation Gain: 120 feet

Difficulty: Easy/moderate

Hiking Season: April through November

irections to the Trailhead: From Graeagle go north on Highway 89 for 1 mile to Highway 70, and turn right. Drive 14 miles, passing through Portola, and just before reaching Beckwourth turn right on the paved Beckwourth-Calpine Road (County Road A-23). The road bridges the Feather River Middle Fork, and then crosses the Union Pacific Railroad main-line tracks. Immediately after the tracks, turn right on a signless dirt road that heads west, paralleling the tracks. In 250 yards, the road crosses a cattle guard and enters an area with the designation National Wild and Scenic River Area, although at this point the countryside is neither very wild nor scenic. Just after the cattle guard, the road divides, with the left branch going to a ranch. Take the right branch, which continues to parallel the tracks and, in ½ mile, bumps over another cattle guard, as you leave the wild and scenic area. The sizable ruts in the road indicate that this stretch is probably unsuitable for normal cars when muddy. In another 200 yards, where a less well used road forks left, continue straight on the dirt road (23N03YA), which crosses the northern edge of Ross Ranch Meadow. Where a dry creek (which might be wet in spring) intersects the road, you'll experience a sizable bump. At this writing, it isn't a four-wheel-drive-vehicle-only bump yet, but, if it looks too rough for your car to handle, just back up to the intersection with the dim road and start your walk from there. If you go slow and cross the creeklet, drive just a bit farther, cross another cattle guard, and again enter the National Wild and Scenic River Area. The trail-

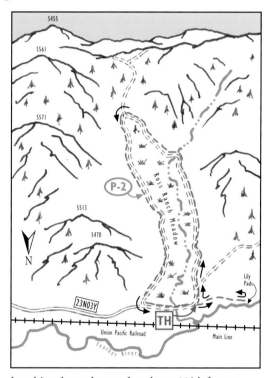

head is where the road makes a 90° left turn.

Comments: The best time to take this hike is in spring or early summer when the meadow is green, but if it has recently rained the road might be muddy. Also, I found ample evidence that the upper meadow was still being used during part of the year by members of the bovine species. If, indeed, a large herd is visible in the upper meadow as you drive to the trailhead across the bottom of the lower meadow, you might have to share the path with some critters. On the bright side, the views of Beckwourth Peak close-at-hand are nice and the meadow, before it dries out in the late summer, is beautiful. A short side trip from the trailhead to see the Feather River lily ponds might also be of interest.

The Hike: At the trailhead, a fence line indicates the boundary of the National Wild and Scenic River Area. Either before or after doing the loop, you might want to take the ¼-mile side trip on the path that leads away from the road and toward the river. I was pleased with the sign posted on the walk-around barrier, which says "Foot Traffic Welcome." I had hoped that the nice-looking trail would offer a delightful stroll along the river for a couple of miles. The stroll is delightful, but it lasts for only about ¼ mile before willows on the riverbank block the path very effectively. I tried some detours, but the trail never resumes. However, I enjoyed finding several side ponds covered with water lilies, along the quietly flowing river, a sight not often seen in the Sierra. A picnic at this seldom visited part of the Feather River would be nice and peaceful, except when a fast freight roared by on the nearby Union Pacific Railroad tracks.

The loop hike starts at the trailhead where the road makes a 90° left turn just after the cattle guard. The route is all on the seldom used (but not dusty or rocky) dirt road that skirts the meadow. Arthur W. Keddie's 1892 Map of Plumas County shows the first half of this loop to be a minor wagon road that connected the main east-west wagon road (now State Highway 70) with several ranches to the south.

In 150 yards a dirt road forks right, and soon another (23N03YB) does the same, but you need to stay on the main road paralleling the western edge of the meadow. An electric fence separates your route from the meadow itself. There's not much shade along this stretch so, on a hot day in late summer, it can get rather warm. Wear a hat, or put sunscreen on your bald spot if you have one.

The meadow ends 1½ miles from the trailhead, and the road starts to curve left. When you see a large pile of rocks on your right, you need to decide whether to take the cow trail or the loop road back to the trailhead. There is something nice about being on a single-track trail versus a dirt road, although this road is seldom used. The cow trail follows along the edge of the meadow starting in the grove of trees on the left at the point where the rock pile can be seen. On the cow trail, you'll have to step over cow pies, especially when the trail enters a grove where the cows lounge in the shade on hot days. The road isn't a bad choice, so you might decide to stay on it. In another 100 yards you come to a Y at which you take the left branch. The road is shouting distance from the cow trail, and the meadow soon comes into view on your left.

A tumbled-down fence line whose only evidence now is a bunch of rotting fence posts runs along the road on the meadow side. About ¾ of a mile from the Y, a gate blocks the road, and a fence line from the gate runs across the meadow. As you approach the gate, expecting to have to climb over, you get a pleasant surprise: there's no lock on it. A courteous sign merely says, "Please! Close the Gate," so, please do. If you took the meandering cow path, it has by now become such a big pain in the neck to follow that you probably have already walked the short distance to the road and reached the gate by road.

Across the meadow is a very nice view of Beckwourth Peak rearing it's attractive profile 2 miles away. The ½-mile walk from the gate back to the "main" road (23N03YA) is uneventful. Where the two intersect, turn left, and walk across the northern edge of the meadow on the road on which you drove in. In spring you'll probably have to jump across the creek (dry in summer) that runs the length of Ross Ranch Meadow.

The 1882 book *History of Plumas County* doesn't list any Rosses, but Keddie's 1892 map of Plumas County shows three separate Ross parcels for the ranch. One, north of the river, is listed as

Lily pads on a calm part of the Feather River near Ross Ranch Meadow

owned by J. L. Ross. The second, where the meadow is, has the name J. B. Ross. A third, adjoining J. B.'s on the east, is titled simply "Mrs. Ross." Hence, the Rosses (including momma?) must have been prominent citizens in the area.

Camping: None.

Winter Use: The access road is not plowed in winter. However, snowshoeing or cross-country skiing in shouldn't be too tough, and the level topography is conducive to these activities. That said, the area does not get as much snow as other parts of the Feather River country, so any winter use is probably confined to a few days after major storms.

P-3 Boca-Loyalton Railroad Grade Loop

Distance: 6-mile loop (with the big loop, 8¾ miles)

Highest Point: 6,022 feet

Total Elevation Gain: 745 feet

Difficulty: Strenuous

Hiking Season: April through June (July and August are too hot)

Directions to the Trailhead: From Graeagle go north on Highway 89 for 1 mile to Highway 70, turn right, and drive 14.5 miles, through Portola, to Beckwourth. Turn left on the Beckwourth-Genesee Road (Forest Road 177), and travel north on this paved road for 3.0 miles to a dirt road leading right with a sign "Sugar Loaf 2,

Dotta Neck 4." Continue on Road 177 another .85 mile, and turn right on an unsigned dirt road there. In about 100 yards you come to a dirt road on your left that goes back to Road 177, thus forming a small triangle. Park here.

Comments: This hike isn't for everyone, because much of it isn't a beaten trail or easily followed jeep road, but it does have its merits. The first half follows the historic circuitous route of the old Boca-Loyalton Railroad. Long ago, after the railroad was no longer in operation, every inch of rail was ripped up and sold for scrap. However, the wooden ties were left to rot, a process they are accomplishing nicely. Although this hike is classified as strenuous because of all the vegetation you have to tramp on, over, or around, much of the railroad route is grass covered. Before starting this hike, you might read Appendix H, which has tips about how to hike an old railroad right-of-way. To prevent scraped legs (from walking through brush), I suggest that you wear long pants, but carry shorts along to change into when the brushy part is over.

The Hike: Before we start, let me give you a little information on the Boca-Loyalton Railroad, whose old route you will be following. The BLRR was founded in 1902. At its peak, the company had 56 miles of tracks throughout the Sierra Valley and up into Mapes Canyon, where it connected with the Clover Valley Lumber Company tracks. Now, 56 miles of tracks may not sound like much of a railroad, but 23 other railroad companies who once operated in Plumas County (most owned by log-

ging companies) were smaller. Only the Sierra Valley Railroad (later known as the Nevada, California, and Oregon Railroad) and the Western Pacific Railroad were bigger. By 1917, lumber trucks had begun to make logging railroads obsolete, thus ending the life of the BLRR.

From your parking place, the 100-yard stretch of road forming the top leg of the aforementioned triangle is the rail grade, so follow it due west for 100 yards to the paved road. Walk directly across the paved road and bear slightly to the left, avoiding a right turn onto an old logging track headed downhill. You soon encounter a large fill where the level route crosses a gully. On your left, the country "opens up" and the forest disappears, giving you a nice view of the treeless upper part of Mapes Canyon (named after George W. Mapes, an early rancher in the area), with Peak 6344 (high, but evidently not prominent enough to get named) behind it. The fill seems to be a ridge, so stay on it—even though this requires tromping on silver sagebrush—rather than dropping down into the less-brushy valley. The railroad grade makes a long sweeping turn right. Soon you pass a stagnant pond (it may be dry late in the summer) on your right, below the fill, and then a small grassy meadow on your left. Evidently a spring feeds the pond, because the track, now in a cut, becomes grassy and a bit boggy.

Junk starts to appear in the trail, and all of a sudden a 1937 or 1938 rusting Chevrolet (or Buick —or Oldsmobile—you decide), full of bullet holes, appears. This signals the fact that you're almost at the second crossing of Forest Road 177. As you reach 177, on your left is a dirt road, on which you will return in an hour or two. Cross the paved road, and head a bit to the left. The correct route isn't particularly visible, but it immediately appears on top of a fill over a small intermittent creek, which runs through a corrugated culvert. Look for this culvert, and make sure you are on top, rather than down at rivulet level.

The route makes a looping right turn and parallels the paved road above it for a few hundred yards before making a looping left turn. A couple of logging tracks intersect your route, but just keep on the level. At this point you'll be slogging through (or on top of) bitterbrush and manzanita and wondering why you thought that hiking a historic route like this was worth a try.

As the trail bends right, you encounter a flat area where the railroad grade is erased by a logger's route. The correct path is easy to find by keeping to the right. You'll note a few 55-gallon steel drums slowly rusting away in the gully to your right. Whether these were left by loggers or railroaders, who knows, but it is sad to see pollution of the landscape out here in the boonies. Conventional tin cans, I've discovered, take a little over 100 years to rust into nothing, but a heavy-duty drum will take a bunch of centuries to disappear.

At this point you find cedar and white fir added to the predominant ponderosa pine cover. A red USFS sign saying "Subdivision Boundary" appears, and the walking gets easier. The route makes a big hairpin turn left, then back right again. Why all these loops and zigzags while Road 177 goes fairly straight? Well, the grade of the paved road is too steep for trains, so the tracks had to wind back and forth, picking up altitude slowly. The loop-de-loops aren't as apparent when you're hiking the route, but they sure look funny on the map. Continue walking through a grassy cut, and then cross an old loggers' track that intersects at 90°. Your route bends right, paralleling the road and close enough to hear the sound of traffic.

A pile of rocks across the track signals the approach of the third crossing of Road 177. A forest road (marked 24N41) also intersects on the right. It's easy to pick up the railroad grade as you cross the paved road, and, in a few hundred yards, you come to the knocked-down remains of an old cabin, followed soon by a USFS benchmark. Here the smooth trail glitters in the noontime sun due to all the flakes of iron pyrites (fool's gold) in it. You pass a sandpit, and walking becomes a pleasure on the hard-packed, sandy, smooth, plantless road. Then you reach a double berm across the road. (If you've done Hike CM-1, you'll recognize these berms and the nice road beyond them, with all the little ponderosas springing up in the plow marks in them.)

After you cross the berms, pay attention to the route as it bends slightly right, then slightly left, then slightly right. About ¼ mile from the double berms, at the finish of this last right bend, a dim jeep trail cuts off left. This crummy road is shown on the Plumas National Forest map but not the topo map. If you're tired, you can turn around here, retrace your steps to the third crossing of Road 177, and then walk the paved road back to your car. However, if you feel like extending this hike into a bigger loop, turn left on the jeep track, which leaves the old railroad grade route. You come immediately to an old barbed wire fence, lying mostly on the ground, so you can step over instead of having to open the once-upon-a-time gate. The route you want is slightly to the left. It heads downhill on a logger's track, which turns into an unused jeep trail that is easy to follow as it descends rapidly. In about ½ mile, the Big Grizzly Creek Valley appears before you. Off to the left you see a dirt road (which you'll soon be on) and hear from ahead the sound of traffic. Upon looking at the map, you find that you're not far from Big Grizzly Creek Road and all the houses along it. A round water tank appears on your left just before you reach an intersection with a much better dirt road (23N53, although there's no sign to tell you so).

Make a left onto this jeep road, which crosses an intermittent stream, makes a sharp right turn, and heads uphill. If the day is hot, this is a good spot to change into shorts for cooler hiking. During the next stretch, take in the view of unnamed Peak 6344 ahead and Big Grizzly Creek Valley to the

right. In a mile, you reach a saddle just below Peak 6344, and your climb is completed just before taking a sharp left turn downhill. The rewarding view from this side overlooks Mapes Canyon and much of the railroad grade route you were on earlier. You cross a cattle guard and descend in a bunch of zigs and zags toward Road 177. Just before reaching 177, look into the gully below you (which is actually a cut in the railroad grade) and you'll spy the bullet-riddled 1930s car you passed earlier. At Road 177 make a right turn, and you will whiz back to your car on the gradually descending paved road.

Camping: None.

Winter Use: Maybe the route could be done on snowshoes, but there are a lot better places to "shoe" than this.

P-4 Charles Valley and Lawton Meadow Trail

Distance: 7 miles out and back

Highest Point: 5,438 feet

Total Elevation Gain: 443 feet

Difficulty: Moderate

Hiking Season: May through October

Directions to the Trailhead: From Graeagle, take Highway 89 north for 1 mile, and turn right onto Highway 70. Drive for 10 miles to Portola, and turn left on West Street toward Lake Davis Recreation Area. At 1 mile, watch on the right for a yellow sign saying "State Game Refuge—All Hunting, Shooting and Possession of Firearms Prohibited—State of California—Department of Fish & Game." Park here at a wide place in the road.

Comments: When I use almost a full roll of 36-exposure film on a hike, I know its scenery quotient is way above average. The moderate difficulty rating of this hike is only because of its distance—the route is smooth and nearly level. Spring or early

summer is best for the Charles Valley, before the meadow loses some of its beauty and the upper section of the creek dries up, although the bright yellow aspen leaves in October are also special. In summer you might share the path with some mooey animals; cow paths crisscross your route in numerous places. Most of the Charles Valley and ranch is private property, so please do not cross over any fence lines other than the two barbed wire gates described in the hike.

The Hike: The first activity of the hike is to remove the wire loop from the top end of the barbed wire gate and hop through the opening. Please be sure to refasten the gate. The trail at this point is an almost never used single-lane dirt road—two side-by-side tracks—making it easy to walk alongside a companion. Exchanging "Wow!" exclamations about the scenery is better done side by side than in single file.

The route immediately swings left and parallels the main road for a few hundred yards before reaching the edge of Charles Valley Meadow. Ahead and across the meadow are a group of ranch buildings that look like they could be part of a western movie set. The trail runs along a fence line separating it from the eastern side of the meadow. This part of the trail is within a small part of Plumas National

Forest. About 1 mile from the trailhead, you come to another barbed wire gate, probably at the point where the path leaves the national forest. Now the route turns easterly, away from the main stretch of meadow through which Charles Valley Creek flows. In ¼ mile, the path reaches the side of an intermittent creek. Keep an eye out for a track that heads left off the road to an easy crossing of the creeklet.

From here a dimmer path heads back to the main meadow. (Yes, you could have cut across this side meadow earlier, but traipsing through a fragile meadow merely to save a few hundred steps is not an ecologically wise move.) The track now runs nearer Charles Valley Creek, as the main meadow becomes narrower, albeit no less beautiful. Watch for a large boulder on your left with an old rusty barrel on top of it, a sight seldom seen in the Sierra (thank goodness). Just past the boulder, turn left off the trail, and carefully cross the creek on some logs laid in the stream for that purpose. The track now heads away from the creek and becomes heavily eroded.

Several hundred yards after passing a huge pile of tree limbs and scraps left by loggers (very unsightly but a nice hotel for small animals), you reach a T intersection with a dirt road. Turn right, and continue northerly toward the upper end of Charles Valley. In ½ mile, you're at a Y intersection with a USFS sign pointing right to Road 23N02Y, which leads to another remote section of Plumas National Forest. Take the left fork, however, and admire the dilapidated split-rail fence that parallels the trail. Shortly, the lower end of Lawton Meadow appears. On your left a marvelous stand of tall, stately aspens lines the edge of the meadow. In the distance, the sharp point of Smith Peak provides a photogenic backdrop to the scene.

Just past an old fence posted with a small yellow survey marker, take the left fork (the right fork is quite dim), and continue north for another ½ mile to where the trail makes a sharp left turn, crossing over Charles Valley Creek, which flows through a culvert. By midsummer, this upper portion of the creek is dry. This is the turnaround place and a nice lunch site, particularly when the small gurgly creek is still flowing. On the way back, it's easy to miss the left turn onto the trail that leads to the log crossing over Charles Valley Creek. (This turn is about 100 yards past a small triangular sign on the left side of the road.) Near the end of the hike, as you come to the lower part of Charles Valley Meadow, enjoy the view across the meadow of distant Beckwourth Peak.

I hate to sound like a nagging parent, but please make sure you securely refasten all the barbed wire gates after passing through.

Camping: None.

Winter Use: West Street out of Portola is plowed in winter, so access to the trailhead is possible. However, places for trailhead parking aren't very wide, and I'm sure they are not plowed in winter.

Aspens in early spring on the Charles Valley Trail

CP-1 Calpine Lookout Trail

Distance: 3 miles out and back

Highest Point: 5,936 feet

Total Elevation Gain: 701 feet

Difficulty: Moderate

Hiking Season: May through October

Directions to the Trailhead: From Graeagle take Highway 89 south for 12.3 miles to a dirt road to the right (1.6 miles past the "Summit 5,441 feet" sign on 89). A sign (facing south) says "Calpine Lookout 1.0" (the 1.0 mile is erroneous; it is actually almost 1.5 miles to the lookout). Park on the opposite side of the highway in a wide flat area or in a turnout .1 mile beyond the trailhead on 89.

Comments: This is one of the few places in the Feather River country where you can reach a great 360° view summit via a short, smooth, gradual uphill hike. Although the trail is a dirt road, there is no traffic because a gate across it near the trailhead is always closed and locked. The lookout tower has an open balcony all the way around for enjoying the views in every direction. The stairs up the tower are about as unscary as tower stairs can be, so even then makes a wide loop up to a shallow saddle, ¼ mile from the summit. To this point, the forest cover has blocked easterly views of Sierra Valley. At the saddle is the first of several marvelous view sites. Soon the lookout tower looms into view directly ahead. You have fine views without climbing the stairs to the top floor of the lookout, but the best views are from its sturdy balcony.

Almost due north, Beckwourth Peak is the nearest large mountain. Circling clockwise around the balcony you see the spread of extensive Sierra Valley, with the tiny town of Loyalton due east at its far edge. To the southwest, the sharp crest of Haskell Peak comes into view. Mount Elwell, flatter-topped Penman Peak, and Smith Peak with its lookout tower round out the prominent mountaintops as you complete the 360° circuit of the balcony. Near the base of the tower, numerous nice boulders make an inviting lunch spot with a commanding view of Sierra Valley. The way back to the trailhead is, naturally, all downhill, making it about the easiest 1½ miles you'll ever encounter.

those subject to vertigo and fear of heights should be able to enjoy Calpine Lookout.

The Hike: The hike is uphill all the way to the summit, but the grade is moderate and the path well cushioned with pine needles. You come to a hefty locked gate in ¼ mile. The route heads south and

Camping: None.

Winter Use: Because the trailhead is on Highway 89, which is open all year, the hike to the lookout is a fun snowshoe. I have even snowshoed to the top in March when the snow cover had melted in places. Fortunately, the bare areas were mostly covered with pine needles and free of rocks, so my snowshoes hardly noticed the lack of snow for short stretches. The route is too steep for most folks' cross-country skiing ability.

Calpine Lookout

CP-2 Lunch Creek and Three Knobs Ski Trail Loop

Distance: 5½-mile loop

Highest Point: 7,416 feet

Total Elevation Gain: 973 feet

Difficulty: Moderate

Hiking Season: June through October

Directions to the Trailhead: Follow the directions for Hike C-4, but, instead of turning left off Highway 49 into Chapman Creek Campground, continue east on 49 until, 5.5 miles from Bassetts, you come to a road on the left with several signs. One says "Begin [Forest Road] 09, Chapman Saddle 5." Another large sign on a tree has a useless map and the words "Lunch Creek Nordic Ski Trailhead." Drive on 09 for about 50 yards, and park to the right just before the road makes an abrupt left turn over Lunch Creek.

Comments: This hike is unique because it follows the route of two cross-country (Nordic) ski trails, both of which are well marked with blue diamonds nailed to trees and blue arrows pointing the direction at sharp turns. For about two-thirds of the way, the blue diamond markers follow seldom used back roads (well, the final 1¾ miles on Forest Road 09 does have a bit of traffic), but the other one-third is trailless. This cross-country part is particularly easy and fun, because all you have to do is walk through the forest following the blue diamonds and arrows.

The Hike: At the trailhead, as Forest Road 09 makes a sharp left turn crossing over Lunch Creek, a sign pointing left along 09 says "Lunch Creek and Three Knobs Ski Trail." Instead, take the road (09-22) heading straight on the east side of Lunch Creek. (The Lunch Creek hiking trail shown on the topo map on the west side of the creek no longer exists.) Logically, this should be called Lunch Creek Ski Trail, because it goes along the east side of Lunch Creek for 1½ miles, but the fact is that the sign with that name points left instead of straight.

Along this first part, Lunch Creek is too far from the trail for you to enjoy the gurgle of the stream as you proceed uphill. Continue on the main jeep road for about 1¼ miles, until you encounter a right turn in the road, with a blue arrow pointing left along a less-well-traveled old road, marked with blue diamonds to follow.

When you come to Lunch Creek, it is so tiny that you can step across without jumping. You might think a watercourse this small would be dry by the end of summer, but when my wife and I took this hike in October the creek was about as big as it is in early summer. Just after the creek crossing, you come to the only place on the loop that is not well marked. Although the old loggers' road continues straight, you need to make a 90° right turn, in spite of the fact that there is no blue arrow. Hooray! You see a telltale blue diamond ahead.

The next ½ mile is one of the trailless portions of the hike, bearing some good news and bad news. The good news is that the route plunges into a beautiful alpine meadow. The bad news is that, even in autumn, the meadow is very boggy, and wet feet are guaranteed if you follow the path up the middle suggested by the blue diamonds. Naturally skiers will be on three feet of snow over the marshy area. On foot, your best bet is to walk along the right edge of the meadow on the dry land in the forest. At the upper end of the meadow a blue arrow directs you to the right, and soon the blue diamonds begin following an old logging road. Not far beyond the

meadow this dim road ends at an intersection with a more prominent dirt road. Orange diamonds indicate that it is a snowmobile route. Turn left, and hike ¼ mile to another road branching off to the left. When you walk a few steps along this branching road, a welcome blue sign tells you that this is the Three Knobs Ski Trail. According to the sign, the orange marked road on which you have been walking is also the Three Knobs Trail, and a third arrow points in another direction with the words "To Lunch Ski Trail." Well, all this makes a person wonder which trail goes where, but the answer isn't important because the left-leading road with its blue diamonds is the route to follow.

In about ¼ mile, the road ends at what I surmise is one of the three knobs—this one consisting of three adjoining prominent rock formations jutting up out of the forest. (Might these three be the three knobs, or are two similar formations nearby? I guess I'll never know, because the maps

Might these three bolders be the three knobs?

don't describe any knobs, and there is no edifying signage.) A blue arrow advises a right turn onto the next trailless section, which begins just to the right of the knob. The blue diamonds lead you through a beautiful forest. My wife and I enjoyed the "game" of seeing who could first spy the next blue diamond.

The diamonds will lead you onto a treeless crest with (perhaps) the second rock knob. The route through this dry meadow is clearly marked, and, at its south end, a blue arrow directs you onto a seldom used dirt road. Another ½ mile brings you to a road intersection at which there is a turn-to-the-left blue arrow. This part of the route provides a good view of pyramid-shaped Haskell Peak (a

monument of stones piled up by hikers is visible on top). Directly ahead, the jagged profile of Sierra Buttes dominates the skyline. In a little more than ¼ mile, the road meets Forest Road 09. Turn left on 09 and hike 1¾ miles back to the trailhead.

Camping: None.

Winter Use: Well, the whole loop is a designated Nordic ski route, but it would take a skier with a heck of a lot better ability than I have to accomplish it. I could manage on snowshoes, but not on skis. Nonetheless I guess it can be done, because the folks who put up those blue arrows and diamonds know more about Nordic skiing than I do.

RP-1 Sugar Loaf and Table Rock Cross-Country

Distance: 7 miles out and back from Trailhead A; 9 miles out and back from Trailhead B; extension up Reconnaissance Peak adds 6 miles

Highest Point: 6,396 feet

Total Elevation Gain: 1,849 feet

Difficulty: Strenuous

Hiking Season: April through October

Directions to the Trailhead: From Graeagle drive north on Highway 89 for 1 mile to Highway 70, turn right, and drive 14.5 miles to Beckwourth. At the Beckwith Tavern (different spelling), turn left on the Beckwourth-Genesee Road (Forest Road 177), and continue on the paved but narrow road for 3.1 miles to a road on the right (24N32) with a sign "Dotta Saddle & Sugar Loaf." The USFS Plumas National Forest map shows this as a well-graded dirt road, which perhaps it was once, but it cannot be classed as that now, by any stretch of the imagination. I wouldn't call it a four-wheel-drive jeep road, but you need to drive it slowly and to have something other than a low-slung car. When you're 1.4 miles from Forest Road 177, an even crummier road branches right (23N72). If you

have a rugged four-wheel-drive vehicle, you can drive a mile farther in on 23N72 to Trailhead A. If not, park here at Trailhead B, and walk the mile on 23N72 to Trailhead A.

Comments: Cross-country hiking means hiking without the benefit of a trail. In most Feather River country cross-country hikes, you have to navigate through forest, bushes, rocks, and whatnot. However, the cross-country part of Hike RP-1 can be accomplished without any threat of losing your way or becoming turned around: The route is nearly devoid of trees, and the way in and out can be easily seen. Of course, no trees means no shade, so don't choose this hike for the hottest day of the year. The views from the top of Sugar Loaf, and, to a lesser extent, Table Rock, are outstanding. If you've never done a trailless hike but would like to give it a try, this is a good one for you.

The Hike: Walk easterly on 23N72 as it winds around without much elevation gain or loss. For much of the next 2 miles on this dirt road you will enjoy views to your right. Nice as they are, they are but a foretaste of those awaiting you from the top of Sugar Loaf. To your left, the dark sheer face of Table Rock makes a good photo, unless the sun is at a wrong angle.

As the track becomes rougher, it loses a bit of altitude, until you reach nearly the level of the ranchland over which you have been looking toward the distant mountains. The road, at this point merely a rough jeep trail, starts uphill toward the saddle you can see between Sugar Loaf and Table Rock (a saddle is a low place between two higher places, a flattish pass, or, in Europe, a col). At the saddle, you now have a choice of which to do first— Sugar Loaf or Table Rock. Sugar Loaf was the more inviting to me, so I climbed it first.

From here you will be trailless, but, no big deal, just start due south up the ridge toward the obvious top of Sugar Loaf. An old barbed wire fence can be seen along part of the route but only about 1 percent of it would keep a cow out; 99 percent is either on the ground or missing completely. The ridgeline you follow steeply uphill is a lava flow that emanated from the volcano Sugar Loaf once was. The easiest route is just to the east of the lava ridge crest. Keep an eye out for interesting lava caves and formations.

After the lava ridge ends, merely make a bee-line for the top. To ease the steepness, do a bunch of zigs and zags—a series of mini-switchbacks. The many flat spots and flat rocks like stair steps help make the steep climb enjoyable, if you go slow and easy. Every now and then, pause to catch your breath and enjoy the views of the peaks to the north, highlighted by formidable Reconnaissance Peak, 7,629 feet high.

Nearer the top, you encounter a few large ponderosa pines, which bring some welcome shade but also create a mini-hazard. They have dropped hundreds of cones that can act like roller skates underfoot and send you on a short unwanted excursion downhill. No problem—just walk where they aren't.

At last the top comes into sight, and there you are, with a magnificent view in every direction. The full extent of Sierra Valley spreads out far below you to the south. This is a great spot for a lunch break, because the summit isn't sheer, and there are plenty of good rocks on which to sit and admire the view without feeling vertigo.

Head down the same way you came up, although you certainly need not find exactly the same route. You can easily see the saddle below, so just aim for that, and zigzag a bit to ease the grade.

Once back at the saddle you can decide if you have enough time (45 minutes) and energy (300 calories) to do the not-too-tough climb (493 feet) up Table Rock. If the answer is yes, start north uphill in almost the same direction you were going while descending Sugar Loaf. The easy way up, however, is around the right side of the promontory, which avoids the supersteep places. Here, too, the top of Table Rock where you are heading is obvious, and getting lost for lack of a trail is unlikely. The hillside is almost devoid of trees, and you can easily see the most expedient route.

Once on top of Table Rock you will mutter to yourself that the table must have a couple of short legs because it's a bit slanted and not absolutely flat. If you hadn't already sampled the much superior views from Sugar Loaf, you would be mighty pleased with the views to the north and west from Table Rock, but, by now, you are probably jaded.

If you're game to extend your hike, from Table Rock, it looks like an easy cross-country trek to the somewhat distant top of Reconnaissance Peak (2 miles as the crow flies). I decided to save it for an-

A balancing rock lava formation below the top of Sugar Loaf looking toward Table Rock

other day. Later, I tried several other approaches cross-country to reach Recon Peak, but, alas, none was suitable. Hence, several weeks later, I wound up using the trailhead on Road 23N72. Instead of walking to the saddle, I walked up the steep ravine to the left of Table Rock until I was level with its summit. If you do the Recon Peak hike as an extension of Hike RP-1, this is where you should join the route up to the peak. Head northeasterly cross-country to the left of Peak 6645 and Peak 6817. After passing these promontories, you traverse an area blackened by forest fire to reach the top of Recon with a little bushwhacking. Return by the same route to your car.

Camping: None.
Winter Use: None.

Deer Lake with Sierra Buttes in the distance (Hike GL-1)

Appendix A

History of Early Feather River Country Railroads, Plus Tips for Hiking a Rail Trail

The prosperity of early-day Plumas County was closely tied to railroads. Wagon roads were slow, got muddy, sometimes became impassable, and did not allow transporting heavy loads so, 100 years ago, trains helped bring goods to and from the Feather River country. Likewise, prior to the use of trucks for hauling logs out of the backwoods, a logger could use *only* ox- or horse-drawn carts or rail. Naturally, rail was faster, easier, and capable of carrying a much larger volume, so most sawmills bought steam locomotives (mostly second- or third-hand for economy's sake) and laid their own track.

Because the sawmill operator had no wish to connect his track to others, the purchaser of a used locomotive did not pay much attention to its gauge. Track widths were laid to match whatever the used engine required. Thus, many different gauges were in use by loggers in the Feather River country. In 1886, the "standard gauge" of 4′8½″ was adopted in the United States. It is used by all domestic railroads today. (The standard gauge width was determined some 2,000 years ago as the distance between the wheels of a "standard" Roman chariot—or so I've read.) But, whatever the gauge was originally, I enjoy walking along an old railroad grade, envisioning an old locomotive huffing and puffing along the path I'm on.

If the rails were still in place, following the route of a long-gone railroad line would be no problem. However, every bit of rail for each of the 25 long-since-defunct railroads operating in Plumas County (most of them short lines owned by lumber companies) has been removed and sold for scrap. An occasional spike can be found, but most of them also became scrap iron. You might expect that, before the use of old railroad ties for garden retaining walls came into vogue, at least the wooden ties would remain, thus making a hike along a railroad grade easy to follow. Not so. In many instances, the ties too have disappeared, and not enough time has elapsed for them to have rotted away completely. Indeed, where the old ties remain, the rotting process has not progressed to the point where a ripped-up rectangular tie is unrecognizable. The old ties that do appear along the railroad bed are scattered around and do not lie in their original, orderly, parallel pattern.

So, finding your way along an old railroad grade may take a bit of detective work. For some reason, manzanita, ponderosa pine, silver sage, and bitterbrush love to grow on the old rights-of-way, thus, in some places, camouflaging the very path on which you need to hike. These century-old routes have little foot traffic (possibly more today, now that a few adventuresome hikers have taken to following some of the rail hikes in this book), so beaten paths are lacking. In a few instances, loggers have driven their heavy machinery across or along the railroad grade, altering its appearance.

The first thing to remember is that the old railroad right-of-way is virtually flat, by design, because steam engines couldn't go up much of an incline. So, if the rail route you're following starts to go up-hill or downhill even slightly, stop and go back a few paces to where you left the level. Look sharp for the level route—it will always be there.

Second, except in places where the ties were taken away or loggers have "done their number," you can, along some routes, spy rotting ties that signal the correct direction. If, all of a sudden, the wood you are stepping over looks like rotting round tree limbs rather than square-cut wooden ties, stop and go back to where you last saw ties, and make sure your chosen route is correct.

A third obvious clue is to follow the map. The maps in this book, I trust, will aid you in finding the route, and, in some instances, the old railroad grades are shown as dashed lines on the topo maps.

Fourth, recognize that, owing to hilly terrain, the railroad builders had to span gullies with dirt fill or a wooden trestle, although all trestles have collapsed and most were washed away long ago. If the railroad designer couldn't go around a hill, he'd cut through it to make a level rail bed. These man-made cuts and fills are obviously not "natural" terrain, so they remain as clues to the right path. Likewise, if the route follows along a soft meadow, as in Hike CM-1, the rail bed would have to be built up slightly, using firmer soil to keep the rails from sinking into soft ground.

Lastly, particularly on fill or raised areas, don't always feel that you need to tromp along the rail route itself, especially if there is heavy growth in the way that cannot easily be stepped over, on, or around. In many instances I will drop down from the crest of the grade itself and walk parallel to it

along its lower edge where walking is easier. I suggest wearing sturdy, long pants and boots rather than sneakers or running shoes, because some tromping through brush on the right-of-way is inevitable.

I hope you try a few of the rail-trail hikes described in this book. The challenge of finding the right route is fun, and, if these tips are followed, you will find pathfinding easy. However, if you are a novice hiker or get easily confused unless the trail is obvious and well worn, then I recommend "passing" on the rail-trail hikes. Or, perhaps you can team up with a companion who is more comfortable and experienced with the pathfinding process.

The nonprofit Rails-to-Trails Conservancy has now converted over 10,000 miles of abandoned railroad rights-of-way to multiuse fitness trails. *Cooking Lite Magazine,* in its May 1998 issue, reported that during the previous year more than 1 million walkers, runners, cyclists, and inline skaters used the rail trails. In many cases, local government agencies and volunteer groups have adopted the more than 1,000 ongoing projects occurring in all 50 states. Perhaps some day we can get Plumas County's old railroad rights-of-way in better shape. (The Conservancy's website is www.railtrails.org, if you'd like to help start a Feather River country project.)

On the PCT above Milton Creek (Hike HV-7)

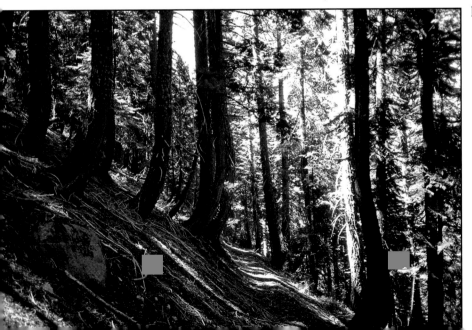

Appendix B

History of Plumas-Eureka Mine and Johnsville

In May 1851, a group of nine miners wandered eastward into country that theretofore had been explored only by its local residents, the Maidu Indians and earlier tribes. The prospectors were seeking more productive mining opportunities than those that were available in the feverish gold-panning activity along Nelson Creek (Hike BN-3). The group set up camp in the shadow of Eureka Peak. On May 21, two men from the party, named Merethew and Peck, climbed to the top of the peak to take observations of the surrounding territory. On their way up, they stumbled across a quartz out-cropping with a spectacular vein of gold (Hike J-7). The group of nine celebrated that they had discov-ered a "bonanza." Indeed they had, because this find was the top of the famous Eureka Chimney, an enor-mous deposit of gold-bearing quartz that became the highly profitable Eureka Mine (later renamed the Plumas-Eureka Mine).

The lucky nine (called the Nine Originals) sent word of their great strike back to Nelson Creek. Their friends rushed to the site, and a company of 36 men was hurriedly organized on June 5, 1851, claiming 30 square feet for each member as well as claiming the water rights from Eureka Lake. (A "company" was merely a group of men who banded together to mine a "find.") Latecomers began pour-ing in, only to find the best ground already claimed. The latter group, being in the majority, without the benefit of a court of law but possessing superior numbers and more weaponry, reduced the claim size of the 36 men to 20 square feet, thus leaving room for the newcomers. The 76 newcomers named their newfound location "Washington," in the "spirit of 1776." The next 40 miners to arrive staked out claims farther south on the peak, naming their mine (appropriately) the Rough and Ready Mine. An-

other 80 men formed the Mammoth Mine to the north of Eureka Mine (Hike J-5).

These four mines were not all immediately successful. The 76 failed within a year because the miners had invested too heavily in equipment and site improvements. They also laid out a town site, which they called the City of 76, but their plans never came to fruition. The Rough and Ready (seemingly too rough and not enough ready) oper-ated sporadically for several years but closed down in 1857, remaining idle for many years thereafter.

Even the richer Eureka and Mammoth Mines struggled because of lack of funds, supplies, and equipment. Unlike their two overspending neigh-bors, the Eureka and Mammoth Mines didn't rush to build expensive stamp mills but, instead, crushed their ore by cheaper arrastras or chile wheels, a pro-cess learned from Mexican and Chilean miners they had worked with. In 1855, harnessing water from Eureka Lake as hydropower, the Eureka Company built an efficient stamp mill 1 mile from its mine. A year later, the Mammoth group erected a 12-stamp mill near Jamison Creek.

Soon after mining started at the four mines, the town of Jamison City, named after a pioneer in the area, sprang up on Jamison Creek. The town quickly earned a reputation as a wild and woolly place where brawls and fistfights became a favorite pastime on Sundays (see Hike J-12).

As the two successful mines continued mak-ing progress, miners spread out to other nearby re-gions, establishing various other mines that you can visit by hikes described in this book. In nearby Mohawk Valley, farms were established to supply food for the miners (Hikes B-6 and J-13). Timbers in the mine tunnels, ties for the ore-car rails, and miles of wooden flumes for bringing water to the

The ridge above Jamison Creek (Hikes GL-13, 14, and 15)

Concurrently with the hardrock mining occurring on Gold Mountain, mining activity flourished along Jamison Creek in the form of gold panning and placer (hydraulic) mining. The washed-away hillsides still seen on Hikes J-12 and J-17 bear witness to the devastation caused more than a century ago by the powerful "water cannons" used in the hydraulic mining operations.

mines for water power—all created a need for sawmills. Indeed, the lumber industry has far outlasted the mining industry in the Feather River country.

By 1856, approximately $250,000 of Eureka Company profits had been paid out to its investors. This was an enormous sum in those days, and many believed that the mine was still in its infancy. However, by 1870, all four of the mines on Gold Mountain (as it was then called, instead of Eureka Peak) had new ownership: the successful Eureka and Mammoth via purchase, and both the unsuccessful 76 and the Rough and Ready by foreclosure.

Profitability of the mines was hampered by having to close, often for seven months, during the long winters, as heavy snow prevented effective mining. In contrast, during dry years the water supply for hydropower for the stamp mills ran short by late summer, thus allowing the mills to operate for only a few high-activity weeks.

Mining techniques still used sledgehammers and hand-held drills to drill holes for blasting powder. The ore cars were loaded by hand by miners who earned $60 per month—a princely sum in those days, yet probably fair compensation for the rigorous and dangerous work.

By 1871, an investor named John Parrott had gained control of the mines, with the exception of a disputed claim to a partial ownership of the Mammoth Mine by one Bill Elwell, for whom Mount Elwell (Hikes GL-15 and GL-16) is named. After much haggling and litigation, Elwell relinquished his claim but pocketed $50,000 (a small fortune in those days) in the process. Upon clearing title to all four properties, Parrott sold out to the Sierra Buttes Company of London, England, for a staggering $1 million. Ironically introducing the new owners to the financial perils of mining on Gold Mountain, one of the two stamp mills at Eureka Lake collapsed, thus severely curtailing production. The well-capitalized new owners responded immediately by building a much more efficient, better located, 40-stamp mill near the mouth of Upper Mammoth Tunnel (the foundations of which can be seen on Hike J-5). This event coincided with the new owner's development of a new town named Eureka Mills on the mountainside (the ghost of which is also visited on Hike J-5). The town expanded quickly and soon included a 200-bed bunkhouse, a school, a church, a hotel, and three saloons.

Numerous homes for miners with families were built in addition to the necessary stables, blacksmith shop, and company offices. All this construction required massive quantities of lumber, resulting in the cutting down of all the trees on Gold Mountain. It is interesting to compare the late 1800s photos of Eureka Mills (posted in the state park museum near Johnsville), showing the denuded hillside, with today's dense forest cover of tall pines and firs. How quickly Mother Nature responds to a change for regrowth—well, maybe a time span of 100 years isn't really that short (although the second growth trees had reached full maturity when I first explored this area 30 years ago).

In 1873, a new headman, William Johns, took over mining operations of the mine complex, whose name by then had been changed to Plumas-Eureka Mine. Under Johns, new machinery and mining techniques were introduced, increasing the profitability of the venture. A steam engine was installed to power the stamp mill during the dry summer period. Even the long-dormant Rough and Ready Mine was profitably reopened, and consolidated Plumas-Eureka profits jumped from a 10 to a 15 percent return for the London investors. This was a huge return for that era, compared with the "satisfactory" 2 to 3 percent return yielded by investors in New England cotton mills.

Eureka Mills flourished and became a sedate town, partly because it was composed mostly of families, unlike the single-man makeup of the rough-and-tumble Jamison City. Games of baseball (invented in 1839 by Abner Doubleday) and the first ski races in America (then called snowshoe races) were held near town. New wagon roads allowed more supplies to reach the area, and a Western Union telegraph line reached Eureka Mills in 1874.

Johns, the headman, was determined to continue his successes, so he built a second, huge, 40-stamp mill for crushing gold ore at the bottom of the hill. Called Mohawk Mill, it stands today in partially restored splendor near the state park museum.

After completion of the Mohawk Mill, Johns decided that development of a new town near the new mill would be his next venture. He originally named the company town Johnstown (after himself, naturally); you can explore it in Hike J-12. It sported two hotels, a school, a church, three "merchandising establishments," and the usual bunch of saloons. Even with this glitzy new community, Jamison City continued to attract the scruffy and raw unmarried miners. The brewery was located in Johnstown, although it had to be rebuilt after being wiped out by a landslide.

However, by 1878, the mine complex, which had been called "the best gold mine on the coast," began to recede in productivity. The richest veins had been mined out, and all work stopped at both the Rough and Ready and the 76. Dividends plummeted to 10 percent in 1884, and, by 1886, were a disappointing 2½ percent. Rather than continue the downslide, the owners of Sierra Buttes Company sold out. By 1897 the mountain had been virtually played out, although unsuccessful sporadic attempts at revitalization occurred well into the 1940s.

On your hikes, make sure to visit the Plumas-Eureka State Park Museum, housed in the old Johnsville boarding house, as well as the restored historic mine buildings near the museum. Likewise, I think you'll enjoy taking Hikes J-7 (Gold Discovery Site Trail), J-5 (Mammoth Mill, Mammoth Mine, and Eureka Ghost Town Trail), J-12 (Jamison Creek Mining Site Overlook and Johnsville Loop), J-10 (Loop around Eureka Lake), and J-17 (Jamison Creek Lower Falls and Swimming Holes Trail).

Appendix C

History of Jamison Mine

Compared to the Plumas-Eureka Mine complex, located on Eureka Peak across Jamison Creek Canyon, Jamison Mine is a relative newcomer. Nonetheless, in its heyday Jamison was one of the most profitable mines in the Sierra.

Although only 2 miles from the fabulous strike at Eureka in 1851, the Jamison site did not reveal gold until the late 1880s. The Jamison Mine Company was formed on January 19, 1887. The mine immediately got off to a rocky start and, for the first two years after incorporation, was involved in litigation to secure land title to 590 acres.

Once title was secured, operations took off, with the drilling of a 400-foot tunnel alongside the main vein. This exploration resulted in great enthusiasm because it disclosed that the vein lay directly in line with the richest gold vein at the highly profitable Plumas-Eureka Mine on the other side of the canyon. In 1890 a vertical shaft was added.

The patient Jamison investors wisely didn't rush into mining immediately and, instead, took time to secure rights to the abundant water of Grass, Jamison, Rock, and Wades Lakes (visited on Hike GL-13), located upstream on Little Jamison Creek. The flume system from the lakes to the mine site provided uninterrupted water power to the Pelton waterwheels, which turned electrical generators. Thus, the newer Jamison Mine was blessed with electricity for powering air compressors used to operate pneumatic drills in the mine. One of the old waterwheels can be seen lying on the bank of Little Jamison Creek: Spot it by looking over the edge of the cliff above the stream near the still-standing boardinghouse at the mine complex.

These expensive pre-mining activities only added to the exuberance of the newspaper reporters who, in November 1890, wrote in *The Plumas National*, "It is to be confidently expected that the best hopes of the company will be realized, and that the mine will soon add its quota of wealth to the circulating medium of the county."

Costly ongoing improvements to the complex were continued and further successful exploration completed, yet by June 1892, no gold ore had been removed. A fifth levy on the stockholders for additional funds was voted by the board of directors of the corporation, but some disgruntled shareholders refused to pony up. The company responded that if these deadbeat renegades failed to pay by mid-July, all their stock would be auctioned off a month later in Quincy. This hard-nosed response by the directors evidently produced results.

Still, the disgruntled shareholders failed to spur the company into productive activities. Almost four years later, in February 1896, the Plumas newspaper reported, "What will be done at the Jamison Mine during the coming summer has not yet been determined, at least no program has been made public. It is hoped, however, that a [stamp] mill will be erected. It seems well settled that there is sufficient good ore in sight to justify its erection." Indeed, the plans for a 10-stamp mill came to fruition and on December 26, 1896, the mill commenced operation (the mill remains are seen on Hike GL-24). By the summer of 1897, the workforce was increased to 40 men, and another 10 stamps were added to the mill.

For those unfamiliar with how a stamp mill works, a heavy steel hammerhead, or "stamp," was raised by cams and levers, using waterpower, and was then dropped on gold ore, fed under when the stamp was raised. The large chunks of ore were crushed into smaller pieces from which the gold could then be removed by various processes.

The now-operating mine became an instant success as a result of all the extensive pre-mining activities. The most modern electrical equipment, made possible by the electricity-generating waterwheel, included hoist, compressor, mill, rock crusher, circular saw, drill press, grindstone, and electric lights. In particular, the use of electric lights in the mine was a huge improvement over earlier gas lights because they were safer, more economical, brighter for better visibility in the tunnels, and even cheaper in terms of fire insurance.

In May 1889, a fire destroyed the hoisting works, causing the mine and mill to shut down until September. It reopened with an expanded crew of 60. A fire-sprinkler system and fire hydrants were added to help prevent further fire-caused shutdowns.

Production continued through 1900, but during the summer of 1901 a scarcity of water caused operations to dwindle. The mine crew was reduced to 35 men. Fortunately, a winter of heavy snowfall followed, and by April 1902 mine employment was back up to 55, a level that lasted through the next four years.

In 1904 disaster struck the mine in two separate cave-ins, killing two miners, both of whom were natives of Italy. Both accidents were judged to be accidental and merely part of the unforeseen events that plague such a dangerous occupation. The fact that both men were of foreign ancestry underscores that a high percentage of the miners had come to the Sierra from other countries. A visit to the Johnsville cemetery (Hike J-12) reveals the names and a wide variety of places of birth called out on the gravestones.

Between 1905 and 1908 the mine remained profitable, in contrast to the other gold mines throughout the West that had by then been mostly mined out. During this period, John Redstreake became mine superintendent. He gained additional local fame as a champion downhill skier, or, as it was then known, snowshoer. His tombstone in the Johnsville cemetery commemorates his many successes in the local ski races.

Jamison Mine's old generator lying in Little Jamison Creek (Hikes GL-13, 14, and 15)

By 1908, water shortages again slowed mine production, although new drifts (horizontal tunnels, one of which can be seen on Hike GL-24) opened fresh ore deposits. Between 1910 and 1916, the lack of sufficient water for power again caused the mine to operate only part of each year. Although water problems continued in ensuing years, a closure in November 1917 resulted because the state required more adequate provisions for depositing tailings from the stamp mill. (It is surprising and pleasing to note that California had some ecological awareness back in 1917!) During the First World War a shortage of workers also reduced operations after the tailings problem had been solved.

Slowly but surely, the good ore of Jamison Mine became mined out, and in 1921 the investors sold out to Plumas-Eureka Annex Company. Various operators leased the mine over the next several years, and another sale occurred in 1925. Although output continued to dwindle, Jamison was still regarded as the highest-producing gold mine in the county, probably because almost all others had closed.

Various new owners came and went until the 1930s, but by 1919 the valuable ore had all been extracted. From 1941 through 1943, however, a rebirth of activity occurred when lessees extracted additional gold from the old tailings, using the new, more-effective amalgamation and concentration method of processing.

That spurt of reprocessing work ended with the permanent closure of the mine. In 1959, the Jamison Mine complex became part of Plumas-Eureka State Park. Many of the buildings at the mine can be visited today, although they all are boarded up. The trailheads for Hikes GL-13, GL-14, and GL-15 are at the site and can be visited by following the "Directions to the Trailhead" for Hike GL-13.

One outstanding feature of Jamison Mine was the large boardinghouse located in the complex. It provided mine workers with accommodations "unequaled in any mining district," reported the editor of the county newspaper. Besides being famous for its fine food and generous servings, the boardinghouse had unique (at least for miners) features, such as electric lights, iron bedsteads, spring mattresses, and hot baths. The boardinghouse escaped disaster in May 1906 when the cook discovered that curtains in the sitting room had caught on fire. He was able to alert workers in the hoist building, which had been rebuilt with a modern fire-alarm system after it had been destroyed by the fire of 1889. The fire whistle summoned miners not only from Jamison Mine but also from Plumas-Eureka Mine on the other side of the canyon. The conflagration was quickly extinguished with only minor damage done.

Besides suggesting that you visit the complex of buildings, I hope you try Hike GL-24 (Upper Jamison Mine Trail), which passes the ruins of the stamp mill, and Hike GL-17 (Mount Washington Runoff Falls Trail). When reading about either of these hikes, please heed the "Caution" paragraph, which warns of the extreme danger posed by the open drift tunnel for Hike GL-24 and the even more dangerous vertical shaft near the turnaround point of Hike GL-17. You will enjoy visiting these historic parts of Jamison Mine, but make sure all kids and any goofing-off teenagers in your party are kept under close control.

Appendix D

History of Jim Beckwourth and His Emigrant Trail

The remarkable Jim Beckwourth was born in Virginia in 1798. His grandfather, Sir Jonathan Beckwith (the change of spelling has several undocumented explanations), inherited his title and baronage from *his* father, Sir Marmaduke, a wealthy Virginia landowner who, in turn, had inherited his title from a long list of relatives who were knights in England. Although titles were supposedly voided by the American Revolution and subsequent independence from England, Sir Jonathan's son, Jim's father, was called Sir Jennings throughout his life. Sir Jennings was married to one Catherine Miskell (who had a large inheritance, including several slaves), but the name of Jim's own mother was never officially recorded. She is referred to as Miss Kill, and sources confirm she was of African-American descent. She probably was a slave, thus technically making Jim himself a slave.

Jim's handsome, swarthy features reflected his African-American heritage. A 29-cent US postage stamp issued in 1994 as part of the Legends of the West commemorative series features a portrait of Beckwourth and honors him as one of the nation's foremost frontiersmen.

Sir Jennings moved his family, which included several sons born to Catherine and several other slave offspring, to Saint Charles, Missouri. In the early 1800s it was not customary for slaves, even the sons of their masters, to be sent to school, but Sir Jennings broke the custom and sent Jim to boarding school in Saint Louis. After about four years of schooling Jim, who at some point was freed from slavery by his father, became an apprentice blacksmith. At 19, Jim became restless, and upon quarreling with the man to whom he was apprenticed, he skipped town. This was his only option,

because, as the story goes, Jim had beat up his employer and "with well-loaded pistol in hand" made further threats, resulting in the constable's being called.

Jim obviously stood in good favor with his father. When the young man returned home and described his troubles with his former boss, Sir Jennings gave him $500, a good horse, and a saddle and bade him Godspeed.

From that point on, Jim's life became one huge adventure. His multitude of professions included trapper, Indian scout, government agent, trader and shopkeeper, rancher, Pony Express mail carrier, trail guide, mule trader, horse thief (reportedly), saloon keeper (supposedly the "best" in Santa Fe), prospector, explorer, gambler ("one of the West's best *monte* dealers"), and even Indian chief. The latter title was as a member of the Crow Nation, with whom he lived for several years.

Many of these exploits earned him considerable amounts—particularly his prowess at gambling—but, as one writer describes it, "Money was an incumbrance to which he would not submit." Occasionally, at a saloon he would spend lavishly and have every man in town drunk, thus depleting his bankroll. This would allow (or require) him to drift on to his next endeavor.

Besides English, Beckwourth was fluent in French, Spanish, and the Crow language. He also spoke and understood several other Indian dialects, thus allowing him to serve as interpreter, guide, and negotiator with many of the tribes in the western United States.

His marital life was affected by his wanderlust. His first wife, Elizabeth, bore him a son and a daughter (who died in infancy), but soon thereafter Jim took up living with a Crow woman named

Sue. Crows and Cheyennes often visited Jim and Sue that first summer, and often as many as 15 or 20 tepees were set up around the Beckwourth cabin.

The feat for which he will be long remembered in the Feather River country began in 1849 when he and two companions wandered through what is now Plumas County, looking for gold. On this trip they discovered a pass over the Sierra that seemed lower than any other. As the book on his life (dictated by Jim and written by another man) relates, "This I at once saw would afford the best wagon-road into the American Valley [now the site of Quincy]." Beckwourth and his companions began laying out a road over this pass in 1850.

One feature of his proposed road was that it would indeed be much lower in elevation than the then commonly used Truckee Emigrant Trail, now known as the Donner Trail (after the ill-fated 1846 Donner party). The Donner party disaster was well known to emigrants, so a less-hazardous route would be welcomed.

Another feature was that its western terminus would be Marysville instead of Sacramento, at that time the end of the Truckee route. Jim cleverly saw the enormous benefit to Marysville and other settlements along the route. As he states in his book, "When I reached Bidwell's Bar and unfolded my project the town was seized with a perfect mania for the opening of the route." Pledges for payment upon completion amounted to $500. From there Jim traveled to Marysville, a thriving town that would derive the biggest benefit from the new route and could even out-prosper rival Sacramento. Jim explained his plan to the mayor, who readily saw that Beckwourth's route would "receive an impetus that would advance Marysville beyond all her sisters on the Pacific shore." Upon completion of the road, the mayor promised, Jim would receive a large payment based on pledges from the town's merchants.

So road building commenced, with a small crew paid by Jim out of his own pocket. He led the first wagon train over his route in 1851, arriving in Marysville on August 31. Alas, the previous night the entire town had burned to the ground. The mayor explained to the crestfallen road builder that no payment could be made, because all the merchants' funds would have to go toward store rebuilding and stock replenishing. A few liberal-minded citizens gathered $200 for him, and that was the extent of his remuneration from Marysville.

In the long run, Jim received adequate benefit for his labors because he profitably operated the only store along the route (near today's town of Beckwourth) between Truckee Meadows (now called Reno) and Bidwell's Bar.

Later, Jim's health began to deteriorate, as a result of his many overindulgences and rough life. He returned to the Crows, who again wished him to be their chief. Illness prevented him from accepting this honor for a second time, and, in late 1866, his condition became acute. His death occurred soon thereafter, and the Crows buried him in an unmarked grave, the site of which is unknown.

Well before his death, his famous Emigrant Trail received smaller and smaller amounts of traffic as the shorter Truckee route became more highly improved, thus, again, recapturing the emigrants' favor.

Today, the route of Beckwourth's trail has been researched thoroughly by use of early maps, emigrant diaries, and surveying of the land. In 1992, President George Bush signed a bill making all the emigrant routes into California part of the National Trails System. Thereafter, the Oregon-California Trails Association completed the research of the route. Trails West, Inc. has placed markers along the route in the form of a series of steel railroad rails placed vertically in the ground; on top of each has been welded a short horizontal piece of rail bearing a commemorative plaque, usually containing a quote from an immigrant's diary about the locale. Part of the trail is obscured by paved highways, and a section of it lies under Lake Davis, which wasn't a lake until Big Grizzly Creek was dammed by California in the 1960s.

Several of the trails in this book follow Beckwourth's famous route: GV-2, GV-3, GV-4, and SG-1. Try 'em—you'll enjoy 'em, now that you know something about Chief Jim.

Appendix E

Sources of Information, Maps, and Medical Care

Information Services

This book can be purchased at most of the following locations. (All area codes are 530 unless otherwise noted.)

● California Department of Fish and Game, 1701 Nimbus Rd., Rancho Cordova 95670, 916/358-2900. (Fish Plant recording: 916/351-0832.)

● California Division of Forestry, 326 E. Main St., Quincy 95971, 283-1792.

● Eastern Plumas Chamber of Commerce, 73921 Highway 70, Portola 96129, 832-5444.

● Plumas County Museum, 500 Jackson St., Quincy 95971, 283-6320.

● Plumas County Visitors Bureau, 91 Church St., Quincy 95971, 800/326-2247.

● Plumas-Eureka State Park, County Road A-14, Johnsville 96103, 836-2380.

● US Forest Service
Plumas National Forest
  • Headquarters, 159 Lawrence
    Quincy 95971, 283-2050.
  • Quincy Ranger Station, 39696 Highway 70
    Quincy 95971, 283-0555.
  • Mohawk Ranger Station, 23 Mohawk Hwy.
    Blairsden 96103, 836-2575.
Tahoe National Forest
  • Headquarters, 631 Coyote St.
    Nevada City 95959, 916/265-4531.
  • Sierraville Ranger Station, 317 Highway 89
    Sierraville 96126, 994-3143.
  • Camptonville Ranger Station, 15924 Hwy. 49
    Camptonville 95922, 288-3231.

Map Sources

● USGS topographical maps:
Plumas County Museum listed above.
USGS, 345 Middlefield Rd., Mail Stop 532, Menlo Park 94025, fax 650/329-5130 (mail and fax orders only).
The Map Shop, 2440 Bancroft Way, Berkeley 94704, 510/843-8080.
REI stores: Berkeley, Concord, Reno, Sacramento, San Carlos, Saratoga.
The Sierra Mountaineer, 1901 Silverado Blvd., Reno 89512, 775/358-4824.

● USFS maps:
Sold at ranger stations listed above.
Sold at REI stores listed above.

Medical Care

● Eastern Plumas Hospital, 500 First Ave., Portola 96122, 832-4320.

● Eastern Plumas Clinic, 7595 Highway 89, Graeagle 96103, 836-1122.

● Plumas District Hospital, 1065 Bucks Lake Rd., Quincy 95971, 283-2121.

● Sierra Valley District Hospital, 700 Third St., Loyalton 96118, 933-1225.

Posted Rules of the Sierra Mine Bunkhouse, Circa 1870

(In the 1870s the lights were gas, not electric, hence the mine owner's concern about a bunkhouse fire.)

1. Every bunk numberd—no changing.
2. Seats at table numbered corresponding to berth.
3. No candlesticks in boarding house—Lights out 9:30.
4. Lamps in buildings under special charge of appointed person who will light and extinguish and no one allowed to meddle.
5. Every employee protect against fire—if fire, sound alarm and work to extinguish the fire.
6. No gambling or betting.
7. No person in dorms except at bedtime.
8. No smoking on-duty or in dorm off-duty.
9. No spirits, wine or intoxicating liquors of any kind.
10. Any intoxicated employee at work or absent for same cause shall be immediately discharged.
11. Every employee pays 50¢/month as Hospital Dues. Free of expense.

A Bit about Me, the Author

I developed a fondness for hiking as a Tenderfoot Boy Scout at Camp Geronimo near Payson, Arizona. Several years later, I earned an Eagle Scout award, which included merit badges in hiking, camping, pathfinding, pioneering, forestry, fishing, rocks and minerals, bird study, first aid, and safety. For many years I enjoyed serving as an assistant scoutmaster, directing the hiking, backpacking, and car-camping activities of a troop.

My first vacation and hiking experience in the Feather River country came in 1965. Smitten by its beauty, my family and I vacationed in Graeagle for many years thereafter. Each visit allowed us to

The author and Daisy, his 1953 Willys (the world's original SUV)

sample the fine trails of the region. In 1992, we built a log house on the outskirts of Graeagle, thus allowing us to spend many more hours walking the wonderful trails of the Feather River country.

I have explored many nooks and crannies of the region, both on and off trail. Often relatives, friends, and neighbors join me on hikes, and I enjoy introducing the joys of the Feather River country to them and other visitors as well. One hiking friend jokingly calls me "the John Muir of the Feather River country," not because I am anything like this great master of the mountains, but because I have walked so extensively throughout the area. Absolutely nobody can compare to the peerless John Muir. Still, even though I cannot match his accomplishments, you and I can both match his enthusiasm for and appreciation of the mountains.

My trail experience includes having hiked much of the High Sierra, the Coast Range of California, and many trails in Austria, France, Italy, Germany, Luxemburg, and Switzerland.

I am a graduate of Stanford University and am now retired from a career in commercial real estate.

Index

DO✓THIS™

☐ Simple Actions
☐ To Eliminate Debt and
☐ Create Wealth

Dennis E. Johnson, C.P.A.

Minor Street Publishing
Denver, Colorado

ISBN-13: 978-0-9791288-0-6
ISBN-10: 0-9791288-0-3

The information included in this book is intended to provide general
guidelines on matters related to personal finances. The impact of tax laws
and financial strategies can vary widely among individuals based on the
facts and circumstances involved. Readers are advised to consult legal,
financial and tax professionals regarding the application of specific strategies to their situation. The authors and publishers disclaim any responsi-
bility for positions taken by taxpayers in their individual cases or for any
misunderstanding on the part of readers.

This book is available at quantity discounts for use as premiums and
in training programs. For additional information, please contact the
National Sales Director, Minor Street Publishing, 1660 S. Albion Street,
Suite 712, Denver, CO 80222-4045. Or send e-mail to:
denjohnsoncpa@aol.com

Visit our web site at www.DOTHIS.org

Cover design and layout by Cherished Solutions, llc

Printed in Canada

DO THIS™ is a Trademark of Minor Street Publishing.

Simple Actions To Eliminate Debt and Create Wealth

Acknowledgements

I have received the support and assistance of many people in bringing this book to fruition. I would like to thank my illustrator, Benjamin Hummel, for his patience in transferring my thoughts to pictures. I would like to thank my editor, Janet Lynne Roots, for her attention to detail and her diligence in meeting deadlines. I would like to thank book designer, Cherish Flieder, for her vision of what this book could be. And most importantly, I would like to thank my wife Donna for her support and patience as I completed this effort.

Life is really simple, but men insist on making it complicated.

Confucius

DO✓THIS™

Simple Actions To Eliminate Debt and Create Wealth

Preface

All of my life I have wondered why some people were wealthy while most others struggled. I was especially intrigued with individuals from modest backgrounds who had achieved comfortable levels of wealth. How were people who were able to acquire comfortable levels of wealth different from people who never seemed to be able to get ahead? How did their actions and attitudes differ? What did these people do that most other people don't do? During my more than 25 years as a practicing C.P.A., I have observed the habits of individuals who always seem to get a little bit ahead of the game each year. I have also observed the habits of individuals who always seem to spend at least one dollar more than they make, no matter how much they make. This book is the result of those observations along with hundreds of hours of research.

Wealth and financial security are not created by accident. They are generally the result of taking the right actions over an extended period of time. J. Paul Getty, who was a billionaire before it became fashionable, said, "we are made or broken by the habits that we form." Our small daily acts do determine our fate. There is a right way and a wrong way of doing most things. There is a smart way and dumb way of doing most things. This is especially true when it comes to how you manage your money. Bad financial moves result in mounting debt and financial difficulties. Smart financial actions can have a profound impact on your finances and your life. Most people recognize that they should be doing a better job of managing their money but are not sure exactly how. *Do This* shows you how. If you take the actions set forth in this book you will reduce your debt, increase your net worth and secure your financial future.

Sow an act ... reap a habit;
Sow a habit ... reap a character;
Sow a character ... reap a destiny.

George Dana Boardman

DO✓THIS™

Simple Actions To Eliminate Debt and Create Wealth

Simple Actions To Eliminate Debt and Create Wealth

DO✔THIS™

Simple Actions To Eliminate Debt and Create Wealth

Compared to what we ought to be, we are only half awake. We are making use of only a small part of our physical and mental resources. Starting the thing broadly, the human individual thus lives far within his (her) limits. He (she) possesses power of various sorts, which he (she) habitually fails to use.

William James

1

Determine What Is Important To You

'Would you tell me, please, which way I ought to go from here?' said Alice.
'That depends a good deal on where you want to get to,' said the Cat.
'I don't much care where,' said Alice.
'Then it doesn't matter which way you go,' said the Cat.

Lewis Carroll,
Alice's Adventures in Wonderland

There is an old saying that if you don't know where you are
going, any road will get you there. It is also true that if you haven't
given much thought to what is really important to you, it is unlikely
that your daily actions will be devoted to your highest priorities.
When we are young we are given direction by our parents. We begin
attending school at age five because that's what we are told to do. In
school there is a pre-planned curriculum. We continue through high
school and college based on a plan that is often laid out or suggested
by others. Most people go through life without giving any thought to
what they want out of life. Tony Robbins, the internationally known
coach and motivational speaker, says that the turning point in his life
was when he made a list of everything that he wanted to accomplish
and experience in life. If you haven't decided what you want in life,
it is very unlikely that you will achieve it. Ralph Waldo Emerson, the
great philosopher, noted, "those who cannot tell what they desire
or expect still sigh and struggle with indefinite thoughts and vast
wishes." In other words, people who haven't decided what they really want kind of wander through life aimlessly.

In deciding what is important, consider the following:

1.   Who are the most important people in my life? The ability to do things for family, friends and loved ones can be one of life's greatest joys.

2.   What were the most enjoyable times in my life? This is an indication of what gives you joy and pleasure.

3.   What places in the world would I like to visit? How many of these places have you visited? Why haven't you visited more? Did the lack of financial resources factor in? That can all change.

4.   Where would I live if I could live anywhere in the world? You can in fact live anywhere in the world that you choose.

5.   When was the last time I had fun? Has it been a long time? Why?

6.   What does my dream home look like? Thinking about this can be a lot of fun.

7.   Have I reached my full potential as a human being? If not, why not?

8.   What is a perfect day for me?

9.   Who do I admire most in history? What is it about that person that you most admire?

Develop a list of everything that you would like to do during your lifetime.
The purpose of this exercise is to get you to think seriously about what is important to you and what gives you joy and pleasure. This list will also be motivational. It is why you get up in the morning to go to work. You can update this list whenever you desire but review the list on a regular basis.

You might use a format like the one set forth below.

Description	✓	Date Achieved

Get Started

"No one ever got lost on a straight road."

Proverb

2

Determine Where You Stand

"A life unexamined is not worth living."

Socrates

It is important for you to determine the current state of your finances so that you know what you need to do to get to where you want to be. The state of your personal finances is reflected, to a great extent, by what you own and what you owe. The things you own are your assets. Your liabilities, or what you owe, represent the other side of the coin. Assets can be broken into two categories, those that increase in value over time and those whose value will decrease over time.

Assets Whose Value Increases Over Time Include:

- Common Stocks
- Money Market Accounts
- Mutual Funds
- Retirement Plans
- U.S. Government Bonds
- Real Estate

Assets Whose Value Decreases Over Time Include:

- Automobiles
- Furniture
- Home Furnishings
- Clothing
- Appliances

Examples of Good Debt Include:

- Home Mortgage
- College or Educational Loans
- Business and Investment Debt

As you can see, the list of items that constitute good debt is a short list.

Bad debt can be defined as debt that is used to acquire things that will decrease in value over time. It is often incurred to purchase items that become worthless before the debt is paid off. This is true with credit card debt, the ultimate form of bad debt. This debt is all too easy to get because it is extremely profitable to credit card companies and merchants while being extremely unprofitable for you the consumer. Like many things that are bad for us, using this kind of debt can be habit forming. These are the kind of habits that can and must be broken if you are serious about securing your financial future and living the kind of life that you deserve.

Examples of Bad Debt Include:

- Credit Card Debt
- Car Loans
- Merchant Charge Accounts
- Rent to Own Contract Debt

Your goal should be to use good debt properly and to reduce and eventually eliminate all bad debt.

John and Jane Smith, a couple in their mid-to-late twenties, decided that they wanted to get a grip on their personal finances. One Sunday afternoon they gathered all of their financial records and listed all of their assets and liabilities.

John and Jane Smith		
Personal Balance Sheet		
Date December 31, 2006		
Appreciating Assets		(Source)
Checking Accounts	$500	Check Book Bal.
Money Market Accounts	1,500	Bank Statement
Mutual Funds	2,000	Account Statement
U.S. Savings Bonds	100	Est. Cash Value
Home	175,000	Est. Value
Other Real Estate	0	
Other Investment	0	
Retirement Account	25,000	Statement Balance

Total appreciating assets	204,100	

Depreciating Assets		
Automobile	4,500	Estimate - FMV*
Automobile	3,500	Estimate - FMV*
Furniture	11,500	Estimate - FMV*
Appliances	5,500	Estimate - FMV*
Other Household Furnishings	1,500	Estimate - FMV*
Clothing	500	Estimate - FMV*

Total Depreciating Assets	27,000	

Total Assets	$231,100	
	========	

*FMV = Fair Market Value

John and Jane Smith		
Personal Balance Sheet (continued)		
Date December 31, 2006		
Liabilities		
Bad Debt		
Credit Card /One	$3,750	Credit Card Statement
Credit Card / Two	2,500	Credit Card Statement
Credit Card / Three	1,750	Credit Card Statement
Auto Loan	3,500	Loan Statement
Department Store Charge Account	750	Credit Card Statement
Other debt	0	

Total Bad Debt	$12,250	

Good Debt		
Home Mortgage	150,000	Mortgage Statement
Student Loan	3,500	Loan Statement

Total Good Debt	153,500	

Total Liabilities (Debt)	$165,750	
	========	
Total Assets	$231,100	
	========	

Their net worth is computed as follows:

John and Jane Smith		
Computation of Net Worth		
Date December 31, 2006		
Total Assets		231,100
Less: Total Liabilities (Debt)		(165,750)
Net Worth		**$65,350**

Evaluating John and Jane Smith's financial position

John and Jane Smith's Balance Sheet

A personal balance sheet should be evaluated in terms of the following: available cash, liquid assets, appreciating assets, retirement assets, "bad" debt, and net worth.

Available Cash. The amount of one's available cash on hand is one of the most obvious indicators of someone's financial condition. The Smith family has $2,000 in checking and savings accounts. According to their monthly cash flow analysis, their monthly cash expenditures total $4,150. It is advisable to have cash in checking and savings accounts equal to one to three months' total family expenditures. Their $1,500 is short of the $4,150 to $12,450 that they should have in their bank accounts.

Liquid Assets. Liquid assets are assets that can be converted to cash in a short period of time, a week or less. Examples of liquid assets include cash in checking, savings and money market accounts. The Smiths have only $3,500 in liquid assets.

Appreciating Assets. Appreciating assets are assets whose value increases over time. Examples of appreciating assets include personal residences, rental properties and common stocks. The Smith's have $204,100 in appreciating assets.

Retirement Assets. Retirement assets are assets, generally investments, that are designated for one's retirement. They include investments in employee retirement plans and individual retirement accounts. The Smiths have only $25,000 in retirement assets.

Bad Debt. The concept of bad debt will be discussed in our chapter on debt, but it consists primarily of credit card and charge account debt. This couple has $12,250 in credit card or bad debt. While this is not as high as the credit card debt for many couples in their age group, it is too high nevertheless.

Net Worth. The Smiths' net worth, the difference between the value of what they own and what they owe, is $65,350. This is much too low for a couple in their age group.

This is the beginning point of the process. On the following pages are sample forms that you may use to compile important financial information. It is a good idea to record this information in a spiral notebook. The date each statement is prepared should always be included to facilitate comparison and measuring of financial progress.

DO THIS™

> **Make a list of everything you own; all of your assets. Your list of assets should be broken down into two categories: assets that will appreciate, or increase in value over time, and assets whose value will decrease over time. You build wealth by acquiring assets that increase in value.**

Name(s):		
Personal Balance Sheet		
Date:		
Appreciating Assets		
Savings Accounts		
Money Market Accounts		
Mutual Funds		
U.S. Savings Bonds		
Home		
Other Real Estate		
Other Investment		
Retirement Account		
Total appreciating assets		

Depreciating Assets		
Automobile		
Automobile		
Furniture		
Appliances		
Other Household Furnishings		
Clothing		
Total Depreciating Assets		
Total Assets		

Make a list of all of your debts, your liabilities. The list of your liabilities should also be broken down into two categories, good debt and bad debt.

Name(s):		
Personal Balance Sheet		
Date:		
Liabilities		
Bad Debt		
Credit Card /One		
Credit Card / Two		
Credit Card / Three		
Auto Loan		
Department Store Charge Account		
Other debt		
Total Bad Debt		

Good Debt		
Home Mortgage		
Student Loan		
Total Good Debt		
Total Liabilities (Debt)		
Total Assets		

Name(s):		
Personal Balance Sheet		
Date:		
Total Assets		
Less: Total Liabilities (Debt)		
Net Worth		

Meeting your financial obligations can be a real juggling act.

Keep your eye on the ball when it comes to your money.

3

Develop A Cash Flow Plan

*"Each person should frame life so that at
some future hour fact and his dreams meet."*

Victor Hugo

The way you manage your money today will determine how wealthy, or poor, you will be tomorrow. If you spend your money wisely today, you can expect to enjoy a future that is free of financial difficulty. If you continue to run up your credit card debt and are unable to find money to save and invest, you are likely to have financial problems for most of your life.

You should prepare a cash flow statement so you have a clear picture of where your money is going. Your cash flow statement identifies where your money comes from and where it goes. It is an important indicator of financial health because it illustrates the extent to which you have adequate income to meet your obligations. It will also help you identify funds for saving and investment.

Your Cash Flow Plan

Your cash flow plan includes sections for your sources of income and your planned monthly expenditures. The expenditures should be broken down into two categories: fixed expenditures and variable expenditures. Fixed expenditures are items that don't change from month to month. They remain constant, at least for the short term. Your mortgage payments are fixed at least until you refinance your loan or there is an increase in your property taxes or homeowner's insurance. Installment loan payments for purchases of autos or major appliances are generally fixed for the term of the loans. We have included utility bills in the fixed category (even though they will vary from month to month) because you generally have little control over this expense and it probably will not vary too much during each season. You should think long and hard before entering into a transaction that will result in another fixed obligation as they tie your hands, financially.

Variable expenditures, on the other hand, may change from month to month based on your behavior. Examples of variable expenditures include credit card payments and amounts spent for clothing, food, and entertainment.

Example: After preparing their personal balance sheet, John and Jane Smith prepare a monthly cash flow analysis.

John and Jane Smith	
Monthly Cash Flow Analysis, 2007	
Income Sources	
John - take home pay	$ 3,000
Jane - take home pay	1,750

Total income sources	$ 4,750

Expenditures	
Fixed:	
Mortgage payment	$ 1,500
Utilities	250
Insurance	150
Auto loan payment	250

Total fixed expenditures	$ 2,150

Variable:	
Credit card payments	$ 400
Food	450
Clothing	300
Medical	150
Entertainment	200
Savings	200
Other	300

Total variable expenditures	2,000

Total budgeted expenditures	$ 4,150

Excess of cash income over budgeted expenditures	$ 600
	========

What do these statements tell us about John and Jane Smith? In many ways they are like most Americans. They have very little in the way of savings (less than one month's living expenses) and no investments. Their cash flow looks very good on paper. It shows a $600 excess of monthly income over budgeted expenses. Despite this, they seldom have anything left at the end of the month. Like many people, they manage to spend all of the money that comes into their possession. Perhaps they should set more aside for investment. They have two children whom they hope will attend college some day, but they have no idea how these educations will be financed. They are putting nothing away for their children's college education. They would like to retire comfortably early enough to enjoy their retirement years, but they have no idea whether social security and employer-sponsored retirement plans will enable them to retire in the fashion they desire. Additionally, if one of them were laid off, the family would probably face a serious financial crisis. These are all good reasons why they should be investing more.

THIS™

> **Develop a cash flow plan for you and your family using the format on the next page.**

Name(s):		
Monthly Cash Flow Plan		
Date:		
Income Sources	**Husband**	**Wife**
Take home pay		
Take home pay		
Investment income		
Other income		
Total income sources		
Expenditures		
Fixed:		
Mortgage or Rent payment		
Utilities		
Auto loan payment		
Auto Insurance		
Auto loan payment		
Other loan payments		
Other		
Total fixed expenditures		

Name(s):		
Monthly Cash Flow Plan (continued)		
Date:		
Variable:		
Groceries		
Heating		
Electricity		
Water		
Phone		
Internet		
Cell Phone		
Trash/Recycle		
Credit card payments		
Credit card payments		
Credit card payments		
Clothing		
Medical		
Entertainment		
Investment		
Savings		
Other		
Total variable expenditures		
Total budgeted expenditures		
Planned receipts over (under) budgeted expenditures		

4

Control Your Bank Account

"A penny saved is a penny earned."

Ben Franklin

You just got a cut-off notice on your utility bill. Your utility company has to have the past due balance of $215.00 in their office within three days or your electricity is going to be cut off. That means you have to put a check in the mail today for them to receive it on time. You pick up your checkbook and have no way of telling how much available money there is in your account. You've had checks bounce before and can't afford to give your utility company another bad check.

Your checkbook is another important cash management tool. You need to maintain an accurate balance in your checkbook to effectively manage your finances. Balancing your checkbook will insure that it reflects the amount of available cash in your checking account. Keeping an accurate balance will also save you time and aggravation. An inaccurate checkbook can result in bounced checks, overdraft charges and embarrassment. Balancing your checkbook will enable you to avoid all of that. Balancing your checkbook is actually a lot easier than you might think. All you have to do is know how to add and subtract. In most instances it is just a matter of subtracting the checks that you have written but that have not cleared your bank from the ending balance on your bank statement.

Example: John Smith has just received his June 30 bank statement, which shows an ending balance of $675.00. John goes through his checkbook and puts a check mark by each check that has cleared the bank. After he completes that process he notices that there are no check marks next to check numbers 1476, 1475 and 1470. These are checks that John has written but that have not cleared the bank by the time the bank statement was issued. They will clear the bank later, probably very soon. They must therefore be subtracted from the bank statement in order to arrive at John's correct checkbook balance. John arrives at his correct checkbook balance by subtracting the total amount of the checks that have not cleared the bank ($185.50) from the ending balance on the bank statement ($675.00) to arrive at his correct checkbook balance of $489.50 as of June 30, the cut off date of his bank statement.

John Smith bank reconciliation:

Balance on bank statement		$ 675.00
Less: Checks written that have not cleared the bank.		
Check No.		
1475	$ 75.00	
1476	10.50	
1470	100.00	
	--------------	(185.50)
Other items: (not included on bank statement)		
Add: Deposit made but not yet on bank statement		0

Correct Checkbook Balance		$ 489.50
		========

D✓THIS

Keep track of how much money you have in your checking account by keeping your account register up-to-date. Record all checks when you write them and other transactions when you make them. And don't forget to subtract any bank fees.

Don't forget to pay attention to your ATM withdrawals and fees as well as debit card purchases and online payments. It is a good idea to enter these transactions in your checkbook just as you list your checks and bank charges.

Choose one day each month to enter amounts being deducted from your account for automatic bill payments.

Balance your checkbook every month. This, along with entering all transactions in your checkbook, is the surest way to avoid bounced checks and overdraft charges.

You can use the form on the back of the bank statement or the blank form that appears below.

Balance on bank statement		$
Less: Checks written that have not cleared the bank.		
Check No.		
	$	
Other items: (not included on bank statement)		
Add: Deposit made but not yet on bank statement		

Correct Checkbook Balance		$
		========

Protect Yourself From Bounced Checks

Having checks bounce is expensive and embarrassing. The best way to prevent bounced checks is to balance your checkbook each month. Mistakes can happen, however, even if you do that. For that reason, you might want to consider some of the services that banks offer that will protect you against bounced checks.

Overdraft Protection. The bank gives you a short-term loan, up to a certain amount, when there are insufficient funds in your account to cover a check that you have written. Checks presented for more than the funds in your account and the amount of your overdraft protection will be returned. While this protection can be very beneficial, you should keep in mind that it is really just a high interest short-term loan. Funds should be deposited in your account as soon as possible to cover both the amount of your overdraft and any bank fees. Keep in mind that some banks may not cover your ATM withdrawals or other electronic transactions that overdraw your account. Check with your bank to be sure of what is covered.

Link Checking Account to a Savings Account. Many banks allow you to link your savings account to your checking account. When this is done, the bank transfers funds from your savings account to your checking account to cover overdrafts. The bank may charge you a transfer fee for this.

Overdraft Line of Credit with the Bank. If you link a line of credit to your checking account, the bank will lend you the funds by using your line of credit to cover overdrafts. You will be charged interest on this loan, and there may be an annual fee associated with the line of credit.

Link Checking Account to a Credit Card. If you link your account to a credit card, the amount of any overdraft becomes a cash advance on your credit card. You will probably be charged a cash-advance fee, and interest charges on the advance will start immediately. The cost of this option depends on the interest rate on your credit card and how long you take to pay the advance back.

Typical Costs Of Dealing With Bank Overdrafts

Options for covering overdrafts	Typical cost
Good account management	$0
Link to savings account	$5 transfer fee
Overdraft line of credit	$15 annual fee + 12% APR
Link to cash advance on credit card	$3 cash-advance fee + 18% APR
Courtesy overdraft-protection plan	$20 to $30
Bounced check	$40 to $75 ($20 to $40 bank fee + $20 to $35 merchant fee)

Reduce Your Banking Costs

Banks pay the important role of enabling you to execute your financial transactions efficiently. They allow you to deposit your paycheck and write checks to pay your bills and conduct other business more economically than you can by any other means. Currency exchanges and check cashing outfits are much more expensive. You can save even more dollars each year by reducing the monthly fees and other banking costs.

Review your bank statement every month
to determine how much you're paying in fees and other charges. Contact your bank and ask them about ways to reduce or eliminate certain charges.

Compare the bank fees your bank charges
you with what other banks in your area are charging. You should do this at least every year or two. You may find a great bargain elsewhere or discover a better deal at your current bank. Concentrate on the accounts and services you actually use when comparison-shopping. Don't be concerned about analyzing every product or fee you see listed.

Look into special deals. Banks often offer customers who have multiple accounts at the bank, maintain a certain balance, have direct deposit of their paychecks, or do a lot of banking electronically, special deals.

Try to limit or avoid "surcharges" (access fees) at the ATM by using your own bank's machines or those owned by institutions that don't charge fees to non-customers. If you do pay a fee, cut down on your number of transactions by making large withdrawals instead of numerous small ones.

If you incur a charge for a late payment
or a bounced check, ask your banker to refund/abate the fee. They will often do this if you're a good customer with a clean record and the offense is your first one. Also check to see if you can get a lower interest rate on a credit card or other loan. It never hurts to ask.

Check to see if you qualify for no-fee or low-fee banking. Banks want as much of your business as they can get. Therefore if you have more than one account at the bank you may qualify for a discount or special offer.

Check into special deals for keeping a certain amount in your account, arranging for direct deposit, or doing a lot of your banking electronically (ATMs, banking at home by computer). If you have money in both checking and savings accounts, ask whether the balances could be combined for the purposes of meeting the bank's minimum balance requirements.

Determine whether you qualify for special offers or savings available to certain groups, such as senior citizens.

Consider buying checks from mail-order companies, especially if you write a lot of checks each month and the cost savings could be significant. Before placing your order, ask your local Better Business Bureau or state consumer protection office whether the company is legitimate.

If you can dream – and not make dreams your master;
If you can think – and not make thoughts your aim;
If you can meet with triumph and disaster – and treat those two imposters just the same...

Rudyard Kipling

5

Set Goals

"A journey of a thousand miles begins with one step."

Lao-Tzu

Michael Jordan is considered by many, including yours truly, to be the greatest basketball player of all time. If you placed a blindfold over Michael Jordan's eyes and walked him around the basketball court a couple of times, it is very unlikely that he would be able to hit a basket. If Michael Jordan can't hit a goal that he can't see, how can you hit a goal you don't have? You can't. Whether it is climbing a mountain or completing college it all starts with a goal. Goal achievement involves three steps:

1. Set goal you are serious about achieving
2. Set date by which goal will be achieved
3. List actions you are going to take to achieve goal

Set Goals

You should only set goals that you are serious about achieving. A goal should be more than a wish or a whim. Every New Year's Eve, Jerry makes a list of resolutions. One year he says he is going to lose weight and get in better shape. Another year he plans to save more money and get his finances in order. Millions of people set New Year's resolutions each year. Few people, however, develop a serious action plan for achieving their New Year's resolutions and most are forgotten before the end of January.

Set Date for Attainment

You should set specific dates by which each goal will be achieved. This will help you avoid procrastination and force you to begin to take the actions required to achieve your goals.

Act

One of the reasons that people don't achieve their goals is that they give little or no thought to what actions are required on their part to achieve the goals they have set. This always requires doing things that you are not doing now and/or doing things in a different way. It does little good to set a goal if you don't identify and commit to taking the actions required to achieve the goal.

Short-Term Goals

Goals can be classified into short-term and long-term goals. Short-term goals are goals that you can achieve in less than a year. You may set some short-term goals that you plan to achieve in three months or less. Setting short-term goals is a good way to get started in this process because it will enable you to experience the joy of achievement. That experience will give you confidence as you go on to achieve more challenging goals. You will find it useful to set goals for various time frames.

One-Month Goals:

- To develop a cash management plan
- To open a mutual fund investment account
- To prepare personal balance sheet and compute personal net worth (see Chapter Two)
- To begin monthly purchase of U.S. Savings Bonds through payroll deductions

Six-Month Goals:

- To accumulate ½ of your monthly living expenses in a savings account
- To decrease credit card debt by 20%
- Identify ways to decrease monthly expenses by 15%

Other Examples of Short-term Goals:

- Begin investing though automatic withdrawals from paycheck or checking account
- Start an adult education class
- Accumulate 1 month's living expenses in savings and investment account

Long-Term Goals

Long-term goal are goals that require a year or longer to achieve. Some long-term goals require five, ten years or more to achieve. The achievement of these goals can be most satisfying and life changing.

One-Year Goals:

- Save down payment for home purchase
- Increase personal net worth by 25%
- Begin educational fund for children
- Decrease credit card debt by 25%

Other Examples of Long-term Goals:

- Purchase new home
- Eliminate all credit card debt
- Purchase sports car for cash
- Accumulate $500,000 in investment assets

DO✓THIS™

> **Develop three short-term goals and three long-term goals. For each goal that you set, set a date for its achievement along with actions that you will take that will enable you to achieve that goal.**

Short-Term Goals	Target Date	Date Achieved
Reduce credit card debt by 30 %	June 30, 2007	
1.		
2.		
3.		

Short-Term Goals	Actions To Take
Reduce credit card debt by 30 %	Pay an extra $100 per week on credit cards
1.	
2.	
3.	

Long-Term Goals	Target Date	Date Achieved
Eliminate credit card debt	June 30, 2008	
1.		
2.		
3.		

Long-Term Goals	Actions To Take
Eliminate credit card debt	Pay an extra $100 per week on credit cards
1.	
2.	
3.	

6

Improve Your Credit Score

"A jug fills drop by drop."

Buddha

Your credit score is the result of your cumulative financial transactions. It tells the world how you conduct your business. It tells them whether you are a reliable and trustworthy person who pays bills on time. It tells them whether you are the kind of person they want to do business with or perhaps employ. Your credit score therefore plays a major role in your ability to navigate in today's society. In many respects, your credit score is society's opinion of how good your word is. When you purchase something on credit, a sweater or a car for example, you agree to make payments by a certain date each month. If you are in the habit of keeping your word regarding such matters and make these payments in a timely manner, you will have a good credit score. You will be able to take credit for the manner in which you conduct your business because banks, mortgage companies and others will want to do business with you. If you don't keep your financial commitments, you will have a poor credit score. Banks, mortgage companies and other businesses will not be very anxious to do business with you and will require you to pay higher interest rates when they do business with you.

Credit Scoring

Most credit bureaus use what are termed "FICO scores," which are computed using software developed by Fair Isaac and Company.

These scores range from 375 to 900. The higher your FICO score, the better. The national average FICO score is 725.

FICO Score	Credit Standing
Below 500	Substandard
501-619	Below Average
620-699	Average
700-719	Good
720-760	Very Good
Over 760	Excellent

Factors That Influence Your FICO Score

Your FICO score is influenced by your:

- Payment history
- Outstanding debt
- Credit history
- Types of credit in use
- Pursuit of new credit

Payment History. Your payment history carries more weight than any of the other factors. Negative factors include:

- Late payments
- Judgments
- Accounts turned over to collection agencies
- Accounts written off by your creditor

Outstanding Debt. The amount of your outstanding debt is second to payment history in influence on your credit score. Negative factors include:

- High balance (compared to credit limit) owed on accounts
- Large number of bank or national revolving accounts

- Large number of credit accounts with balances
- High average outstanding balance

Credit History. Credit history follows in influence on your credit score. Negative factors in this category include:

- Account payment history is too new
- Too few accounts with recent payment information
- No payment history

Types of Credit In Use. The type of credit you have also influences your credit score. Negative factors include:

- Lots of credit cards
- Department store charge accounts
- Installment loans

Pursuit Of New Credit. Recent applications for credit influence your credit score. Negative factors include:

- Several recent applications for credit
- Numerous inquiries (regarding you) to credit bureau from creditors

Pay your bills on time. Forming the habit of paying your bills on time is the most effective thing that you can do to improve your credit score. This is the factor that is given the most weight in credit scoring systems.

Reduce the amount of outstanding debt.
Credit scoring systems compare the amounts you owe on your accounts with the credit limits. Maxing out your credit cards lowers your credit score. Reducing the amount you owe on your credit cards, in comparison to your credit limits, will increase your credit score. For example, if you have an outstanding balance of $4,750 on a credit card that has a $5,000 credit limit, you need to reduce the amount owed on that card as soon as possible.

> **Pay off credit card balances.** Paying off account balances improves your credit score. If you have accounts with small outstanding balances, pay them off as soon as you can.
>
> **Retain credit cards that have low or no balances.** Your credit score is improved when the amount of your available credit increases. Your available credit is the difference between your credit limit and your outstanding balance.

Your Credit Report

William Blake and his wife Shirley submitted an application for a mortgage to purchase the home of their dreams. They had enough income to qualify for the loan so a good credit score was the only thing standing between them and the home of their dreams. They anticipated no problems because they had always paid their bills on time and had no bankruptcies or other negative credit factors.

They were shocked when their credit score came back at 605, much lower than they needed to qualify for the loan at the interest rate they expected. When they reviewed their credit report with the mortgage broker they discovered several errors on the report. There were charge offs and late payments on accounts that did not belong to William and Shirley Blake, at least not this William and Shirley Blake. There was another William and Shirley Blake, from Wisconsin, whose credit information was erroneously included in their report. Now they had to rush to get this matter cleared up in time to meet the deadline contained in their offer to purchase the home.

> **Review your credit report at least twice each year.** It is important to review a copy of your credit report at least three or four months prior to seeking financing for a major purchase like an automobile or a home.

Obtaining A Copy of Your Credit Report

You may obtain a free copy of your credit report if you have been denied credit, insurance, or employment because of information included on your credit report. You should contact the credit agency for a free copy of your report within 60 days of receiving a denial notice. You may also get a free copy of your report if you certify in writing that:

- You are unemployed and plan to look for a job within 60 days,

- You are on welfare, or

- Your report is inaccurate because of fraud.

If you do not meet any of the aforementioned criteria, you can get a copy of your report by contacting the Credit Reporting Agency and paying the fee charged by them.

They can charge up to $8 to supply you with a copy of your report. You can get the addresses and telephone numbers of credit reporting agencies by looking in the yellow pages under "credit" or "credit rating reporting." You might want to contact each credit bureau listed because more than one agency probably has a file on you and some may have different information. While you are waiting to receive a copy of your credit report, gaining an understanding of how the credit reporting system works will be useful.

The three major credit-reporting agencies are:

Equifax
1-800-525-6285, and write: P.O. Box 740241, Atlanta, GA 30374

Experian
1-888-397-3742, and write: P.O. Box 9532, Allen, TX 75013

TransUnion
1-800-680-7289, and write: P.O. Box 6790, Fullerton, CA 92834

DO THIS™

Credit agencies are required to remove inaccurate negative information from your credit report.

Request credit agencies to remove inaccurate negative information from your credit report. This can improve your credit score and reduce your cost of credit. To have incorrect negative entries removed you should write each of the three major credit agencies and point out the errors contained on your credit report.

The following is a sample letter requesting a Credit Reporting Agency to remove inaccurate information from your credit report.

Sample Letter to Credit Reporting Agency

Date

Your name
Your address
Your city, state and zip code

Name of credit reporting agency
Attn: Complaint Department
Address (or P.O. Box)
City, state and zip code

Dear Sir or Madam:

I am writing to dispute the following information in my credit file. The items I dispute also are encircled on the attached copy of the report that I received.

Items Disputed   Why item is incomplete or incorrect

Please reinvestigate these matters and delete or correct the disputed items as soon as possible.

Sincerely,

Accurate Negative Information

Beware that when your credit report contains accurate negative information, sometimes only the passage of time can assure its removal. Accurate negative information generally can stay on your credit report for seven years. Exceptions include:

- Bankruptcy information may be reported for 10 years

- Credit information reported in response to a job application for a job with a salary of more than $75,000 has no time limit

- Information about criminal convictions has no time limit

- Credit information reported because of an application for more than $150,000 worth of credit or life insurance has no time limit

- Information relating to the default of a U.S. government-insured or guaranteed student loan can be reported for seven years after certain guarantor actions

- Information about a lawsuit or an unpaid judgment against you can be reported for seven years or until the statute of limitations runs out, whichever is longer.

DO☑THIS™

Request that credit agencies include an explanation of the circumstances pertaining to any accurate negative information on your credit report.

This might indicate when the obligation has been satisfied and why your circumstances have changed since this occurrence.

Example: Jerry Williams lost his job three years ago when the company that he was working for went out of business. He was out of work for 18 months. During that time he was unable to pay several of his creditors. As a result, he had several "charge-offs" on his credit report. Jerry sent a letter to all three credit bureaus with an explanation of the cause for those charge-offs. The letter also pointed out that Jerry has not had a late payment in over a year. His explanation was attached to Jerry's credit report and was helpful when Jerry applied for a home mortgage.

Control Your Debt

Is credit card debt weighing you down?

7

Control Credit Card Debt

"Money is a good servant, but a poor master."

Dominique Bouhours

Money that you invest is your servant. Money that you owe is your master. The biggest difference between the wealthy and most other people is that the wealthy use money as their servant while most other people are servants for their creditors. If your paycheck is spent before you get it, going to pay credit card bills and other debts, you need to ask yourself who you are working for. When you owe credit card companies, banks and other creditors, you are in fact working to pay those monthly bills. If you intelligently manage your money you will be able to reduce your debt and control your life.

Prepare a credit card control record. This control will assist you with tracking and controlling your credit card debt.

This worksheet should list all of the family's credit cards and should indicate credit limits and current balances. Preparing this worksheet periodically will give you a clear picture of your credit card debt and will assist you in measuring your progress toward reducing and eventually eliminating this kind of debt. Six month intervals is a good time period to track your balances.

Credit Card Control Record

Credit Card Co.	Credit Limit	Interest Rate	Balance at _____	Balance at _____	Balance at _____	Customer Service Number

Beware Tell-Tell Signs/Too Much Credit Card Debt

The following are tell-tell signs that you have more credit card debt than you can handle. If two or more of these signs apply to you, you have too much credit card debt.

1.   You are only able to make minimum payments on your credit cards. This is a very bad situation to be in. This means that you will virtually never get out of debt. If you have $5,000 in credit card debt and are making only the minimum payment each month it will take you 20 years to pay off the debt. During this time you would have paid approximately $ 6,731 in interest. This assumes an interest rate of 18% and a minimum payment of $20.

2.   You have to use your credit cards to purchase groceries or other basic living expenses.

3.   Your credit card debt payments exceed 20% of your monthly take home pay

4.   You have three or more credit cards with significant outstanding balances.

5.   You are at maximum levels on all or most of your credit cards.

6.   You have to borrow from friends or relatives to meet unexpected cash needs because you are unable to access funds through commercial credit channels.

7.   Your credit card debt is increasing.

8.   You borrow money to meet debt obligations. This is often known as borrowing from Peter to pay Paul. It is all you can do to keep your creditors at bay. It is only a matter of time before it all comes apart.

9.   You regularly incur late payment fees.

10.   You dread going to the mailbox to pick up your mail because all you receive are bills.

11.   You don't know exactly how much you owe in credit card debt because you are afraid to sit down and total up all of your credit card debt.

DO✓THIS™

List the number of the items above that apply to you. If two or more apply, you need to act aggressively to reduce your credit card debt.

Reducing Credit Card Debt

Credit cards are the most common form of bad debt and the most dangerous. They are easy to get and easier to use. Do you want to purchase a sweater and pair of shoes but don't have cash? Just flip out your credit card and charge it! "Buy now and pay later" has become a way of life for all too many today. It is, however, one of the worst habits that anyone can form. When you pay later you have to pay more later, a lot of the time much, much more. By continuing to overuse your credit cards, you are digging yourself into a hole that is very difficult to get out of.

Bob Nightingale went to his doctor to find out what was the best way to lose weight. The doctor asked Bob about his eating habits. What kinds of foods do you eat, in what quantities? Bob went on to describe his love of many kinds of foods including sweets and starches. The doctor suggested that he cut out all desserts and reduce portions of all other foods. When he reached his targeted weight he could eat desserts, but only in moderation. This was not what Bob wanted to hear. He wanted some type of magic potion that would take away the weight without any effort or sacrifices on his part. Many people are the same way about their debt situation. They say they want to get out of debt but they are unwilling to make the life style changes required. Controlling your spending is the first step to getting control of your debt and is an important step toward taking control of your finances.

DO THIS™

Take steps to reduce your credit card debt if you have any significant level of credit card debt. The following are actions that you can take that will help you reduce your credit card debt.

It is best for you to pay your entire credit card bill when it comes every month. If you can't do that, pay as much on your credit card bill as you can.

Don't apply for more credit cards than you need.
Don't apply for a card just because you are offered free merchandise or because there is no annual fee.

Carry only one credit card at a time. Carrying a lot of credit cards on your person may increase the temptation to use them.

Go on a credit card diet. Stop using your credit cards for a specific period of time, the longer the better. Put them in the freezer for a while. This may be the best strategy of all. When you buy things on credit you are generally buying things that you don't need with money you don't have.

Pay your bills on time. Late payment fees on credit cards can run as high as $35 or more per month, regardless of your balance or the amount of the payment due. Billy Jones was late with his $25 minimum credit card payment. He was charged a $50 late fee. Late payments can also hurt your credit score, which could result in the credit card company increasing your interest rate, reducing your credit limit and even canceling your card.

Stop using your credit card to purchase expensive impulse items. You should never make an expensive purchase on the spur of the moment.

Identify Expenditures To Reduce or Eliminate

It has been said that most people spend money that they don't have on things they don't need to impress people they don't like. Getting your debt under control requires you to get your spending under control. This is something that people who are determined to get out of their credit card debt have to do. Mary Spendthrift was a compulsive shopper. She went to the shopping mall for the same reason that Sir Edmund Hillary gave for climbing Mt. Everest: " Because it was there." She did not go shopping to purchase a particular article of clothing. She just went there to shop. Her closets were filled with clothing that she had worn only once. What have you purchased over the last six months that you could do without? Identify expenditures that you can reduce or eliminate and don't purchase anything that you can do without until your credit card debt is at an acceptable level.

Identifying Additional Sources of Income

Mary Smith got mad one day. She was tired of going to her mailbox and receiving nothing but credit card bills. She was tired of living from paycheck to paycheck. It had gotten to the point where she felt that she was working for her creditors.

She decided that she was going to do whatever it took to get out of debt and once she got out, she vowed never to get in her present situation again. One morning as she was reading the daily newspaper and drinking a cup of coffee, she noticed an ad for newspaper carriers. The ad indicated that individuals could earn up to $800 per month. That amounted to about $600 after taxes. Immediately Mary's wheels started to turn. She would just have to get up a few hours earlier every morning. Wouldn't it be great if she could apply an additional $600 every month toward her credit card debt? What was the downside? What if some of her friends saw her throwing newspapers? Why should she care? Besides, none of them were up that early anyway. Could she do it? It's worth a shot, she thought. She called the number on the flyer and started her route the next week. Getting up earlier required her to turn in about one hour earlier each evening. She later commented that she had traded watching the local news and late night shows for her credit card debt. It was one of the best trades that she had ever made.

This is not to say that you have to get a job throwing papers, but getting any type of part-time job to assist you in paying off your debts can be one of the best investments of your time that you can make. The important thing is your commitment. If you are truly committed to debt reduction you will find a way as Mary did.

| Use Automatic Transfers To Pay Bills |

Paying your bills through automatic transfers from your checking account is convenient and easy. You may pre-authorize direct withdrawals so that recurring bills, such as insurance premiums, mortgages, and utility bills, are paid automatically. This ensures that these bills will be paid on time, preventing late charges and improving your credit score. If you use this technique, be sure to deduct automatic transfers from your checkbook balance.

| Use Tax Refund to Pay Down Credit Card Debt |

Using all or part of your income tax refund to pay down credit card debt is one of the best uses that you can make of your tax refund. Many people have a difficult time finding money to pay down credit card debt. Using your income tax to pay down credit card debt will reduce your interest charge and result in more of your payment going toward interest.

All great masters are chiefly distin-
guished by the power of adding
a second, a third, and perhaps a
fourth step in a continuous line.
Many a man has taken the first step.
With every additional step you
enhance immensely the value of
your first.

Ralph Waldo Emerson

8

Avoid Easy Credit Sources

"There is no free lunch."

Milton Freedman

Avoid easy credit sources. They are much too expensive. People who make a habit of using these credit sources generally find themselves in a vicious cycle of increasing credit card debt and deteriorating financial health.

Avoid Rent To Own Stores

Individuals with poor credit scores often go to rent to own stores because they can't get credit from anywhere else. These stores represent one of the highest cost forms of credit. Their sales pitch offers you the opportunity to rent appliances for a low monthly charge. The monthly rent can be applied toward the purchase of the product. The problem is that you generally wind up paying two or three times the retail price for a product.

TV Set

Monthly charge per contract	$ 45
Total months to own	x 36
Total amount paid to own	1,620
Retail value	$ 650
Amount paid over retail	$ 970
	=====

Avoid Payday Loans

With a typical payday loan, you might write a personal check for $115 to borrow $100 for two weeks (until payday). You are paying $15 in interest to borrow $100 for two weeks. That computes to an annual percentage rate (APR) in this example of 390 percent! If you don't pay within two weeks, there are additional charges. It's little wonder that payday loans are illegal in some states.

Avoid Instant Tax Refund Loans

Instant tax refund loans are short-term advances against an anticipated income tax refund. According to the Center for Responsible Lending, annual percentage rates (APR) for these loans can range from 40% to over 700%.

Bill Jones receives his W-2 form from his employer in late January. Expecting a refund, he puts his W-2 form in a drawer and forgets about it. Two months later he goes to see his accountant. He learns that he has a $2,000 refund coming. He is advised that he will get his refund in approximately two weeks if he e-files his income tax return and elects to have the refund deposited directly into his bank account or two days if he elects to get an instant refund. The fee for getting an instant refund is $350. He would like to have his money right away. He reasons that for $350 he is getting $2,000 (immediately). Bill is actually paying $350 to get $2,000 two weeks earlier. He is paying $350 for the use of $2,000 for two weeks. That computes to an astronomical rate of interest. Conducting his business that way, it is little wonder that Bill can never seem to get ahead.

9

Act To Avoid Identity Theft

"Regard your good name as the richest jewel you can possibly possess."

Socrates

Identity theft is the crime of the 21st century. It is a crime that you have an excellent chance of being a victim of if you don't take certain precautions.

Identity Thieves:

- Call your credit card company and change the billing address on your account. The thief then runs up charges on your account. It may be months before you realize there's a problem, because the bills are being sent to a different address.

- Open new credit card accounts in your name. When they use the credit cards and don't pay the bills, the delinquent accounts are reported on your credit report.

- Establish phone or wireless service in your name.

- Open bank accounts in your name and write bad checks on the account.

- Counterfeit checks or credit or debit cards, or authorize electronic transfers in your name, and drain your bank account.

Identity thieves cannot commit these crimes without your help. They need you to allow them to access your personal identification information (social security numbers, account numbers, etc.).

Mary Jones gets a call from her first cousin. Beth Smith was Mary's favorite cousin but they haven't communicated much in the last ten years. Mary had heard that Beth had been through some difficult times in the last few years. She had recently been divorced and had been reportedly convicted on bad check and shoplifting charges. Mary did not know much detail about those things but she was happy to hear from Mary when she called.

Beth: "I'm going to be in your neck of the woods for a few days next week."

Mary: "I insist on you staying here with us. John (Mary's husband) is working a lot of hours these days and Billy (Mary's son) will be away on a field trip with his class, so we will have the house pretty much to ourselves."

Beth: "That would be wonderful, that would give us a chance to catch up."

Beth comes to visit and she and Mary have a wonderful time. They talk about everything from old boy friends to their most difficult teachers in high school. One morning Beth asks to borrow Mary's car to go into town. Mary has some things to do around the house so it is no problem. While Beth is away Mary notices that her purse is not in the place where she thought she left it. She doesn't need it right then and so goes back to doing her housework. Beth comes back in the afternoon and Mary finds her purse. She never gives this incident a second thought until two months later.

She calls her credit card company because she hasn't received her bill in two months. When the company requests that she confirm her address they notice that a change of address has been filed on the account. Further investigation reveals that a cash advance of $10,000 (the maximum) has been drawn against the account. In addition, another $15,000 has been charged. It didn't take her long to put two and two together and realize that Beth was the culprit. Mary is beside herself. How could Beth do such a thing to her? What would she tell her husband (who was never a big fan of Beth's)?

Mary, in a panic, calls almost every relative in the family until she tracks Beth down. Much to Mary's amazement, Beth doesn't see this as much of a big deal. She needed the money and Mary had good credit.

Beth: *"You and your husband live in that big house. You are doing all right."*

Mary: *"What has that got to do with you stealing $25,000 from me?"*

Beth: *"It's not really stealing, I'll pay you back when I can. Just consider it a loan."*

Mary: *"And just how are you ever going to be able to pay me back $25,000?"*

Beth; *"Just you wait and see. My ship will come in someday."*

If her ship did come in, Mary would have loved to have thrown her overboard. Mary has to hang up at this point. She is so angry that she can't see straight. Beth seems unwilling to accept the fact that what she did was wrong, very wrong. Now Mary faces a very difficult decision. Should she file formal charges against Beth? She may have to for the credit card company to make good on her losses. If she does that, Beth could face up to five years in prison. As angry as she is, Mary does not want to see Beth go to prison. And yet, she cannot afford to kiss off $25,000.

What should Mary do?
What would you do?

This is not an easy situation to be in. Mary may have to file charges against her cousin. Beth made her own bed. Maybe it's time for her to sleep in it.

DO THIS™

Take these actions to avoid identity theft.

Make sure that documents that contain your social security number or account numbers are secure whether you are at home or work. Do not leave your wallet or purse unattended, especially when strangers or visitors are present.

Guard your social security number. Do not carry it in your wallet and do not give it to anyone unless you are sure adequate safeguards are place.

Carry a minimal number of credit cards on your person. Keep department store charge cards in a secure place at home and pull them out only on days when you plan to use them. Do not carry PIN numbers with your credit cards.

File or destroy receipts from restaurants, stores, gasoline pumps or ATMs.

Buy a shredder and shred documents that contain your social security number and account numbers before putting them in the trash.

Avoid pre-printing your Social Security number or driver's license number on your checks.

Use strong passwords for your ATM, credit and debit cards. Strong passwords containing a combination of numbers, letters and symbols are especially good.

Sign new credit and debit cards as soon as you receive them.

Destroy expired and unneeded credit, debit and ATM cards so that typed numbers and magnetic strip cannot be read.

Delete personal information from your personal computer before discarding or giving it away.

Beware of people looking over your shoulder when typing in your PIN number at the cash register or ATM.

Act Quickly If You Are A Victim Of Identity Theft

If you discover that you have been victimized by identity theft, it is important that you act quickly to minimize the damage. Every hour that you delay reporting the theft is another hour the thief has to do damage to your credit. While resolving credit problems resulting from identity theft can be time-consuming and frustrating, the good news is that there are procedures under federal laws for correcting credit report and billing errors, and stopping debt collectors from contacting you about debts you don't owe.

Correct Your Credit Report

The Fair Credit Reporting Act (FCRA) establishes procedures for correcting mistakes on your credit record and requires that your record be made available only for certain legitimate business needs. Under the FCRA, both the credit bureau and the organization that provided the information to the credit bureau (the "information provider"), such as a bank or credit card company, are responsible for correcting inaccurate or incomplete information in your report. To protect your rights under the law, contact both the credit bureau and the information provider.

What To Do If You Are Victimized

1.   Call and then write letters to all banks and credit card companies to report lost or stolen credit, debit or ATM cards. Be sure to get names and titles of everyone that you talk to.

2.   Review your monthly credit card and bank statements and report any unauthorized transactions immediately. You should write to the creditor at the address given for "billing inquiries" to report the unauthorized transactions. Tell the creditor or other information provider in writing that you dispute an item. Again, include copies (NOT originals) of documents that support your position. Many information providers specify an address for disputes. If the information provider then reports the item to any credit bureau, it must include a notice of your dispute. In addition, if you are correct—that is, if the disputed information is not accurate—the information provider may not use it again. Be sure to include your name, address, account number and a description of the unauthorized transaction or billing error.

3.   Contact at least one of the three nationwide credit bureaus to place a fraud alert in your credit file. When you contact one of the three national credit bureaus they are required by law to contact the other two. Tell them what information you believe is inaccurate. Include copies (NOT originals) of documents that support your position. In addition to providing your complete name and address, your letter should clearly identify each item in your report that you dispute, give the facts, explain why you dispute the information, and request deletion or correction. You may want to enclose a copy of your report with circles around the items in question. Your letter may look something like the Sample

Dispute Letter in the appendix. Send your letter by certified mail, and request a return receipt so you can document what the credit bureau received and when. Keep copies of your dispute letter and enclosures.

Credit bureaus must investigate the items in question, usually within 30 days, unless they consider your dispute frivolous. They   also must forward all relevant data you provide about the dispute to the information provider. After the information provider receives notice of a dispute from the credit bureau, it must investigate, review all relevant information provided by the credit bureau, and report the results to the credit bureau. If the information provider finds the disputed information to be inaccurate, it must notify any nationwide credit bureau that it reports to, so that the credit bureaus can correct this information in your file.

Disputed information that cannot be verified must be deleted from your file. If your report contains erroneous information, the credit bureau must correct it. If an item is incomplete, the credit bureau must complete it. For example, if your file shows that you have been late making payments, but fails to show that you are no longer delinquent, the credit bureau must show that you're current. If your file shows an account that belongs to someone else, the credit bureau must delete it.

When the investigation is complete, the credit bureau must give you the written results and a free copy of your report if the dispute results in a change. If an item is changed or removed, the credit bureau cannot put the disputed information back in your file unless the information provider verifies its accuracy and completeness, and the credit bureau gives you a written notice that includes the name, address, and phone number of the information provider.

If you request it, the credit bureau must send notices of corrections to anyone who received your report in the past six months. Job applicants can have a corrected copy of their report sent to anyone who received a copy during the past two years for employment purposes. If an investigation does not resolve your dispute, ask the credit bureau to include your statement of the dispute in your file and in future reports.

4. File a police report with your local police department. Be sure to obtain a copy of the report and store it in a safe place with the names and telephone numbers of all the police officers that you spoke with.

5. Report the incidents to the Federal Trade Commission (FTC). The FTC keeps track of these crimes and shares the information with law enforcement throughout the country. The FTC can also assist you in restoring your identity. See their web-site at www.consumer.gov/idtheft.

6. Obtain a free copy of your credit report from each of the three major credit bureaus (Equifax, Experian and Transunion) to determine if there are erroneous entries on your credit report.

10

Buy A Home

**"Home is an invention
on which no one has yet improved."**

Ann Douglas

For most Americans, home ownership is the first step in the
wealth-building process. Your home is your most important asset. It is
the place where you raise your family and where you come to relax
after a hard day of work. It also represents the foundation of your
financial base, providing immediate and long-term financial benefits.
If you do not currently live in a home that you are purchasing, you
should begin taking the necessary steps to enable you to purchase
a home when the time is right. If you live in a home that you are
purchasing, you should begin taking steps to pay off the mortgage
as soon as possible. Paying off your home mortgage will give you
security and peace of mind. You do not have to wait until you reach
retirement age to experience that.

Time To Buy?

The following factors are key indicators of whether or not
the time is right for you to purchase a home.

You should have a steady source of income (a job). You
should have been employed on a regular basis for the last two to

three years. According to the FHA, monthly mortgage payments should be no more than 29% of gross income, while the mortgage payment, combined with non-housing expenses, should total no more than 41% of income. With a conventional loan, this qualifying ratio allows only 28% toward housing and 36% towards housing and other debt.

Example:

Your annual income is $60,000.
Your gross monthly income is $5,000.

$5,000 x 28% = $1,400.

So you would probably qualify for a conventional home loan that requires monthly payments of $1,400.

- You expect to live in the same area for a minimum of three years.

- You and your spouse, if you are married, should have a credit score of at least 650.

- You need to have saved enough money for a down payment. The amount of cash that you will need for a down payment and closing costs will depend on the purchase price of the home you are buying and the type of financing that you obtain. If you are planning on getting FHA financing, you must have a down payment of at least 3% of the purchase price. On average, closing costs run approximately 2% to 3% of the purchase price of the house. Therefore, if you purchase a home with a price of $200,000, you will need $6,000 for the down payment and $4,000 to $6,000 for the closing costs. Most affordable loan programs offered by private lenders require a 3% - 5% down payment, with a minimum of 3% coming directly from the borrower's own funds. Under those loan programs you would need $6,000 to $10,000 on the purchase of a home with a purchase price of $200,000.

- Your other debt payments such as car payments, loan payments and credit card obligations should not be significant enough to make it difficult to make your mortgage payments. You should start paying down your consumer debt, particularly credit card debt when you first begin thinking about purchasing a home.

After you have determined that the time is right to buy a home, you are ready to begin your search.

Determine Your Priorities

Do you want to be near a certain school or your job? Do you need access to public transportation? How many bedrooms do you need? What kinds of amenities are you looking for? You should establish a set of things that a house must have for you to consider it. You should communicate these things to your realtor and be sure your realtor is clear about everything you're looking for. This will save you from spending time looking at houses that do not meet your requirements.

Prepare a checklist to take with you when viewing homes. This checklist should include your priorities and the following items:

- Is there enough room for both the present and the future?
- Are there enough bedrooms and bathrooms?
- Is the house structurally sound?
- Do the mechanical systems and appliances work?
- Is the yard big enough?
- Do you like the floor plan?
- Will your furniture fit in the space? Is there enough storage space? (Bring a tape measure to better answer these questions.)
- Does anything need to be repaired or replaced? Will the seller repair or replace the items?
- Imagine the house in good weather and bad, and in each season. Will you and your family be happy with it year-round?

Take your time and think carefully about each house you see. Ask your real estate agent to point out the pros and cons of each home from a professional standpoint.

Prepare A List of Questions To Ask The Present Homeowner. Many of your questions should focus on potential problems and maintenance issues.
Does anything need to be replaced? What things require ongoing maintenance (e.g., paint, roof, HVAC, appliances, carpet)? Also ask about the house and neighborhood, focusing on quality of life issues. Be sure the seller's or real estate agent's answers are clear and complete. Ask questions until you understand all of the information they've given. Making a list of questions ahead of time will help you organize your thoughts and arrange all of the information you receive.

DO THIS™

Visit Many Houses. There isn't a set number of houses you should see before you decide. Visit as many as it takes to find the one you want.
On average, homebuyers see 15 houses before choosing one. If possible, take photographs of each house: the outside, the major rooms, the yard, and extra features that you like or ones you see as potential problems. And don't hesitate to return for a second look.

Loan Application

Your real estate agent is probably the best source for recommendations on potential lenders. You should also ask family, friends and business professionals. There are advantages to working with a lender that has the authority to approve and process your loan locally because it will be easier for you to monitor the status of your application and get answers to your questions.

You'll need the following information for your loan application:

- W-2 forms for the past two years
- Pay stubs for the past two to three months
- Information on long-term debts
- Recent bank statements
- Tax returns for the past two years
- Proof of any other income
- Address and description of the property you wish to buy
- Sales contract

During the application process, the lender will order a credit report and a professional appraisal of the property you want to purchase. The application process typically takes from one to six weeks. It is important that you remember the following during the lending process of obtaining a mortgage:

- Be sure to read and understand everything before you sign
- Refuse to sign any blank documents
- Do not buy property for someone else
- Do not overstate your income
- Do not overstate how long you have been employed
- Do not overstate your assets
- Accurately report your debts
- Do not change your income tax returns for any reason
- Tell the whole truth about gifts
- Do not list fake co-borrowers on your loan application
- Be truthful about your credit problems, past and present
- Be honest about your intention to occupy the house
- Do not provide false supporting documents

Source of Down Payment and Closing Costs: Besides your own funds, you may use cash gifts or money from a private savings club. If you can do certain repairs and improvements yourself, your labor may be used as part of a down payment (called "sweat equity"). If you are doing a lease purchase, paying extra rent to the seller may also be considered the same as accumulating cash.

Protect Your Home Equity

Homeowners are confronted with various schemes and scams designed to rob them of the precious equity they have in their homes. The following are some that you should be aware of and avoid.

Bait-and-switch schemes: A mortgage broker or lender promises one type of loan or interest rate but, without good reason, gives you a different one. You may be charged a higher (and unaffordable) interest rate that doesn't kick in until months after you have begun to pay on your loan.

Equity stripping: The broker or lender encourages you to borrow heavily from the equity in your home (the amount you own free and clear of your mortgage) as an easy way to get additional money, consolidate debt, or fund home repairs. The fees and payments are so high that you are not able to make the mortgage payments. In the worst case, the lender forecloses on the loan, and takes possession of your home.

Loan flipping: The broker or lender encourages you to get additional cash by refinancing your mortgage again and again. This tactic significantly increases your debt because fees (often exorbitant) are tacked on to each loan transaction, and you may pay a higher interest rate than with your original loan. You become saddled with higher payments and higher debt.

Home improvement scams: A contractor talks you into costly or unnecessary repairs and steers you to a high-cost mortgage lender to finance the job. Under this arrangement, the loan proceeds are to be sent directly to the contractor. All too often, the contractor performs shoddy or incomplete work, and the homeowner is stuck paying off a long-term loan that puts the house at risk.

Mortgage servicing scams: After getting the loan, you're told you owe additional money for bogus taxes, insurance, legal fees, or late fees. Or, if you try to pay off the loan, the lender provides inaccurate information that causes you to pay too much or discourages you from refinancing with another lender.

Tips For Financing or Refinancing Your Mortgage

Be sure and find a reputable mortgage broker if you decide to refinance your home mortgage. Compare data from several lenders or brokers. You should compare more than just the amount of the monthly payment and the interest rate. Obtain a list of each lender's current mortgage interest rates and determine whether the rates you are being quoted are the lowest for that day or week.

Determine annual percentage rate (APR) for any loan being offered you. The APR takes into account all costs of the loan, including interest rate, broker fees and certain other credit charges.

Determine if the loan is a fixed or adjustable rate. Interest rate on adjustable rate mortgages can go up causing your monthly payment to increase.

Determine maximum increases allowable (annually and during the period of the loan) for any adjustable rate mortgages.

Be mindful of points you are being charged.

Points are fees charged by the lender and/or broker for processing the loan. Points are often tied to the interest rate. You can often get a lower interest rate by paying additional points. That may be beneficial when you plan on owning the home for a long period of time.

Determine what other fees you are being charged.

A home loan often involves many fees, such as underwriting fees, broker fees, and transaction, settlement, and closing costs. Every lender or broker should be able to give you an estimate of fees. Many of these fees are negotiable. Some fees are paid when you apply for a loan (such as application and appraisal fees), and others are paid at closing. In some cases, you can borrow the money needed to pay these fees, but doing so will increase your loan amount and total costs. "No cost" loans are sometimes available, but they usually involve higher interest rates.

DO THIS™

Take Household Inventory

Take an inventory of what you have in your home. An inventory of the contents of your home is one of those things that may appear unimportant until you need it and don't have one. This is useful and valuable for a number of reasons. The most obvious need arises when you have a burglary and must complete a report for the insurance company. It also tells you what you have in your home. This may help avoid the purchase of unnecessary items. A sample household inventory worksheet follows. If you don't know the exact date you acquired something or exact amount you paid for an item, use your best estimate.

Sample Household Inventory Worksheet				
Date Acquired	Description Number	Number	Cost Each	Location

Get Smart And Stay Smart

Find one hour every week to study and plan. There are few better uses of your time.

11

Learn Investing ABCs

"Today knowledge has power;
It controls access to opportunity and advancement."

Peter Drucker

One can go so far as to say that in the 21st century, you cannot consider yourself to be a truly educated person, regardless of your schooling or degrees, if you do not have a certain level of financial literacy. If you are financially illiterate, you put the financial well-being of yourself and your family in the hands of others. Brokers, salesmen, etc., are primarily interested in their financial well-being, not yours. While professionals have their roles, it is important that you be in charge. In order to be in charge you must know what is happening. That requires having an understanding of basic investment principles.

Basic Investment Principles

Risk vs. Reward

John Bigtimer worked as an electrician. While he made a decent salary, he was by no means rich. He had managed to accumulate $16,000 in a savings account over ten years. John was the kind of person who always dreamed of making a killing. He played the lottery regularly though he had never won more than a few dollars.

He was easy prey when he received a telephone call from a sales-man marketing an interest in an oil-drilling program. The minimum investment was $15,000. John had a chance to turn his $15,000 into $150,000 if enough of the wells came in. John was full of excitement as he withdrew $15,000 from the bank and sent it, in certified funds, to the broker. He could hardly wait for the drilling to start.

The drilling started about six months later as did the bad news. The results of the drilling produced one dry hole (no oil) after another. John's $15,000 investment was now worthless. John was in shock. He had reasoned that even if the drilling did not result in the value of his investment growing to $150,000 it would at least be worth $40,000 or $50,000. He never imagined that his $15,000 would turn to zero in what seemed like overnight. He contributed his loss to bad luck and didn't understand why this was the wrong investment for him.

John did not understand the risk/reward relationship. The risk/reward relationship is probably the most important investment principle. It will not only tell you whether a particular investment is suitable for you but will help you identify scam investments. This principle states that the higher the potential reward of any invest-ment, the greater the probability that you will lose part or all of your investment. There are no exceptions to this rule. John was not aware of this principle. If John had been aware of this principle, he would have known that there was a high degree of risk that he would lose part or all of his investment. He would have also known that this was not the type of investment that he should be investing over 90% of his life savings in.

Another good example of this concept is a lottery ticket. When you go to the corner store to purchase a lottery ticket, your potential reward or return can run into the millions of dollars. On the other hand, your risk of losing your entire investment is astro-nomical to the point that it is almost a certainty. When the risk and potential reward is this high you are not investing, you are gambling.

Example: Bill goes to the convenience store on his block and purchases a power ball lottery ticket for $1. The power ball jackpot that week is $175 million. If Bill's ticket contains the winning number the return on his $1 purchase would be astronomical. His chances of winning, however, are about 1 in 200 million. Bill did not win the power ball drawing. Well, maybe next time.

On the other end of the spectrum are conservative investments with little or no risk and very low return. Conservative investments include treasury bills and savings accounts, which are federally insured. They offer little or no risk and pay modest interest rates. There are many other types of investments that fall inbetween these two extremes. These investments enable you to build wealth slowly but surely.

DO✓THIS

Build a portfolio that consists of investments with varying degrees of risk. The majority of your investments should have moderate risks and offer moderate returns. High-risk investments that offer the possibility of great profits should represent a small portion of your portfolio.

A good allocation of your investments might look something like this:

High-risk investments (high-flying stocks, new issues, etc.)	10%
Investments with moderate risks and returns (diversified mutual funds)	50
Real Estate (excluding your personal residence)	30
Money Market funds	10

Total	100%
	=======

Liquidity

Liquidity represents the time it takes to convert an investment into cash. Investments that are instantly convertible to cash are considered to be very liquid. These include savings accounts, stock or bonds that are traded on a major stock exchange, and funds invested in money market accounts. Assets that have little liquidity include real estate, stocks of closely held corporations, and collectibles. These are assets that take an extended period of time to convert to cash. Smart investment planning requires a certain dollar amount of your assets to be in liquid assets. In allocating resources to various asset categories, liquidity should be a major consideration. This factor is important because not only does it determine the ease with which you can get your money back when needed, it also indicates how fast you can get money out of an investment once its value starts to head in the wrong direction.

You should keep part of your assets in liquid investments. There are few things worst than not have cash when you really need it. You should cash or liquid investments equal to two or three months living expenses.

Types of Investments

Debt vs. Equity

Investments can generally be classified in one of two broad categories: debt investments or equity investments. An understanding of these two categories of investment is important for determining the extent to which each is to be included in your portfolio. Your investment objective, the make-up of your portfolio and other factors will determine whether debt or equity investments are best suited for you.

Debt investments, generally in the form of bonds, represent obligations or debt of the issuer. The issuer is obligated to pay the owner of the bond the stated rate of interest. When corporations or governmental entities (local, state, or federal) want to borrow money from the investing community, they issue bonds. When you purchase a bond you are in effect a creditor of the issuer. The issuer owes you money. The bonds have a specific maturity date and pay interest at a specified rate of interest. The amount of interest to be paid is determined by multiplying the face amount of the bond by the stated rate of interest. A $10,000, 6% bond will yield annual interest of $600 ($10,000 / .06).

Example: XYZ Corporation needs to raise money for plant expansion. They decide to issue or sell $10 million in corporate bonds through a major brokerage firm. The terms of the bonds call for investors to be paid an interest rate of 7% per year on the entire amount of principal, with any unpaid interest due and payable in 15 years. The bonds are then sold to individual and institutional investors. These bonds are then traded over one of the major stock exchanges.

Examples of debt investments include:

- U.S. Savings Bonds (you can purchase from your bank or directly from the U.S. Government)
- Corporate bonds
- Municipal bonds
- Municipal bond funds
- U.S. treasury bills or bonds

DO THIS

Purchase debt investments such as U.S. Bonds or municipal bond funds. They are good investments for rounding out your investment portfolio. You should have 10% to 15% of your investment in U.S. bonds and or other bonds.

Equity investments represent ownership interests. The most common equity investments are common stocks. Companies issue shares of stock to raise capital for various reasons. The investor becomes an owner of the issuing company. Values rise and fall with the fortunes of the companies.

These stocks are available for purchase by the public upon issuance, new offering, or through a stockbroker. These investments generally don't have any specific rate of return. Income received, generally in the form of dividends, is based on earnings.

Example: ABC Corporation needs to raise money to expand the business. It decides to sell common stock to the general public. This is often referred to as going public. This common stock represents an ownership interest in ABC Corporation. ABC wants to raise $100 million by issuing 10 million shares of common stock at $10 per share. It hires a major brokerage firm as the underwriter. The stocks are then sold to individual and institutional investors. These stocks are then traded over one of the major exchanges. The fortunes of the company will determine future stock prices and dividend payments.

Examples of equity investment include:

- Common stock
- Preferred stock
- Ownership of small business
- Rental real estate

Keep the majority (70% to 80%) of your investment portfolio in equity investments. This is particularly important for your retirement accounts. Equity investments have historically performed better over the long term than other types of investments. You should lower the level of equity investments when you near retirement age.

Commit to Lifetime Learning

You should commit to lifetime learning. If recent corporate and accounting scandals have taught us anything, it is that one should not entrust the financial well-being of one's family to stockbrokers, financial advisors, or any other so-called experts. You should not depend on the kindness or expertise of strangers for the management of your life savings or investments. There was a time when you could invest in your company's retirement plan and be assured of having an adequate retirement income. So-called experts have one primary objective. They are concerned about increasing their net worth and securing the financial future of their families a lot more than they are worried about yours. Recent events have also revealed that many of these experts are far from infallible when it comes to valuing investments. This is not to say that all of these people are unethical, but enough of them are to give one pause. And even the honest ones are more concerned about their financial security than yours. So the bottom line is this: Continually educate yourself about financial matters so that you can make the right choices yourself, turning to the experts for clarification rather than giving them complete control.

Subscribe to and read magazines on personal finances. Good ones include Kiplinger's Personal Finance and Consumer Report.

Watch television programs that deal with investments and personal finances. Good ones include Lou Dodd's Tonight (CNN) and Business Report (Public TV).

Read business section of your local newspaper everyday.

Read books on money and finances.

Read national publications. Good ones include USA Today, the Wall Street Journal and Barron's.

Ten Dumbest Financial Moves

In a nutshell, the following are ten financial moves that are the most ill-advised. Each one can be costly; some can cause irreparable damage to your financial health. You should make your best effort to avoid them.

1. Running up credit card debt.
This is the greatest cause of financial difficulty and bankruptcy. High interest charges can result in you paying two or three times the purchase price for goods and services.

2. Taking withdrawals from your retirement.
This is probably the worst move that you can make from a tax and retirement standpoint. It generally results in you paying up to 50% of your withdrawal in income taxes and penalties. It also causes a substantial reduction in the money that will be available to you when you retire.

3. Purchasing an expensive car that you cannot afford.
Purchasing a more expensive car than you can afford can severely damage your financial health. This is especially damaging to young people just starting out.

4. Borrowing against the equity in your home.
Ads encourage you to cash out equity in your home as if you were withdrawing money from a savings account. You are not. You are borrowing against the equity in your home, one of your most valuable assets. Using home equity financing on a shopping spree is a gross misuse of this valuable asset. Home equity financing should be implemented only after considering all of the financial ramifications.

5. Gambling with money you can't afford to lose.
You are all but certain to lose the money that you gamble with. Enough said. I hope!

7. Under-withholding your income taxes.
This results in a little extra money in your paycheck and big headaches down the road. Be careful. Working overtime or getting a part time job is a much better option.

6. Making high-risk investments without doing your homework. Beware of anyone who promises you high returns with little or no risk. Do your homework before making any major investment. Get a second opinion from someone you trust, your C.P.A., lawyer, etc. Your best defense against high-pressure sales people is to just hang up.

8. Taking part in a network marketing scam.
These are generally a waste of time and a waste of money. I don't know anyone who has made any money in a network-marketing program. Do you?

9. Late filing your income tax returns.
This can result in penalties that are completely avoidable. All you have to do is file for an extension and/or get up off the couch and get your taxes done.

10. Obtaining instant tax refund loans.
These loans are very costly. A much better option is to e-file your taxes early.

Ten Smartest Financial Moves

Smart people do smart things. Here are ten financial moves that will make you look smarter and improve your financial health.

1. Make a financial plan.
When you fail to plan you plan to fail. Your financial plan does not have to be complex or expensive. It might just involve an automatic investment program and strategies for reducing your debt.

2. Pay off your credit card debt.
One of the best investments that you can make. Banks pay out 1-4% on savings accounts. Can you afford to pay the credit card company up to 18% on your credit card debt?

3. Purchase a home.
Probably the best investment that you will ever make. Buying a home early in life is a great way to start building net worth. In addition to providing great tax benefits, the appreciation on your home is a wealth builder.

4. Start automatic investment program.

Create wealth one paycheck at a time. Its been said that you don't miss money that you haven't seen. Using an automatic program to purchase shares in a high quality mutual fund is a very smart move.

5. Pay your bills on time.

This is great for your credit rating. You will avoid expensive late fees and reduce your interest costs. Automatic bill paying may help.

6. Invest in 401(k) plan.

Excellent way to amass retirement assets, particularly when your employer matches your contribution. Participating in a 401(k) plan allows you to put pre-tax dollars into a retirement plan. These dollars grow tax-free.

7. Read.

Easy way to continue your education for your entire life. We live in what has been described as an information age, and information has become a very valuable commodity. Knowledge used properly can be very powerful. We've all heard the expression "knowledge is power." It's true. Ignorance on the other hand can be expensive, very expensive. This is especially true in the area of money and finances. So you miss an episode of "I Pity The Fool."

8. Buy dependable used car.

There is nothing like not having an auto loan payment. You will have a smaller loan payment on a dependable pre-owned car and a shorter loan term. These savings can be applied to debt reduction and investment.

9. Monitor your credit report.

Catch errors early. Your credit report can have a profound impact on many aspects of your life. Your credit standing determines the availability and cost of credit (money) to you. Be alert for identity thieves.

10. Pay off your home mortgage.

You don't really own your home until you pay off your mortgage. Until then, it is owned by you and the bank and the bank is in "first position."

12

Fund Your Children's Higher Education

*"Every addition to true knowledge
is an addition to human power."*

Horace Mann

Providing for your children's education is one of the best investments that you can make. If you have children you should begin a college fund. A child born in 2006 will probably start college in the year 2024, when a private college education could cost over $65,000 a year! Clearly, it helps to begin saving early, preferably as soon as the child is born. The idea is to save or invest as much money as you can and pay taxes on as little as possible. It's like buying a house: the more you've saved ahead of time, the less you'll need to borrow. The sooner you begin to set aside or invest something each month, the better.

Options For Funding College Education

Educational Savings Accounts

A savings account called a Coverdell Education Savings Account (CESA) is probably your best option for funding your children's education. This account can be used to pay qualified expenses of elementary, secondary and higher education expenses. Contributions are allowed until your child reaches 18, and contributions may not exceed $2,000 per child per year. The $2,000 limit is phased out for joint filers with income above $190,000 and less than $220,000 and for single filers with income above $95,000 and less than $110,000. While there is no tax deduction for contributions, the funds accumulate tax-free. Withdrawals from education savings accounts are not taxable if used for qualified higher education expenses. These include tuition and books and room and board if the student is enrolled on at least a half-time basis in an eligible institution.

All money in the account should be withdrawn before the beneficiary reaches age 30. The designated beneficiary can be changed to a member of the beneficiary's family.

Example: You start a Coverdell Education Savings Account for your elder son, Tyrone. When Tyrone graduates from college there is $7,500 left in his CESA.

Tyrone instructs the trustee of his account to change the name of the beneficiary on his account to that of his sister, Helen. This enables him to avoid paying tax on the distribution of the remaining amount in the account and provides his sister with money for her college education.

DO THIS™

> **Contact your banker or investment advisor to open a Coverdell Education Savings Account to fund your child's education.** Begin making contributions to this account as soon as possible even if you cannot make the maximum contribution to the account.

Prepaid Tuition Plans

Certain states, such as Alabama, Alaska, Colorado, Florida, Massachusetts, Michigan, Ohio, Pennsylvania, Tennessee, and West Virginia, offer various types of prepaid tuition plans, generally for students attending state schools. Residents of these states can buy a contract or bonds at a fixed price, based on the rates of college tuition today. Payments can be made in lump sums or monthly installments. The state, in turn, invests the money to earn the difference between the amount you are paying and the projected cost of tuition at the time your child reaches college age. Those who sign up are fully protected, as the state assumes all the risk of the investments. Check with your state's commission on higher education to see if a prepaid tuition plan is available where you live.

Prepaid tuition plans are not for everyone. They mostly attract middle-income families who tend to be more conservative in their investments. Lower-income families using this option may jeopardize their chances for state aid and forfeit money needed for immediate essentials. If you're interested and a plan is offered in your state, you'll want to know whether it covers only the cost of tuition, or room and board, too. Also, check to see whether it applies to other than state schools. Finally, confirm that your original deposit will be returned if your child attends a private or out-of-state college, is not accepted at a state school, or chooses not to attend college at all.

Other Considerations

Even if you start early, it may be impossible to save enough for your child's college education. That doesn't mean, however, that college is out of the question. You have other cost-saving options available.

Student Strategies

Many college students, particularly those who commute to a local school, are able to work part-time and summer jobs to help subsidize their tuition. Be aware, however, that money earned by the child prior to college may reduce his or her eligibility for financial aid. Some colleges offer cooperative education programs where students rotate study with periods of career-related work, allowing them to earn money and credits at the same time. However, it may take more than four years to complete a degree through a cooperative education program. Ask the college admissions office about the specifics of their program.

Depending on a child's scholastic ability, he or she may be able to earn college credits by taking college courses or advance placement exams while still in high school. First- and second-year college students can also take College Level Examination Program tests for course credit. These options can represent a significant savings over the cost of a full-semester course in the classroom. Check with your child's high school guidance counselor or with the college admissions office for eligibility requirements and program specifics.

Another cost-saving possibility is to attend a Community College for the first year or two, then transfer to a four-year college to complete a degree. This can be a more affordable approach to receiving a degree from a prestigious institution; one that you may have been unable to afford for four years or that may have been more competitive to gain entrance as a freshman.

Financial Aid

Think of this in broad terms. You needn't be the sole source of funding for your child's higher education. For example, when your child receives a gift of money, put it into a college fund. When grandparents ask what to give for birthdays, suggest college fund contributions. And don't forget the traditional sources of financial aid: scholarships, grants, work-study programs, and government loans. Your child's scholastic record, course of study, athletic ability, and choice of college are just a few of the variables that may affect the availability of these options.

If your family meets certain financial criteria, the federal government has a program of low-interest loans with extended payment terms. Relying too heavily on loans, however, is costly and can burden graduates with large debts just when they are working to establish their financial independence. Also, you should be aware that government financial aid programs are subject to change.

Loans

If you plan to take out a loan to help pay for your child's college expenses, the interest may now be deductible. Generally, if the taxpayer's adjusted gross income is below $130,000 for joint filers and below $65,000 for single filers the interest may be deductible. The deduction is phased out ratably from $50,000 to $60,000 for single filers and from $100,000 to $130,000 for joint filers. Students may claim this deduction only if they are not claimed as dependents on parents' returns.

It's important to note, too, that tax laws are constantly changing and this discussion of tax rules provides a general overview. Consult your tax advisor before you begin investing, and then check back regularly. If changes in the tax laws negatively affect your college investments, you may want to move the money. How and when you move the funds can also affect your taxes so be sure to talk to your tax advisor first. In particular, some of the tax provisions discussed above are due to expire after December 31, 2010.

Build Financial Security, One Brick At A Time

Investing something out of every paycheck is a sure-fire way to create wealth.

13

Invest Early And Often

"We are what we repeatedly do."

Aristotle

Albert Einstein said that compound interest was the greatest mathematical discovery of all time. Some refer to "the magic of compound interest." Compound interest is the process of earning interest on interest while earning interest on the original amount invested. The consistent use of compound interest is a sure avenue to accumulating wealth. You will accumulate a significant sum of money by regular investing over a long period of time using the magic of compound interest.

Example: If you invest $100 a month, earning 6% annually, you will accumulate: $7,012 in 5 years and $16,470 in 10 years. I don't know anyone who couldn't find $100 a month to invest, if they really tried. That's just a little more than $3 per day, less than a pack of smokes or a fancy coffee drink. If you invest more, you will have more. You will have $10,518 in five years and $24,705 in ten years if you invest $150 per month and earn 6% annually.

How nice would it be for you and your family if you had started an investment program five years ago? Start now so that you aren't asking yourself that question five years from now.

It pays to have financial assets. There is nothing like having money when you need it.

Money Accumulated By Investing $100 Per Month					
Rate of Return	5 Years	10 Years	15 Years	20 Years	25 Years
4%	$ 6,652	$ 14,774	$ 24,691	$ 36,800	$ 51,584
5%	6,800	15,593	26,840	41,104	59,799
6%	7,012	16,470	29,227	49,435	69,646
7%	7,201	17,409	31,881	52,397	81,480
8%	7,397	18,417	34,835	58,902	95,737
9%	7,599	19,497	38,124	67,290	112,953
10%	7,808	20,655	41,792	76,570	133,789
11%	8,025	21,899	45,886	87,359	159,058
12%	8,249	23,234	50,458	98,926	189,764

Example: Joe Smith left high school early to take a job and help support his family after his father died. While he did what he felt he had to do, it always concerned him that he did not graduate from high school. Joe recalled that his grandmother had always stressed the importance of savings. She gave Joe and his siblings piggy banks when they were young. When each turned 12, she would open a savings account for him or her. Joe never forgot the lesson his grandmother taught him. When he turned 18 he began purchasing U.S. savings bonds. He instructed his bank to deduct $100 from his checking account each month to purchase U.S. savings bonds. As the years passed, Joe didn't pay too much attention to the savings bonds that were accumulating in his safety deposit box. He just subtracted $100 from his checking account balance each month. Joe married his childhood sweetheart on his twenty-fifth birthday. They had a son two years later and a daughter three years after that. Joe was now working for the local school district as a janitor. His wife worked part/time as a checker at the neighborhood grocery store. The two incomes allowed them to live a modest lifestyle. On Joe's thirty-second birthday he and his wife talked about how great it would be if they could purchase their own home. They began to look around in neighborhoods that they liked. After about a week of looking, they found what they considered their dream home. It had three bedrooms, a large back yard and even a basement. Their realtor informed them that, based on their incomes, they could only qualify for a loan that would require them to make a down payment of $25,000. $25,000? Where were they going to get that kind of money? They both made modest salaries. No one in either of his or her families had that kind of money. At breakfast one morning, his wife asked, "What about the savings bonds?" "They can't be worth that much," Joe responded, " I've only been buying $100 worth per month." "Well, let's at least see what they are worth," she demanded. That day, in Joe's lunch hour, she and Joe went to the bank. They removed the bonds from their safe deposit box and solicited the aid of a teller to determine their value. Joe's jaw almost dropped to the floor when the teller informed them that the savings bonds' current value was $28,954. They got their home, and of course Joe is still purchasing $100 worth of savings bonds each month.

Many investment advisors would have advised Joe that there are a lot better investments out there than U.S. savings bonds. And he probably would have made more money investing in a high quality mutual fund. Joe didn't know anything about stocks or mutual funds. He invested in something that he understood. He did it consistently for a long number of years. Joe still does not have a high school diploma, but his investments turned out a lot better than those of the Wall Street experts who invested in Enron.

Mutual Funds

Mutual funds are a convenient form of investment. A mutual fund is a company that pools money from many investors and invests the money in stocks, bonds or other securities. They hire experts, known as fund managers, to make investment decisions. When you purchase a share in a mutual fund you are purchasing a proportionate ownership of the fund's holdings (stocks, bonds, etc.) and the income those holdings generate. Each share represents an investor's proportionate ownership of the fund's holdings and the income those holdings generate.

Advantages of investing in mutual fund. Every investment has advantages and disadvantages. But it's important to remember that features that matter to one investor may not be important to you. Whether any particular feature is an advantage for you will depend on your unique circumstances. For some investors, mutual funds provide an attractive investment choice because they generally offer the following features:

1. Professional management.
Professional money managers research, select, and monitor the performance of the securities the fund purchases.

2. Diversification.
Diversification is an investing strategy that can be neatly summed up as "Don't put all your eggs in one basket." Spreading your investments across a wide range of companies and industry sectors can help lower your risk if a company or sector fails. Some investors find it easier to achieve diversification through ownership of mutual funds rather than through ownership of individual stocks or bonds.

3. Affordability.
Some mutual funds accommodate investors who don't have a lot of money to invest by setting relatively low dollar amounts for initial purchases, subsequent monthly purchases, or both.

4. Liquidity.
Mutual fund investors can readily redeem their shares at the current net asset value (NAV) — minus any fees and charges assessed on redemption — at any time.

Disadvantages of investing in mutual fund. Mutual funds also have features that some investors might view as disadvantages, such as:

1. Costs despite negative returns.
Investors must pay sales charges, annual fees, and other expenses

(which we'll discuss below) regardless of how the fund performs. And, depending on the timing of their investment, investors may also have to pay taxes on any capital gains distribution they receive, even if the fund went on to perform poorly after they bought shares.

2. Lack of Control.

Investors typically cannot ascertain the exact make-up of a fund's portfolio at any given time, nor can they directly influence which securities the fund manager buys and sells or the timing of those trades.

3. Price uncertainty.

With an individual stock, you can obtain real-time (or close to real-time) pricing information with relative ease by checking financial web sites or by calling your broker. You can also monitor how a stock's price changes from hour to hour — or even second to second. By contrast, with a mutual fund, the price at which you purchase or redeem shares will typically depend on the fund's NAV, which the fund might not calculate until many hours after you've placed your order. In general, mutual funds must calculate their NAV at least once every business day, typically after the major U.S. exchanges close.

Types of Mutual Funds

When it comes to investing in mutual funds, investors have literally thousands of choices. Before you invest in any given fund, decide whether the investment strategy and risks of the fund are a good fit for you. The first step to successful investing is figuring out your financial goals and risk tolerance, either on your own or with the help of a financial professional. Once you know what you're saving for, when you'll need the money, and how much risk you can tolerate, you can more easily narrow your choices.

The following are mutual funds which fall into one of three main categories: money-market funds, bond funds (also called "fixed-income" funds), and stock funds (also called "equity" funds). Each type has different features and different risks and rewards. Generally, the higher the potential return, the higher the risk of loss.

Money Market Funds. The assets in these funds typically consist of U.S. Treasury bills, Certificates of Deposit (CDs) and other commercial investments. You'll find them on the lowest rung of the risk ladder. On the other hand, they also offer the lowest potential for return and may not beat inflation. These funds are generally not insured nor guaranteed by the U.S. Government and there is no guarantee that they can maintain a stable net asset value.

Bond Funds. Bonds represent loans to federal or local governments or to a corporation, with a promise to repay at a set interest rate in a predetermined period of time. Bonds are generally considered a more conservative investment than stocks. However, they are sensitive to interest rate fluctuations. This means their value will rise and fall with changes in general market interest rates. In addition, long-term performance may be outpaced by inflation. In general, high-grade bond funds are low- to moderate-risk investments, with a few categorized on the high-risk side.

Balanced Funds (Life Style Funds or Asset Allocation Funds). Blending both stocks and bonds, these funds allow diversification with potentially lower risk than pure stock funds, but also with a lower potential for return.

Stock Index Funds. These funds attempt to "mirror" the performance of stock market indexes, such as the S&P 500. Index funds invest in most or all of the same stocks found in the corresponding index and, accordingly, seek to closely match the performance of that index. This middle-of-the-road approach puts index funds at the low end of the risk spectrum for stock funds.

Growth and Income Funds. Such funds invest in companies with strong growth potential that also have a solid record of paying dividends (income). Growth and income funds fall in the middle of the risk spectrum.

Growth Funds. Investing in relatively stable and established companies, which may or may not pay dividends, these funds try to identify companies whose stock values are expected to increase. Growth funds are considered higher risk, so expect significant fluctuation in share price in exchange for a potentially higher return.

Aggressive Growth Funds. These funds are comprised of stocks with greater-than-average potential for growth. Such stocks may include start-up companies, smaller companies or companies in high-risk industries. As a result, these funds also have a high degree of risk and a high potential for return.

International or Global Equity Funds. International stock funds invest only in stocks from countries outside the U.S., while global funds invest in both foreign and U.S. companies. Investors in these funds take on a higher degree of additional risk, since international issues contain risks not present with domestic issues, such as currency exchange rate fluctuations and different economic conditions, governmental regulations, and accounting standards. The risks and potential rewards are very high.

Each type of investment has its own degree of certainty and uncertainty. Since all investments perform differently, one way to manage risk is to diversify your portfolio by investing in a blend of different types of assets.

The Payoff

When you invest in mutual funds, you can make money from dividend payments, capital gains distributions and increases in the value of the fund.

Dividend Payments. A fund may earn income in the form of dividends and interest on the securities in its portfolio. The fund then pays its shareholders nearly all of the income (minus disclosed expenses) it has earned in the form of dividends.

Capital Gains Distributions. The price of the securities a fund owns may increase. When a fund sells a security that has increased in price, the fund has a capital gain. At the end of the year, most funds distribute these capital gains (minus any capital losses) to investors.

Increased Net Asset Value (NAV). If the market value of a fund's portfolio increases after deduction of expenses and liabilities, then the net asset value of the fund and its shares increases. The higher NAV reflects the higher value of your investment.

With respect to dividend payments and capital gains distributions, funds usually will give you a choice: the fund can send you a check or other form of payment, or you can have your dividends or distributions reinvested in the fund to buy more shares (often without paying an additional sales load).

How to Buy and Sell Shares

You can purchase shares in some mutual funds by contacting the fund directly. Other mutual fund shares are sold mainly through brokers, banks, financial planners, or insurance agents. All mutual funds will redeem (buy back) your shares on any business day and must send you the payment within seven days.

The easiest way to determine the value of your shares is to call the fund's toll-free number or visit its web site. The financial pages of major newspapers sometimes print the NAVs for various mutual funds. When you buy shares, you pay the current NAV per share plus any fee the fund assesses at the time of purchase, such as a purchase sales load or other type of purchase fee. When you sell your shares, the fund will pay you the NAV minus any fee the fund assesses at the time of redemption, such as a deferred (or back-end) sales load or redemption fee. A fund's NAV goes up or down daily as its holdings change in value.

The following are some of the leading mutual funds per the 2007 Forbes Fund Survey. You are advised to review their prospectus. Past performance is no guarantee of future performance.

Mutual Funds	6 Year Average Annual Return	Annual Expense Ratio	Minimum Initial Investment	Telephone
Bond Funds				
Fidelity Ginnie Mae	4.8	.45	$2,500	800-343-3548
TCW Total Return	6.2	.44	2,000	800-386-3829
Vanguard High Yield Tax Exempt	5.6	.16	3,000	800-662-7447
Balanced Funds				
Oakmark Equity & Income	11.2%	.89	$1,000	800-625-6275
Vanguard Wellington	8.1	.29	3,000	800-662-7447
Vanguard Star	6.8	.36	1,000	800-662-7447
Growth & Income Funds				
Bruce Fund	28.2	1.14	1,000	800-872-7823
Growth Funds				
Vanguard Strategic Equity	12.1	.59	1,000	800-662-7447
Fidelity Value Fund	13.9	.84	2,500	800-343-3548
Global Equity Funds				
Polaris Global Value	17.7%		$2,500	888-263-5594
Vanguard Global Equity	13.9		3,000	800-662-7447

DO THIS

Establish Emergency Fund

You should establish an emergency fund before you begin an investment program. Your emergency fund is for unexpected family emergencies such as loss of employment, illness or other needs for cash. A money market account is a good vehicle for holding emergency fund cash. Money market accounts are insured by the Federal government and pay a higher interest rate than most savings accounts. These accounts generally require a minimum initial deposit to open (often $1,000) and penalize you if your balance falls below that level. You can generally write up to three checks a month from these accounts without a charge.

Jerry East used his tax refund to open a money market account. His financial plan called for him to maintain an emergency fund equal to two paychecks. He opened the account with $1,000 and deposited $100 from each of his paychecks until he reached this goal.

Invest Something Every Month

Invest early and often. Form the habit of investing something every month. Often referred to as paying yourself first, adopting this practice is among the smartest financial moves that you can make. You should invest as much as you can but you will benefit even if you can only invest a small amount. Forming the habit of regular investing will reap you a lifetime of benefits.

What The Experts Say About the Future

Ibbotson Associates is recognized as the definitive authority on historical investment returns on stocks and bonds. Ibbotson Associates forecasts investment returns through the year 2025.

Ibbotson's Forecast for Investment Returns Through the Year 2025	
Security	**Projected Median Annual Return**
Large Cap Stocks (Large Companies)	12.5%
Small Cap Stocks	11.6%
Government Bonds	5.4%
Treasury Bills	4.5%

DTHIS™

Keep Accurate Records of Your Investments

Keep accurate investment records. This is important for a number of reasons. First of all it makes it easy to determine, at any point in time, where you stand in terms of profit or loss as it relates to any of your holdings. It is also important for tax purposes when you sell a security and have to report the purchase and sale price on your income tax return.

Jim Smith purchased 250 shares of Vanguard Star fund on December 18, 2006. He paid $35.15 per share. He files his account statements in his home office file. He records this purchase as follows:

Investments							
Date: December 31, 2006							
Date Acquired	Type	Description	Number Of Shares	Cost Per Share	Market At 1/31/07	Total Value	Location Statements or Certificates are Kept
12/18/06	M	Vanguard Star Fund	250	35.15	37.00	9,250	Office File
Note Type: B – Bonds, S – Stock, M – Mutual Funds							

The greatest of all mistakes is to do nothing because you can only do a little. Do what you can.

Sydney Smith

14

Gamble Only With Money You Can Afford to Lose

"When I lose, I lose too much. When I win I don't win enough."

Charles Barkley on his gambling

During a discussion on athletics with gambling problems, TV commentator and NBA hall of famer Charles Barkley lamented, "When I lose, I lose too much, when I win, I don't win enough." That statement, more than any other that I have heard, puts the fate of every gambler in a nutshell. You will win now and then but your winnings will never be sufficient to recoup your losses. They only encourage you to gamble more. Casino managers, for their part, are brilliant in their marketing. They create an atmosphere in which losing is acceptable. Patrons often brag about how much they have lost. As the saying goes, they do not spend hundreds of millions of dollars building casinos so that they can give money to you. The adage "you cannot beat the house" is true. Habitual gambling is dangerous.

Gambling has proliferated in almost every state, city and neighborhood in the United States. More than half the states have casinos and 48 states allow some form of legalized gambling. There is more money wagered in this country than is spent on groceries. Gambling in this country was originally controlled by the underworld. It now operates under the umbrella of so-called legimate business. A week hardly passes without the announcement of plans for the construction of a new and expensive casino. The reason for this growth is simple. Gambling is very profitable for the house. Gambling is not so profitable for gamblers. Habitual gamblers are increasing in numbers by the hour. Many families and fortunes are among gambling's victims.

In June of 1999 Dr. James Dobson, Commissioner on the National Gambling Impact Study Commission, issued the findings of a two year study on gambling. This was the first time in more than 20 years that the issue of gambling had been looked at by a federal commission. The major findings of this Commission included the following:

- Problem and pathological gambling is a growing problem that affects millions of Americans. Problem gamblers have persistent and recurrent preoccupation with gambling.

- Gambling addiction is devastating to those whom it touches, with demonstrated links to bankruptcy, suicide, crime, divorce, domestic violence, child abuse and neglect and homelessness.

- Lotteries prey on the poor on minorities and subsist on a small percentage of very heavy players (average expenditures of $3,800 per year or about $73 per week).

- Gambling is having a devastating effect on America's youth. Eighty-five percent of young people on everything from card games to sports teams to casinos and lotteries.

The American Psychiatric Association defines pathological gambling as an impulse control disorder that is a chronic and progressive mental illness. Persons having five or more of the following criteria could be suffering from pathological gambling.

1. Preoccupation.
One constantly thinks about gambling.

2. Escape.
Gambling is used to improve mood or escape problems.

3. Chasing.
There are constant attempts to win back gambling losses.

4. Lying.
There is lying to family, friends and others to hide the extent of one's gambling.

5. High gambling tolerance.
Larger and/or more frequent wages are needed to experience the same "rush."

6. Withdrawal.
Attempts to cease or reduce gambling cause restlessness or irritability.

7. Loss of Control.
There have been several unsuccessful attempts to reduce gambling.

8. Damaged relationships.
Gambling has caused damage to friendships, marriage or employment.

9. Debt.
Gambling has resulted in borrowing from friends, family and others.

10. Crime.
Crimes are committed to obtain money to gamble or recoup gambling losses.

DO☑THIS™

Always set a limit on the amount you can lose whenever you go into a casino or do any kind of gambling. Never gamble with money that you cannot afford to lose. Going to the casino for entertainment, with a limited budget, is one thing. Going to a casino expecting to win money is another. Visits to Las Vegas can be fun and exciting, as long as you know your limits.

15

Avoid Scams and Swindlers

"Life gives nothing to man without labor."

Horace

The chances are pretty good that at some point in your life you will be approached by someone to take part in a sure-fire get rich quick opportunity. The pitch will very likely be long on hype and short on specifics. There is a good chance that it will involve some sort of pyramid scheme. These scams are just below gambling in terms of activities that are wealth drainers. They rate below gambling because with gambling at least you have some chance of winning, however thin. I know of no one who has ever gained anything as a result of being involved in any of these schemes. You should avoid get rich quick schemes like the plague.

 THIS

Beware Of Scams!

Internet Auctions

The Bait: Shop in a "virtual marketplace" that offers a huge selection of products at great deals.

The Catch: After sending their money, consumers say they've received an item that is less valuable than promised or, worse yet, nothing at all.

The Safety Net: When bidding through an Internet auction, particularly for a valuable item, check out the seller and insist on paying with a credit card or using an escrow service.

Internet Access Services

The Bait: Free money, simply for cashing a check.

The Catch: Consumers say they've been "trapped" into long-term contracts for Internet access or another web service, with big penalties for cancellation or early termination.

The Safety Net: If a check arrives at your home or business, read both sides carefully and look inside the envelope to find the conditions you're agreeing to if you cash the check. Read your phone bill carefully for unexpected or unauthorized charges.

Credit Card Fraud

The Bait: Surf the Internet and view adult images online for free, just for sharing your credit card number to prove you're over 18.

The Catch: Consumers say that fraudulent promoters have used their credit card numbers to run up charges on their cards.

The Safety Net: Share credit card information only when buying from a company you trust. Dispute unauthorized charges on your credit card bill by complaining to the bank that issued the card. Federal law limits your liability to $50 in charges if your card is misused.

Miracle Health Care Products/Services

The Bait: Items not sold through traditional suppliers are "proven" to cure serious and even fatal health problems.

The Catch: Claims for "miracle" products and treatments convince consumers that their health problems can be cured. But people with serious illnesses who put their hopes in these offers might delay getting the health care they need.

The Safety Net: Consult a health care professional before buying any "cure-all" that claims to treat a wide range of ailments or offers quick cures and easy solutions to serious illnesses.

Avoiding Swindlers

The first line of defense against investment fraud is your inalienable right to ask questions and –until you get the right answers–to say no and mean no. Not surprisingly, this is usually an investment swindler's first point of attack. To keep you from asking questions, he asks them! Invariably, the questions have "yes" answers. "You would at least be interested in hearing about such a fantastic investment opportunity, wouldn't you?" or he will ask "You would like to make a large amount of money in a short period of time with little or no risk, right?"

One difference between a reputable investment firm and a swindler is that reputable firms encourage you to ask questions, to obtain as much information as possible, to clearly understand the risks involved, and to be entirely comfortable with any investment decision you make. The only thing a swindler wants is your money.

Questions to Ask Before Investing

1. Where did you get my name? If the response is that you were chosen from a "select list of intelligent and prudent investors," that select list may be the telephone directory, or a purchased list of persons who've bought certain types of books, subscribed to particular magazines, or responded to newspaper ads. If you have made ill-advised investments in the past, you can be pretty sure your name is on someone's alumni list. It's the list swindlers prize most: easy preys who are eager to recoup (but are doomed to repeat) their earlier losses.

2. What risks are involved in the proposed investment?
Except for obligations of the U.S. Treasury, which are considered risk-free, all investments involve some degree of risk. And some investments, by their nature, involve greater risks than others. Keep in mind that if the salesman had knowledge of a sure-thing, big-profit investment opportunity, he wouldn't be on the phone talking with you.

3. Can you send me a written explanation of your investment so I can consider it at my leisure? For someone peddling fraudulent investments, that can be a double turn-off. For one thing, most crooks are reluctant to put anything in writing that might cause them to run afoul of postal authorities or provide material that, at some point, might become evidence in a fraud trial. Secondly, swindlers don't want you to do anything at your leisure. They want your money now. It's a good rule of thumb that any investment that "absolutely has to be made immediately" shouldn't be made at all.

4. Would you mind explaining your investment proposal to some third party, such as my attorney, accountant, investment advisor, or banker? If the answer goes something along the lines of "normally, I'd be glad to, but there isn't time for that," or if the salesman snaps back by asking "can't you make your own investment decisions?" These are virtually certain clues that your final answer should be an emphatic no.

5. Can you give me the names of your firm's principals and officers? Although some persons who establish and operate dishonest firms change their own names as often as they change their firms' names, even the hint that you are the kind of investor who checks into things like that can be a fast turnoff for a swindler.

6. Can you provide references? Don't settle for just another list of other investors who supposedly became fabulously wealthy (the names you get may be the salesman's boss or someone sitting at the next phone), but reputable and reliable recommendations such as a bank or well-known brokerage firm that you can easily contact.

7. Do you have any documents such as a prospectus or risk disclosure statement that you can provide? This may not be available in connection with all types of investments but in many investment areas—such as securities, futures, and options trading—it's required. And there can be requirements that you be provided with this information and acknowledge in writing that you have read and understood it. Obviously, it's not the sort of information a swindler is likely to distribute.

8. Are the investments you are offering traded on a regulated exchange, such as a securities or futures exchange? Some bona fide investments are and some aren't, but fraudulent investments never are. Exchanges have strict rules designed to assure fair dealing and competitive price determination. There are also mechanisms to provide for rule enforcement and to impose severe sanctions against those who fail to observe the rules.

9. What governmental or industry regulatory supervision is your firm subject to? If the salesman rattles off a list that ranges from the FBI to the Boy Scouts, tell him you'd like to check the firm's good standing before making an important investment decision. Then verify the response. Few things discourage a swindler faster than the thought that his first visitor the next morning may be from a regulatory agency. If, on the other hand, you are told his particular area of investment isn't subject to regulation (perhaps because everyone in his business is an ethical, upstanding citizen), take that explanation for whatever you think it's worth. At the very least, keep in mind that any ongoing supervision that isn't being provided by a regulatory organization or agency will have to be provided by you.

10. How long has your company been in business? In any kind of business activity, there can be advantages to dealing with a known, established company. This isn't to say that new businesses aren't starting up all the time or that the vast majorities aren't perfectly reputable. But if you find yourself talking with someone who doesn't seem to have a past, it can be worthwhile to find out why.

Many swindlers have been running scams for years but understandably aren't anxious to talk about it.

11. What has your track record been? Before you accept a salesman's assurance that he can make money for you, you have the right to know what his performance has been in making money for others. And ask to have the information (if there is any) in writing. Boasting over the phone is one thing; putting it down on paper is quite another. In any case, even if you are able to obtain a documented performance record, don't lose sight of the fact that past performance in itself provides no assurance of future performance.

12. When and where can I meet with you or with another representative of your firm? Chances are a crooked operator—particularly if he is operating out of a telephone boiler room—isn't going to take time to visit with you and even more certainly doesn't want you to see his place of business.

13. Where, exactly, will my money be? And what type of regular accounting statements do you provide? In many investment areas, such as futures trading, firms are required to maintain their customers' funds in segregated accounts at all times. Any mingling of investors' funds with those of the firm or its principals is prohibited. You might also want to find out what, if any, routine outside audits the firm's account records are subject to.

14. How much of my money would go for commissions, management fees and the like? Also ask whether there will be other costs such as interest or storage charges, or whether the investment agreement involves any type of profit-sharing arrangements in which the firms' principals participate. Insist on specific answers, not glib and evasive responses such as "that's not important" or "what's really important is how much money you are going to make." And, again, get it in writing, just as you would any other type of contract.

15. How can I liquidate (i.e., sell the item I'd be investing in) if and when I decide I want my money? If you find that the investment is illiquid, or there would be substantial costs if liquidated, or that you are unable to get straight and solid answers, these are all things to consider in deciding whether you want to invest.

16. If disputes should arise, how can they be resolved?
Short of having to go to court to sue someone, does the company or regulatory organization provide a mechanism for resolving disputes equitably and inexpensively through arbitration, mediation, or a reparations procedure? Aside from seeking important information, you may be able to detect whether the sales person is uncomfortable or impatient with this line of questioning. Swindlers generally will be.

D✔THIS

Be wary of extravagant claims about performance or earnings potential. Get all promises in writing and review them carefully before making a payment or signing a contract. Read the fine print and all relevant links. Fraudulent promoters sometimes bury the disclosures they're not anxious to share by putting them in teeny-tiny type or in a place where you're unlikely see them.

Look for a privacy policy. If you don't see one, or if you can't understand it, consider taking your business elsewhere. Be skeptical of any company that doesn't clearly state its name, street address and telephone number. Check it out with the local Better Business Bureau, consumer protection office, or state attorney general.

D✔THIS

Check Out Stockbrokers Before Investing.

You can do a background check on any stockbroker or brokerage firm before investing with them. Anyone selling securities (stocks, bonds, mutual funds, etc.) is generally required to be licensed or registered. The Central Registration Depository system (CRD) maintains the following information on stockbrokers:

- Employment history for the past ten years

- Securities examination scores

- Status of license or securities registration

- Pending written complaints alleging sales practice violations

- Civil judgments and arbitration decisions in securities and commodities disputes involving public customers

- Disciplinary actions (if any)

- Criminal convictions or indictments

- Employment terminations due to allegations of fraud, theft or violations of securities regulations

- Bankruptcies filed within the last ten years and outstanding judgments and liens

You can obtain a CRD report about a stockbroker or brokerage firm that you are thinking about doing business with by contacting your state securities regulating agency. You can find out who your state securities regulating agency is by contacting the North American Securities Administrators Association at (202) 737-0900 or on their web site at www.nasaa.org (click on "Find Regulator").

16

A Few Shopping Tips

"If we triumph in the little things of our hours, we are sure to triumph in our lives."

Unknown

You can save thousands and thousands of dollars over the coming years just by being a smarter shopper. Common mistakes that people make on a regular basis cost them a lot of money. The following are actions that can save you money.

Make A Shopping List

Form the habit of preparing a shopping list whenever you go grocery shopping. This will not only aid in not forgetting needed items but will also aid in avoiding buying things that you don't need and really don't want.

Clip Coupons

It pays to clip coupons and use them when you shop for groceries. I know families whose annual incomes exceed six figures ($100,000) that regularly clip coupons for grocery shopping. I've been in line at the grocery store when the person ahead of me had a coupon for what seemed like every item that they had. I was a little annoyed because it took a little extra time to ring up their order until I noticed that they saved over 60% off their bill. Then I was jealous. If you generally spend $500 per month on groceries and are able to knock 25% off that bill by using coupons, you will save about $125 per month and $1,500 per year.

Your best source of coupons is your Sunday newspaper. You should be on the lookout for items that you use regularly. Other sources of coupons include:

- Company's 800 number. The company's 800 number is often listed on the label or package.
- The Internet. Many companies have web sites from which you can print coupons. You should also visit these web sites
    - → www.coolsavings.com
    - → www.grocery-store-coupons.info
    - → www.couponcraze.com

Be sure to organize your coupons so that they are easy to access when you need them. There are many inexpensive coupon organizers available that do a great job.

Compare Prices

It pays to compare prices. Things are not always as they appear. For example, you don't always get the best deal when you purchase bulk quantities of items. You can lose out in a couple of ways. First of all, you may pay more per ounce or unit price when purchasing goods in bulk than you would if purchasing a smaller quantity. Warehouse stores are the rage now. We've all seen people loading up their RV with huge sacks of various products. Their actual savings on these purchases may be illusionary.

Always compare the price per ounce, etc. of bulk purchases with that of regular size purchases. A twenty-pound sack of rice costs $15 at a warehouse outlet. A one-pound bag costs 69 cents. Which is a better buy? You are paying 75 cents per pound ($15 / 20 = .75) if you buy the twenty-pound bag. The pound bag is therefore a better deal at 69 cents. Stores are now required to post the price per unit (ounce, pound, etc.) next to their products. Most people pay little attention to this. Don't be one of them.

Send In Mail-In Rebates

One of the reasons that companies offer mail-in rebates on purchases of their product is because many people neglect to redeem them. Advertised prices often factor in the amount of the mail-in rebate. You see an ad in your daily newspaper for a brand name computer priced at $400. You look closer and you notice an asterisk and a notation, "after mail-in-rebate of $200." You go down to the store and purchase the computer for $600 but forget to complete and mail in the rebate forms.

Whenever you purchase a product that offers a mail-in rebate, you should complete and mail in the rebate forms as soon as you get home. This will reduce the chances that the forms will be lost or you will just forget to submit the required paperwork. It often takes six to eight weeks for you to receive your rebate. You want to get the process going right away.

DO☑THIS™

Shop intelligently. Prepare a shopping list before you go shopping and only buy the items on the list.

Quantity	Item	Regular Price	Total

17

Buy An Automobile That You Can Afford

"He is richest who is contented with least."

Socrates

You are what you drive. That's what many people believe. An automobile is a status symbol. That is why when many people come into money one of the first things they do is to buy a new car. The neighbors see this and of course acknowledge their new status. The kind of car that you drive may say something about you, but not what advertisers tell you. It may say that you are likely to struggle with your finances because you are driving more car than you can afford. When you fall into the cycle of continuing to purchase more expensive automobiles than you can afford, you put a tremendous strain on your finances. This is especially true for young people who are trying to establish themselves. You take on debt to acquire an asset, a car that loses value as soon as you drive it out of the lot and continues to decrease in value as long as you own it.

Example: Billy Wheels purchased a new car on December 19, 2006, his birthday. He put down $1,000 and got a $24,000 loan. He got a five-year loan so that he would have a lower monthly payment. It will not take very long before Bill is "upside down" in his loan. Upside down is a term commonly used to describe a situation when the amount of your loan exceeds the value of the property that secures it.

Date	Car's Value	Loan Amount
Purchase Date	$25,000	$24,500
December 2007	20,000	23,500
December 2008	15,000	18,500
December 2009	10,000	16,000
December 2010	7,500	12,500

Never Purchase A Car Before The Loan on Your Present Car Is Paid Off

Many dealers offer to pay off the loan on your old car when you trade it in on a new or used automobile. This generally has two very negative effects on your financial health. First of all, it results in your having a larger monthly car payment than you would normally for the type of vehicle that you are driving. This will also result in a situation in which the vehicle is worth less than the amount owed on it almost immediately after the purchase.

Example: Joe Walker is still making payments on a 2003 model that he purchased new in January of 2004. His monthly payment was $325 and the loan has an outstanding balance of $6,500. Joe is tired of driving his car and decides to buy a new car. Joe has the admiration of many of his friends who wonder how he is able to continue to drive new cars on his salary. In January of 2006, he responds to a radio ad in which a local automobile dealer offers to pay off the loan on a vehicle used as trade-in on a new car. The amount owed on the old loan is just added to the new loan. Joe's new monthly car payment is $475 for the next five years. In October of 2006 Joe gets restless again. He goes into a dealer's showroom to check out the new models. He is told that his car is valued at $12,000. The loan balance on the car is $18,000. Joe leaves the car lot in shock.

Buying a New Car

Think about what car model and options you want and how much you're willing to spend. Do some research. You'll be less likely to feel pressured into making a hasty or expensive decision at the showroom and more likely to get a better deal.

A new car purchase is the largest purchase that many people make, outside of their home. It should not be undertaken lightly. Making a good car purchase can mean years of dependable driving at an affordable cost. Making a bad car purchase can put you in a big financial hole. Before purchasing a car, you should:

- Determine what you can afford to pay for a car. Prepare a list of your current monthly obligations. Now add your new car payment and related expenses (insurance, etc.) to that figure. Is your income sufficient to cover that number?

- Check publications at a library, bookstore, or on the Internet, that discuss new car features and prices. These may provide information on the dealer's costs for specific models and options.

- Do some research. It is well worth your time. Shop around to get the best possible deal by comparing models and prices in ads and at dealer showrooms. You may also want to contact car-buying services to make comparisons.

- Plan to negotiate on price. Dealers may be willing to bargain on their profit margin, often between 10 and 20 percent. Usually, this is the difference between the manufacturer's suggested retail price and the invoice price.

- Because the price is a factor in the dealer's calculations regardless of whether you pay cash or finance your car — and also affects your monthly payments — negotiating the price can save you money.

- Consider ordering your new car if you don't see what you want on the dealer's lot. This may involve a delay, but cars on the lot may have options you don't want — and that can raise the price. However, dealers often want to sell their current inventory quickly, so you may be able to negotiate a good deal if an in-stock car meets your needs.

Trading in Your Old Car

Discuss the possibility of a trade-in only after you've negotiated the best possible price for your new car and after you've researched the value of your old car. Check the library for reference books or magazines that can tell you how much it is worth. This information may help you get a better price from the dealer. Though it may take longer to sell your car yourself, you generally will get more money than if you trade it in.

Considering a Service Contract

Service contracts that you may buy with a new car provide for the repair of certain parts or problems. These contracts are offered by manufacturers, dealers, or independent companies and may or may not provide coverage beyond the manufacturer's warranty. Remember that a warranty is included in the price of the car while a service contract costs extra. Before deciding to purchase a service contract, read it carefully and consider these questions:

- What's the difference between the coverage under the warranty and the coverage under the service contract?
- What repairs are covered?
- Is routine maintenance covered?
- Who pays for labor? The parts?
- Who performs the repairs? Can repairs be made elsewhere?
- How long does the service contract last?
- What are the cancellation and refund policies?

Buying a Used Car

Before you start shopping for a used car, you will need to think about your driving habits, your needs, and your budget. You can learn about car models, options, and prices by reading newspaper ads, both display and classified. There is a wealth of information about used cars on the Internet: enter "used car" as the key words and you'll find additional information on how to buy a used car, detailed instructions for conducting a pre-purchase inspection, and ads for cars available for sale, among other information. Libraries and bookstores also have publications that compare car models, options, and costs, and offer information about frequency-of-repair records, safety tests, and mileage. Many of these publications have details on the do's and don'ts of buying a used car. Once you've narrowed your car choices, research the frequency of repair and maintenance costs on the models in auto-related consumer magazines. The U.S. Department of Transportation's Auto Safety Hotline (1-800-424-9393) gives information on recalls.

Some dealers are attracting customers with "no-haggle prices," "factory certified" used cars, and better warranties. Consider the dealer's reputation when you evaluate these ads.

Before you purchase from a dealer, ask about the dealer's return policy, get it in writing and read it carefully. Dealers are not required by law to give used car buyer's a three-day right to cancel. The right to return the car in a few days for a refund exists only if the dealer grants this privilege to buyer's. Dealers may describe the right to cancel as a "cooling-off" period, a money-back guarantee, or a "no questions asked" return policy.

Buyer's Guide

The Federal Trade Commission's Used Car Rule requires dealers to post a buyer's guide in every used car they offer for sale. This includes light-duty vans, light-duty trucks, demonstrators, and program cars. Demonstrators are new cars that have not been owned, leased, or used as rentals, but have been driven by dealer staff. Program cars are low-mileage, current-model-year vehicles returned from short-term leases or rentals. Buyer's Guides do not have to be posted on motorcycles and most recreational vehicles. Anyone who sells less than six cars a year doesn't have to post a Buyer's

Guide. The Buyer's Guide must tell you whether the vehicle is being sold "as is" or with a warranty, and what percentage of the repair costs a dealer will pay under the warranty.

Remember that spoken promises are difficult to enforce. It is wise to get all promises in writing. Keep the Buyer's Guide for reference after the sale. Ask to have the car inspected by an independent mechanic before you buy. When you buy a used car from a dealer, get the original Buyer's Guide that was posted in the vehicle, or a copy. The Guide must reflect any negotiated changes in warranty coverage. It also becomes part of your sales contract and overrides any contrary provisions. For example, if the Buyer's Guide says the car comes with a warranty and the contract says the car is sold "as is," the dealer must give you the warranty described in the Guide. When the dealer offers a vehicle "as is," the box next to the "As Is - No Warranty" disclosure on the Buyer's Guide must be checked. If the box is checked but the dealer promises to repair the vehicle or cancel the sale if you're not satisfied, make sure the promise is written on the Buyer's Guide. Otherwise, you may have a hard time getting the dealer to make good on his word. Some states don't allow "as is" sales for many used vehicles.

Implied Warranties

State laws hold dealers responsible if cars they sell don't meet reasonable quality standards. These obligations are called implied warranties—unspoken, unwritten promises from the seller to the buyer. However, dealers in most states can use the words "as is" or "with all faults" in a written notice to buyer's to eliminate implied warranties. There is no specified time period for implied warranties. If you have a written warranty that doesn't cover your problems, you still may have coverage through implied warranties. That's because when a dealer sells a vehicle with a written warranty or service contract, implied warranties are included automatically. The dealer can't delete this protection. Any limit on an implied warranty's time must be included on the written warranty.

Warranty of Merchantability. The most common type of implied warranty is the warranty of merchantability: the seller promises that the product offered for sale will do what it's supposed to. That a car will run is an example of a warranty of merchantability. This promise applies to the basic functions of a car. It does not cover everything that could go wrong.

Breakdowns and other problems after the sale don't prove the seller breached the warranty of merchantability. A breach occurs only if the buyer can prove that a defect existed at the time of sale. A problem that occurs after the sale may be the result of a defect that existed at the time of sale or not. As a result, a dealer's liability is judged case by case.

Warranty of Fitness for a Particular Purpose. A warranty of fitness for a particular purpose applies when you buy a vehicle based on the dealer's advice that it is suitable for a particular use. For example, a dealer who suggests you buy a specific vehicle for hauling a trailer, in effect, is promising that the vehicle will be suitable for that purpose.

Written Warranties

Dealers who offer a written warranty must complete the warranty section of the Buyer's Guide. Dealers may offer a full or limited warranty on all or some of a vehicle's systems or components. Most used car warranties are limited and their coverage varies. A full warranty includes the following terms and conditions:

- Anyone who owns the vehicle during the warranty period is entitled to warranty service.

- Warranty service will be provided free of charge, including such costs as removing and reinstalling a covered system.

- You have the choice of a replacement or a full refund if, after a reasonable number of tries, the dealer cannot repair the vehicle or a covered system.

- You only have to tell the dealer that warranty service is

needed in order to get it, unless the dealer can prove that it is reasonable to require you to do more.

• Implied warranties have no time limits.

If any of these statements doesn't apply, the warranty is limited.

A full or limited warranty doesn't have to cover the entire vehicle. The dealer may specify that only certain systems are covered. Some parts or systems may be covered by a full warranty while others are covered by a limited warranty. The dealer must check the appropriate box on the Buyer's Guide to indicate whether the warranty is full or limited.

You have the right to see a copy of the dealer's warranty before you buy. Review it carefully to determine what is covered. The warranty gives detailed information, such as how to get repairs for a covered system or part. It also tells who is legally responsible for fulfilling the terms of the warranty. If it's a third party, investigate their reputation and whether they're insured. Find out the name of the insurer, and call to verify the information. Then check out the third-party company with your local Better Business Bureau. Make sure you receive a copy of the dealer's warranty document if you buy a car that is offered with a warranty.

Service Contracts

Like a warranty, a service contract provides repair and/or maintenance for a specific period. But warranties are included in the price of a product, while service contracts cost extra and are sold separately. To decide whether you need a service contract, consider whether the service contract duplicates warranty coverage or offers protection that begins after the warranty runs out. Does the service contract extend beyond the time you expect to own the car? If so, is the service contract transferable or is a shorter contract available?

Questions to ask:
• Does the service contract covers all parts and systems.

Check out all claims carefully. For example, "bumper to bumper" coverage may not mean what you think.

- Is a deductible required and, if so. The amount and terms

- Does the contract covers incidental expenses, such as towing and rental car charges while your car is being serviced.

- Do repairs and routine maintenance, such as oil changes, have to be done at the dealer.

- Is there a cancellation and refund policy for the service contract and, whether there are cancellation fees?

- Is the dealer or company offering the service contract . reputable? Read the contract carefully to determine who is legally responsible for fulfilling the terms of the contract.

If you have a problem that you think is covered by a warranty or service contract, follow the instructions to get service. If a dispute arises, there are several steps you can take.

First, try to work it out with the dealer. Talk with the salesperson or, if necessary, the owner of the dealership. Many problems can be resolved at this level. However, if you believe you're entitled to service, but the dealer disagrees, you can take other steps. If a car manufacturer backs your warranty, contact the local representative of the manufacturer. The local or zone representative is authorized to adjust and decide about warranty service and repairs to satisfy customers. Some manufacturers also are willing to repair certain problems in specific models for free, even if the manufacturer's warranty does not cover the problem. Ask the manufacturer's zone representative or the service department of a franchised dealership that sells your car model whether there is such a policy.

You also might consider using a dispute-resolution organization to arbitrate your disagreement if you and the dealer are willing. Under the terms of many warranties, this may be a required first step before you can sue the dealer or manufacturer. Check your warranty to see if this is the case. If you bought your car from a franchised dealer, you may be able to seek mediation through the Automotive Consumer Action Program (AUTOCAP), a dispute-resolution program coordinated nationally by the National Automobile Dealers Association and sponsored through state and local dealer associations in many cities. If none of these steps is successful, small claims court is an option. Here, you can resolve disputes involving small amounts of money, often without an attorney. The clerk of your local small claims court can tell you how to file a suit and what the dollar limit is in your state.

The Magnuson-Moss Warranty Act also may be helpful. Under this federal law, you can sue based on breach of express warranties, implied warranties, or a service contract. If successful, consumers can recover reasonable attorneys' fees and other court costs. A lawyer can advise you whether this law applies.

Pre-Purchase Independent Inspection

It's best to have any used car inspected by an independent mechanic before you buy it. For about $100 or less, you'll get a general indication of the mechanical condition of the vehicle. An inspection is a good idea even if the car has been "certified" and inspected by the dealer and is being sold with a warranty or service contract. A mechanical inspection is different from a safety inspection. Safety inspections usually focus on conditions that make a car unsafe to drive. They are not designed to determine the overall reliability or mechanical condition of a vehicle.

To find a pre-purchase inspection facility, check the yellow pages under "Automotive Diagnostic Service" or ask friends, relatives, and co-workers for referrals. Look for facilities that display certifications like an Automotive Service Excellence (ASE) seal. Certification indicates that some or all of the technicians meet basic standards of knowledge and competence in specific technical areas.

There are no standard operating procedures for pre-purchase inspections. Ask what the inspection includes, how long it takes, and the price. Get this information in writing.

If the dealer won't let you take the car off the lot, perhaps because of insurance restrictions, you may be able to find a mobile inspection service that will go to the dealer. If that's not an option, ask the dealer to have the car inspected at a facility you designate. You will have to pay the inspection fee.

Once the vehicle has been inspected, ask the mechanic for a written report with a cost estimate for all necessary repairs. Be sure the report includes the vehicle's make, model, and vehicle identification number (VIN). Make sure you understand every item. If you decide to make a purchase offer to the dealer after considering the inspection's results, you can use the estimated repair costs to negotiate the price of the vehicle.

Financing Your Auto

Consider all of your financing options when purchasing a car. While 80% of all car purchases are financed through the dealer, this may not be the best choice for you. Dealers and lenders offer a variety of loan terms and payment schedules. Shop around, compare offers, and negotiate the best deal you can.

Most dealerships have a finance and insurance (F&I) department, which provides one-stop shopping for financing. The F&I department manager will ask you to complete a credit application. Information on this application may include: your name; Social Security number; date of birth; current and previous addresses and length of stay; current and previous employers and length of employment; occupation; sources of income; total gross monthly income; and financial information on existing credit accounts. The dealership will obtain a copy of your credit report, which contains information about current and past credit obligations, your payment record and data from public records (for example, a bankruptcy filing obtained from court documents). For each account, the credit report shows your account number, the type and terms of the account, the credit limit, the most recent balance, and the most recent payment.

Dealers typically sell your contract to an assignee, such as a bank, finance company or credit union. The dealership submits your credit application to one or more of these potential assignees to determine their willingness to purchase your contract from the dealer. These finance companies or other potential assignees will usually evaluate your credit application using automated techniques such as credit scoring, in which a variety of factors, like your credit history, length of employment, income, and expenses, may be weighted and scored. Since the bank, finance company, or credit union does not deal directly with the prospective vehicle purchaser, it bases its evaluation upon what appears on the individual's credit report and score, the completed credit application, and the terms of the sale, such as the amount of the down payment. Each finance company or other potential assignee decides whether it is willing to buy the contract, notifies the dealership of its decision and, if applicable, offers the dealership a wholesale rate at which the assignee will buy the contract, often called the "buy rate."

Your dealer may be able to offer manufacturer incentives, such as reduced finance rates or cash back on certain models. You may see these specials advertised in your area. Make sure you ask your dealer whether the model you are interested in has any special financing offers or rebates. Generally, these discounted rates are not negotiable, may be limited by a consumer's credit history, and are available only for certain models, makes, or model years.

When there are no special financing offers available, you can negotiate the annual percentage rate (APR) and the terms for payment with the dealership, just as you negotiate the price of the vehicle. The APR that you negotiate with the dealer is usually higher than the wholesale rate described earlier. This negotiation can occur before or after the dealership accepts and processes your credit application. Your credit history, current finance rates, competition, market conditions, and special offers are among the factors that influence your APR.

Sometimes, dealers offer very low financing rates for specific cars or models, but may not be willing to negotiate on the price of these cars. To qualify for the special rates, you may be required to make a large down payment. With these conditions, you may find that it's sometimes more affordable to pay higher financing charges on a car that is lower in price or to buy a car that requires a smaller down payment.

DØ THIS

If you decide to finance your car, be aware that the financing obtained by the dealer, even if the dealer contacts lenders on your behalf, may not be the best deal you can get.

When financing a car, put down the largest down payment that you can afford. This will reduce the overall cost of the loan.

Contact lenders directly. Compare the financing they offer you with the financing the dealer offers you. Because offers vary, shop around for the best deal, comparing the annual percentage rate (APR) and the length of the loan. When negotiating to finance a car, be wary of focusing only on the monthly payment. The total amount you will pay depends on the price of the car you negotiate, the APR, and the length of the loan.

Avoid credit insurance to pay off your loan if you should die or become disabled. You can get a better deal by purchasing life or disability insurance from your insurance agent.

18

Stay Out Of Trouble With The IRS

"First do no harm."

Hippocrates

One of the most important pledges ever created is the Hippocratic oath taken by new physicians. The oath says, in part, to "first, do no harm." This is indeed a worthy objective. It is desirable no matter what the pursuit. It is particularly relevant in the area of tax planning. The most costly outcomes often result from the ill-advised actions that people take. Effective long-term tax management involves not just making smart tax moves, but also avoiding dumb tax moves. It often takes years for those with tax problems to free themselves from the clutches of the IRS. The first objective of intelligent tax management, therefore, should be to first do no harm; in other words to just stay out of trouble.

Filing Your Income Tax Returns

Your U.S. and state (if applicable) income tax returns are due on April 15th. You are subject to late filing penalties if your income tax returns are not filed on time and late payment penalties and interest if your taxes are paid late.

If you are unable to complete your tax returns by April 15, be sure to get an extension and include a check for the amount of taxes that you expect to owe with the return. If you can't pay all of the taxes that you expect to owe, pay as much as you can, then file the return as soon as possible. Many people make the mistake of not filing a tax return because they expect to owe additional taxes. This only makes a bad situation worse.

Withholding Exemptions

Many people claim more exemptions (for withholding tax purposes) than they are entitled to in order to increase their take-home pay. Individuals often claim ten, 15 or more exemptions so that their employers withhold little or no income taxes from their wages. While this will increase their take-home pay it can cause big problems when their income tax returns are filed. Insufficient withholding can result in the taxpayer owing taxes and penalties for under withholding of income taxes. If the practice of under withholding occurs over several years, it can result in mounting taxes, interest and penalties. It often takes years for those who owe taxes to free themselves from the clutches of the IRS.

DO THIS™

Claim no more withholding exemptions than you are entitled to. When you claim more withholding exemptions than you are entitled to you are in effect borrowing money from Uncle Sam. The interest and penalties charged by the IRS make this one of the most expensive loans that you can get. Avoid the temptation to generate what appears to be easy cash by claiming more withholding exemptions than you are entitled to. Instead, prepare a cash flow plan if you are having trouble making ends meet.

Early Withdrawals From Retirement Plans

Taking an early withdrawal from your retirement plan is among the worst tax and financial moves that you can make. This situation is generally the result of deficiencies in other areas of cash management. It is one of the worst things you can do from a tax standpoint. These withdrawals are subject to a 10% penalty in addition to being added to your taxable income.

Example: John and Mary Late have total income of $105,000 and taxable income of $70,000. They have decided to withdraw $20,000 from John's 401(k) plans to purchase new furniture that they have wanted for quite some time. They will also take $5,000 of the withdrawal to pay down credit card debt. They justify the withdrawal by rationalizing that since they are paying down credit debt this is a positive action. Let's see whether it is:

Penalty on withdrawal:	$20,000 x 10% =	$2,000
Income tax	20,000 x 35% =	7,000
State income tax	20,000 x 5% =	1,000

Total taxes and penalties on $20,000		$ 10,000
		=======

When John and Mary took an early distribution from their retirement account, 50% of their money went to taxes and penalties. Had the money been left in the account, it would have grown to $64,442, assuming 8% annual earnings, if it had remained in John's 401(k) account for 15 years when he reached retirement age.

Avoid Early Withdrawals From Retirement Plans.
People take early withdrawals from their retirement plans to meet emergency cash needs. This situation is generally the result of deficiencies in other areas of their cash management. It is often seen as a source of last resort. It is, nevertheless, a very poor option. A better option would be to borrow from your 401(k) plan. Many 401(k) plans allow you to borrow. You avoid being taxed and penalized if you pay back the loan by the due date of the loan.

19

Pay No More Income Taxes Than Necessary

"In the middle of difficulty lies opportunity."

Albert Einstein

It has been said that death and taxes are the only sure things in this life. We pay many kinds and forms of taxes. There are sales taxes on purchases of goods. We pay property taxes and of course income taxes. Federal, state and local taxes consume between 25% and 60% of our income. The manner in which you manage your tax obligations is an important piece in the wealth-building puzzle. Despite all the talk about tax cuts, taxes are likely to represent the single largest annual expenditure now and for the foreseeable future. It is therefore important for you to take advantage of all tax deductions available to you. The following are positive actions you can take to improve your tax picture.

Tax Saving Opportunities

Multi-Support Agreements. You are generally required to contribute over half of the support of a relative in order to claim a dependency exemption for them on your tax return. If you and another person or persons contribute to the support of someone, a Multiple Support Agreement (IRS form 2120) allows you to take turns claiming the dependency exemption for that person. The Multiple Support

Agreement spells out who can claim the dependent in any given year.

Example: Mary and her two brothers, William and Bobby, all pitch in to support their elderly mother. Her monthly expenses are:

Rent	$ 750
Utilities	250
Groceries	500
Prescriptions	125
Other	250

Total	$ 1,875
	======

Their mother's only source of income is her $900 monthly social security check. Mary and her two brothers make up the difference, each contributing $325 each month toward her support.

Agnes Williams – Source of Support

Social Security benefits	$ 900
Mary Jones	325
William Williams	325
Bobby Williams	325

Total	$ 1,875
	======

Since Mary and her two brothers combine to provide more than 50% of their mother's support, they may take turns claiming her as a dependent on their tax returns.

Tax-Free Income From Sale of Home. A married couple is allowed to exclude, from their taxable income, up to $500,000 of profit from the sale of their personal residence if they have owned and lived in it for two years. Single taxpayers can exclude $250,000.

Example: Erik and Edie Monroe paid $150,000 for their home in 1994. Their children have all left home and they have decided that they don't need all of the space that this house provides and they no longer want to incur the cost of its upkeep. They decide to put the house on the market. It sells for $325,000. Their gain, after commissions and other sales expenses, is $155,000. They are not taxed on any of this gain.

Donate Old Clothing and Furniture to Charitable Organizations. You are allowed a tax deduction for the fair market value of property that you donate to a church or qualified charitable organization. This is particularly advantageous because it allows you to get a tax deduction without an outlay of cash.

Donation of Auto to Charitable Organizations. Your deduction of a car, boat or airplane to a qualified charitable organization generally is limited to the organization's gross proceeds from the sale vehicle. If the organization sells the car (you donated) for $500 or less, you can deduct the smaller of $500 or the fair market value of the car on the date of the contribution. If the value of the vehicle is more than $500, you can take a tax deduction for the amount the organization's gross proceeds from the sale or the car's fair market value on the date of the contribution, whichever is smaller. You should obtain a written acknowledgement (form 1098-C) from the charity within 30 days of the donation. This form provides documentation of the use or disposition of the vehicle including the amount of gross proceeds received by the charity. A copy of this form should be attached to your income tax return.

Take Educational Tax Credits. You are allowed tax credit when you pay for post-secondary education costs. The Hope Credit provides a credit of up to $1,500 per student for each of the first two years of college. The Hope Credit is based on qualified education expenses you pay for yourself, your spouse or a dependent you claim on your tax return. Generally, the credit is allowed for qualified education expenses paid during the tax year for a school period beginning during the tax year in the first three months following the end of the tax year.

Example: You paid $3,500 in December 2006 for qualified tuition for the Spring 2007 semester beginning in January 2006. You use the $3,500 in figuring your deduction or credit for 2006. Eligible educational institutions include colleges, universities, vocational schools, and other post-secondary educational institutions.

DⓋTHIS™

Take Dependent Care Credits. You are allowed a tax credit when you pay dependent care expenses for:

1. Your qualifying child who is your dependent

2. Your spouse who was physically or mentally not able to care for himself or herself and lived with you for more than half of the year, or

3. A dependent, who was physically or mentally not able to care for himself or herself, lived with you for more than half the year.

Example: Bill and Mary Smith are married with two pre-school children, ages two and four. Their adjusted gross income is $78,500. Bill earned $60,000 and Mary earned $18,500. During the year, they pay work-related expenses of $3,000 for childcare for their son Daniel at the neighbor's home and $2,800 for their daughter Alice at the Peachtree Nursery School. They are allowed to use $5,800 to compute their childcare tax credit.

DⓋTHIS™

Maintain Good Tax Records.
Maintaining good records is the key to identifying eligible tax deductions and supporting the deductions you claim if you are required to do so by the IRS. The statute of limitations for the IRS to assess additional tax to your income tax return is three years from the later of the due date of the return or the date it was filed.

Example: Darius and Lillian Carver filed their 2006 income tax return on March 1, 2007. Since the due date of the return is April 15, 2007, the IRS has until April 15, 2010 to audit and assess additional income tax to this income tax return.

The statute of limitations is extended to six years if more than 25% of gross income has been omitted from the tax return. There is no statute of limitation when a taxpayer files a fraudulent return.

File Returns Using the Most Advantageous Filing Status. Your filing status determines what tax schedule you must use to compute your tax liability. Married filing jointly is the filing status with the most favorable tax rates, followed by head of household, single and married filing separately. In order to file as married filing jointly a couple must be legally married on December 31st. (The IRS does not recognize same sex marriages.) Unmarried persons who provide a home for a qualifying child or parent can file as head of household.

Take Deductions for Unpaid Loans. You can take a bad-debt deduction when you are unable to collect money that you are owed. A personal loan that becomes worthless is treated as a non-business bad debt and is reported as a short-term capital loss on your income tax return. To be deductible, non-business bad debt must be totally worthless. The debt must also arise from a debtor-creditor relationship based on a valid and enforceable obligation to repay a fixed or determinable sum of money. It is more difficult to claim a tax loss for loans to relatives. The IRS often questions tax losses claimed for loans to relatives, particularly loans to parents, siblings, or children. To protect your ability to get a tax deduction for any loans that become worthless, especially those to relatives, you should:

- Get the borrower to sign a note that includes a repayment schedule and an interest rate.

- Obtain collateral. Even if the value of the collateral doesn't cover the entire amount of the loan, this is further evidence that monies being advanced are a loan and not a gift.

- Attempt to collect the loan if it is unpaid after the due date. These attempts could be evidenced by demand letters, documented telephone calls, and other efforts.

DO✓THIS™

Deduct Stock Loss. You are able to deduct up to $3,000 in stock losses against your ordinary income each year. If your capital losses are more than your capital gains, you are able to offset up to $3,000 of capital gains against your other income. Any capital losses in excess of $3,000 may be carried over to future years.

Example: Mike and Gloria Wells sold property in 2006 that resulted in an $8,000 capital loss. They are allowed to deduct $3,000 on their 2006 tax return. The unused part of the 2006 loss ($8,000 - $3,000) is carried over to 2007.

DO✓THIS™

Take Deductions for Charitable Mileage. An often-overlooked tax deduction is the one allowed for mileage incurred when doing work for your church or non-profit organization. You are allowed to deduct $.16 per mile for charitable mileage.

Example: Lora does volunteer work for her church. Two days a week she goes to her church to pick up food baskets for delivery to sick and shut-in members. She travels 25 miles each of those days during this work. Her charitable miles total 2,600 for the year. During 2006 she is entitled to a tax deduction of $416.00. This is reported as a cash contribution on schedule A of her income tax return.

The following are the most commonly asked questions that I get in my practice as a certified public accountant.

Questions and Answers

Q. *What is the difference between a tax deduction and a tax credit?*

A. A tax deduction reduces the amount of income that you are taxed on. A tax credit reduces your actual income tax.

Impact of $1,000 Tax Deduction (A) and $1,000 tax credit (B):

	A	B
Income	$ 50,000	$ 50,000
Itemized deductions	(5,000)	(5,000)
Exemptions	(5,500)	(5,500)
	------------	------------
	39,500	39,500
Less: $1,000 tax deduction	(1,000)	(0)
	------------	------------
Taxable income	38,500	39,500
	------------	------------
Tax on taxable income	7,583	7,877
Less: 1,000 tax credit	(0)	(1,000)
	------------	------------
Tax	7,583	6,877
Income tax withheld	7,500	7,500
	------------	------------
Tax owed	$ 83	(0)
Refund due	(0)	$ 623
	========	=======

Q. *My wife and I do a lot of work for our church. Can we deduct the value of our time and expenses that we incur when doing work for our church?*

A. You cannot deduct the value of the time you spend doing work for a church of charity. You can, however, deduct the following:

- Mileage incurred going to your church or charity to do volunteer work and mileage incurred in the performance of this work
- Travel expenses (hotel, airfare, etc.) incurred while doing church work, if those expenses are not reimbursed
- Out of pocket expenses incurred while doing charitable work.

Q. *We hear a lot about the so-called marriage penalty that many couples incur when both husband and wife work. What is the marriage penalty and can we avoid it by filing separate returns?*

A. The marriage penalty is the additional income tax that two-income married couples incur when they file a joint return over the amount they would have paid had they filed separate returns as two single taxpayers. Filing separate income tax returns generally results in higher income taxes for married couples. Married couples who file separately are subject to higher tax rates and are denied certain deductions.

Q. *My mother just moved into our home. She has no income other than her social security check. My wife and I provide for her total support including the cost of having a caretaker for her while we are at work. What tax benefits are we entitled to?*

A. By providing more than half of her total support, you are entitled to claim your mother as an exemption. You may also deduct any of her medical expenses that you pay.

Additionally, because your mother is physically incapable of caring for herself, you may claim a tax credit of 20% to 30% of the cost of having someone care for your mother while you and your wife are at work.

Q. *Can I take a tax deduction for loans made to friends or family that are not repaid?*

A. In order for an unpaid loan to be deductible as a bad debt you must be able to establish that the debt is worthless, that it arose from a debtor-creditor relationship, and that there was a valid and enforceable obligation to repay the money.

20

Make Sure You Are Covered

"Patch the roof before it starts raining."

John F. Kennedy

Insurance is something you need just in case you don't live forever and you don't live a life in which nothing ever goes wrong. Comedians have been known to describe life insurance as something you purchase with money that you could be using to enjoy your life so that others can enjoy their lives after you are dead. All jokes aside, responsible money management requires that you have adequate insurance coverage. Being without insurance when needed can result in financial disaster for you or your loved ones. Insurance should be something, however, that you buy and not be sold. In other words, you should not be sold a policy based on an elaborate presentation that you don't understand. You should buy insurance based on your understanding of your needs and the policy's features.

Having insurance coverage that you don't need is a waste of money. It is therefore important that you know what type of insurance coverage you need and don't need. Life, health, disability and auto insurance are types of insurance coverage that almost everyone needs.

Life Insurance

The purpose of life insurance is to provide cash to your family if something happens to you. The money your dependents will receive (the "death benefit") is an important financial resource: It can help pay the mortgage, run the household, and ensure that your dependents aren't burdened with debt. The proceeds from a life insurance policy could mean that they won't have to sell assets to pay outstanding bills or taxes. What's more, there is no federal income tax on life insurance benefits. One rule of thumb is to buy life insurance equal to five to seven times your annual gross income.

Permanent Insurance

Permanent insurance provides lifelong insurance protection. With permanent insurance, you will have life insurance coverage as long as you pay the insurance premiums. This type of policy makes sense for you if you keep it for a long period of time. They become very expensive if they are canceled after a few months or a few years.

Permanent life insurance is sold under a variety of names: whole life, ordinary life, universal life, variable life and adjustable life. The distinguishing feature in a permanent life insurance policy is a feature known as "cash value" or "cash surrender value." This feature, which is not found in most term insurance policies, provides you with the following options:

- You can cancel or "surrender" the policy—in total or in part—and receive the cash value as a lump sum. There is generally little or no cash value in the early years of a life policy.

- You can use the cash value to continue your current insurance protection for a specified time or to provide a lesser amount of protection for your lifetime, if you need to stop paying premiums.

- You usually can borrow money from the insurance company, using the cash value in your life insurance as collateral. The insurance company will give you this loan regardless of your credit score. There will, however, be a reduced death benefit if the loan and accrued interest is not repaid.

You should keep in mind that the cash value of a policy is different from the policy's face amount. The face amount is the money that will be paid at death or policy maturity. Cash value is the amount available if you surrender a policy before its maturity or your death. The cash value increases over time as you pay premiums.

Advantages of permanent insurance include:

- As long as the premiums are paid, protection is guaranteed for life.

- Premium costs can be fixed or flexible to meet personal financial needs.

- The policy accumulates a cash value against which you can borrow. (Loans must be paid back with interest or your beneficiaries will receive a reduced death benefit.) You can borrow against the policy's cash value to pay premiums or use the cash value to provide paid-up insurance.

- The policy's cash value can be surrendered—in total or in part—for cash or converted into an annuity. (An annuity is an insurance product that provides an income for a person's lifetime or a specific period.)

- A provision or "rider" can be added to a policy that gives you the option to purchase additional insurance without taking a medical exam or having to furnish evidence of insurability.

Disadvantages of permanent insurance include:

- Required premium levels may make it hard to buy enough protection.

- It generally costs more than term insurance in the early years.

Term Insurance

Term insurance is best suited for meeting temporary insurance needs. Many people cannot afford to purchase permanent insurance for all the life insurance coverage they need. This is particularly true for young families when the bread-winners are just getting started in their careers. Term or some combination of term and permanent insurance is often the best option in that situation. Term insurance provides insurance coverage for a specific period of time. It pays a benefit only if you die during the term. Some term insurance policies can be renewed when you reach the end of the term, which can be from one to 30 years. The premium rates increase at each renewal date. Many policies require that you present evidence of insurability at renewal to qualify for the lowest rates. A couple with young children might purchase 15-or 20-year term policies that provide insurance coverage until their children reach their majority.

Advantages of term insurance include:

- Initial premiums generally are lower than those for perma nent insurance, allowing you to buy higher levels of coverage at a younger age when the need for protection often is greatest.
- It's good for covering needs that will disappear in time, such as mortgages or car loans.

Disadvantages include:

- Premiums increase as you grow older.
- Coverage may terminate at the end of the term or become too expensive to continue.
- The policy generally doesn't offer cash value or paid-up insurance.

Health Insurance

There is nothing more important than having adequate health insurance when you need it. Health care costs are high, and getting higher. You need health insurance to protect you and your family against large unexpected medical bills. Most Americans get health insurance through their employer.

Employer Sponsored Plans

Persons who get health insurance through their employers generally have to choose between Health Maintenance Organization (HMO's) and Preferred Provider Organizations (PPO's).

Health Maintenance Organizations (HMO's)

A Health Maintenance Organization, commonly referred to as an HMO, is an organization of hospitals and doctors that have contracted with an insurance company to offer their services for a fixed price. When you have medical insurance coverage with an HMO you are required to select a primary care physician, who manages all aspects of your healthcare. Health maintenance organizations are pre-paid health plans. As an HMO member, you pay a monthly premium. In exchange, the HMO provides comprehensive care for you and your family, including doctors' visits, hospital stays, emergency care, surgery, lab tests, x-rays, and therapy. The HMO arranges for this care either directly in its own group practice or through doctors and other health care professionals under contract. Usually, your choices of doctors and hospitals are limited to those that have agreements with the HMO to provide care. However, exceptions are made in emergencies or when medically necessary.

There may be a small co-payment for each office visit, such as $5 for a doctor's visit or $25 for hospital emergency room treatment. Your total medical costs will likely be lower and more predictable in an HMO than with fee-for-service insurance.

Because HMO's receive a fixed fee for your covered medical care, it is in their interest to make sure you get basic health care for problems before they become serious. HMO's typically provide preventive care, such as office visits, immunizations, well-baby checkups, mammograms, and physicals. The range of services covered varies in HMO's, so it is important to compare available plans. Some services, such as outpatient mental health care, often are provided only on a limited basis.

Many people like HMO's because they do not require claim forms for office visits or hospital stays. Instead, members present a card, like a credit card, at the doctor's office or hospital.

However, in an HMO you may have to wait longer for an appointment than you would with a fee-for-service plan. There may be limits on medical tests, surgery, mental health care, home care, or other services offered.

In almost all HMO's, you either are assigned or you choose one doctor to serve as your primary care doctor. This doctor monitors your health and provides most of your medical care, referring you to specialists and other health care professionals as needed. You usually cannot see a specialist without a referral from your primary care doctor who is expected to manage the care you receive. This is one way that HMO's can limit your choice.

What is the service area of the HMO? Where are the facilities located in your community that serves HMO members? How convenient to your home and workplace are the doctors, hospitals, and emergency care centers that make up the HMO network? What happens if you or a family member are out of town and need medical treatment? What will the HMO plan cost? What is the yearly total for monthly fees? In addition, are there co-payments for office visits, emergency care, prescribed drugs, or other services? How much?

Preferred Provider Organizations (PPO's)

The preferred provider organization is a combination of traditional fee-for-service plans and an HMO. As in an HMO, there is a limited number of doctors and hospitals to choose from. When you use those providers (sometimes called "preferred" providers, other times called "network" providers), most of your medical bills are covered.

When you go to doctors in the PPO, you present a card and do not have to fill out forms. Usually there is a small co-payment for each visit. For some services, you may have to pay a deductible and coinsurance.

As with an HMO, a PPO requires that you choose a primary care doctor to monitor your health care. Most PPO's cover preventive care. This usually includes visits to the doctor, well-baby care, immunizations, and mammograms.

There may be limits on medical tests, out-of-hospital care, mental health care, prescription drugs, or other services.

In a PPO, you can use doctors who are not part of the plan and still receive some coverage. At these times, you will pay a larger portion of the bill yourself (and also fill out the claims forms). Some people like this option because, even if their doctor is not a part of the network, it means they don't have to change doctors to join a PPO.

Other Health Insurance Options

If you do not get health insurance through a plan sponsored by your employer, you need to obtain it through other means. One option is to buy an individual policy. But you should compare your options and shop carefully because coverage and costs vary from company to company. Individual plans may not offer benefits as broad as those in-group plans. Try to get a non-cancellable policy (also called a guaranteed renewable policy), then you will receive individual insurance under that policy as long as you keep paying the monthly premium. The insurance company can raise the cost, but cannot cancel your coverage. Many companies now offer a conditionally renewable policy. This means that the insurance company can cancel all policies like yours, not just yours. This protects you from being singled out. But it doesn't protect you from losing coverage.

Key Health Insurance Terms

Coinsurance: The amount you are required to pay for medical care in a fee-for-service plan after you have met your deductible. The coinsurance rate is usually expressed as a percentage. For example, if the insurance company pays 80 percent of the claim, you pay 20 percent.

Coordination of Benefits: A system to eliminate duplication of benefits when you are covered under more than one group plan. Benefits under the two plans usually are limited to no more than 100 percent of the claim.

Co-payment (co-pay): Another way of sharing medical costs. You pay a flat fee every time you receive a medical service (for example, $5 for every visit to the doctor). The insurance company pays the rest.

Covered Expenses: Most insurance plans, whether they are fee-for-service, HMO's, or PPO's, do not pay for all services. Some may not pay for prescription drugs. Others may not pay for mental health care. Covered services are those medical procedures the insurer agrees to pay for. They are listed in the policy.

Deductible: The amount of money you must pay each year to cover your medical care expenses before your insurance policy starts paying.

Exclusions: Specific conditions or circumstances for which the policy will not provide benefits.

HMO (Health Maintenance Organization): Prepaid health plans. You pay a monthly premium and the HMO covers your doctors' visits, hospital stays, emergency care, surgery, checkups, lab tests, x-rays, and therapy. You must use the doctors and hospitals designated by the HMO.

Managed Care: Ways to manage costs, use, and quality of the health care system. All HMO's and PPO's, and many fee-for-service plans, have managed care.

Maximum Out-of-Pocket: The most money you will be required to pay a year for deductibles and coinsurance. It is a stated dollar amount set by the insurance company, in addition to regular premiums.

Non-cancellable Policy: A policy that guarantees you can receive insurance, as long as you pay the premium. It is also called a guaranteed renewable policy.

PPO (Preferred Provider Organization): A combination of traditional fee-for-service plans and an HMO. When you use the doctors and hospitals that are part of the PPO, you can have a larger part of your medical bills covered. You can use other doctors, but at a higher cost.

Pre-existing Condition: A health problem that existed before the date your insurance became effective.

Premium: The amount you or your employer pays in exchange for insurance coverage.

Primary Care Doctor: Usually your first contact for health care. This is often a family physician or internist, but some women use their gynecologist. A primary care doctor monitors your health, diagnoses and treats minor health problems, and refers you to specialists if another level of care is needed.

Provider: Any person (doctor, nurse, dentist) or institution (hospital or clinic) that provides medical care.

Third-Party Payer: Any payer for health care services other than you. This can be an insurance company, an HMO, a PPO, or the federal government.

Buying Health Insurance

Before you buy any health insurance policy, make sure you know what it will pay for and what it won't. To find out about individual health insurance plans, you can call insurance companies or other providers in your community, or speak to the agent who handles your car or house insurance.

Tips when shopping for individual insurance:

- Shop carefully. Policies differ widely in coverage and cost. Contact different insurance companies, or ask your agent to show you policies from several insurers so you can compare them.

- Make sure the policy protects you from large medical costs.

- Read and understand the policy. Make sure it provides the kind of coverage that's right for you. You don't want unpleasant surprises when you're sick or in the hospital.

- Check to see that the policy states the date that the policy will begin paying (some have a waiting period before coverage begins), and what is covered or excluded from coverage.

- Make sure there is a "free look" clause. Most companies give you at least ten days to look over your policy after you receive it. If you decide it is not for you, you can return it and have your premium refunded.

- Beware of single disease insurance policies. There are some policies that offer protection for only one disease, such as cancer. If you already have health insurance, your regular plan probably already provides all the coverage you need. Check to see what protection you have before buying any more insurance.

Disability Insurance

Disability insurance replaces income you lose if you have a long-term illness or injury and cannot work. Disability insurance is one of the most important types of insurance coverage. It is also one of the most overlooked. If you are between the ages of 15 and 65, you are much more likely to be disabled than you are to die. Keep in mind that disability insurance does not cover the cost of rehabilitation if you are injured. Check your major medical insurance to see whether it is covered there. Some employers offer group disability insurance and this may be one of the benefits where you work. Or you might be eligible for some government-sponsored programs that provide disability benefits. Many different kinds of individual policies are also available.

When purchasing disability insurance you should be aware of the elimination period, benefit period, benefits paid and the degree of disability required to qualify for a benefit.

Elimination period: This represents the amount of time that you have to wait (after you become disabled) before you begin to receive benefits. Elimination periods may be 7, 30, 60 or 90 days. The premium is lower for longer elimination periods.

Benefit period: The benefit period is the maximum period of time in which you can receive disability benefits. The benefit period is generally stated in a number of years. It may also be stated "to age 65." Disability policies generally do not pay beyond age 65.

Benefits paid: This is the amount of monthly income that you will receive after the elimination period.

Definition of disability: The definition of disability is the most important provision in your disability policy. Policies are generally as "own occupation" or "any occupation" basis. Under an "own occupation" policy, you are eligible for benefits when you cannot work in your present occupation. Under an "any occupation" policy, you are eligible for benefits when you cannot work in any occupation. The "own occupation" policy is much more desirable.

DO☑THIS™

> **Purchase disability insurance if you do not presently have disability coverage. Obtain a policy that has an "own occupation" definition of disability. You can elect a 30- or 60-day elimination period if that makes the policy affordable for you.**

Auto Insurance

If you drive a car, you must have auto insurance. There are four types of auto insurance coverages: liability insurance; medical insurance; uninsured insurance; and physical insurance.

Liability Coverage (Coverage A)

Liability coverage insures you when you are held responsible for the losses of others. Bodily injury coverage insures against bodily injury to others, including pedestrians. Your policy should have limits of least 100,000/300,000. This means you have coverage of $100,000 for each person injured and up to $300,000 per accident.

Property damage covers damage to another vehicle, road signs or buildings. You should have at least the greater of $25,000 or the required minimum in your state.

Medical Payments Insurance (Coverage B)

This insurance covers medical expenses, incurred because of an auto accident, of driver or passengers. This insurance also covers family members of the insured who are injured while passengers in any car, or who suffer injuries when on foot or riding a bicycle.

Uninsured Motorist Insurance (Coverage C)

This insurance protects you against losses incurred in an accident when the other driver, who is at fault, is uninsured or underinsured. Uninsured motorist protection with 50/100 limits provides up to $50,000 coverage per person and $100,000 per accident. This coverage is generally a good buy, often costing as little as $50 per year.

Physical Damage (Collision) Insurance (Coverage D Collision)

Collision coverage pays for the cost of repairs to your car for damage that results from an auto accident, regardless of who is at fault.

Purchasing the Collision Damage Waiver (CDW) can nearly double your daily rate. A much better option is to ensure that you have this coverage through other sources. Your auto policy probably covers rental cars if you have collision and comprehensive coverage on that policy. If not, you may still be covered if you charged the rental to a Visa, MasterCard, American Express, or Discover card. You should check with your auto insurance company or credit card company to determine the coverage offered for rental cars.

Comprehensive

Comprehensive coverage covers theft and pays for damage to your car that results from fire, flood, vandalism, and other random acts.

DO✓THIS™

Make sure that you have adequate automobile insurance coverage. While state laws generally require that you have policy limits of 100,000/300,000 you should get a policy with at least $300,000/500,000 of coverage. The additional coverage is well worth the additional cost. Your auto policy should also include uninsured motorist protection with 50/100 limits ($50,000 coverage per person and $100,000 per accident).

Determine the rating of the insurance company before you purchase one of their policies. The following are the leading companies that rate insurance companies.

A.M. Best – www.ambest.com
Fitch Ratings – www.fitchratings.com
Moody's Investors Services – www.moodys.com
Standard & Poor's – www.standardandpoors.com
Weiss Ratings – www.weissratings.com

List the key information on all of your insurance policies and retain it in one location.

Insurance Control Record

LIFE				
Insurance Company	**Insured**	**Policy Number**	**Coverage**	**Contact Number**

HEALTH				
Insurance Company	**Insured**	**Policy Number**	**Coverage**	**Contact Number**

DISABILITY				
Insurance Company	**Insured**	**Policy Number**	**Coverage**	**Contact Number**

Insurance Control Record (Continued)

AUTO				
Insurance Company	**Insured**	**Policy Number**	**Coverage**	**Contact Number**

HOMEOWNERS / RENTERS				
Insurance Company	**Insured**	**Policy Number**	**Coverage**	**Contact Number**

OTHER INSURANCE				
Insurance Company	**Insured**	**Policy Number**	**Coverage**	**Contact Number**

Happiness is not pleasure, it is victory.

Zig Zigler

21

A Few Words About Retirement

**"They talk of the dignity of work. Bosh.
The dignity is in leisure."**

Herman Melville

It is never too early to start preparing for retirement. The actions that you take early in life will determine when you will be able to retire and the quality of your retirement. Doing little things today can make a big difference later on. When it comes to your retirement, there are two pertinent questions.

- How much retirement income will I need?

- Where will my retirement income come from?

How Much Retirement Income Will You Need?

Your retirement income requirements will depend on the kind of retirement you want to enjoy. Someone who plans to live a quiet, modest retirement in a low-cost part of the country will need a lot less money than someone who plans to be active, take expensive vacations, and live in an expensive region. Expenses typically decline for retirees: income taxes generally decrease and work-related costs usually disappear. Your medical expenses, however, will probably increase. If you still have a home and a mortgage your overall expenses may not decline much. An easy rule of thumb is that you'll need to replace 70 to 90 percent of your pre-retirement income. If you're making $50,000 a year (before taxes), you will probably need $35,000 to $45,000 a year in retirement income to enjoy the same standard of living you had before retirement.

How Long Will You Live in Retirement?

Based on current estimates, a man retiring at age 55 today can expect to live approximately 23 years in retirement. A female retiring today at age 55 can expect to live approximately 27 years. These are average figures and how long you can expect to live will depend on factors such as your general health and family history. In general though, people are living longer today than they did in the past, and virtually all experts expect the trend toward living longer to continue.

Where Will Your Retirement Income Come From?

401(k) Plans

A 401(k) is an excellent vehicle for building investment as-sets. A 401(k) plan is a retirement plan established by your employer for the benefit of the employees. This plan allows you to set aside a percentage of your pay, often with matching contributions from your employer. Your contributions to your employer-sponsored 401(k) plan are exempt from federal and state income tax. Both the employer contributions (if any) and any growth in the 401(k) are tax-deferred until withdrawn. Similar to an individual retirement account (IRA), a 401(k) is designed primarily as a retirement savings plan. The IRS will penalize you for any withdrawals taken before you reach the age of 59½, except for special circumstances. The earlier in life that you start investing for retirement, the easier it will be for you to retire comfortably. You need only invest a fraction of the money, in your twenties, that you would have to invest in your forties to meet your retirement needs.

Example: May Brooks' first job out of college was with a prestigious law firm in her hometown. She was hired as an administrative assistant to a group of lawyers. She was 21 years old. After being on the job for six months she was allowed to participate in the firm's 401(k) plan. Under the terms of the plan she was allowed to contribute up to 5% of her salary to the plan, with the firm matching her contributions up to the first 3% of her salary. May made the maximum contribution to the 401(k) plan each year of her employment. May worked at the law firm for five years and then left to start a family. The growth in her 401(k), assuming 8% annual earnings, account was as follows:

May's Age	Salary	May's Contribution	Employer Contribution	Total For Year	Growth To Age 65
22	$40,000	$2,000	$1,200	$3,200	$70,400 *
23	42,000	2,100	1,260	3,360	73,250 *
24	44,100	2,205	1,323	3,528	76,644 *
24	46,300	2,315	1,389	3,704	80,000 *
25	48,600	2,430	1,458	3,888	83,200 *
Total	$221,000	$ 11,050	$ 6,630	$17,680	$383,349
* Approximate					

After working only five years, May has a retirement account that will be valued at over $383,000 when she reaches the age of 65. May contributed $11,050 to her 401(k) account with her employer adding $6,630. This fantastic growth is due to the fact that these funds are allowed to grow for approximately 40 years. She will have over $383,000 available to her at retirement even if she never works another day in her life. May plans to earn 20 additional quarters before she reaches retirement age so that she will also be eligible to receive social security benefits.

Let's compare May's situation with Bob Later who doesn't give any thought to his retirement until he reaches the age of fifty.

Bob Later has lived in the fast lane most of his adult life. He has always had good paying jobs but he spent money as fast as he earned it. "Tomorrow will take care of itself," was his motto. The light finally went on when he turned 50. He had one child, a son, who was now married and living in another state. Many of Bob's friends were approaching retirement age. They often discussed their plans for retirement.

Bob began to think about what he would need in the way of retirement income and had a severe panic attack. He went to the company's human resource department to get information about his employer's 401(k) plan. Under the terms of the plan he was allowed to contribute up to 5% of his salary to the plan with the firm matching up to the first 2% of his contributions. He immediately signed documents that called for him to make the maximum contribution. The growth in his 401(k) account until his retirement is as follows:

Bob's Age	Salary	Bob's Contribution	Employer Contribution	Total For Year	Growth To Age 65
51	$70,000	$3,500	$1,400	$4,900	$14,392
52	73,500	3,675	1,470	5,145	13,992
53	77,175	3,859	1,543	5,402	16,603
54	81,000	4,050	1,620	5,670	13,220
55	85,000	4,250	1,700	5,950	12,845
56	89,250	4,462	1,785	6,247	12,488
57	93,700	4,685	1,874	6,559	12,140
58	98,400	4,920	1,968	6,888	11,805
59	103,300	5,165	2,066	7,231	11,474
60	108,500	5,425	2,170	7,595	11,159
61	113,925	5,696	2,278	7,974	10,848
62	119,600	5,980	2,392	8,372	10,546
63	125,600	6,280	2,512	8,792	10,255
64	131,900	6,595	2,638	9,233	9,972
65	138,495	6,925	2,770	9,695	9,695
Total	$1,509,345	$ 75,467	$30,186	$105,653	$177,544

Bob and his employer contributed a total of $105,653 to Bob's 401(k) account over a 15-year period. This had grown to $177,544 when Bob reached retirement age. May's account grew to over $383,000 even though she and her employer contributed only $17,680 to her 401(k) account. May started early. While Bob started late, he was still better off than he would be if had not started at all.

DⒸTHIS

Start investing for your retirement as soon as possible. The sooner you start putting money into a retirement account, the easier it will be for you to retire in style.

You should allocate 100% retirement plan assets to common stock fund (not your company stock) until you are within ten years of retiring.

Then you should start allocating a percentage of retirement assets to high-rated bond funds. At age 55, you should put 20% of your retirement assets in high-rated bond funds.

At age 60 you should have 25% of your retirement assets in high-rated bond funds and you should continue to increase the allocation of your retirement assets to high-rated bond funds by 5% every five years.

Employer Defined Contribution Plan

A defined contribution pension plan is a pension plan in which your employer contributes a specific amount to your retirement account each year. Under this type of arrangement your pension benefits will be determined, in part, by how well the investments in the plan do.

Employer Defined Benefit Plan

A defined benefit pension plan is a pension plan in which the benefits that you are to receive are based on a mathematical formula. Your employer is required to make sufficient contributions to produce the income needed to pay you the benefits that you are entitled to based on the formula. The benefit is generally based on salary and years of service. These plans are becoming rare because employers don't want to guarantee pension benefits to their employees.

Traditional IRA

A traditional Individual Retirement Account (IRA) allows you to make contributions to your own private retirement account. Contributions and investment earnings are not taxed until they are distributed. Individuals younger than 70½ years old may set up an IRA.

Roth IRA

A Roth Individual Retirement Account (Roth IRA) allows you to make contributions to your own private retirement account. You do not receive a tax deduction for making a contribution to a Roth IRA but distributions taken after the age of 59½ are tax- free. The amount you able to contribute to an IRA may be limited by your adjusted gross income and taxable compensation.

Social Security

Social Security benefits replace a percentage of your earnings when you retire, become disabled or die. As you work and pay taxes, you earn Social Security "credits." You can earn up to four credits per year. Most people need 40 credits (ten years of work) to qualify for benefits. Younger people need fewer credits to be eligible for disability benefits or for family members to be eligible for survivor's benefits when the worker dies.

DOTHIS™

> **Review the annual statement that you receive from the Social Security Administration. This statement shows your earnings history and an estimate of the retirement, disability, and survivor's benefits you and your family may receive based on those earnings.**
>
> When you receive your statement, check your earnings history carefully. Make sure all of your earnings are accurate. Be sure to report any errors to the Social Security Administration. That is important because your benefits will be based on your lifetime earnings. You can obtain a copy of your Social Security account statement by requesting one at www.socialsecurity.gov.

Simple Actions To Eliminate Debt and Create Wealth

Appendix

Sample Complaint Letter

Date

Your name
Your address
Your city, state and zip code

Name of Contact Person (If available)
Company Name
Customer Services (If you have no specific contact)
Street Address
City, State, Zip Code

Dear (Contact Person or Sirs:)

On (date) I (bought, leased, rented, or had repaired) a (name of the product with model and serial number or description of service provided) at (location).

Unfortunately, your (product or service) has not performed well (or the service was inadequate) because (state the problem). I am disappointed because (explain the problem: for example, the product does not work properly, the service was not performed correctly, I was billed the wrong amount, something was not disclosed clearly or was misrepresented, etc.).

To resolve this problem, I would appreciate your (state the specific action you want-money back, credit card credit, repair, exchange, etc.). Enclosed are copies (do not send originals) of my records (include receipts, guarantees, warranties, canceled checks, contracts, model and serial numbers, and other documents).

I look forward to you reply and a resolution to my problem, and will wait until (set a time limit) before seeking help from the Better Business Bureau and the appropriate Federal agency. Please contact me at the above address or by phone at (home and/or office numbers with area code).

Sincerely,
Your Name

Document Retention Guidelines

Document	Keep	Suggested Location	Where Document is Kept
Appliance manuals, warranties	While Owned	File Cabinet	
Auto title, license documentation	While Owned	Safe Deposit Box	
Birth certificates	Permanently	Safe Deposit Box	
Bank statements	2 Years	File Cabinet	
Credit card statements	2 Years	File Cabinet	
Insurance policies	While In Force	File Cabinet	
Investment statements	While Owned	File Cabinet	
Investments stock certificates	While Owned	Safe Deposit Box	
Loan Documents	3 Years After Loan Is Paid Off	File Cabinet	
Social Security records	Permanently	Safe Deposit Box	
Tax return copies	10 years	File Cabinet	
Tax returns, supporting receipts, documentation	6 years	File Cabinet	
Wills and power of attorneys	Permanently	Safe Deposit Box	

Top Ten Web Site You Should Visit

Web Site	Contents
Charities www.charitynavigator.org	Lists and ratings on more than 5,000 charities. Charities are classified according to the type of service that they provide (education, human service, religion, etc.) and rated according to efficiency and how effective they are in carrying out their mission.
Health & Fitness Tips www.health-fitness-tips.com	Health and fitness tips and for improving health and achieving a high quality life.
Investor Guide www.investorguide.com	Research and education tool for stocks. Answer Center contains answers to over 1,000 commonly asked investing questions.
Kiplinger's Personal Finance www.kiplinger.com	Kiplinger Personal Finance magazine. Online calculators.
Legal Advice and Information www.nolo.com	Clear advice on information on various topics including family law, living wills, real estate issues.
Library of Congress www.loc.gov	Library of Congress is the largest library in the world. Site includes access to millions of items.
Mind Tools www.mindtools.com	Called food for the mind, this sight offers techniques for improving mental skills. Topics include Goal Setting, Managing Stress and Time Management.
Money Magazine www.money.com	Advice and news on personal finance issues. Prior Money Magazine issues.
Volunteer www.volunteermatch.org	Volunteer opportunities in your community. Type your zip code and specify your area of interest to view a list of volunteer opportunities near you.
Yahoo Finance www.finance.com	Articles on numerous personal financial issues including taxes, health care and managing credit card debt.

Sample Dispute Letter — For Existing Credit Accounts

Date

Your name
Your address
Your city, state and zip code

Your Account Number
Name of Creditor
Billing Inquiries
Address
City, State, Zip Code

Dear Sir or Madam:

I am writing to dispute a fraudulent (charge or debit) attributed to my account in the amount of $_____. I am a victim of identity theft, and I did not make this (charge or debit). I am requesting that the (charge be removed or the debit reinstated), that any finance and other charges related to the fraudulent amount be credited as well, and that I receive an accurate statement. Enclosed are copies of (use this sentence to describe any enclosed information, such as police report) supporting my position. Please investigate this matter and correct the fraudulent (charge or debit) as soon as possible.

Sincerely,

Your name
Enclosures: (List what you are enclosing.)

Sample Dispute Letter — Credit Bureau

Date

Your name
Your address
Your city, state and zip code

Complaint Department
Name of Credit Bureau
Address
City, State, Zip Code

Dear Sir or Madam:
I am writing to dispute the following information in my file. The items I dispute also are circled on the attached copy of the report I received. (Identify item(s) disputed by name of source, such as creditors or tax court, and identify type of item, such as credit account, judgment, etc.) I am a victim of identity theft, and did not make the charge(s). I am requesting that the item be blocked to correct my credit report. Enclosed are copies of (use this sentence if applicable and describe any enclosed documentation) supporting my position. Please investigate this (these) matter(s) and block the disputed item(s) as soon as possible.

Sincerely,
Your name

Enclosures: (List what you are enclosing)

Simple Actions To Eliminate Debt and Create Wealth

Glossary

401(k) plan: A tax-deferred investment and savings plan that serves as a personal retirement fund for employees.

Acceleration Clause: A stipulation in a loan contract stating that the entire balance becomes due immediately if other contract conditions are not met.

Amortization: The rate at which a debt is paid off by making periodic payments over a certain period.

Adjustable-Rate Loans: Also known as variable-rate loans, these usually offer a lower initial interest rate than fixed-rate loans. The interest rate fluctuates over the life of the loan based on market conditions, but the loan agreement generally sets maximum and minimum rates. When interest rates rise, generally so do your loan payments; and when interest rates fall, your monthly payments may be lowered.

Annual Fees (Credit Cards): The annual fee that most credit card issuers charge for use of their credit card. These fees range from $50 to $75 for most cards, and from $150 and up for premium "gold" or "platinum" cards.

Annual Percentage Rate (APR): This is the cost of credit expressed as a yearly rate. The APR includes the interest rate, points, broker fees, and certain other credit charges that the borrower is required to pay.

Annuity: A series of equal payments made at regular intervals, with interest compounded at a specified rate.

Appreciation: An increase in the value or price of something.

Asset: An item possessing value.

Automated Teller Machine (ATM): An electronic terminal that enables you to bank almost any time. They allow you to withdraw cash, make deposits, or transfer funds between accounts when you insert an ATM card and enter your PIN. Some financial institutions and ATM owners charge a fee, particularly to consumers who don't have accounts with them or on transactions at remote locations. Generally, ATMs must tell you they charge a fee and its amount on or at the terminal screen before you complete the transaction. You should be sure of what bank fees your bank charges.

Average Daily Balance Method: (Computing Credit Card Interest) (including or excluding new purchases) The average daily balance method gives you credit for your payment from the day the card issuer receives it. To compute the balance due, the card issuer totals the beginning balance for each day in the billing period and deducts any payments credited to your account that day. New purchases may or may not be added to the balance, depending on the plan, but cash advances typically are added. The resulting daily balances are added up for the billing cycle and the total is then divided by the number of days in the billing period to arrive at the "average daily balance." This is the most common method used by credit card issuers.

Balance: The amount owed on a loan or credit card or the amount in a savings or investment account.

Balance Sheet: A financial statement showing a "snapshot" of the assets, liabilities and net worth of an individual or organization on a given date.

Bankruptcy: A legal proceeding declaring that an individual is unable to pay debts. Chapters 7 and 13 of the Federal Bankruptcy Code govern personal bankruptcy.

Base Price: This is the cost of the car without options, but includes standard equipment and factory warranty. This price is printed on the Monroney sticker.

Budget: An itemized estimate of probable income and expenses for a given period.

Capital: Cash or other resources accumulated and available for use in producing wealth.

Cash Flow: Money coming to an individual or business less money being paid out during a given period of time.

Certificate Of Deposit (CD): A type of savings account that earns a fixed interest rate over a specified period of time.

Collateral: Asset pledged to secure a loan.

Common Stock: An ownership interest in a corporation that entitles the investor to share any profits remaining after all other obligations have been met.

Compound Interest: Interest computed on the sum of the original principal and accrued interest.

Conventional Loans: These are mortgage loans other than those insured or guaranteed by a government agency such as the FHA (Federal Housing Administration), the VA (Veterans Administration), or the Rural Development Services (formerly known as Farmers Home Administration, or FMHA).

Credit: The granting of money or something else of value in exchange for a promise of future repayment.

Credit Bureau: An organization that compiles credit information on individuals and businesses and makes it available to businesses for a fee.

Credit Card: A plastic card from a financial services company that allows cardholders to buy goods and services on credit.

Credit Report: A loan and bill payment history, kept by a credit bureau and used by financial institutions and other potential creditors to determine the likelihood a future debt will be repaid.

Credit Score: A rating of an individual's credit worthiness.

Credit Union: A cooperative organization that provides financial services to its members.

Creditor: A person, financial institution or other business that lends money.

Dealer Sticker Price: Usually on a supplemental sticker, this the Monroney sticker price plus the suggested retail price of dealer-installed options, such as additional dealer markup (ADM) or additional dealer profit (ADP), dealer preparation, and undercoating.

Debt: Money owed; also known as a liability.

Debt Service: Periodic payment of the principal and interest on a loan.

Debit Charges to an account.

Debit Card: A plastic card similar to a credit card that allows money to be withdrawn or the cost of purchases paid directly from the holder's bank account.

Delinquency: The failure to make timely payments under a loan or other credit agreement.

Direct Deposit: Process that allows you to authorize specific deposits, such as paychecks and Social Security checks, to your account on a regular basis. You also may pre-authorize direct withdrawals so that recurring bills, such as insurance premiums, mortgages, and utility bills, are paid automatically.

Discount Broker: A broker who buys and sells stock. Since such brokers do not usually provide customers with other services, notably research, they tend to have lower fees than those of major brokerage firms.

Diversification: Spreading investments among different companies in different fields. Another type of diversification is offered by the securities of many individual companies whose activities cover a wide range. The purchase of varying assets in order to minimize the risk associated with a portfolio.

Dividend: A share of profits paid to a stockholder.

Dividend Rate: The indicated annual rate of payment of dividend's to shareholders.

Dollar (Cost) Averaging (DA): A system of buying securities at regular intervals with a fixed dollar amount. The investor buys by the dollars' worth rather than by the number of shares. If each investment is of the same number of dollars, payments buy more shares when the price is low and fewer when it rises.

Dow Jones Industrial Average (DJIA): An average computed from 30 leading blue-chip industrial securities, utilizing an unweighted arithmetic mean, and quoted in terms of points rather than dollars. DJIA is used as a representative indicator of the movement of markets in general, but specifically on the NYSE.

Earnings Per Share (EPS): Synonymous with the net income per share of common stock.

Employee Stock Ownership Plans (ESOPs): Programs that allow workers to purchase stock in the company they work for.

Escrow: The holding of money or documents by a neutral third party prior to closing. It can also be an account held by the lender (or servicer) into which a homeowner pays money for taxes and insurance.

Equity: Ownership interest in an asset after liabilities are deducted.

Face Value: The principal amount of a bond, which will be paid off at maturity.

Fair Market Value: The price a willing buyer will pay and a willing seller will accept for real or personal property.

Federal Deposit Insurance Corp. (FDIC): A federally chartered corporation that insures bank deposits up to $100,000.

Fixed-Rate Loans: Generally have repayment terms of 15, 20, or 30 years. Both the interest rate and the monthly payments (for principal and interest) stay the same during the life of the loan.

Finance Company: A company that makes loans to individuals.

Financing Fee: The fee a lender charges to originate a loan. The fee is based on a percentage of the loan amount; one point is equivalent to 1 percent.

Foreclosure: The legal process whereby the property is sold to satisfy the payment of debt secured by the property

General Obligation Bond: A type of municipal bond backed by the full faith and credit of the governmental unit that issues it.

Individual Development Account (IDA): A type of savings account, offered in some communities, for people whose income is below a certain level.

Individual Retirement Account (IRA): A retirement plan, offered by banks, brokerage firms and insurance companies, to which individuals can contribute each year on a tax-deferred basis.

Industrial Bond: A financial instrument issued by businesses primarily to fund expansion or acquisitions.

Interest: The cost of borrowing money expressed or the amount earned when placed in an interest bearing account.

Interest Rate: The percentage charged for a loan or earned on money lent or placed in an interest-bearing account.

Investor: An organization, corporation, individual or other entity that acquires an ownership position in an investment, assuming risk of loss in exchange for anticipated returns.

Installment Plan: A plan requiring a borrower to make payments at specified intervals over the life of a loan.

Investing: Purchasing securities or other assets for income and or future appreciation.

Invoice Price: The manufacturer's initial charge to the dealer. This usually is higher than the dealer's final cost because dealers receive rebates, allowances, discounts, and incentive awards. Generally, the invoice price should include freight (also known as destination and delivery). If you're buying a car based on the invoice price (for example, "at invoice," "$100 below invoice," "two percent above invoice"), and if freight is already included, make sure freight isn't added again to the sales contract.

Leverage: The ability to use a small amount of money to attract other funds, including loans, grants and equity investments.

Liability: Money an individual or organization owes; same as debt.

Lien: A creditor's claim against a property, which may entitle the creditor to seize the property if a debt is not repaid.

Liquidity: The ease with which an investment can be converted into cash.

Load: The fee a brokerage firm charges an investor for handling transactions.

Loan: A sum of money lent or borrowed.

Loan Origination Fees: Fees charged by the broker or lender for processing the loan, often expressed as a percentage of the loan amount.

Lock-in: Refers to a written agreement guaranteeing a home buyer a specific interest rate on a home loan provided that the loan is closed within a certain period of time, such as 60 or 90 days. Often the agreement also specifies the number of points to be paid at closing.

Management Fee: The fee paid to a company or individual for managing investments or property

Market Value: The amount a seller can expect to receive on the open market for merchandise, services or securities.

Maturity: The time when a note, bond or other investment option comes due for payment to investors.

Money Market Savings Account: A type of savings account offered by a financial institution.

Monroney Sticker Price (MSRP): Shows the base price, the manufacturer's installed options with the manufacturer's suggested retail price, the manufacturer's transportation charge, and the fuel economy (mileage). Affixed to the car window, this label is required by federal law, and may be removed only by the purchaser.

Mortgage: A document, signed by borrower(s) that pledges property as collateral for a loan. Mortgage gives the lender a right to take possession of the property if the borrower fails to repay the loan under the terms set forth in the loan document.

Municipal Bond: A bond issued by cities, counties, states and local governmental agencies to finance public projects, such as construction of bridges, schools and highways.

Mutual Fund: A pool of money managed by an investment company and invested in stocks and or bonds.

Net Worth: The difference between a company or individual's total assets and total liabilities.

On-line Banking: The process of doing banking transactions via your personal computer. For instance, you may use your computer to view your account balance, request transfers between accounts, and pay bills electronically.

Pay-by-Phone Systems: System that allows you to call your financial institution with instructions to pay certain bills or to transfer funds between accounts. You must have an agreement with the institution to make such transfers.

Points: Fees paid to the lender for the loan. One point equals 1 percent of the loan amount. Points are usually paid in cash at closing. In some cases, the money needed to pay points can be borrowed, but doing so will increase the loan amount and the total costs.

Pre-tax: Income or deductions before state and federal income taxes are calculated or paid.

Predatory Lending: Targeting loans to elderly, low-income and other people to take advantage of their financial status or lack of financial knowledge.

Prime Rate: The lowest interest rate on bank loans, offered to preferred borrowers.

Principal: The unpaid balance on a loan, not including interest; the amount of money invested.

Private Mortgage Insurance (PMI): Protects the lender against a loss if a borrower defaults on the loan. It is usually required for loans in which the down payment is less than 20 percent of the sales price or, in a refinancing, when the amount financed is greater than 80 percent of the appraised value.

Promissory Note: A written promise on a financial instrument to repay the money plus interest.

Qualified Plan: A retirement plan in which pretax contributions are made.

Risk: The possibility of loss on an investment.

Return: The profit made on an investment.

Savings Account: A bank account that earns interest where people deposit money for future use.

Stockholder: A person who owns stock in a company.
Term The period from when a loan is made until it is fully paid.

Terms: Provisions specified in a loan agreement.

Thrift Institution: A general term for savings banks and savings and loan associations.

Transaction Fees and Other Charges: A credit card also may involve other types of costs. For example, some card issuers charge a fee when you use the card to obtain a cash advance, when you fail to make a payment on time, or when you go over your credit limit. Some charge a flat monthly fee whether or not you use the card.

Transaction, Settlement, Or Closing Costs: Charges such as application fees; title examination, abstract of title, title insurance, and property survey fees; fees for preparing deeds, mortgages, and settlement documents; attorneys' fees; recording fees; and notary, appraisal, and credit report fees. The Real Estate Settlement Procedures Act requires that a borrower receive a Good Faith Estimate of closing costs at the time of application or within three days of application.

Treasury Bill: A short-term investment issued by the U.S. government for a year or less.

Treasury Bond: A government security with a term of more than 10 years; interest is paid semi-annually.

Treasury Note: A government security with a maturity that can range from two to 10 years; interest is paid every six months.

U.S. Savings Bond: A nontransferable, registered bond issued by the U.S. Government in denominations of $50 to $10,000.

Simple Actions To Eliminate Debt and Create Wealth

Sources

Building a Better Credit Report, Federal Reserve Board

Buying a New Car, Federal Trade Commission

Buying a Used Car, Federal Citizen Information Center

Currents and Undercurrents: Changes in the Distribution of Wealth, 1989-2004, Arthur B. Kennickell

FDIC Consumer News, Federal Deposit Insurance Commission

Forbes Fund Survey

I.D. Theft: What's It About? Federal Trade Commission

Internal Revenue Service Publication 503

Internal Revenue Service Publication 523 - Selling Your Home

Internal Revenue Service Publication 526 – Charitable Contributions

Internal Revenue Service Publication 544 – Sales & Dispositions of Assets

Internal Revenue Service Publication 547 – Casualties, Disasters and Thefts

Internal Revenue Service Publication 550 – Investment Income & Expenses

Internal Revenue Service Publication 970 – Tax Benefits for Education

Preventing Identity Theft: A Guide for Consumers, National Crime Prevention Council

Protecting Yourself From Overdrafts & Bounced Checks, Federal Reserve Board

Scams and Frauds, Federal Citizen Information Center

The HUD Home Buying Guide, U.S. Department of Housing and Urban Development

There's a Lot To Learn About Money, Federal Reserve System

U.S. General Services Administration Consumer Action Handbook

Your Credit Scores, Federal Citizen Information Center